BRAZEN

Big Banks, Swap Mania and the Fallout

BRAZEN
Big Banks, Swap Mania and the Fallout

A. Rashad Abdel-khalik
University of Illinois at Urbana-Champaign, USA

 **WS Professional**

NEW JERSEY · LONDON · SINGAPORE · BEIJING · SHANGHAI · HONG KONG · TAIPEI · CHENNAI · TOKYO

Published by

WS Professional, an imprint of
World Scientific Publishing Co. Pte. Ltd.
5 Toh Tuck Link, Singapore 596224
USA office: 27 Warren Street, Suite 401-402, Hackensack, NJ 07601
UK office: 57 Shelton Street, Covent Garden, London WC2H 9HE

Library of Congress Cataloging-in-Publication Data
Names: Abdel-Khalik, A. Rashad, author.
Title: Brazen : big banks, swap mania and the fallout / A. Rashad Abdel-Khalik
    (University of Illinois at Urbana-Champaign, USA).
Description: New Jersey : World Scientific, [2018] | Includes bibliographical references.
Identifiers: LCCN 2018041491 | ISBN 9789813275560
Subjects: LCSH: Banks and banking--Moral and ethical aspects--United States. |
    Nonprofit organizations--United States--Finance. | Swaps (Finance)--United States. |
    Public welfare--United States.
Classification: LCC HG2491 .A23 2018 | DDC 332.10973--dc23
LC record available at https://lccn.loc.gov/2018041491

British Library Cataloguing-in-Publication Data
A catalogue record for this book is available from the British Library.

For any available supplementary material, please visit
https://www.worldscientific.com/worldscibooks/10.1142/11136#t=suppl

Desk Editors: Dr. Sree Meenakshi Sajani/Shreya Gopi

Typeset by Stallion Press
Email: enquiries@stallionpress.com

Printed in Singapore

To the Memories of my beloved Parents

Preface

In July 2014, street demonstrators in the City of Detroit held up banners reading, "Gave banks $537 million and shut off the poor's water." Following that demonstration and at the invitation of concerned citizens, the United Nations sent to the City of Detroit a team of experts to investigate alleged violation of human rights. Other demonstrators in the City of Chicago carried boxes containing 88,000 collected signatures of citizens protesting against big banks to the local office of the Securities and Exchange Commission. That was followed by a larger demonstration organized by the Chicago Teachers Union whose members marched to the branch of Bank of America on LaSalle Street to close the Union's account in protest. At the same time, the Chicago Teachers Union joined a class action suit filed by the City of Baltimore alleging injury from big banks' violation of antitrust law. Students at the University of California wearing orange-colored cloths, calling themselves "Prisoners sentenced to debt" carried banners reading "Your fee hikes go towards *Wall Street*." They were referring to the obligations of the University of California to big banks for some contracts called interest rate "swaps." In Philadelphia, after dismissing more than 3,700 teachers, teachers' aids and school staff in 2012 to free up funds to pay the banks for the same types of contracts, a City Councilman, James Kenney, who is the current Mayor, introduced a bill to the City Council back then to stop doing business with Citigroup and Bank of America.

Nonprofits across the country including universities, public schools, health centers, hospitals and transit authorities alleging injuries caused by big banks pushing specific type of contracts to exchange fixed rate of interest for a variable rate. The claimed damages are in the billions of dollars. Many of these entities had already filed class action suits against big banks for causing them harm by manipulating the interest rate benchmark to which these contracts were linked.

> *Were the bankers mad?*
>
> *Were they evil?*
>
> *Or were they simply grotesquely greedy?*
>
> Gillian Tett, *Fool's Gold* (The Free Press, New York, NY, 2009)

Billions and Trillions

Large numbers have been creeping into our daily conversations and events ranging from the U.S. budget deficit to the stock market information. However, we have not encountered as large numbers as the count of financial derivatives traded behind closed doors. It is in the hundreds of trillions of dollars. [*A financial derivative is a contract that generates or derives its value from some other externally determined factor such as changes in interest rates, changes in commodity prices, currency exchange rates or even weather.*] While stocks and bonds have fundamentals because they represent investment in real resources, financial derivatives are means of wealth transfer and have no fundamentals of the same type. The majority of financial derivatives do not trade on organized exchanges where there is transparency. Instead, they are traded privately in the dark in settings to which the name Over-the-Counter (OTC) is attached.

In the first half of 2016, the Bank for International Settlements reported the worldwide total face amounts of OTC derivatives as $553 trillion ($553,000,000,000,000) as Appendix 3 reveals.[1] Of this amount, $446 trillion ($446,000,000,000,000) were for contracts related to interest rates. At the same time, outstanding face amounts of financial derivatives held by the largest 25 bank holding companies in the USA reportedly stood at $250 trillion ($250,000,000,000,000).[2] Of that amount, $231 trillion ($231,000,000,000,000) belonged to the top five bank holding companies alone. Because of the similarity of this method of trade to the traditional way of old fashion purchasing commodities from any store, this dark market for financial derivatives was also named Over-The-Counter (OTC).

Based on the reports by the Bank for International Settlements, if all OTC financial derivatives contracts world-wide were to be settled or terminated in the first half of 2016, all participants worldwide would have to transfer among themselves the fair market value of $21.0 trillion ($21,000,000,000,000) or 3.9% of the face amounts.[3] Total amounts of fair values dropped to $11 trillion ($11,000,000,000,000) in the second half of 2017. Using the same relationships, U.S. bank holding companies would need to transfer nearly $10 trillion ($10,000,000,000,000) to counterparties to settle all outstanding financial derivatives in the second half of 2016 and about $5 trillion in the second half of 2017. This amount is called the "fair" market value or the price at which the holders of these financial derivatives contracts could sell them to others. Unlike the face (notional) amounts of these contracts, the "fair" value numbers are not hypothetical; they are the estimated financial assets for one side of these contracts and estimated financial obligations on the other side that should change hands to settle all the contracts. However, these "fair" values were not generated by free competitive market forces. Instead, they are based on rules designed by big banks and others accept them

---

[1] https://www.bis.org/statistics/d5_1.pdf.

[2] U.S. Office of the Comptroller of the Currency, which is in the U.S. Department of the Treasury,

    https://www.occ.gov/topics/capital-markets/financial-markets/derivatives/derivatives-quarterly-report.html.

[3] This relationship changes with changes in global interest rate.

without questioning their economic validity. Chapter 34 provides reasons why the so-called "fair market value" is hardly "fair."

Exchanging Interest Rates with Nonprofit Organizations

About 80% of all the OTC market is related to contracts betting on the movements of interest rate, which is the "price" of money. The contracts of relevance in the cases provided in this book are agreements to exchange interest rates, mostly one party pays a fixed rate and receives from the counterparty a variable rate, and vice versa. Entering into these agreements is one way to modify cash flow requirements. To draw analogy with mortgages, one mortgage contract might make monthly or quarterly payments based on a fixed rate of interest, while another mortgage contract might make payments based on an adjustable (variable) rate of interest. If the fixed-rate mortgage holder wishes to modify her/his interest payment schedule, she/he could seek refinancing the mortgage and chooses adjustable rate instead. Similarly, if the adjustable rate mortgage holder wants to modify her/his schedule of payments, she/he could refinance to switch from adjustable rate to fixed rate. Refinancing mortgages is also an OTC-type of transaction because it is privately carried out between the banks and the mortgagees.

However, refinancing is costly and an alternative method of modifying interest payments less expensively came on the scene accidentally in 1982 when the Students Loan Marketing Association (Sallie Mae) entered into an agreement with another institution to exchange interest payments on a fixed rate bond for interest payments on a variable rate bond. That was the first time such an agreement existed and the year of 1982 was indeed the birth year of contracts to exchange interest rates, which has the Wall Street's more common name of "interest rate swaps."

Interest rate exchange (swap) contracts are essentially betting instruments between two counterparties. One party pays interest at a fixed rate and receives interest at a variable rate. This party is betting or counting on future increases in market interest rate. The higher the market interest rate, the higher the dollar amounts of interest this party would receive for a variable interest rate. The counterparty, on the other hand, receives fixed rate and pays variable rate. This party is betting on future decreases in market interest rate. The two counterparties exchange the difference between the fixed and the variable rates periodically. Thus, interest rate exchange (swap) contracts are means of *wealth transfer not wealth creation*.

This book focuses on interest rate exchange (swap) for a sample of cases in the nonprofit sector. By hook or crook, big banks were able to persuade hundreds of hospitals, city and state governments, public school districts, universities, and transit authorities across the country to commit heavily to these interest rate exchange (swap) contracts. For close to 25 years since the start of the Swap Mania, these nonprofit entities have literally lost "their shirts" by transferring billions of dollars to the vaults of big banks to settle swap contracts to which they had agreed although they did not understand. Strangely enough, officials at these nonprofits had easily agreed to adopt the big banks' propositions to restructure their approach to debt financing, including entering into interest rate exchange (swap) contracts. Unlike contracts with the corporate sector, the time to maturity of interest rate exchange (swap) contracts with nonprofit organizations extends up to 30 years or longer. Thus, entering into these contracts exposes the nonprofit counterparties to assured times of liquidity crises.

Moreover, big banks and swap dealers proved to be very aggressive. With the full knowledge that every (bilateral) interest rate exchange (swap) contract could have only one winner, swap dealers set up a contracting process that assures the banks of being the winners on average and sold them to charitable hospitals. In addition, they relied on the gullibility of the priests and sisters running these hospitals to sell them a bill of goods that ended up adding to their debt hundreds of millions of dollars.

There is much more in the store of mishaps and abuse of the fallibility of officials at nonprofits. However, the space in this book allowed for including only a sample of these cases from public schools, universities, hospitals and health-care centers, state governments, cities and local government agencies, and transit authorities.

The "ISDA"

It was in the mid-1980s when big banks became enthused about the possibility of writing, selling and buying interest rate exchange (swap) contracts to make more money. They established an association to set the rules and to lobby on their behalf. The first name of that association was the "International Swap Dealers Association." To be more encompassing of all derivatives, the name changed later to be the "International Swap and Derivatives Association," which retains the acronym of "ISDA."

Ten big banks founded ISDA in 1985 and currently 19 of its 26 managing board members are big banks. Thus, it is not surprising that ISDA lobby for the interests of big banks anywhere, everywhere and at all times. The alleged independence and impartiality, especially in designing the guide template to contracts called "Master Agreement," are simply a façade.

A. Rashad Abdel-khalik
Champaign, Illinois
June 30, 2018

Acknowledgments

I am particularly indebted to G. Nicolaus Dupre, Shane Moriarity, and Madhubalan Viswanathan for providing insightful comments helping to shape the direction of the manuscript that formed the basis for this book. I am also indebted to my student, Dongyi (Donny) Wang, who helped me in discussing and searching some issues for which I needed assistance and for preparing many of the financial charts. Margaret Ann Justh and Haibotullah Sami have generously provided their time and support by reading and commenting on an early draft of the manuscript and providing helpful comments. Sarah Vaughen drew all the sketches including those images for which I could not obtain copyright release.

Among friends and colleagues who discussed some related issues with me or gave me specific comments, I would like to thank Heba Badawy, Sasson Bar-Yosef, Richard Crowley, Ed Giroux, Adel Nematallah Naguib Ibrahim, Ravi Jagannathan, Kacie Jones, Ashraf Khalaf, Bartosz Kurek, Doug McInnis, Ira Solomon, Theodore Sougiannis, and Wangjing (Jenny) Zhu. Of course, the analyses, conclusions, and inferences as well as any errors remain my own.

Finally, I want to thank my dear wife, Nayer Purkhosrow, for her continuous support and interest in my completing this project.

Contents

Thunder from the Far East

V.K. Sharma, a former executive director of the Reserve Bank of India (RBI), marked his recent departure by giving an almighty kicking to India's over-the-counter interest-rate derivatives market. In a speech at the end of 2012, he called it "disturbing, preposterous, perverse, the antithesis of responsible financial innovation, weird and warped."

The Economist. Interest-rate swaps in India. "Derivatiff: A retiring official raises the alarm about derivatives in Inst, February 16, 2013.

Retrieved from https://www.economist.com/news/finance-and-economics/21571901-retiring-official-raises-alarm-about-derivatives-india-derivatiff.

A Rumble from the Near East

Over the last 12 months, I have seen five different managing directors refer to their own clients as "muppets," sometimes over internal e-mail.

. . . . .

You don't have to be a rocket scientist to figure out that the junior analyst sitting quietly in the corner of the room hearing about "muppets," "ripping eyeballs out" and "getting paid" doesn't exactly turn into a model citizen.

Greg Smith. "Why I am leaving Goldman Sachs," The New York Times, March 14, 2012.

Retrieved from http://www.nytimes.com/2012/03/14/opinion/why-i-am-leaving-goldman-sachs.html?_r=0.

The Hard Reality

Municipal borrowers from Detroit's utilities to Harvard University in Cambridge, Massachusetts, have paid billions of dollars to banks to end privately negotiated interest-rate bets sold as hedges. The Federal Reserve's policy of holding its benchmark-borrowing rate near zero since 2008 has turned many of the swaps into wrong-way bets.

Darrell Preston, May 10, 2013. Denver Pays Wall Street $216 Million as Swaps Fail: Muni Credit. Bloomberg

http://saberpartners.com/press/articlepages/bloomberg_05_10_13.html.

https://saberpartners.com/press/bloomberg-news-5/.

CHAPTER 1

What Is This Book All About?

Introduction

Could you imagine paying nearly $2,900,000 to obtain a $780,000 loan? Regrettably, this is a true episode. A school superintendent was overheard lamenting that an 81-year-old building in his school district was falling apart and the State could not provide the funds to fix it. Then a voice came from across the seating area saying, "I can help you; just stop by my office at the bank tomorrow and we will work something out." That was the voice of an executive at the JPMorgan Chase office in the neighborhood.

The deal would provide the school district about $780,000 for repairing and taking care of the old building if the district agreed to a contract of exchanging interest rates. Under the terms of this contract, the school would pay the bank amounts of interest calculated at a fixed rate, and the bank would pay the school amounts of interest calculated at an adjustable rate. When asked about the cost of that agreement, the banker said, "I cannot quantify that to you." When the school turned to the "financial advisor" it had hired to help navigate the contract terms, the answer proved to be an ideal form of financial rubbish generated by bunching together seemingly mythical terms such as zero-coupon rate and yield curve, LIBOR, hedge, and so on. There was no sign that the so-called financial advisors were any different from the participants from the school district — none had understood these new and complex types of contracts.

1

A short time later, the bill for the cost of underwriting the interest rate exchange agreement arrived at the desk of the school's superintendent; it was for $1 million! The school board went into frenzy — requiring a fee of $1 million for making a loan of $780,000 sounded unreal! The school district board had no recourse and activated emergency measures. It arranged for transactions with another bank to find money to pay the $1 million underwriting fees to JPMorgan Chase, the fees of the financial adviser and legal counsel, and others. When it was all over, the cost of obtaining $780,000 in cash using that prepaid interest rate exchange (swap) contract has reportedly totaled $2.9 million! Indeed, this story could fit in a book of fairy tales, except for the fact that it is true; it is the case of the Erie City School District, PA elaborated in Chapter 13.[1]

The deal between JPMorgan Chase and Erie City School District was one of the new set of contracts (called derivatives) that was not known until 1982 and big banks began to sell them and spread them like a plague to nonprofit entities all over the country starting late 1990s.

A **derivative** is a contract between two parties that generates, or derives, its value from something else called "the underlying."

An **interest rate swap** is a contract to exchange one interest rate for another. This type of contract generates its value from changes in market interest rates. Thus, interest rate swaps are derivatives; they do not have fundamentals like stocks or bonds. In fact, interest rate swaps are financial instruments and are not securities.

The **most common** form of interest rate swaps is a fixed-payer contract requiring one type to pay interest at a fixed rate and the counterparty to pay interest at a variable or floating rate. This is also known as "plain vanilla" swap.

This **book** addresses how big banks used these contracts to drain enormous amounts of money form the nonprofit sector.

---

[1] The setup of meeting at a gathering drinking beer does not describe the initial meeting; it is only for emphasis.

Changes in Financing Strategies of Nonprofits

Historically, nonprofit entities have used the municipal bond market to raise funds for their operations. The traditional method was selling bonds that pay fixed rates of interest, giving the issuing organizations predictable cash outflow patterns. In addition, the interest income that investors earned from municipal bonds was typically tax-exempt and predictable. Many institutional investors, pension funds, and retirees found security and assurance by investing in the $3.77 trillion municipal bond market. However, the phenomenal growth of interest-rate-exchange (swap) contracts starting late 1990s led big banks to pursue a radically different strategy of financing nonprofit entities, a strategy that shook the stability of the market for both the investors and the borrowers. The shock is still lingering on for many large and small nonprofits.

Strictly pursuing their own self-interest, big banks encouraged nonprofit entities to move away from selling bonds that pay fixed interest rates and pursue instead a two-pronged financing strategy.

(i) To issue bonds at floating (variable) rates that could change frequently — quarterly, monthly, weekly or even daily.[2]
(ii) To concurrently sign interest-rate-exchange contracts with the same bonds, underwriter banks to pay fixed rates and receive variable (adjustable, floating) rates.

The adjustable rates of swap contracts are typically tied to a known and generally acceptable benchmark rate such as London Average Interest Rate (LIBOR) or Municipal Bond Average Interest Rate (SIFMA) and are typically adjusted quarterly or semiannually. If the variable cash flow receivable from the swap covers the variable cash flow payable on the bond, the net interest cost to the nonprofit counterparty would be the fixed rates payable on the swap. Thus, coupling the bond contract with an interest rate swap agreement, the counterparties that issued the bonds would have succeeded in mimicking the conventional fixed rate bonds and call the result "synthetic fixed rates." That synthetic-fixed interest rates could

---

[2]This is the auction rate we will discuss in more detail below.

be "lower" than the straight-fixed rates of interest was a major sale pitch big banks had adopted.

Commonly Used Benchmark Interest Rates

London Average Interest Rate (LIBOR):

An average of the interest rate that big banks could pay to borrow funds from one another. Until 2012, the British Bankers Association announced the rate daily in London at 11:30 AM. Following the discovery of the LIBOR scandal (see Chapter 32) this task moved the U.S. Intercontinental Exchange. The acronym LIBOR stands for London InterBank Offered Rate. LIBOR is a worldwide reference benchmark rate. (Elaborated in Chapter 32.)

- Libor is based on a process not too much different from polling a panel of selected large international banks.

The Municipal Bond Average Interest Rate (SIFMA):

An average of municipal bond interest rates announced weekly in New York by Bloomberg for the Securities Industry Financial Markets Association.

- SIFMA is based on actual trades.

Uses:

Both LIBOR and SIFMA are the most referenced benchmark interest rates in the swap contracts sold by big banks to non-profit entities. Most variable or adjustable rates of interest include one of these two benchmarks plus or minus percentage points. The variable rate of the contract changes with the movements of the benchmark rate.

Up until late 1990s, many states did not allow government agencies to be parties to any type of derivative contracts. Nonetheless, big banks lobbied hard and succeeded in removing those restrictions; the legislatures in many states, including California, Illinois, New York, and Pennsylvania changed their laws in early 2000 and allowed any government agency to enter into derivatives contracts without seeking further significant authorization.[3] Although the financial revolution that ensued continued to grow in private, dark markets called over-the-counter (OTC), it had actually created strange bedfellows.[4] Interestingly, it became possible to conceive of a common thread between Harvard University and Jefferson County, Alabama, or between charitable hospitals like the Sisters of Charity of Leavenworth Health System and the New York Metropolitan Transportation Authority. The existence of these contracts made such common threads among these nonprofits and many others an unmistakable reality. A thick common thread loaded with money — billions of dollars lost every year to benefit big banks.

A Critical Contract Design Feature

The design of an interest-rate-exchange (swap) contract employs some mathematical formulas to determine the fixed rate of interest that equates the values of the stream of future fixed-rate payments with the stream of future variable-rate payments at inception (the time of signing the agreement). As "Exhibit 1A" shows, the variable rates generated from that process have a distinct pattern that is expected to take three different stages:

(a) For approximately the first half of the life of the agreement, the variable rate falls below the fixed rate but keeps on increasing over-time because of changes in the time value of money and the risk exposure during that stage. In this stage, the fixed rate payer makes

---

[3]Every state had some superficial limitations. For example, the State of Illinois allowed (Public Act 93-9 in 2003) the practice of entering into financial derivatives for any entity that qualifies to borrow more than $10 million.

[4]OTC market is independent of the organized official exchanges and had no regulation of any kind until 2010 when the Dodd–Frank Act allowed the Commodity Futures Trading Commission to oversee the market. Although the OTC market is multiple the size of organized exchanges, it still has minimal regulation.

cash payments to the variable rate payer equal to the excess of the
fixed rate over the variable rate — i.e., the fixed rate payer would
be the loser.
(b) The growth trajectory of the variable rate is expected to continue until
the variable rate equals the fixed rate at about the mid-range of the life
of the contract.
(c) For the remainder of the life of the agreement, the variable rate is
expected to keep on increasing above the fixed rate. In this stage, the
fixed rate payer receives cash payments from the variable rate payer
equal to the excess of the variable rate over the fixed rate — i.e., the
fixed rate payer would be the winner.

Graphically, "Exhibit 1A" displays this pattern distinctly. While the
cash flow from the fixed rate remains unchanged, the cash flow from the
floating, variable rate changes such that, from the point of view of the
fixed rate payer, the present value of the gains expected in the second half
equals the present value of the losses expected in the first half. Thus, at
the start of the agreement, the present value of the cash flow stream of the
fixed leg equals the present value of the expected cash flow stream of the
variable leg. Under this condition, neither one of the two sides has an
economic advantage over the other at the start of the agreement.
Accordingly, the value of that agreement itself at inception is zero.[5]

As "Exhibit 1A" shows, there is always an expectation of having difference between the cash amounts of the fixed interest rate and the cash
amounts of the floating interest rate. The two counterparties exchange this
difference periodically, perhaps every six months. However, the cash flow
profile in "Exhibit 1A" is an expectation at the start of the agreement
which provides a tool or a theory that academia love to discuss. But they
will tell you, realization is different; the actual cash flow may and generally will differ from these expectations, as we will see in the rendering of
the specific cases in this book.

---

[5]There is no difference in values at the instant of signing the contract. However, usually
that equality does not last for long. It should be emphasized, however, that this presentation always ignores "Transaction Cost." Regrettably, this is true in all the reports, books or
publications I examined. Chapter 34 discusses the impact of including the relatively high
"Transaction Cost" of swap contracts.

Exhibit 1A
The Theoretical Relationship between the Fixed
and Variables Legs of the Swap

A TYPICAL SWAP TRANSACTION AT INCEPTION

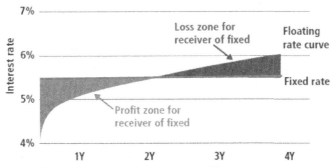

When an investor enters into a swap, the difference between
the fixed rate payments and the expected future floating rate
payments should be zero (the blue zone equals the green zone)

Source: Adapted from PIMCO. Understanding Interest Rate Swaps — Education

Retrieved from https://global.pimco.com/en-gbl/resources/education/understanding-interest-rate-swaps.

Creating Values "on Paper"

Without consideration of any item of the relatively significant "Transaction Cost," the terms of a swap contract guarantee that the beginning value of the contract is nil given the economic environment at the time of signing the agreement.[6] But, the macroeconomic factors of that environment change in unpredictable ways. These external causes alter the cash flow patterns of the floating leg of swap contracts because the variable rate of the swap adjusts with the changes in the benchmark rate. With every change, the value of the contract deviates from the initial equality:

- An increase in the adjustable rate will generate:
  - Gains for the receiver (the nonprofit entity) and
  - Losses for the payer (the bank).

---

[6]These conditions include macroeconomic indicators such as the term structure of the zero-coupon rate and the forward interest rate.

- A decrease in the adjustable rate will generate:
  - Losses for the receiver (the nonprofit) and
  - Gains for the payer (the bank).
- The loss of one counterparty is the gain of the other — i.e., the swap contract is a "zero-sum" game.

On every settlement date, the two counterparties take two actions:

(i) Settle in cash the differences between the amounts of interest dollars calculated at the fixed interest rate and the amounts of interest dollars calculated at the variable interest rate for the current period.

(ii) Calculate the present value of all expected future settlement amounts for the remaining life of the contract under the assumption that the current period settlement will continue for the entire contract duration modified only by the known and somewhat predictable changes (based on the forward yield curve). The resulting amount would be recorded on the balance sheet as a non-current, long-term liability designating expected future losses and would be reported as a long-term asset designating expected future gains for the counterparty.

Under the current conventions of swap agreements, if the contract is terminated before maturity for whatever reason, the holder of the non-current, long-term asset will demand collection of the entire amount from the counterparty.[7] And, the holder of the non-current, long-term liability would be obligated to pay. In the course of this book, we shall see how this type of arrangement came about and why it is a manifestation of an unconscionable contracting process that led to unjust enrichment.

How does it Work? An Example: A Swap Contract from the NY MTA Portfolio

Exchanging or swapping interest rates came on the scene in 1982.[8] The growth of these contracts as a mainstream method of generating profits

---

[7] Exceptions may be noted in cases of bankruptcy.

[8] When the Student Loan Marketing Association (Sallie Mae) swapped the interest payments on an issue of fixed-rate debt for variable-rate interest payments indexed to the

increased significantly in the 1990s and early 2000 when swap dealers invaded hundreds of organizations across the country and solidified the existence of the Swap Mania. A contract from the huge swap portfolio of New York Metropolitan Transportation Authority should help as a case to understand how swap contracts work to cause financial damage, often unacknowledged by officials at the transit authority.

In 2002, the NY MTA sold a variable rate bond issue for $200 million as "Exhibit 2A" illustrates. The bond is set to mature in November 2032. The coupon interest rate of this bond issue is 0.69 of LIBOR.[9] Thus, the interest payments will increase with any increase in LIBOR,

Exhibit 2A
NY Metropolitan Transportation Authority Bond Issue in 2002

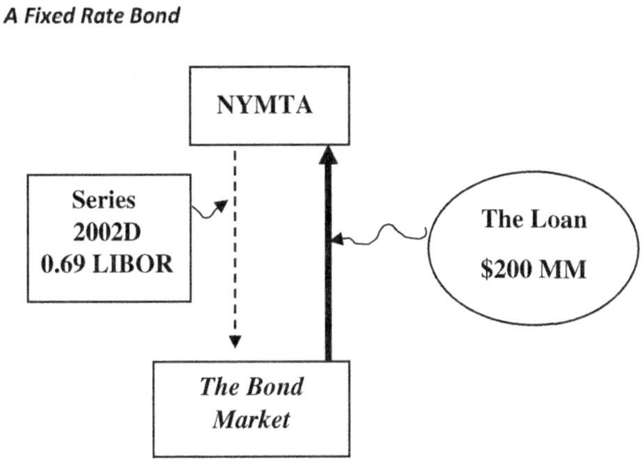

A Fixed Rate Bond

Note: LIBOR is the London average interest rate.

---

three-month US Treasury bills. See the story in Douglas Skarr, "The Fundamentals of Interest Rate Swaps," *Issue Brief*, California Debt and Investment Advisory Commission, October 2004.

Retrieved from http://www.treasurer.ca.gov/cdiac/reports/rateswap04-12.pdf.

[9] LIBOR rates are stated for different durations: overnight, one week, one month, three months, …, 12 month. The relevant LIBOR index here is the one-month LIBOR.

which poses exposure to interest rate risk that the officials at NY MTA did not want to bear. To mitigate that risk exposure, NY MTA entered into a separate contract with JPMorgan Chase (JPMC) on a reference notional (hypothetical face) amount of $200 million to swap interest rates: NY MTA pays JPMC interest at 4.45% and receives from JPMC interest at 0.69 of one-month LIBOR. The swap is noncancelable and is set to mature thirty years later, at the same time as the related bond — "Exhibit 3A" presents the cash flow depicted by this contract between NY MTA and JPMC.

The combination of the contract of the bond issue and the swap contract with JPMC results from a circular transaction converting the variable interest rate on the bond into a "fixed" rate. In this illustration, NY MTA collects 0.69 of one-month LIBOR from JPMC and pays it to the bond market, ending up with a net interest rate payment of 4.45%. Coming to this seemingly fixed rate is not by the conventional means of selling a fixed rate bond, but rather by an artificial and contrived process of combining two agreements. This is how the name "synthetic" fixed rate came about to highlight the artificial process of fixing the rate (see Exhibit 4A).

In 2002, LIBOR averaged 1.88% and in December 2017, LIBOR was 1.49%. In the interim, LIBOR ranged between 0.24% and 5.4%. Yet, 0.69 of LIBOR has *never* exceeded 3.726% from the inception of the swap contract in 2002 to this day in 2016. Simply put, MTA was always paying JPMC for the difference between 4.45% and the variable interest rate.

Exhibit 3A
NY Metropolitan Transportation Authority
Swap Contract with JPMorgan Chase

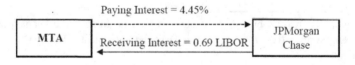

Notional (Face) Amount $200 million

Exhibit 4A
NY Metropolitan Transportation Authority
The Combination of the Bond Issue
& the Swap Contract with JPMorgan Chase

A Synthetic Fixed Rate Bond

Two contracts: A variable rate bond contract & an interest rate exchange (swap) contract

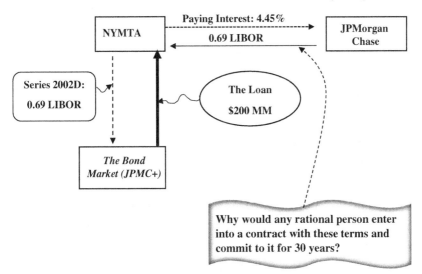

Every year, NYMTA had to take two actions and has the option on a third one.

1. Pay to JPMC the difference in amounts of interest between the fixed rate and the stated variable rate. That difference thus far averaged about $5.4 million annually. For example, the actual dollar amounts of this difference for the two anchor dates noted above were $6,251,600 in 2002 and $6,830,000 in 2016.
2. Estimate the future liabilities related to the contract assuming that this annual loss will continue until the contract matures. From December 2016 up to contract expiry in 2032, NY MTA estimated a future loss

of $67 million, which it reported as a long-term non-current liability on the balance sheet of the year ended December 31, 2016.[10]

3. If NY MTA decided to terminate the contract in December 2016, it would have been required to pay JPMorgan Chase at that time the $67 million estimated future obligations. We shall show later that such a payment would be actually giving away money for services that were not, and will not be, provided; paying money for nothing!

This circular composite transaction and the actions of officials at NY MTA cannot escape two ironic events:

(a) NY MTA had purchased the swap contract from JPMorgan Chase in the hope of reducing borrowing costs. This was the advertised motivation, although the true incentives are not known and might become known in the ongoing litigation. Instead, the cost of borrowing had increased. NYMTA did not need to enter into a swap contract in order to sell a bond issue at a variable rate.

(b) NY MTA continued to enter into similar contracts as if no lessons were ever learned from existing swaps.

Incidentally, these characteristics are not limited to NY MTA alone; we shall see how these situations, with some exceptions, repeatedly replicated themselves in the sample of nonprofit organizations presented in this book. Unfortunately, any proposed inferences that one could draw from these facts at this time are inexplicably complex defying logic and rationality at any level. This book offers more details throughout and provides a summary analysis in Chapters 34 and 35.

Paying Enormous Termination (Fees) Penalties

Any organization whether profit-making or nonprofit enters into interest rate swaps for one or all of three reasons:

• Hedging (offsetting or counteracting) interest rate risk. That is the risk of paying more interest on variable rate bonds or receiving less interest on variable rate assets.

---

[10] NY MTA CAFR (2016, p. 107).
The reported $67 million is the present value of expected losses, which is the discounted cash flow. The actual amounts would be larger.

- Managing exposure to interest rate risk by changing the patterns of receivable and payable cash flow with the goal of lowering the cost of borrowing.
- Betting or gambling on the movement of interest rates.

Purchasing interest rate exchange (swap) contracts has the potential of achieving any or all of the three objectives. However, when swap contracts are terminated as called for by either side of the contract, the results are not ambiguous:

○ The hedge is no longer a possibility.
○ Swap contracts will not be active in modifying the pattern of cash flow in managing interest rate risk or lowering the cost of borrowing.
○ Succeeding (or even failing) in gambling would be an impossibility because the instrument of gambling will no longer exist.

More specifically, upon terminating interest rate swap contracts, all of the claimed services also terminate, but somehow the benefits to big banks do not cease! Interest rate swaps are often described as "zero-sum" game in that the gains of the banks are the losses of nonprofit counterparties, and vice versa. Big banks believe they have the right, which is more like a self-empowered entitlement, to collect amounts of money equal to the losses that the counterparty could have accrued for the entire life of the contract. Because the contracts terminate in this instance, if a nonprofit entity does not pay big banks the amounts of money it could have lost up to the original contract maturity date, it would be depriving big banks from what could have been their future gains. If challenged, bankers have reasons to be puzzled: how dare could nonprofits do this to the big banks that tried to help them in reducing their cost of borrowing? How could the counterparties goad big banks and deprive them of having what could have been their future gains even though the benefits of these contracts to counterparties no longer exist? In evaluating this conflict, it does not matter to big banks that terminating swap contracts would have absolutely no impact on the object of the betting transaction, which is the movement of the economy-wide term structure of interest rate. Moreover, the termination of swap contracts would not in any shape or form prevent big banks from entering into other contracts. Nonetheless, big banks built in an implicit clause of self-generated entitlement that counterparties have not thus far gathered the courage to challenge. They all seem to have given into big banks mandate: big banks must and do collect the huge payments (penalties) upon termination in spite of the recognition that any and all services will end with terminating the contracts. It has been rare that termination payments go the other way. It is critical to know that big banks do not admit using the term "penalties." Instead, they are "fair" values.

These amounts are enormous and are probably as large as the Gross Domestic Product of some small countries. For example, for terminating swap contracts with big banks, the City of Detroit had to pay nearly $900 million; Harvard University paid $1.25 billion and the State of New Jersey paid nearly $800 million. All were funds out of the doors of these organizations to satisfy self-generated and self-empowered artifice rights that: give banks lots of money for nothing received or expected. There is more of the same problem in the sample of cases presented in this book.

What if Big Banks' swap-termination style were to be introduced at a Las Vegas Casino

The above-described method of calculating the termination payment is rather mystifying and bizarre. To show how bizarre it is, let us talk about what a similar setting in a real gambling casino would be like. Assume you have rented a gambling machine in a Las Vegas casino for one hour. You paid the nominal amount of rent for the full hour in advance and have agreed to pay the casino amounts equal to your losses and receive from the casino amounts equal to your gains. This is exactly the setting of a plain vanilla interest rate swap contract. In the first minute, you lost $10,000, which you paid to the Casino promptly. However, that loss made you decide to quit. Using the approach developed by big banks, if you leave the machine after one minute, you would have deprived the casino owner from grabbing the amounts of money that you could have lost during the full hour. Thus, as you terminate your contract after one minute, you would be obligated to pay the casino an amount of money equal to what you

---

(*Continued*)

(Continued)

could have lost during the entire hour. In substance, this payment is a penalty, although big banks like to call it "fair" value. The amount of penalty in this illustration would be $590,000, which is calculated as the $10,000 loss in the first minute times the 59 minutes remaining in the contract. Nonetheless, everyone knows that, when you leave after one-minute time, you will not be benefitting by the machine in any shape or form. Furthermore, the machine will be free and in excellent working order so that the casino could rent it to someone else. But these factors are totally irrelevant for the purpose of calculating the penalty that you must pay using the model that big banks have developed (through the conduit ISDA) for calculating the penalty of terminating interest rate swaps. But the casino owner might not have the guts to call it the "fair" market value as bankers do. *In summary, you pay for what you lost and pay for what you could have lost!*

Clearly, casinos from Las Vegas to Macau would never accept the approach that big banks had adopted in determining the termination penalty of betting on interest rate movements. Otherwise, most of their clients would simply disappear!

Because of what some people might call naïveté, under education or gullibility, officials at nonprofit organizations entered into interest rate swap contracts having maturity durations matching the durations of the related bonds, which could extend for periods as long as 40 years. Firms in the corporate sector would find this practice totally alien; more than 70% of their swap contracts are for maturities of five years or less.[11] In all cases, the number of years remaining in the life of a contract after termination is an important ingredient in determining the amounts of penalties. Thus, the longer the time to maturity, the greater the estimated expected losses of the counterparties and the greater the expected gains of big banks.

Whether the management reported the expected losses as long-term liabilities or paid them as termination fees or penalties, the large amounts

---

[11] https://www.occ.gov/topics/capital-markets/financial-markets/derivatives/dq216.pdf.

have created devastating economic and social effects. To meet the unexpected demands created by these claims, cities and states went to the extremes of depriving people from having running water at their homes (e.g., the City of Birmingham, AL, and the City of Detroit). Similarly, public schools dismissed teachers and staff (e.g., the City of Chicago, the City of Philadelphia and Denver), hospitals restricted their additions to infrastructure, universities raised fees or cut down the services offered, and transit authorities raised transportation fares and eliminated some essentials. All of these actions had succeeded in threatening and eroding the fabric of this society. In the meantime, big banks kept on accumulating huge bags full of money siphoned through interest rate swaps sinkholes.

Are Nonprofit Officials Equipped to Deal with Swaps?

Joseph S. Fichera, the CEO of the New York-based financial advisory firm of Sabre Partners, LLC, expressed his view of the possible mismatch between the skills of swap dealers (i.e., big banks) and the skills of officials of nonprofits.[12]

> "One might wonder how a government employee could know about all this [swaps complexity] when evaluating financing and determining whether it is a good deal for citizens. How evenly matched are the $80,000 per year salaried public servant and the $500,000 a year, big-bonus Wall Street banker?"

He further answered another question, if these officials do not have the skills that puts them at par with swap dealers of big banks, could they depend on swap advisors?

> "Governments often hire advisers to help negotiate with the banks. Until the Dodd-Frank Act reforms, however, these advisers were unregulated

---

[12] Joseph S. Fichera, "Were Detroit's Interest-Rate Swaps Not Fair," *Bloomberg*, January 27, 2014.
    Retrieved from https://saberpartners.com/press/bloomberg-view/.

and unlicensed, and there were no professional standards. My grandfather, a barber, had to have a license, but municipal advisers didn't."

We shall see these issues throughout this book starting with the case of *Smith Barney v. Dade* County. Back at the start of the Swap Mania in late 1990s, Dade County, FL sought proposals from investment banks for selling a fixed rate bond issue. Smith Barney offered to help but proposed an alternative financing scheme consisting of issuing the bonds at variable, floating rates and coupling that with interest rate swap contracts requiring the county to pay fixed and receive variable. In their communication with Dade County, the representatives of Smith Barney pressed hard to emphasize the expected savings from entering into these contracts. After many negotiation sessions, numerous presentations and multiple lies, Dade County agreed to the alternative financing arrangements proposed by Smith Barney. It did not take long to find out how costly and wasteful was that financing arrangement. Michael Lissack was the executive at Smith Barney involved in the case. He later blew the whistle on Smith Barney and himself informing the Federal Bureau of Investigation (FBI) of the deceit and fabrication of "facts" in which he was involved to perpetrate fraud on Dade County. In this case, the financial advisor was deceptive and the officials at Dade County believed the promises he made. Furthermore, they did not have the ability to sort out the plausible from the impossible. Only when they saw millions of dollars going out of the door, the fear of escalating the cash outflow led the county to file a complaint with the Securities and Exchange Commission. More discussion about this case is in Chapter 3.

The case of the City of Detroit was not exactly the same as that of Dade County but it was not much different — the officials did not have the requisite knowledge to deal with complex contracts such as interest rate swaps. They had no idea what risks swap contracts posed and accepted the arrangements swap dealers brought their way. They signed onto noncancelable contracts for periods extending up to 30 years as if they had the ability to foretell and manage interest rate risk for that long time in the future. Not knowing much about swap contracts, they believed the swap dealers' sales pitch and the advice they received from the rather incompetent "swap advisors."

Subsequently, the operations managed by these same officials began to experience liquidity crises exacerbated by the impact of trusting the promises made by the self-serving swap dealers. To terminate the city's swap contracts, the city was faced with paying nearly $900 million for termination penalties in 2012 alone before Judge Steven Rhodes, the bankruptcy judge, intervened and helped lower the penalties. However, this was not all; when the previous year's termination payments were added, total termination penalties and fees amounted to $896 million. More about the plight of the City of Detroit is in Chapter 4.

In the State of Pennsylvania, the widespread mishaps of interest rate swaps were perhaps the best gauge of reflecting the financial management abilities of the officials everywhere in the state. The finance personnel at nonprofits did not show signs of having the skills or incentives to understand the risks and rewards of swap contracts. Big banks began to hound them when this type of contracting was new and seemed exotic. Almost 108 public school districts and nearly 105 other government agencies in Pennsylvania entered into interest rate swap contracts only to lose hundreds of millions of dollars a year. Jack Wagner, the former Auditor General of the Commonwealth (State) of Pennsylvania, led a crusade against the purchased swap contracts related to total debt of $17.4 billion. The reluctance and indignation that comes with admitting unfamiliarity with the contracts that swap dealers presented to them with confidence led officials at many nonprofits in the state to fall for the slick and polished salesmanship of swap dealers as if they were speaking the "truth." We shall know more about different organizations in the Commonwealth of Pennsylvania in several chapters of this book. We shall also see a reference to a known occasion when a school board voted to sign with the banks then walked out to say "they did not understand the contract."

There can be no doubt that the actions of all officials at nonprofits from the very small to the very large speak aloud of the lack of understanding the nuances and complexity of interest rate swap contracts. It is true, nonprofit officials were dealing with other people's money and ended up costing their organizations massive amounts of wealth for nothing of value received in exchange. It is most difficult, however, to understand how officials at top universities also fell victims of the Swap Mania just the same as officials at a small public school district or a small hospital. Top universities such as Harvard, North Carolina at Chapel Hill, the University of Texas System, the University of California, Dartmouth College and many others did not seem to exhibit any more astute knowledge or cautionary actions than the officials whose vocation was not in the knowledge industry.

The lack of skill and insights showed up in cases that border on foolhardiness. For example, the Denver Public Schools (DPS) system sold a bond issue to Royal Bank of Canada (RBC), and then hired the same bank to be a "swap advisor" to help DPS write a swap contract also with the same bank, RBC. Naiveté? Perhaps, although it is difficult to claim naïveté or gullibility when DPS claimed to have two in-house financial experts.

In other cases, the swap advisors either did not know or simply lied "in your face" and the officials making decisions were unable to see through the blatantly false information. A case in point is a swap advisor's presentation making a sales pitch to the Board of Commissioners of Dauphin County, PA to enter into a swap contract.[13] He concluded his presentation by repeatedly stating that such a contract has "no exposure to interest rate risk," which is, of course, nonsense. None of the commissioners at the meeting was able to see through the made-up statements he uttered and all agreed to buy the contract! So much for the skill of the officials at nonprofit entities.[14]

It is true though that almost all officials at nonprofit organizations obtained their education before interest rate swaps were taught

---

[13] That was a type of swap known as "basis swap" in which one party pays a variable rate based on one benchmark such as LIBOR and receives from the other party variable rate based on another benchmark such as SIFMA.

Minutes. Dauphin County Board of Commissioners Workshop. April 13, 2005.

Retrieved from http://www.dauphincounty.org/government/About-the-County/Meetings/Minutes/WS041305.pdf.

[14] Swap advisors may not care much about the accuracy of what they say as long as they get paid.

Andrew Kalotay. *SEC Hearing on the State of Municipal Securities Market*, Birmingham, AL, July 29, 2011.

Retrieved from https://www.sec.gov/spotlight/municipalsecurities/statements072911/kalotay.pdf.

anywhere, even in graduate schools. Nevertheless, the lack of formal schooling by itself does not explain or excuse their signing onto non-cancelable contracts to exchange interest rates for 30 and 40 years in the future. Did anyone of them knew that the variable leg of the swap contract depends on the unpredictable and uncontrollable macroeconomic conditions?

Additionally, a more disturbing indicator of the lack of financial skill in the nonprofit sector is their committing to contracts using Auction Rates of interest, which required continuous remarketing (reselling) variable rate bonds once every seven days, 14 days, 28 days or 35 days. Accepting this approach to set variable interest rates on a 30-year bond was problematic because an auction rate bond was typically coupled with swap contracts using different benchmark rates and different rate resetting program. All are decisions and actions border on foolhardiness and signal the absence of any logic or rational thought. Accepting to sell bonds at Auction Rates creates numerous difficulties even without coupling the bond with a swap contract. First, it required paying an annual remarketing fee varying between 0.3% and 0.7%. Second, it required hiring and retaining personnel to oversee the continuous remarketing processes. Third, it subjects the issuing nonprofit entity to the volatility of credit market. Fourth, it gives the market a mechanism to speed up responding to deterioration in the credit rating of the borrowing entity. Finally, when the auctions fail, the new interest rate on the bond would be set at the default rate — i.e., a much higher rate.

Moreover, as if these concerns were not enough to create serious problems, the big banks supporting the Auction Rate Securities carried out clandestine activities. In 2008, the Securities and Exchange Commission (SEC), the New York Department of Financial Services (NYDFS) and a number of investors sued the big banks involved in the Auction Rate Securities (ARS) market alleging they deceived and misled investors. Big banks were forced to admit failing to disclose the increasing risks associated with ARS, including their reduced abilities to support the auctions. (See Linda Chatman Thomsen's Testimony, 2008). By engaging in this conduct, big banks violated the Federal securities laws, including the broker–dealer antifraud provisions. They were all convicted of having committed crimes and were charged heavy penalties. Nevertheless, these convictions did not correct for the bad decisions that nonprofit organizations had already made, almost blindly, using the dreadful Auction Rate system.

Several nonprofits have taken actions to replace the auction-rate bonds. For example, in 2008, Andrew Ackerman wrote that the Texas-based large private nonprofit student loan lender, Brazos Higher Education Service Corporation "may be the first to ask its institutional investors to voluntarily tender, at less than par, roughly $6 billion of outstanding taxable student-loan related auction-rate securities so that it can restructure them as term floating-rate notes."[15]

An Illustrative Case: The Midway Airport Swap

To be more specific and to show how banks profit from interest-rate-exchange contracts beyond charging underwriting fee, we can look at the case of the swap contract related to a bond issue sold by the City of Chicago for Midway Airport.[16] Setting aside the cost of underwriting, insurance and legal fees, the terms of this swap contract are as follows:

(a) The contract has a reference face (notional) amount equal to the face amount of the related bond, which is $152 million in this case. However, it should be noted that the bond and the swap agreement are two separate contracts linked only by purpose.
(b) The contract became effective on December 14, 2004.
(c) The contract is noncancelable for *30 years* and is scheduled to mature on January 1, 2035.
(d) The city pays the counterparty banks a fixed rate of interest at 4.174% per annum.

---

[15] Andrew Ackerman. Lender Is Offering Floating-Rate Notes. *The Bond Buyer*. October 3, 2008.

Retrieved from https://www.bondbuyer.com/news/brazos-asks-investors-to-tender-ars.

[16] The swap contract is related to bond issues, Series 2004C and D.

(e) The city receives from the counterparty banks the Average Municipal Bond Rate of interest (SIFMA) plus 0.05%. By construction, SIFMA is re-measured weekly as the average municipal market rate.[17]

Given that the Municipal Bond Average Interest Rate (SIFMA) was 1.65% at the start of the swap agreement on December 15, 2004, the city would have been paying 4.174% and receiving only 1.7% (1.65% + 0.05%). The 2.474% difference between the two rates was a loss to the city and had to be paid every year although the exact amounts will depend on the movements of the benchmark rate, i.e. SIFMA. In reality, as "Exhibit 5A" shows, the Municipal Bond Average Interest Rate (SIFMA) varied overtime and the city's

Exhibit 5A
The Midway Airport Exhibit

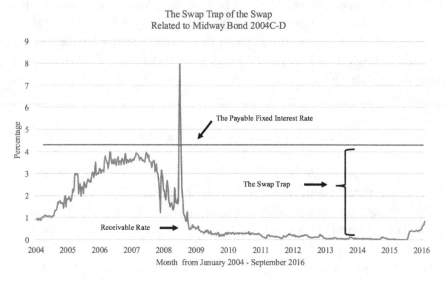

Note: The Municipal Bond Average Interest Rate (or SIFMA) exceeded the swap contract fixed rate during the period September 9, 2008 and October 18, 2008.

---

[17]The SIFMA rate is the weekly average of interest rates of high-grade, variable-rate, tax-exempt municipal bonds compiled and published by the Securities Industry and Financial Market Association.

Retrieved from https://en.wikipedia.org/wiki/Securities_Industry_and_Financial_Markets_Association.

loss in connection with this contract varied with it, but had a special pattern. It (a) was usually a deficit (except for eight months over the past 14 years), and (b) got much worse after the 2008 Financial Crisis. As a reminder, the estimated difference that started at 2.474% excludes other transaction costs such as the cost of swap underwriting, swap advisors, legal counsel, insurance, and the cost of putting up collateral. Furthermore, the difference between fixed and variable rates increased to be close to 4% after the financial crisis of 2008.

It is important to note that the theoretical constructs of designing swap contracts do not account for the continual recurring realization of large losses on one side. As noted earlier, in theory, the adjustable rate should rise gradually until it exceeds the fixed rate at about the midterm of the life of the contract and continues to rise above the fixed rate for the remainder of the contract life up to expiry as "Exhibit 1A" shows clearly. However, that all sounded like academic stuff designed to fit the bankers' paradigm and help them structure means for guaranteed gains.

Exhibit 5A presents the actual results of the Chicago Midway Airport interest rate swap contract for the period between 2004 and 2016. In 2016, the swap contract had 18 years remaining to maturity. Under various conservative assumptions about the movement of adjustable rates, the expected average difference between the fixed rate and adjustable rate multiplied by the notional amount of $152 million calculates to an average of about $3.5 million a year. This is an estimate of the average annual amount of money going from the City of Chicago to Goldman Sachs (until 2011 then to Goldman Sachs and Wells Fargo thereafter until 2035) for this contract alone. To estimate the noncurrent liabilities for future losses, the contract template that big banks follow require projecting the current year's loss into the future until the contract matures in 2035.[18] Under plausible assumptions, the estimated amount of expected long-term liability

---

[18] The "template" or model contract has the name of "Master Agreement," and is designed by a theoretically independent organization by the name of International Swap and Derivatives Association (ISDA). This projection, however, factors in the predicted behavior of yield to maturity and forward interest rates. A short explanation of ISDA's relationship with big banks is at the end of this chapter as well as in Chapter 35.

Usually the two counterparties enter into negotiation to modify the estimated long-term losses. We shall ignore this aspect of the termination penalty because its impact varies from one case to another.

related to this contract could be as high as $54 million (under the assumption of a flat yield curve). However, the city reported $37 million liability in 2012 and $31 million in 2015.[19] As noted earlier, these are services that may never be rendered after termination.

Moreover, as we detail in Chapter 34, the bases for calculating such a liability, which would be the termination penalty if either party chooses that option, are terms of a contract in which unconscionability raised its ugly head though glamorously attributed it to the "Master Agreement".[20]

The swap contract related to the bonds of Midway Airport was a small component of the city's portfolio of swaps. Chapter 6 presents a full picture of the City of Chicago's huge losses on its portfolio of swaps. For example, the amount of long-term liability of the swap contracts reached $549 million in 2012. It is highly likely that the City of Chicago would have not faced the ongoing serious budgetary or spending problems if its officials did not jump into a lake full of "swaps," the intangible snakes. The large amounts of funds the city had diverted to big banks for interest rate swaps as either annual payments, or termination penalties would have gone a long way to avert problems arising from the budgetary shortfall.

The Impetus for the Exponential Growth of Derivatives and Swaps

Some people might, and for good reasons, consider the two years 1999–2000 as the years of *Financial Economics Infamy*. In those two years, Congress and President Clinton sent two powerful messages to big banks and the world:

1. Big banks may acquire and merge with any other organization be it in investment banking, an entity in the insurance industry or any other

---

[19]The city renegotiated $84 million notional amounts and moved them from Goldman Sachs to Wells Fargo. The cost of that transaction is not known except that the fixed rate increases from 4.174% to 4.247%. In 2016, the notional amount was reduced from $152 million to $132 million and the long-term loss was $26 million.

[20]In Chapter 34, we show the identity of the 10 banks that established the International Swap and Derivatives Association (ISDA) and also the names of the 19 big banks currently sitting on the Board of Directors of ISDA.

financial company to grow big and bigger without any limits. (The Gramm–Leach–Bliley Act of 1999 following the Riegle–Neal Act of 1994).
2. Big banks may gamble as much as they wish using any financial instrument they and others develop or invent. (Section 117 in The Commodity Futures Modernization Act, 2000).

Earlier, in 1994, Congress approved and President Clinton signed the Riegle–Neal Interstate Banking and Branching Efficiency Act (Riegle–Neal Act) granting big banks the freedom to erase state lines and branch across state borders of any state that concurs with the act starting on or before June 1, 1997.[21] Increasing bank size because of unlimited branching out into other states was constrained by a maximum relative measure of deposits — no bank should have more than 10% of total market-wide deposits. However, crossing state lines to establish or acquire other banks to facilitate branch banking was not good enough for the banks that wanted to become megabanks with dominant influence on the nation's economic machinery. That kind of growth would come by adding other functions to commercial banking more than just collecting deposits and making loans.

On November 12, 1999, Congress passed, and President Clinton signed the "Financial Services Modernization Act," which has become known as the Gramm–Leach–Bliley Act (GLBA).[22] The major impact of the Act was rolling the clock backward to the pre-1933 conditions and repealing major sections of Glass–Steagall Act.[23] There was no "modernization" in marching

---

[21] David Fettig, David S. Dahl, and Kathy Cobb. Interstate branch banking: Opt in or opt out? *FEDGAZETTE*. The Federal Reserve Bank of Minneapolis. January 1, 1995.

https://www.minneapolisfed.org/publications/fedgazette/interstate-branch-banking-opt-in-or-opt-out.

[22] The three federal Acts, Riegle–Neal Act, The Gramm, Leach and Bliley Act, and the Commodity Futures Modernization Act, use the words "efficiency" or "modernization" in their titles, which is a way of hypnotizing people to think of them as achieving admirable goals. None of them, however, had shown "efficiency" or "modernization" in any uncontestable shape.

[23] One major component of Glass–Steagall Act established the Federal Deposit Insurance Corporation (FDIC). That section was not part of GLB and remained intact.

backward even though the word "modernization" is in the name of the Act; GLBA allows commercial banks to acquire and affiliate with investment banks and insurance companies. GLBA opened the doors to the formation of mega size banks for which Charles Mitchell coined the names of "financial mall" and a "one-stop-shop."[24] Soon after the president signed GLBA, Chase Bank and JP Morgan Company merged to form JPMorgan Chase in 2000. Almost two years earlier, Sanford Weil formed Citigroup that included Citibank and The Travelers Group, which was a collection of insurance and investment banking establishments.[25] Other banks followed suit — GLBA was a call for "merger for all" without discrimination.

The urge to project the "modernization" theme continued in the titles, but not in the substance, of other Acts. On December 20, 2000, Congress passed and President Clinton signed the Commodity Futures Modernization Act (CFMA). This Act was concerned with the organization, structure and operation of OTC financial derivatives market with one ultimate undeclared goal: to prevent the Commodity Futures Trading Commission and its Chair Brooksley Born from regulating OTC market or even requiring the most limited measures of transparency. Signing this Act came back to haunt President Clinton who, in 2010, blamed his signing of CFMA on Robert Rubin (Secretary of the Treasury), Larry Summers (Deputy Secretary of the Treasury) and Alan Greenspan (Chairman of the Federal Reserve Board).[26] In an interview with reporters in March 2010, President

---

[24] Charles E Mitchell was the former CEO and President of New York City Bank, the predecessor of Citibank who built an empire not too much different from what we see as modern financial malls. Mitchell was forced out of the job and his empire was dismantled by the enactment of Glass–Steagall Act in 1933.

See, for example, Michael Perino, *The Hellhound of Wall Street: How Ferdinand Pecora's Investigation of the Great Crash forever Changed American Finance.* (Penguin Books. New York, 2010.

[25] The formation of Citigroup was in 1998 and has its own saga of exemptions and favoritism.

[26] Ryan Chittum. Bill Clinton on deregulation: "The Republicans made me do it!" The ex-president seriously mischaracterizes his record. *Columbia Journalism Review.* The Audit Archive

   http://archives.cjr.org/the_audit/bill_clinton_the_republicans_m.php.

Susie Madrak. I was wrong to listen to Rubin and Summers on Derivatives. Crooks and Liars. April 19, 2010.

   https://crooksandliars.com/susie-madrak/president-clinton-i-was-wrong-listen.

Clinton uttered explanations that boil down to a simple expression, "They made me do it."

There is danger, however, in focusing attention on the failure of CFMA to regulate OTC markets. This misguided attention led everyone to miss or ignore the much more critical section of the Act. That is Section 117, which preempted all state and local laws against gambling on securities and other commodities. Here is a partial text of that section[27]:

> *This Act shall supersede and preempt the application of any State or local law that prohibits or regulates gaming or the operation of bucket shops (other than antifraud provisions of general applicability. (105)*

The "bucket shops" expression referenced in this Act were gambling establishments that flourished in the U.S.A. between 1876 and 1908.[28] The growth of these establishments was never derailed by the U.S. Supreme Court decisions of 1905 and 1906 declaring them as illegal gambling establishment.[29] Achieving the eradication of bucket shops was left for the 1907 Bank Panic and stock market crash. To save New York Stock Exchange from further damage from the encroachment of bucket shops, the State of New York enacted a legislation in May 1908 prohibiting the operation of "bucket shops." Other states followed suit and enacted similar laws.[30] Largely, these laws *remained in effect until December 20, 2000*

---

[27] Commodity Futures and Modernization Act. December 14, 2000. The 106 Congress.
Retrieved from http://www.cftc.gov/files/ogc/ogchr5660.pdf.

[28] David Hochfelder, a known historian in this area, claims that bucket shops were dead by 1915, although Governor Hughes of New York signed the prohibition law in 1908 to become effective on September 1.

David Hochfelder. How Bucket Shops Lured the Masses Into the Market. Bloomberg January 10, 2013.
Retrieved from https://www.bloomberg.com/view/articles/2013-01-10/how-bucket-shops-lured-the-masses-into-the-market.

[29] U.S. Supreme Court. November 16, 1906. ERNEST GATEWOOD, Plff. in Err., v. STATE OF NORTH CAROLINA. 203 U.S. 531 (27 S.Ct. 167, 51 L.Ed. 305). Legal Information Institute, Cornell University.
Retrieved from https://www.law.cornell.edu/supremecourt/text/203/531.

[30] David Hochfelder, September 2006. "Where the Common People Could Speculate": The Ticker, Bucket Shops, and the Origins of Popular Participation in Financial Markets, 1880–1920. *The Journal of American History,* pp. 335–358.

when CFMA came along to re-establish the right of entrepreneurs to run bucket-shop-like operations.[31] Back then, the bankers charted a path to build up the gaming segment of their business. By any logic in any language, enacting a law in 2000 to return to the pre-1908 conditions cannot be "modernization" — it is marching backward that might as well be described as "backwardization."

Except for the similarity between OTC financial derivatives and bucket shops, there was no *prima facie* reason for placing section 117 (preempting all state and local laws against financial gambling) in CFMA. But there is definitely a functional similarity between swap dealers and the bucketeers who owned and managed bucket shops. Interest rate swap contracts are simply bets on the movement of interest rate just as bucket shops operated to bet on prices. In combination, allowing commercial banks to be financial shopping malls (GLBA) coupled with CFMA preemption of anti-gambling laws has led to an explosive growth of OTC derivatives. The graph reported by the U.S. Office of the Comptroller of the Currency, "Exhibit 6A", shows the growth in total notional (face) amounts of derivatives held by the largest 25 U.S. commercial banks up to $192 trillion ($192,000,000,000,000) on March 31, 2016. On the same date, the largest 25 U.S. bank holding companies had a total notional (face) balance of $250 trillion ($250,000,000,000,000) of OTC derivatives.[32] These numbers were only for the notional, face amounts. However, the real values are not difficult to estimate. The derivatives statistics provided by the Bank for International Settlements estimate the actual and real, "fair" market value of OTC derivatives to fall between 2.2% and 3.9% of notional amounts with an unweighted

---

Retrieved from https://academic.oup.com/jah/article/93/2/335/830224.

Brendan Sapien. 2010. Financial Weapons of Mass Destruction: From Bucket Shops to Credit Default Swaps. *Southern California Interdisciplinary Law Journal.*

Retrieved from http://clhc.usc.edu/why/students/orgs/ilj/assets/docs/19-2%20Sapien.pdf.

[31] Eric Lipton and Stephen Labaton. November 16, 2008. Deregulator Looks Back, Unswayed. *The New York Times.*

Retrieved from http://www.nytimes.com/2008/11/17/business/economy/17gramm.html.

[32] Many of the noted commercial banks are also members of bank holding companies.

Exhibit 6A
Growth of OTC Derivatives the Largest
25 U.S. Banks (For 2000–2016)

Derivative Notionals by Type

Insured U.S. Commercial Banks and Savings Associations

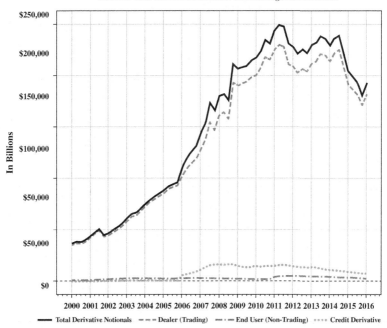

Source: Office of the Comptroller of the Currency. *Quarterly Report on Bank Trading and Derivatives Activities*. First Quarter 2016 (Washington D. C., June 2016).

https://www.occ.gov/topics/capital-markets/financial-markets/derivatives/dq116.pdf.

average of 3.2%.[33] Thus, the real value of OTC derivatives in 2012 would be about $6.1 trillion ($6,100,000,000,000) for the largest 25

---

[33] Notional (Market Value)

$76 trillion ($1.7 trillion) in 2001. Retrieved from https://www.bis.org/publ/otc_hy0112. pdf, p. 5.

$204 trillion ($6.0 trillion) in 2005. Retrieved from https://www.bis.org/publ/otc_hy0511. pdf, p. 7.

U.S. commercial banks and $8.25 trillion ($8,250,000,000,000) for the largest 25 U.S. bank holding companies. About 70% of these amounts are by and large for interest rate contracts.

With these unthinkable numbers for balances of OTC derivatives at one point in time, the average daily volume of trading stood at near $4 billion in 2017. Thus the average annual trade was nearly one and half trillion. It is, therefore, nonsensical to claim that OTC derivatives are used for hedging risk. There are two reasons for making this statement. First, the U.S. Gross Domestic Product (GDP, or the market value of all products and services in 2016) stood at $18 trillion ($18,000,000,000,000) and no one could ever think of having instruments on $250 trillion ($250,000,000,000,000) to hedge that much level of activities. Second, Exhibit 6A shows a picture consistent with the data big banks report: about 98% of their OTC derivatives are held for trading, i.e., profit making in the short run.

Incidentally, the statistics about the amounts of outstanding OTC derivatives does not include the derivatives held by insurance companies, hedge funds and other financial institutions for which the counterparties are not any of the largest 25 U.S. banks. The derivatives traded on organized official exchanges are also not included in the OTC data. When all are added up, the U.S. might be exposed to more than 60% of OTC derivatives worldwide.[34]

The exotic features of interest rate swaps and other derivatives seem to have enthralled the officials at nonprofit organizations to the point of subordinating the core business of their operations to dancing with interest rate swaps. For example, one of the main responsibilities of the

---

$479 trillion ($19.0 trillion) in 2010. Retrieved from https://www.bis.org/publ/otc_hy1011.pdf, p. 13.

$561 trillion ($15.0 trillion) in 2013. Retrieved from https://www.bis.org/publ/otc_hy1311.pdf, p. 19

$438 trillion ($16.0 trillion) in 2016. Retrieved from https://www.bis.org/publ/otc_hy1611.pdf, p. 13.

[34]For completeness of presentation, most of these OTC derivatives are for the corporate sector and the share of the nonprofits is relatively smaller. However, a small loss in the nonprofit causes more damage than a larger loss in the corporate sector — nonprofits spend other people's money taken away from essential services.

administration of the City of Philadelphia, like the governance of any city, is managing the supply of fresh water to homes and businesses and disposing of wastewater. Yet, when compared with interest rate swaps, the roles seem to have been reversed. The 2016 Comprehensive Annual Financial Report of the City of Philadelphia cited the word "swap" 231 times, while the word "water" was repeated only 109 times. For another example, the 2015 Comprehensive Annual Financial Report of NY MTA repeated the word swap 140 times while the words "buses" and "trains" were repeated 124 times.

The Orbit of ISDA: The Inside Shop

Shortly after the accidental invention of interest rate swaps in 1982, big banks began writing more of these contracts. To help them manage the process, they formed a volunteer association in 1985 and called it the "International Swaps Dealers Association" (ISDA) to act as a seemingly independent crutch on which big banks could lean for support and lobbying. (Later, ISDA was renamed "the International Swaps and Derivatives Association.") The original founders of ISDA were the following 10 banks.

Bankers Trust, Citibank, First Boston, Goldman Sachs, Kleinwort Benson, Merrill Lynch, Morgan Stanley, Morgan Guaranty Trust, Salomon Brothers, and Shearson Lehman Brothers.

In his book, *Infectious Greed*, Frank Partnoy notes that the founding 10 banks together made up 80% of the swaps market at that time.[35] Following its establishment, ISDA moved forward in strides to solidify the positions of big banks. This organization was positioned in a way to appear as if it were neutral, independent body governing the industry. ISDA makes enough noise constantly to convince the world it is a

---

[35]Partnoy, *Infectious Greed.* p. 45.

legitimate neutral professional body, although 19 of the 26 ISDA Board members are big banks.

- In 1995, ISDA developed a prototype for swap contracts and called it the "Master Agreement." One goal of the Master Agreement was to determine a highly unorthodox way of measuring what big banks should collect from counterparties in swap contracts in case of premature cancelation.
- According to the terms of the Master Agreement, the amounts that losing counterparties would be required to pay swap dealers upon premature termination of swap contracts should, in essence, be determined as if the following two conditions were satisfied. (a) The agreement was never terminated, and (b) losses of the counterparty in the termination period would have continued at the same level (adjusted by changes in the yield curve) all the way up to the original maturity date of the agreement. However, there is a limited room for negotiation and mediation by other banks.
- Thus, if a counterparty terminates a losing contract, the counterparty must compensate swap dealers and the related banks for the amounts of money the banks could have collected for each year remaining in the original term to maturity. It does not really matter if there was no service or benefit provided. That amount is an unrealized opportunity cost and is surprisingly called "fair" value. It is rare to see the reverse.
- Accordingly, the resulting termination payment is nothing more than a legitimized stealth way of affecting unjust enrichment, perhaps the most skilled in history. This is even more true when it comes to contracts with nonprofits whose peculiar administrators had irrationally signed onto swap agreements to mature in 30 or even 40 years.

If you think for a minute that this characterization is an exaggeration, you will need to know that currently 19 of the 26 ISDA board members are big banks.[36] The names of these banks ware contained in ISDA Press Release on April 23, 2015 and are in "Exhibit 7A."

Relying on the "Master Agreement" template, nonprofit entities have been paying obscenely large amounts of money for terminating swap

---

[36] ISDA Press Release. April 23, 2015. ISDA Elects 12 Board Members.
  Retrieved from https://www.isda.org/2015/04/23/isda-elects-12-board-members-4/.

Exhibit 7A

International Swap and Derivatives Association Press Release Regarding the Composition of its Board of Directors

Composition of ISDA Board (Bank names are in bold).

Two new directors were elected. They are:

- Yasunobu Arima, General Manager, Global Markets Planning Division, **The Bank of Tokyo-Mitsubishi UFJ, Ltd (BTMU).**

- Sam Skerry, Global Head of Structured Products and IST Commercial Support, BP plc.

10 directors were re-elected:

- Keith Bailey, Managing Director, Market Structure, **Barclays.**
- Nitin Gulabani, Global Head of FX, Rates and Credit Trading, **Standard Chartered Bank.**
- Rich Herman, Head of Global Fixed Income & Currencies (FIC), **Deutsche Bank Securities, Inc.**
- Kieran Higgins, Head of Trading, Corporate & Institutional Banking, **The Royal Bank of Scotland** Plc.
- Jonathan Hunter, Global Head of Fixed Income and Currencies, **RBC [Royal Bank of Canada] Capital Markets.**
- J Lim, Global Head of Markets, **UniCredit.**
- Eric Litvack, Managing Director, Head of Regulatory Strategy, **Société Générale Global Banking And Investor Solutions.**
- Christopher Murphy, Global Co-Head of FX, Rates & Credit, **UBS Investment Bank.**
- Ciaran O'Flynn, Managing Director, Global Co-Head of Fixed Income Electronic Trading, **Morgan Stanley.**
- Emmanuel Ramambason, Head of Global Market xVA Trading, **BNP Paribas.**

The directors continuing on the Board are:

- Biswarup Chatterjee, Global Head Electronic Trading & New Business Development, Credit Markets, **Citigroup Global Markets.**
- Bill De Leon, Managing Director, Global Head of Portfolio Risk Management, PIMCO.
- Elie El Hayek, Managing Director, Global Head of Rates, Credit and EM Global Markets, **HSBC Bank Plc.**
- Diane Genova, Managing Director and General Counsel, Global Markets, **JP Morgan Chase & Co.**
- Jonathan Hall, Advisory Director, **Goldman, Sachs & Co.**
- George Handjinicolaou, Deputy Chief Executive Officer, ISDA.
- Ted MacDonald, Managing Director, DE Shaw & Co, LP., Chief Risk Officer, DE Shaw Group.
- Scott O'Malia, Chief Executive Officer, ISDA.
- Richard Prager, Managing Director and Global Head of Trading and Liquidity Strategies, BlackRock.
- Will Roberts, Head of Global Rates, Structured Credit Trading and Counterparty Portfolio Management, **Bank of America Merrill Lynch.**
- Koji Sakurai, Senior Vice President, Head of Business Planning Team, Derivative Products Division, **Mizuho Bank, Ltd.**
- Eraj Shirvani, Head of Fixed Income for EMEA and Global Head of Emerging Markets for Investment Banking, **Credit Suisse Group AG.**
- Emmanuel Vercoustre, Deputy CEO & CFO, **AXA Bank Europe.**

contracts. It is indeed surprising that no one is known to have made the connection between these payments and big banks controlling and engineering the design of ISDA's Master Agreement. Furthermore, there seems to be no awareness that paying termination fees as currently calculated is paying for services not, and will never be, provided. Even the legal experts have tackled the derivatives' problem with big banks from the antitrust angle, not from the persistent indication of unconscionable contracting, and unjust enrichment, as we shall see in various cases presented in this book.[37]

On the other hand, typical financial officers at nonprofit entities may not be all that suspicious when they observe elite knowledge organizations like Harvard University Management Corporation pay a hefty $1.25 billion for terminating their interest rate swaps without making a fuss or even raising doubt about its legitimacy.

After my reading the 40-page "Master Agreement" of ISDA, it became clear that the "Master Agreement" is incomprehensible even to the most highly educated. Officials at nonprofit entities have no comparative advantage to comprehend, understand or decipher the terms and implications of the variations and contingencies thrown into the Master Agreement. I passed the draft I had to two contract-law attorneys to read and both of them came back to me independently noting their strong conviction that the Master Agreement is confusing, convoluted and full of complex terms and contingencies intended, perhaps, to simultaneously impress and confuse normal mortals.

Then again, it is also arguable that if the managers and officials at nonprofit entities had signed onto these contracts without fully comprehending their terms and implications, they might be in violation of their fiduciary responsibilities. These officials should not, therefore, be surprised if the people at Goldman Sachs and other big banks find all the reasons to call them "muppets."[38]

---

[37] See the LIBOR Scandal discussed in Chapter 33.

[38] Greg Smith, March 14, 2012. Why I am leaving Goldman Sachs. *The New York Times.*
Retrieved from http://www.nytimes.com/2012/03/14/opinion/why-i-am-leaving-goldman-sachs.html?_r=0.

Look Who is Guarding the Henhouse!

The Means of Persuasion that
Big Banks had Adopted

(a) *Persuasion: Promising Mirage Benefits*

Finance officials at nonprofit entities come from an educated crowd who most likely had a level of financial sophistication higher than that of the average administrator. This observation, however, begs the question of their incentives or motivation in signing on to interest rate swaps that do not mature for decades and could only increase risk exposure. This behavior could be evidence of not having the requisite knowledge that led them to agree to actions for which no rational explanation can be easily developed.

The biggest lure that swap dealers used in their swap sales pitch was promoting the prospect of lowering the cost of borrowing and saving money for swap counterparties, i.e., nonprofits. At times of shrinking liquidity and facing budgetary shortfalls, offering such a possibility activated a weak button in all types of administrative structures of nonprofit organizations. The sales pitch of big banks typically involved making several presentations to convert a weak button into a panic button, which they could then make an offer to soothe. Big banks did not hesitate in using this weakness to bombard the officials of nonprofit entities with various alternatives that gradually swayed them into believing in the two main promised benefits of swaps: (a) lowering the cost of debt, and (b) managing interest rate risk.

One of the methods adopted for persuasion was the repeated presentations about the different benefits attainable under the suggested financing package. Cases demonstrating this strategy include Smith Barney v. Dade County and Jefferson County vs. JPMorgan Chase. Prior to having any contractual commitment, JPMorgan Chase sent trainers in risk management to Birmingham, Alabama numerous times to make presentations and then partnered with the county administration to cosponsor a high-profile statewide conference on risk management. When the iron was hot, JPMorgan Chase paid Jefferson County $23 million upfront money and signaled its willingness to pay grease money to county commissioners, an act the executives representing the bank appeared happy to perform. The details of this saga are in Chapter 3.

"Giving the sales pitch over and over, I started to believe it" — Theresa Tucker.[39]

This book includes several cases about which the public gained knowledge by virtue of being subjects of litigation. In addition to Jefferson County, the case of Smith Barney and Dade County provides evidence for making several presentations by Michael Lissack and his team from Smith Barney (currently part of Citigroup's Global Corporate and Investment Bank). They kept doing so until they convinced the reluctant county officials that the proposed swap contracts should bring cost savings and benefits to the county. Nonetheless, all turned out to be unrealizable as discussed further in Chapter 2.

Next we will see the case of Peralta Community College District. According to a Grand Jury report, the board of trustees participated in many well-structured demonstrations and presentations by different banks. The presentations introduced interest rate swaps as "an attractive opportunity for potential savings" due to unusual interest rates in effect at that time.

Moreover, we shall see how the City of Chicago had a rough ride with big banks. Jason Grotto and Heather Gillers of the *Chicago Tribune* note the early lobbying by Goldman Sachs to prepare the officials at Chicago Public Schools to join the Swap Mania.

As early as 2000, *a vice president of municipal finance at Goldman Sachs* asked to meet with CPS [Chicago Public School] officials about the possibility of *issuing auction-rate bonds* in a letter circulated to Cepeda (the financial advisor to the Chicago Public Schools Board) and school and city officials. The letter highlighted the potential cost savings, and accompanying materials quoted an *anonymous financial adviser as saying the product had "no downside."*[40] [Emphasis added]

---

[39] Maija Palmer, "You get a thick skin and you learn when not to be at the bar," *Financial Times.* September 27, 2017, p. 5.

Retrieved from https://www.ft.com/content/743cfdc2-715c-11e7-93ff-99f383b09ff9.

[40] Jason Grotto and Heather Gillers, "Risky Bonds Prove Costly for Chicago Public Schools," *Chicago Tribune,* November 7, 2014.

In Chapter 7, we shall see the case of the City of Oakland. After a number of presentations by Goldman Sachs, the city issued a variable rate debt and entered into a swap contract with Goldman Sachs to hedge interest rate risk related to that bond issue. The City was able to pay off the bond issue by the year 2008, but the swap contract continued. After paying off the debt, interest-rate-swap contracts lose the benefits of hedging and risk management and would instead add risk and cost but nothing else. Public appeals to Goldman Sachs to consider the financial difficulties the city was facing and cancel the swaps at no cost to the city went unheeded. The city will continue to pay Goldman Sachs for what is currently costly and useless interest rate swaps until the year 2021.

Another outrageous misuse of public funds was paying for a swap contract related to the promised reductions in the cost of borrowing on a nonexistent bond issue. This was a case with the State of New Jersey; it had paid over $22 million to the Bank of Montreal for a swap contract related to a bond issue that the State had never sold. The story is part of Chapter 9. There was also the case with State College Area Public School in Pennsylvania that paid $9 million for a swap related to bonds that were never sold.

Under the financing strategy that banks touted, if the variable interest receivable from the swap contract covers the variable interest payable on the bonds, the expected combined effect of these two contracts would, presumably, fix the interest rate on the debt artificially (or synthetically). Swap dealers promised that the synthetic fixed rate achievable in this fashion should be lower than the fixed interest rate payable on conventional municipal bonds, but they offered no guarantees. However, even if we stay at that level of discourse and ignore all the other embedded and hidden costly terms, such a promise proved to be a mirage, and the cost of borrowing had actually increased. Furthermore, when the variable rate on the bonds was changing every week (called auction rate), the obtained synthetic rate could not be fixed for more than one week at a time. A weekly auction rate on municipal bonds requires a costly weekly remarketing and seeking bids on interest rates that investors would accept. Similarly, the floating rate that replaced the auction

---

Retrieved from http://www.chicagotribune.com/news/watchdog/cpsbonds/ct-chicago-public-schools-bond-deals-met-20141107-story.html.

rate structure links the interest rate being charged to a benchmark rate such as LIBOR or Municipal Bond Average Interest Rate (SIFMA) with the payable interest rate being adjusted weekly. This was a problem with most of the cases presented in this book — e.g., the University of North Carolina (Chapter 16), Chicago Public Schools (Chapter 14), and the City of Chicago (Chapter 6), wherein the city stated[41]:

> The Series 2004C-D bonds were sold in December with an initial *auction rate* of 1.55 percent and 1.45 percent and maturity dates ranging from January 1, 2012 to January 1, 2035. [Emphasis added]
>
> …
>
> At the discretion of the City, the Series 2004C-D bonds may bear interest at a weekly, flexible, adjustable long, auction rate or fixed rate. *The City issued the bonds in the auction rate mode for a seven-day auction period.* [Emphasis added]

(b) *Persuasion: Providing Near-Term Quick Cash*

Making advance payments to nonprofit entities was another clever way of enticing officials to commit and sign on the dotted line. Although this book covers a small sample of cases, they are sufficient to draw the mosaic of failure that exist in the nonprofit sector due to getting entrapped in the net of the Swap Mania. The injured entities range from cities such as the City of Atlanta, the City of Philadelphia, and the City of Chicago, to public schools such as Bethlehem Area School District, universities such as the University of North Carolina and the University of Texas System, to counties such as Jefferson County, Alabama.

Big banks selling swap contracts made advance payments to counterparties in several ways, two of which were more common. The first method was making outright upfront payments at the time of signing the contracts. In substance, these advance payments were loans, though not recorded as such until recently. The other approach to advancing money to swap buyers was through agreeing to a compound contract called swaption. A swaption is a contract composed of two stages. At

---

[41] City of Chicago, Comprehensive Annual Financial Report, 2004, p. 69.

first, a nonprofit entity sells an option to a bank, giving it the right to compel the nonprofit to enter into an interest-rate-swap contract at a future date to be decided by the bank. The nonprofit entity collects the option premium (sale price) in advance to ease short-term liquidity needs but becomes obligated to sign the swap agreement when the bank exercises the option. However, once the bank decides, the resulting swap contract would not differ from any other swaps; the nonprofit entity typically pays the bank a fixed rate of interest and receives from the bank an adjustable rate of interest.[42]

In both cases of collecting upfront money or selling a swaption, the nonprofit entity would be effectively locked into a noncancelable swap contract for a period equal to the life of the related bond — i.e., 30 years or longer. The power of collecting quick cash to ease short-term liquidity crises was often irresistible. The Jefferson County Commission, for example, found it easy to accept $23 million upfront money offered by JPMorgan Chase that led the county into swap contracts loaded with disasters. The City of Philadelphia accepted over $100 million upfront payments related to swap contracts for four of its component departments (excluding the school district).

Harrisburg, the capital city of Pennsylvania, had also filed for bankruptcy in 2011 after it paid Royal Bank of Canada and other banks more than $105 million to terminate interest-rate-swap contracts in addition to incurring a loss of more than $200 million on re-engineering its incinerator. As we shall see in Chapters 5 and 11, the city and Dauphin County were also the center of attention for the crusade against interest rate swaps led by former Auditor General (2005–2013) Jack Wagner. Wagner began his campaign after observing significant losses from involvement in interest rate swaps in 108 public school districts and 105 government agencies. Yet, after uncovering a significant amount of damage, as we shall see in Chapters 11–13, Dauphin County of Pennsylvania, the home of the capital city, Harrisburg, needed short-term financing and decided on July 9, 2014, to sell a swaption contract to Royal Bank of Canada. The swaption

---

[42]The other type of interest rate exchange agreements is "Basis Swap" which requires exchanging one variable rate for another.

gave the bank the right to force the county to enter into an interest-rate-swap contract at a future date of the bank's own choosing.[43]

In Chicago, Royal Bank of Canada enters the picture again. The bank makes $25 million upfront payment to Chicago Public Schools (CPS). Concurrently, Bank of America paid CPS $18 million upfront. Both of these arrangement were in relation to swaption contracts that CPS sold to the two banks. In spite of allegations of conducting incomplete and primitive analysis before entering into these contracts, Gillers and Grotto of the *Chicago Tribune* note that the city and school officials were blindly attracted to the lure of quick cash. Yet, when the deals backfired and both the city and CPS were drowning in red ink, no one wanted to take responsibility.[44] To this day, after dealing with interest rate swaps for nearly 25 years, the City of Chicago and Chicago Public Schools District (CPS) continue to squabble over assigning responsibility and blame for the mounting losses from swap contracts.

All types of upfront payments, however, served the function of locking the receiving nonprofit entities into long-term commitments from which they could be partially or completely relieved only by bankruptcy or by paying huge penalties.

(c) *Persuasion: Buying Swaps as Seen by a Grand Jury*

The problems noted above were clearly demonstrated in the case of Peralta Community College District (the District), which is the largest

---

[43]The contract is called swaption. The county collected a premium for the option component that gives Royal Bank of Canada (the counterparty) the right to sell an interest-rate-swap contract to the county at a future date of the bank's choosing. The ordinance authorizing this transaction is number 2–2014 and resolution 22–2014.

Minutes Dauphin County Board of Commissioners Workshop, July 9, 2014.

Retrieved from http://www.dauphincounty.org/government/About-the-County/Meetings/Minutes/WS%2007%2009%202014.pdf.

[44]Heather Gillers and Jason Grotto, "Banks kept CPS in shaky bond market," *Chicago Tribune*, November 10, 2014.

Retrieved from http://www.chicagotribune.com/news/watchdog/cpsbonds/ct-chicago-public-schools-bonds-banks-met-20141107-story.html.

community college in the State of California and perhaps the country.[45] The College is funded by public money and is therefore subject to public scrutiny. The District was dealing with several banks: Lehman Brothers, which was replaced by Neuberger Berman after Lehman's bankruptcy; Deutsche Bank; and Morgan Stanley. The District also had five financial advisers who received $1,077,000 in consulting fees between 2005 and 2010. Deutsche Bank and Morgan Stanley gave the District a small upfront payment and emphasized the possibility of lowering the cost of borrowing. The District entered into several swap agreements. When interest rate swaps backfired and the college lost relatively significant amounts of money to Morgan Stanley, investigating the matter became a subject for the Alameda County Grand Jury.[46]

The problem for the District began in 1994 when the Governmental Accounting Standards Board required public entities like the District to project and recognize as debt the expected obligations for postretirement benefits, such as the cost of providing health care to retirees. The term Other-Post-Employment-Benefits (OPEB) describes the newly recognized obligation. To fund OPEB obligations, Lehman Brothers, Deutsche Bank, and other financial consultants[47] advised the college to deviate from the traditional fixed-rate municipal finance and issue six series of bonds that mature consecutively in periods ranging from 10 to 30 years and that pay *auction interest rates adjustable weekly*.[48] According to the

---

[45]Located in northern Alameda County, Peralta Community College District (PCCD) serves more than 220,000 students and operates four college campuses: the College of Alameda, Laney College, Merritt College, and Berkeley City College. The district is governed by a seven-member board of trustees elected by the citizens of Alameda County and funded by taxpayer dollars.

Retrieved from https://www.acgov.org/grandjury/final2010-2011.pdf.

[46]Peralta Community College District Final Report, Other Post-Employment Benefits Program. KNN Public Finance, June 28, 2011.

Retrieved from http://web.peralta.edu/accreditation/files/2012/01/3.-OPEB-Final-Report-June-28-2011-KNN.pdf.

[47]Peralta Community College District entered into contracts to sell adjustable-rate bonds and to exchange (swap) interest rates with Deutsche Bank and Morgan Stanley.

[48]This interest rate is known as the auction rate. However, in the case of PCCD bonds, payment of interest for each bond series was deferred until the end of the series.

Grand Jury's findings, the banks reassured the District of realizing future benefits of interest-rate-swap contracts, as described in the reproduced short history presented in "Exhibit 7A."

Yet, significant losses rendered the advice of swap pushers and advisors to be dysfunctional for two reasons. First, accepting to sell bonds at a <u>weekly adjustable auction rate</u> exposed the District to the risk of credit markets every week. Second, the inability of the board of trustees to understand the intricate complexity of interest rate swaps and the financing packages put forth by bankers.

Exhibit 7A
A Short Summary of the History of Swaps at
Peralta Community College

The banks presented interest rate swaps as "an attractive opportunity for potential savings" due to unusual interest rates in effect at that time. Each interest rate SWAP can be understood as a contract in which PCCD and a financial institution "bet against each other" about the future levels of fixed and variable interest rates. In 2006, the District entered into a number of interest rate SWAPs (derivatives) intended to hedge some of the risk that interest rates would increase before the various series of the bonds were priced…By 2010, the bond obligations and related swaps were a significant drain on the district's [College's] general fund, which contributed to the decision to place the college on probation…Each additional action cited above incurred further transaction fees for the benefit of the same outside financial advisors. Based on a simple bond calculation model, the Grand Jury estimated that [the college's] total…bond cost (principal and interest) would have been $390 million had they been conventional 45-year bonds with an $8.6 million annual payment assuming a 5.19% interest rate. Instead, the district now faces bond costs of nearly $540 million.

Source: Alameda County Grand Jury Final Report, p. 147. Retrieved from https://www.acgov.org/grandjury/final 2010-2011.pdf.

The contracts of Peralta College specify that failure to market the bonds in any week will result in charging the default rate of 17%.
Alameda County Civil Grand Jury, p. 146.
 Retrieved from https://www.acgov.org/grandjury/final2010-2011.pdf.

In the process, the very existence of the college was threatened by fiscal mismanagement. "In July 2010, the Accrediting Commission for Community and Junior Colleges (ACCJC), which operates under the Western Association of Schools and Colleges, placed the District on probation, citing concerns about "fiscal insolvency and stability, jeopardizing the district's accreditation."[49] The grand jury's summary and conclusion highlighted the weak spots of the process that led to entering into swap agreements, which cost the public relatively large sums of money. "Exhibit 8A" presents the text of a segment of these conclusions.

Like numerous other cases, the experience of Peralta Community College District was of no help to other entities facing the same encroachment by swap dealers because that experience remained localized until the grand jury issued its report.

Exhibit 8A
The Conclusion of Investigating Peralta College Swaps

In summary, there were several ways in which the board of trustees "pushed the envelope" of appropriate financing decisions:

- At substantial expense, PCCD restructured its OPEB debt twice and is considering a third restructuring so as to defer payments and release short-term General Fund dollars.
- The use of Convertible Auction Rate Securities exposed the district to poorly understood, complicated and expensive financial risks. 2010-2011 Alameda County Grand Jury Final Report
- The district used interest rate SWAPs (derivatives) not fully understood by the board, expecting to gain additional interest rate advantages to reduce short-term costs and boost revenues for the district.
- The Grand Jury learned of one other California community college district that issued bonds to "pre-fund" its OPEB obligations. The Grand Jury was informed that this other district chose more conventional methods of borrowing money to fund its OPEB trusts and is in a much better position today than PCCD to actually pay for both its OPEB costs and related debt. Most other districts chose the "pay-as-you-go" method.

Source: Alameda County Grand Jury Final Report, pp. 148–149. Retrieved from https://www.acgov.org/grandjury/final2010-2011.pdf.

---

[49] Alameda County Civil Grand Jury Final Report, p. 147.

(d) *Persuasion: Using Economic Dependence: The Glaring Example of the City of Atlanta*

In addition to focusing on the potential for lowering the cost of borrowing as well as providing upfront money, big banks used their strong financial ties with large nonprofits to request them to make certain fundamental changes in their debt financing to benefit these banks. A case in point is the City of Atlanta's history of external financing. In its Comprehensive Annual Financial Reports for the years 2002–2004, the City of Atlanta made the following admissions[50]:

> In March 2001, the System [City of Atlanta] entered into an interest rate swap option agreement with a financial institution in which it agreed to essentially *convert, at the financial institution's request*, $145,000,000 of the System's Water and Wastewater Revenue Bonds, Series 1999, *from 5% fixed rate bonds to floating rate bonds in which the interest rate* is based on the Municipal Swap Index. [Emphasis added]
>
> ……..
>
> Also, in March 2001, the System [City of Atlanta] entered into a similar interest rate swap option agreement with the same financial institution in which it agreed to *essentially convert, at the financial institution's request*, $71,850,000 of the System's Water and Wastewater Revenue Bonds. [Emphasis added]

The financial institution that had asked city officials to rearrange its financial system to fit the bank's goals was reportedly JPMorgan Chase. Interestingly, the Comprehensive Annual Financial Reports for the years following 2004 deleted this particular acknowledgment. Additionally, the city adopted variable interest rates (i.e., auction rates) that are adjustable both *daily* and *weekly*.[51]

Bond Series 2001B:
Interest is payable on a monthly basis at the beginning of each month beginning with February 1, 2002 at *a variable rate of interest as established on a _weekly basis_ by the remarketing agent.* [Emphasis added]

---

[50] City of Atlanta. Comprehensive Annual Financial Report, December 31, 2004, page 70. Retrieved from https://www.atlantaga.gov/home/showdocument?id=729.

[51] City of Atlanta, 2004, P. 68.

Bond Series 2001C:
Interest is payable on a monthly basis at the beginning of each month beginning with February 1, 2002 at *a variable rate of interest as established on a _daily basis_ by the remarketing agent.* [Emphasis added]

Nonetheless, contrary to the promised goals of managing interest rate risk to lower the cost of debt, the effective interest rate almost doubled between 2006 and 2009 and was more than doubled in some years just the same as the case of the Bay Area Tunnel Authority (BATA) presented in Chapter 29. For the city of Atlanta, the synthetic (artificially) and presumed-synthetic-fixed rate increased from 4.105% to 8.13% for swap one and from 4.11% to 7.99% for swap two.[52] For the City of Atlanta, these increases led to an increase in annual settlements and accumulating expected long-term losses as much as $178 million in 2012 and $138 million in 2015.

Why was it difficult to meet with the Actors?

It would have been ideal and would have saved much effort if the responsible officials at the nonprofit institutions that fell for purchasing swaps were not resistant to opening their records and tell us their reasons for getting entangled in the net of the Swap Mania. However, the reality of the prevailing conditions made this alternative impossible to accomplish. Even Sharon Ward, the Director of Pennsylvania Bureau and Budget Center, has reportedly collected the majority of the information she published in *Too Big to Trust: Banks, Schools and the on Going Problems of Interest Rate Swaps* from the official Comprehensive Annual Financial Reports.[53] There are several compelling reasons for the

---

[52]The description "presumed-fixed rate" is in reference to the fact that no synthetic rate would be fixed more than one week when the bond is issued at auction rates that change weekly.

City of Atlanta, Comprehensive Annual Financial Report, 2006.
  Retrieved from https://www.atlantaga.gov/home/showdocument?id=731.
City of Atlanta, Comprehensive Annual Financial Report, 2009.
  Retrieved from https://www.atlantaga.gov/home/showdocument?id=734.

[53]Sharon Ward. January 17, 2012. *Too Big to Trust: Banks, Schools and the Ongoing Problem of Interest Rate Swaps.* Pennsylvania Budget and Policy Center. Harrisburg, PA 17101.
  Retrieved from http://pennbpc.org/sites/pennbpc.org/files/TooBigSwaps.pdf.

evasive attitude of the officials who participated in buying interest rate swap contracts. Most of these reasons have to do with preservation of self-interest, avoiding self-incrimination and, to some extent, the indignation that comes with admitting ignorance of the magic instruments called "swaps." The driving forces for this attitude include the following six reasons.

(a) *Concern for Pending Litigation*

Starting in 2012, a large number of private investors, nonprofits, and corporate entities filed class-action suits against big banks alleging conspiracy and collusion to reduce the interest money the banks paid them on swaps and other variable rate contracts. For example, Chicago Teachers Union filed a class-action suit and also joined the suit filed by the City of Baltimore. The City of Philadelphia and the City of Houston are plaintiffs in two of these suits. The Regents of the University of California System filed its own class-action suit. The Federal Deposit Insurance Corporation and Fannie Mae filed their own suits as well. The list of claimants against big banks is available at LEAGLE: In Re LIBOR-based Financial Instruments Antitrust Litigation.[54] Additionally, Chapter 33 provides a summary information about litigation related to swaps and interest rate manipulation.

All class-action suits related to the manipulation of interest rate benchmark (LIBOR) were consolidated in a multiregional case before the U.S. District Court, Southern District of New York. The plaintiffs allege that big banks had violated antitrust laws by restricting competitive market mechanisms in order to keep monopolistic control over the rates of interest the defendants had been paying for interest rate swaps. In the first round, US district court Judge Naomi Buchwald dismissed the case against the banks on March 29, 2013. In her decision, she concluded that the plaintiffs did not show that their alleged injury was the result of anti-competitive behavior. Subsequently, the plaintiffs appealed and the case

---

[54]LEAGLE. In Re LIBOR-based Financial Instruments Antitrust Litigation, April 29, 2016.
Retrieved from https://www.leagle.com/decision/infdco20160502c87.

was returned to the U.S. District Court, Southern District of New York. Few claimants followed the advice to sue the banks for fraud. Charles Schwab and the Regents of the University of California filed new cases with the District Court of California alleging conspiracy to defraud counterparties in interest-rate-swap contracts.

In a decision dated July 28, 2017, district court Judge Paul A. Engelmayer reversed Judge Buchwald's decision and allowed the antitrust litigation to continue.[55] While big banks are the defendants, the nonprofit entities involved in the noted class-action suits are plaintiffs (claimants) who had no interest in discussing their past actions while litigation concerning these actions is pending. Others who are not directly involved in the noted class-action suits are in the same situation: they are watching and waiting to see how they could benefit from the outcome of the litigation. It is, therefore, understandable that none of the officials who authorized or signed interest-rate-swap contracts was willing to jeopardize the potential of having a favorable court judgment.

A second branch of legal inquiries into the conspiracies and collusion to manipulate the benchmark rate "LIBOR" also began in 2012. Regulatory agencies in the USA, Europe, Japan and elsewhere began investigating the submitter panels of big banks. While class-action suits progressed in the courts, regulatory authorities were negotiating settlements with the same big banks. These settlements involved both criminal and civil violations, resulting in deferred prosecution for criminal violations and sizable financial fines for civil violations. In Appendix 13, we shall see that the sum of the penalties for seven of these large banks added up to $8.7 billion. Although this appears to be a large amount, these penalties represent an infinitesimal proportion of the losses suffered by nonprofit entities for engaging in swap contracts with the same big banks. They also fade in the shadows of the nearly $20 billion annual

---

[55] United States District Court, Southern District of New York, *In Re: Interest Rate Swaps Antitrust Litigation. This Document Relates to All Actions*, Case 1:16-md-02704-PAE. July 28, 2017.

Retrieved from http://www.nysd.uscourts.gov/cases/show.php?db=special&id=562.

profits that big banks in the USA alone realize from dealing in financial derivatives, especially interest rate swaps.[56]

(b) *Novelty and Complexity of Interest Rate Swaps*

According to the statistics reported by the Bank for International Settlements, the face, (reference or notional) amounts of interest rate contracts exceeded $435 trillion worldwide in 2016, which was down from the $561 trillion level of 2013.[57] Nearly one-half of this amount belonged to large banks in the USA. By any measure, this amount is more than six to eight times the size of Gross Domestic Product worldwide.[58] People watching the fast growth in the amounts of outstanding interest rate contracts would probably be shocked to know that this form of contracting did not exist before 1982. The California Debt and

---

[56] United States Office of Comptroller of the Currency, *Quarterly Report on Bank Derivatives Activities*, 1996–2017.

Retrieved from https://www.occ.gov/topics/capital-markets/financial-markets/derivatives/derivatives-quarterly-report.html.

[57] *Statistical release OTC derivatives statistics at end-June 2014*, Bank for International Settlements, Monetary and Economic Department, November 2014.

Retrieved from https://www.bis.org/publ/otc_hy1411.pdf.

Yes, these numbers are in trillion [$1,000,000,000,000] dollars, but that is what we call notional amounts. Appendix 1 explains what *notional amounts* mean. For the time being, it is useful to note that a notional amount is the face value the two parties use to calculate the amounts of interest due to each other. The notional amount does change hands; only the difference between the amounts of interest of both sides changes hands.

[58] *Statistical release OTC derivatives statistics at end-June 2016*, Bank for International Settlements, Monetary and Economic Department, November 2016.

Retrieved from https://www.bis.org/publ/otc_hy1611.pdf.

&

U. S. Office of the Comptroller of the Currency, the Department of the Treasury, 1995 onward.

Retrieved from https://www.occ.gov/topics/capital-markets/financial-markets/derivatives/derivatives-quarterly-report.html.

Investment Advisory Commission described the 1982 birth of interest rate swaps in a short statement[59]:

> "The first interest rate swap was a 1982 agreement in which the Student Loan Marketing Association (Sallie Mae) swapped the interest payments on an issue of intermediate term, fixed rate debt for floating rate interest payment indexed to the three month U.S. Treasury bill. The interest rate swap market has grown rapidly since then."

This incidental discovery of interest rate exchange in 1982 took hold as a possible profit-making instrument soon after 10 big banks formed, in 1985, the trade organization International Swap Dealers Association (ISDA, which changed the name later to International Swap and Derivatives Association). Ever since then, with the help of ISDA, Wall Street has propagated interest rate swaps as a powerful instrument for hedging risk, speculating, investment and gambling.

Swap contracts could range from simple to highly complex. An example of complexity is the contract that Bankers Trust of New York sold to Procter & Gamble. This contract is a subject of Chapter 2. We only know about this contract because it was the subject of a widely discussed litigation. Otherwise, interest rate swap contracts remain private.

(c) *Lack of Knowledge*

Given the novelty of swaps as a financial derivative instrument, it took some years for academics, bankers and the newly minted area of financial engineering to develop knowledge and modeling sufficient to allow some universities to include this type of financial derivatives into their teaching curricula. By that time, the people who were in the administration of non-profit organizations and who authorized and signed swap contracts for their employers had already graduated from college and missed the train. Nevertheless, they thought they knew finance by understanding something about securities such as stocks and bonds and by playing a role in corporate financial management. However, interest rate swaps are not securities, and

---

[59] Douglas Skarr, The Fundamentals of Interest Rate Swaps, *Issue Brief*, California Debt and Investment Advisory Commission, October 2004.
  Retrieved from http://www.treasurer.ca.gov/cdiac/reports/rateswap04-12.pdf.

none of what they had studied or learned was remotely be connected to interest rate swaps. Even to this day, only a very small percentage of college graduates in accounting, finance, and economics know anything about interest rate swaps. Moreover, the complexity of that financial derivative makes it difficult to acquire thorough knowledge by self-teaching.[60]

Ultimately, swaps salespeople were able to overload the thought processes of decision-makers at nonprofit entities, even those with some self-acquired knowledge. Throwing swanky financial engineering jargon at the audience enhanced the believability of the promised cost saving. Sometimes swap sales pushers even drew unwarranted conclusions to appeal to the envisaged needs of the audience. For example, reading the official minutes of the Dauphin County Board of Commissioners in Pennsylvania suggests that some of these commissioners had acquainted themselves with the subject matter well enough to carry on an intelligent dialogue. Yet, they were not able to see through the nuances of the contracts proposed to them by swap advisors who were sales conduits for the banks and who also were not always telling the truth. Appendix 6 presents an example from Dauphin County commissioners' workshop meeting on April 13, 2005, in which the commission authorized entering into one form of interest rate swaps without fully comprehending the implications of the decisions they made.

(d) *Deception and Incomplete Disclosure of Facts and Risks*

Given the focus of this book, Chapter 2 presents only a glimpse of the lies and deceit perpetrated by swap sellers.[61] Once again, the world became aware of some of these cases because what once was private information became public knowledge through litigation.

---

[60] Martin Z. Braun and William Selway, "Schools Flunk Finance," *Bloomberg Markets, Bloomberg,* March 2008.

Retrieved from http://www.bloomberg.com/apps/news?pid=nw&pname=mm_0308_story2.html.

[61] However, the entire book, *Infectious Greed — How Deceit and Risk Corrupted Financial Markets,* by Frank Partnoy (London, Profile Books 2003) is an engaging presentation of many cases of deception linked to Bankers of New York Trust that have come to characterize big banks and the derivatives' markets.

The Five People

I think that in terms of understanding derivative finance [interest-rate-exchange contracts and the like], there are five people who understand [it], they are all locked in a basement on Wall Street and they don't ever let them out.

Source: Alex J. Pollock. September 9, 2008.

Cited in Robin Smith, Southern Discomfort: An Examination of the Financial Crisis in Jefferson County, Alabama, Houston, Business and Tax Law Journal, 2010, pp. 376.

Retrieved from http://www-lexisnexis-com.proxy2.library. illinois.edu/hottopics/lnacademic/?verb=sr&csi=250859.

(a) One of these situations is the case of *Smith Barney v. Dade County* back at the start of the Swap Mania. The executive involved in the case was Michael Lissack, who blew the whistle and informed the Federal Bureau of Investigation (FBI) of the deceit, which he helped perpetrate.

(b) The next pivotal case was the case of Procter & Gamble (P&G). While P & G is a profit-oriented company, the case provides a vivid example of the sales tactics of swap dealers. Facing an amount of loss almost as large as the notional (face) value of the swap contract led the company to sue Bankers Trust of New York. In the course of litigation, investigators uncovered a massive inventory of tape-recorded conversations by the bank's swap sellers that revealed the extent to which they had willingly misinformed and misled Procter & Gamble. A memorable quote by Edwin L. Artzt, the Chairman of the Board of P & G at the time highlights the extent to which Bankers Trust kept P & G in the dark.[62]

"There is a notion that end users of derivatives must be held accountable for what they buy," Mr. Artzt added. "We agree completely, but only if the terms and risks are fully and accurately disclosed," he said.

(c) In 2008, the Securities and Exchange Commission sued the big banks involved in the Auction Rate Securities (ARS) market alleging they deceived and misled investors. In ARS market, bondholders of outstanding bonds may choose to remarket (resell or reprice) their bonds every 7, 14, 28 or 35 days. Remarketing here means putting the bonds up for subscription by new bondholders who would bid on the interest rate they are willing to accept. The banks involved in ARS failed to disclose the increasing risks associated with ARS, including their own reduced ability to support the auctions. By engaging in this conduct, those firms violated the Federal securities laws, including the broker–dealer antifraud provisions. (See the testimony by Linda Chatman Thomsen, September 8, 2008)

---

[62] Saul Hansell. "P. & G. Sues Bankers Trust Over Swap Deal," *The New York Times.* October 28, 1994.

Retrieved from http://www.nytimes.com/1994/10/28/business/p-g-sues-bankers-trust-over-swap-deal.html.

(d) A case involving swap contracts for Denver Public Schools presented in Chapter 15 reveals that Royal Bank of Canada (RBC) acted as both a lender and a swap advisor for the swaps related to loans from the very same bank. With the evident conflict of interest, it is hard to believe that RBC was not able and willing to distort the real risk of entering into swap contracts. As Andrew Kalotay noted, "it is in the best interest of swap advisors to see the deal go through, otherwise they would not get paid."[63]

(e) A much larger picture of deceit was uncovered in 2012. It was the case of conspiring and colluding among large banks to manipulate the most important interest rate benchmark in the world — i.e., the London Interbank Offered Rate (LIBOR) — starting in early 2000 to benefit the banks and their traders.[64] The result was an appreciable drop in the amounts of interest that big banks had been paying to their counterparties on interest rate swaps and other investments linked to LIBOR. This discovery was the impetus for filing numerous class-action suits against big banks, which are continuing in the courts to this day. However, significantly relevant information about this discovery is the acquisition of recorded chat-room conversations within each bank and across banks. Samples of these recorded cheating chats are in Chapter 33 and in Appendix 12; they provide ample details of the extent of the deception and destruction of that scheme.

(f) A more specific example is the 2005 sales pitch the financial advisor Lou Verdelli made before the Dauphin County commissioners in Pennsylvania, persuading them to enter into a contract that swaps one type of variable interest rate for another type of variable interest rate

---

[63] Andrew Kalotay. *SEC Hearing on The State of Municipal Securities Market Birmingham, AL, July 29, 2011.*

Retrieved from https://www.sec.gov/spotlight/municipalsecurities/statements072911/kalotay.pdf.

[64] The banks in consideration here are generally those U. S. and international banks constituting the panel of voters (submitters) of daily interest rate quotation to contribute to the London Average Rate known as London Interbank Offered Rate (LIBOR). This process is discussed in Chapter 32.

(basis swap).[65] This type of swap is simply a contract betting or wagering on the spread between the two variable rates. As a gamble, you may lose if the interest rate you would be receiving falls below the interest rate you would be paying and vice versa. Clearly, this relationship creates an exposure to interest rate risk. Yet, Verdelli concluded his presentation by emphasizing that such a contract has no interest rate risk.[66]

"Basically, this transaction really does not have interest rate risk. It doesn't depend upon the level of interest rates. If…so it is not really interest rate sensitive. Not really interest rate risk."

Appendix 6 presents a major segment of Verdelli's presentation to Dauphin County commissioners that provides many insights into the way swap dealers slant their presentation of proposed swap contracts to bait their clients.

(e) *Key Decision Makers are in Jail*

Persuasion could also take a darker form — that is of bribing officials. Usually, however, litigation is the only means by which this dark side is revealed to the public. Chapter 3 shows details about Jefferson County, a case of bribing officials that is unsurpassed as far as one could detect from public records dealing with financial derivatives. The information about bribing officials to entice them to sign swap contracts became known because it was the focus of the county's bankruptcy litigation and other investigations by the Securities and Exchange Commission. Moreover, the active players from Jefferson County went to jail for periods ranging from a few months to 15 years. For obvious reasons, none of

---

[65]This is the form of 'Basis Swaps' in which interest rate on each side is based on a different benchmark.

[66]*Minutes.* Dauphin County Board of Commissioners Workshop. April 13, 2005.

Retrieved from http://www.dauphincounty.org/government/About-the-County/Meetings/Minutes/WS041305.pdf.

them would be willing to shed light on their decisions related to the activities of entering into swaps.

The same conclusion applies to the City of Detroit's rough encounter with big banks in relationship to interest rate swaps. The former mayor of the city, Kwame Kilpatrick, is completing a 28-year sentence in jail and would have no interest in further self-incrimination.

To obtain similar information about other cases that have not been the subject of litigation requires having access to private records. All the evidence I used in preparing this book came from public sources, official documents, and financial press reports and analysis as well as other public disclosures. For nonprofits, public sources are stores of rich information. Yet, the public is very much unaware of this evidence. Although the information is publicly available, it takes a specialized knowledge, extensive research, and establishing links to understand what is going on.

Nevertheless, as elaborate and extensive as these sources are, they could not provide direct answers to questions like those posed by the Philadelphia city council member Jim Kenney before he became the Mayor of the city in 2016.[67]

> "Whose idea was this?" Kenney wanted to know. "We found it very difficult to find the documentation I would like to have seen, about why the city entered into swaps." Nancy Winkler, the treasurer of the City of Philadelphia under Mayor Nutter, noted the grim reality of corruption in the city: "The city's prior swaps advisers, the principals, *were convicted and are mostly either in prison or awaiting sentence.*" [Emphasis added]

The City of Chicago elders also asked the same questions in connection with the numerous swap contracts that dragged the city and its public schools to the ills of the Swap Mania:

o   Who authorized these contracts?
o   Where are these people now?

---

[67] Joseph N. DiStefano, "Philly Deals: Interest-rate swap strategy backfires, costs city $186M," *The Philadelphia Inquirer,* October 24, 2012.

Retrieved from http://www.philly.com/philly/columnists/joseph-distefano/20121024_PhillyDeals__Interest-rate_swap_strategy_backfires__costs_city__186M.html.

Nonetheless, for some other compelling reasons, no one wants to take responsibility and admit having made costly mistakes. Each was happy to point to others as having made the bad decisions.

(f) *Staff Turnover*

The change in personnel as a result of elections, reassignments, or retirement places serious difficulties on going back one or two decades to identify the officials who were responsible for authorizing and committing their organizations to long-term interest rate swaps. Take, for example, Mayor Rahm Emanuel in Chicago. He blames the previous mayor, Richard M. Daley, for the city's swap disaster.[68]

> The city, primarily in the Richard M. Daley era, entered into millions of dollars of interest-rate-swap transactions. Critics argue these were cavalier agreements, embedded with triggers calling for stiff penalty payments if the city's bond ratings tumbled.
>
> That occurred, and in 2015 City Hall renegotiated its swap deals with banks and also paid millions in related penalty costs.

Would former mayor Dailey admit fault? Of course not! He relied on the advice of big banks and those financial advisors who did not know much about swaps. This is only one example of the difficulties one encounters in getting people to admit making costly mistakes. I simply failed to get the promised information from those whom I had approached.

---

[68] Robert Reed, "Mayor, treasurer Summers at odds over antitrust lawsuit against big banks," *Chicago Tribune*, November 3, 2016.

Retrieved from http://www.chicagotribune.com/business/columnists/ct-kurt-summers-versus-banks-robert-reed-1103-biz-20161102-column.html.

CHAPTER 2

Carol Loomis Described Four Derivatives' Sins: Lies, Leverage, Ignorance, and Arrogance

More than 20 years ago, Carol Loomis, the renowned reporter of *Fortune* magazine, proffered a brutal assessment of the emergence of the Swap Mania.[1] In this respect, she noted four Derivatives' Sins as characterizing Wall Street and big banks. This was only two years before Frank Partnoy published his book *F.I.A.S.C.O.: Blood in the Wall Street*. Twenty years later nothing seems to have changed; Bob Ivry published a book titled *The Seven Sins of Wall Street*.[2]

---

[1] The noun *mania* was imported into business environments in 1636 when the market for Tulips in Holland skyrocketed to sell Tulip bulbs at prices higher than the price of some homes, then suddenly crashed. The euphoria-to-crash cycle became known as the Tulips Mania. See, for example, Jason Zweig. *The Museum of Art and Finance, Gallery 1: Tulipmania.* 2015.

Retrieved from http://jasonzweig.com/the-museum-of-art-and-finance-gallery-1-tulipmania/?utm_content=buffer83e4a&utm_medium=social&utm_source=twitter.com&utm_campaign=buffer.

[2] Frank Partnoy, *F.I.A.S.C.O.: Blood in the Water on Wall Street*, (New York, W.W. Norton. 1997). Bob Ivry, *The Seven Sins of Wall Street: Their Washington Lackeys and the Next Financial Crisis* (New York, Public Affairs, 2014).

> *These red-hot [derivative] instruments proved too tempting for both buyers and sellers. This is the story of how lies, leverage, ignorance — and lots of arrogance — burned some big players.*
>
> Carol Loomis (reprinted on November 21, 2012),
> "Untangling the Derivatives Mess," *Fortune*, March 20, 1995
> Retrieved from http://fortune.com/2012/11/21/untangling-the-derivatives-mess.

(a) Lies and Ignorance — Michael Lissack and Dade County, Florida
(*A Case of Big Banks' Deceitful Sales Tactics*)

This story goes back almost 25 years, but officials in other public service agencies did not learn from it and kept on making the same mistakes over and over again. We shall come across some of these cases in the course of the presentations in this book.

It was June 1993 when Dade County, Florida, issued a request for proposals, seeking a financial security firm to underwrite the sale of $800 million of fixed-rate municipal bonds. Of the numerous responses received, officials at Dade County gave serious consideration to the offer submitted by Smith Barney, an investment unit of the Travelers Group that later merged with Citibank to form Citigroup.

The county had originally planned for the transaction to consist of conventional fixed-rate bonds. However, over the next several months, Smith Barney introduced an alternative financing structure consisting of writing two separate contracts.

(a) Contract one: to sell bonds at adjustable rates of interest.
(b) Contract two: to *enter into interest-rate-exchange contracts requiring the county*:
   (i) *to pay Smith Barney interest at a fixed rate and*
   (ii) *to receive from Smith Barney interest at adjustable rates.*

The thoughts behind this idea seemed simple and plausible. If the money receivable from Smith Barney for the adjustable rate on the interest-rate-exchange contract were equal to the money of the adjustable rate payable to bondholders, then Dade County would be left with paying the fixed rate on the swap to Smith Barney. Apparently, the concern for "fixity" of interest rate overtook the need to understand the cost of funding.

Smith Barney assigned substantial responsibility for structuring and calculating the presumed benefits of the alternative financing structure to Michael Lissack, a managing director with the firm at that time. Lissack and his team made numerous visits and presentations to county officials. Nevertheless, officials at the county offices instinctively knew that issuing variable-rate bonds involves additional costs and risks. For that reason, the county required a certain amount of economic benefits in the form of stated amounts of savings before it would select the alternative financing structure. Additionally, the Federal Reserve Bank increased interest rates by nearly 80% in one year between 1993 and 1994, which gave Lissack a good enough excuse to manipulate the use of certain variables to create the false impression that the selection of the alternative financing structure would still result in savings to the county in excess of its stated threshold. Those presentations ultimately persuaded the county to implement the approach proposed by Smith Barney.

The SEC complaint about the case states the following[3]:

> Accordingly, the presentations to the county showing present value savings were based on intentional manipulations by Lissack of the underlying calculations and assumptions…undertaken to fraudulently present the *Alternative Financing Structure* in an artificially favorable light. The use of these faulty and inaccurate assumptions resulted, under conservative estimates, in an overstatement of the hypothetical

---

[3] United States of America before the Securities and Exchange Commission. *In the Matter of Michael Lissack. Order Making Findings and Imposing Sanctions and a Cease-and-Desist Order*. Securities Exchange Act of 1934. Release No. 39687 Administrative Proceeding File No. 3-9427, February 20, 1998.
  Retrieved from https://www.sec.gov/litigation/admin/34-39687.htm.

savings associated with the Alternative Financing Structure by at least $5 million.

At this point, it was clear that no one in the Miami operation had ever heard of this so-called alternative financing structure until Smith Barney proposed it as an aspiration for achieving two goals: lowering the cost of borrowing and helping to manage interest-rate risk. Adopting the proposed alternative meant the following:

(a) The county would have to give up the tradition of issuing municipal bonds at fixed rates (the so-called plain-vanilla bond).
(b) Instead, the county would issue bonds at an adjustable rate of interest, which would be linked to a commonly acceptable interest-rate benchmark.
(c) Simultaneously, the county would enter into an interest-rate-exchange (swap) contract with Smith Barney. The county would pay interest at a fixed rate and receive interest at an adjustable rate. The adjustable rate of the swap may or may not be linked to the same benchmark rate of the adjustable rate of the bonds.

Dade County officials were reluctant to enter into these alien interest-rate-exchange contracts even if someone said they "reduce cost or risk." No one among the officials knew what these contracts meant or what risks were involved in agreeing to them. There is no doubt in this case that one element of Loomis's Four Derivatives' Sins was at play, namely ignorance. The ignorance sin existed simply because these types of contracts were invented only few years earlier and people outside a small circle of certain bankers had no idea what these agreements were or what they meant. Only those who worked for big banks, who designed and sold these agreements had some knowledge of them. Thus, the touted goals of reducing borrowing cost and risk turned out to be only promises that Lissack and his team highlighted in the multiple sales presentations they made to officials at Dade County. Knowing that bets on interest rates could go either way, no one at Smith Barney was willing to offer any assurance of achieving either promise. As we shall see in other cases, the ideas underlying these goals are only theoretical for the joy of academia and swap dealers but are rarely realized.

For several months, the officials at Dade County debated the alternative financing structure offered by Smith Barney. During that time, Michael Lissack did all he could in the form of presentations and playing different scenarios to make the alternative structure look attractive to county officials. He cooked up favorable scenarios by manipulating the assumptions made about expected future changes in interest rates, the amounts and timing of future cash flows, and the calculated present values (current dollars) of the presumed future savings. After making these bogus assumptions, the alternative financing structure pointed to directions that Dade County officials considered favorable, just at the position where Lissack wanted the county's decision-makers to be. The world got to know that information from the Securities and Exchange Commission's files and Michael Lissack himself after he became a whistleblower.

The repeated presentations by Lissack's team ultimately persuaded the county to implement the alternative financing structure.

The report of the Securities and Exchange Commission (SEC) states[4]:

> The County decided On January 25, 1994, to implement the *Alternative Financing Structure* and, at first, entered into a thirty-year interest-rate-exchange contract (swap) to pay fixed interest rate and receive variable interest rate. Issuing the bonds came out later, on February 2, 1994.

Some years later, Michael Lissack became a whistleblower about a phenomenon called yield burning.[5] He surreptitiously contacted the

---

[4] United States of America, SEC, In the Matter of Michael Lissack. February 20, 1998
[5] Here is how the practice works: To refinance their old expensive debt when interest rates fall, municipalities often sell new bonds and put the proceeds into temporary escrow accounts. By law, those accounts cannot generate a higher rate of interest than the rate on the newly issued bonds. If they do, the excess is considered to be arbitrage profit, and it must be rebated to the federal government. To comply with that law, issuers typically buy a mix of ordinary Treasury securities in the open market or special securities, called slugs, from the Treasury. In yield burning, underwriters sell the issuers Treasury securities at inflated prices, which cuts the yield to levels that appear to meet the escrow requirements

Federal Bureau of Investigation (FBI) to report in unambiguous terms that Smith Barney had used fake and unsupported assumptions in making the calculations that appeared to favor the county. Lissack's disclosure was problematic because Dade County began losing money on the deal and worried that these losses might continue for the entire 30-year lives of the noncancelable interest-rate-exchange contracts. Indeed, long before the financial crisis, Dade County losses were greater than $84 million in 2002, $99 million in 2003, $72 million in 2004, and $74 million in 2005. All these losses represented money that would be taken away from providing education, providing health care, and renovating the infrastructure of Miami and Dade County. With losses mounting and lies exposed, Dade County filed a suit with the SEC against both Michael Lissack and the firm of Smith Barney. In its release of the administrative proceedings, the SEC noted the following[6]:

> The County originally had planned for the [bond] transaction to consist of traditional, fixed-rate bonds, whereby the county would be obliged to pay a fixed interest rate to bondholders over the life of the bonds. However, over the next several months, the National Firm [Smith Barney] raised with the county a different financing structure as an alternative to fixed-rate bonds (the "Alternative Financing Structure"). The Alternative Financing Structure provided for the county to issue variable-rate bonds, and thereafter enter into a contract with a third-party (the "Swap Provider"), whereby the county would exchange its obligation to make variable-rate payments for an obligation to make fixed-rate payments.

---

but that also generate substantial profits for the underwriters. By some estimates, underwriters may have earned $2 billion to $3 billion of illegal profits from yield burning since the late 1970s. Sharon King, "Market Place: Municipal bond investors could wind up in an I.R.S. crackdown," *The New York Times*, July 25, 1996.

Retrieved from http://www.nytimes.com/1996/07/25/business/market-place-municipal-bond-investors-could-wind-up-in-an-irs-crackdown.html.

[6]United States of America, Securities and Exchange Commission, *In the Matter of Michael Lissack*. February 20, 1998.

The SEC penalized both the firm of Smith Barney and Michael Lissack for lying and setting up a ruse that drew Dade County into a costly trap. In the meantime, neither Michael Lissack nor anyone else informed the county that, for any interest-rate-exchange contract, *there could be only one winner* and that Smith Barney was not about to plan a strategy to be on the losing side. However, Dade County officials were not innocent bystanders either. Interestingly enough, no one from the county offices had questioned the validity of the promises made; it was clear that no one in her/his right mind would believe a mendacious story that a bank would structure a contract to lose its own money for the benefit of the buyer.

(b) Arrogance, Lies, and Leverage — Procter & Gamble versus Bankers Trust of New York (*Another Case of Big Banks' Deceitful Sales Tactics*)

At the same time that Smith Barney bombarded Dade County with presentations encouraging the county to enter into interest-rate-exchange (swap) contracts under false premises, Bankers Trust of New York had created other victims. These include Gibson Greetings, Air Products & Chemical Co., Federal Paper Board Company and the large successful company of Procter & Gamble; they all became victims of the same big banks' ruse. They all sued Bankers Trust of New York and all received relatively court-ordered large compensation.

The episode between Bankers Trust and Procter & Gamble is perhaps the most intriguing. Neither the chief financial officer of Procter & Gamble nor anyone on his staff had realized that, the terms of this contract are such that the company could benefit only if interest rates and commercial paper rates declined.[7] Otherwise, if market interest rates increased, P&G would likely suffer a significant loss. The essential formula in the swap contract between P & G and Bankers Trust is in Appendix 8.

---

[7] Frank Partnoy, *Infectious Greed: How Deceit and Risk Corrupted the Financial Markets.* (London, Profile Books, 2003), pp. 51–57.

Sixteen Percent as Much

One might wonder how a government employee could know about all this when evaluating financing and determining whether it is a good deal for citizens. How evenly matched are the $80,000 per year salaried public servant and the $500,000 a year, big-bonus Wall Street banker?

Governments often hire advisers to help negotiate with the banks. Until the Dodd-Frank Act reforms, however, these advisers were unregulated and unlicensed, and there were no professional standards. My grandfather, a barber, had to have a license, but municipal advisers didn't.

Source: Joseph S. Fichera, "Were Detroit's Interest-Rate Swaps Not Fair," Bloomberg, January 27, 2014.

Retrieved from https://saberpartners.com/press/bloomberg-view/.

Nevertheless, Bankers Trust allusion to declining interest rates was no more than illusion. During 1994, the Federal Reserve Bank, under the direction of Chairman Alan Greenspan, began a series of incremental increases in the Federal Reserve Bank benchmark interest rate (the Fed Rate), which is a critical index for all other interest rates, until the Fed Rate increased from 2.92% in December 1993 to 5.25% in December 1994.[8] An 80% increase in interest rate in one year resulted in a serious disruption of balance in all contractual relationships in general, and in the relationship between Bankers Trust of New York and Procter & Gamble in particular.[9] The top management was stunned to find out that swap contracts on $200 million notional (hypothetical reference face) amount obligated the company for nearly $105 million in a very short period after signing the deal.[10] Two factors contributed to creating this rather strange result:

1. The contract had a built-in leverage (weight multiplier) factor.
2. No one understood how the amount claimed by the bank was calculated because Bankers Trust used its own proprietary (secret) model of valuation.

Still, even with these two considerations, Bankers Trust must have used some type of voodoo magic to come up with $105 million loss for exchanging adjustable and fixed rates on $200 million. For this rotten deal, the chief financial officer of the company and some of his top staff

---

[8] The Fed Rate is either the basis for adjustable contracts or is very highly correlated with other indexes such as the London Interbank Offered Rate (LIBOR), to be discussed in this book in reference to banking collusion to falsify the rate. It is unfortunate that Orange County of California got shot by that sharp rate increase, and among other risky investments, it drove the county into bankruptcy.

[9] It is also arguable that such an imbalance contributed seriously to the bankruptcy of Orange County. "Orange County Case," *Finance Train* (Undated).
    Retrieved from http://financetrain.com/orange-county-case/.

[10] Kelley Holland, Linda Himelstein, and Zachary Schiller, "The Bankers Trust Tape." *BusinessWeek*, October 16, 1995.
    Retrieved from http://www.businessweek.com/1995/42/b34461.htm.
    Retrieved from https://www.bloomberg.com/news/articles/1995-10-15/the-bankers-trust-tapes.

lost their jobs, and the company went to court alleging that the bank's employees had defrauded the company and deliberately withheld critical information from Procter & Gamble. The investigation, aided by detective journalists at *Business Week*, revealed that Bankers Trust routinely tape-recorded the conversations of its employees.[11] In the end, the court ordered the release of 65,000 tapes and more than 300,000 pages of written material for use by the financial press and Procter & Gamble in its court proceedings against the bank.

Carol Loomis, the well-known business writer of *Fortune* magazine, summarized the issues as follows[12]:

> P&G claims that before the swaps were signed, Bankers repeatedly assured it that in the early stages of the [interest-rate-exchange contracts] swaps, the company would be able to do lock-ins at acceptable prices. Court papers, in fact, include letters from Bankers that make such assurances, though these consistently cite assumptions of stable or only slightly rising rates. P&G says, however, that on one occasion it "pointedly" asked the Bankers Trust person with whom it was dealing what the lock-in situation on the first swap would be if rates and volatility were not "stable." The answer, P&G says, was that "possible changes in rates or volatilities would not have a material or significant effect" on the company's lock-in position.

Through the course of litigation, the recorded conversations among swap pushers at Bankers Trust revealed that they knew they had

(a) Structured very complex contracts to ensure the bank would be the winner.

(b) Deceived and misinformed Procter & Gamble about the presumed virtues of interest-rate swaps.

---

[11] United States Court of Appeals, Sixth Circuit, "The Procter & Gamble Company, Plaintiff-Appellee, v. Bankers Trust Company, BT Securities Corporation, Defendants-Appellees, The McGraw-Hill Companies, Inc., Appellant." No. 95-4078. March 5, 1996.
   Retrieved from http://caselaw.findlaw.com/us-6th-circuit/1139948.html.

[12] Carol Loomis, "Untangling the Derivatives Mess," *Fortune*, March 20, 1995.
   Retrieved from http://archive.fortune.com/magazines/fortune/fortune_archive/1995/03/20/201945/index.htm.

(c) The confidence that no one in the finance offices of Procter & Gamble could ever know anything about built-in terms (or tricks) in the specific interest-rate swaps written by Bankers Trust.

(d) Explicitly assured P & G that changes in interest rates "would not have a significant effect on P & G's position."[13]

The essence of this rather infamous contract is in Appendix 8.

The tape-recorded conversations released under a court order revealed the lies and cynical attitudes of the employees at Bankers Trust and their making mockery of finance personnel at Procter & Gamble. For example, some employees feared the negative consequences of the potential involvement of the Securities and Exchange Commission[14]:

> P&G claims that around that time, some Bankers employees were themselves worrying about the suitability of their activities. It cites a March 1994, conversation between two employees where one said he had "fears of SEC probes." "This wave was always…made up of polluted water," one says. The other recalls telling a colleague *as soon as we quit selling dynamite, maybe we'll have a good business.*" [Emphasis added]

In his book, *Infectious Greed*, Frank Partnoy provided some details about the interaction between Bankers Trust and P&G.[15] He writes that "P&G certainly didn't seem sophisticated to anyone at Bankers Trust." And when the swap dealer, Kevin Hudson, told his fiancé, Alison Bernhard, about the deal he made with P&G, she sounded alarmed. "In a taped phone call:

BERNHARD: Oh, my ever-loving God. Do they understand that …. What they did?

HUDSON: No. They understand what they did, but they don't understand the leverage, no.

---

[13] Hansell, October 28, 1994.

[14] Holland, Himelstein, and Schiller. The Bankers Trust Tapes, 1995.

[15] Frank Partnoy, *Infectious Greed: How Deceit and Risk Corrupted the Financial Markets,* (London. Profile Books, 2003), p. 55.

BERNHARD: They would never know. They would never be able to
              know how much money was taken out of that.
HUDSON: Never, no way, no way. That's the beauty of Bankers
              Trust."

As it turned out, Hudson was correct, and only through litigation did
the financial experts at Procter & Gamble or anywhere else become aware
of how the bankers had relied on their private knowledge of the swap
contracts they developed to deceive and cheat the buyers and grab money
from anyone and everyone. This strategy was revealed in one of the vide-
otapes seized by the court. One employee was revealing his inner thoughts
out loud to another about what "Bankers Trust can do for Sony and IBM
is get in the middle and rip them off — take a little money." The employee
then added, "Let me take that back. I just realized that I'm being filmed."
But, of course, it was all too late; the cat was out of the bag.[16]

---

[16] Partnoy, *Infectious Greed*... p. 53.

Migrating to the Nonprofit Sector

Starting in the 1990s, big banks fanned their derivatives sales force throughout the country, seeking gullible and uninformed officials at organizations and agencies in the not-for-profit service sector. All along, the officials of these agencies could not fathom the notion that interest-rate-exchange contracts are gaming instruments, as was proclaimed by the civil grand jury of Alameda County, California:

"Each interest rate swap [interest rate exchange] can be understood as a contract in which PCCD [Peralta Community College District] and a financial institution 'bet against each other' about the future levels of fixed and variable interest rates."

Source: "The Civil Grand Jury of Alameda County CA, Final Report 2010-2011," June 27, 2011, p. 148.

Retrieved from https://www.scribd.com/document/58911903/Alameda-County-Grand-Jury-Report-Final-2011.

Cases in Wealth Transfer from Local Government Agencies to Big Banks

CHAPTER 3

The Saga of Jefferson County, Alabama, & JPMorgan Chase

The Visible Shocks

The financial tremor in Jefferson County, Alabama, that began to take shape in late 1990s was felt four thousand miles away when Brian Wheeler of the British Broadcasting Company wrote about it in 2011. The county filed for bankruptcy in November 2011 (see Exhibit 1), but the severe financial effects of that tremor will continue until 2053 and beyond. The shocks came from the disastrous fallout of decisions made by corrupt and inept policy makers in Jefferson County with the misguided encouragement of none other than two executives at JPMorgan Chase.[1] The title of Wheeler's article was quite revealing: "The scandal of the Alabama poor cut off from water." Wheeler wrote about the case of Tammy Lucas, whom he called

> [t]he human face of a financial and political scandal that has brought one of the most deprived communities in America's south to the point of what some local people believe is collapse. She says: "If the sewer bill gets higher, my light might get cut off and if I try to catch up the

---

[1]Brian Wheeler, "The scandal of the Alabama poor cut off from water," *BBC News, Alabama,"* December 14, 2011.

Retrieved from http://www.bbc.co.uk/news/magazine-16037798.

Jefferson Exhibit 1
Demonstrators Against JPMC

Feeling the pinch and seeing the seizure of money from necessities to pay for the sewer and water fees, the citizens of Birmingham, Alabama, became aware of some of the tales of JPMorgan Chase involvement and took to the streets with banners reflecting their frustration:

Sewer rate payers Clarence Muhammad, second from right, and Irene Johnson, right, protest potential sewer rate hikes in front of the Jefferson County, Alabama Courthouse Tuesday, Aug. 2, 2011. (The *Birmingham News*, Joe Songer)

Drawing is based on Jeff Hansen "Timeline: How Jefferson County, Alabama's financial crisis unfolded," *The Birmingham News*, August 05, 2011.

--

Retrieved from http://blog.al.com/birmingham-news-stories/2011/08/timeline_how_jefferson_countys.html.

light, my water might get cut off. So we're in between. We can't make it like this."

Mrs Lucas's monthly sewerage rate bills — the amount levied by the county to flush away waste and provide water for baths and showers — has quadrupled in the past 15 years. She says it is currently running at $150 (£97) a month, which leaves little left out of her $600 social security cheque for food and electricity.

While the story of Mrs. Lucas having to choose between paying for water and paying for heating her home was relayed in 2011, the problem had persisted in the community for many years. In fact, six years earlier, in a 2005 article in *Bloomberg Markets*, Martin Z. Braun, Darrell Preston, and Liz Wilken wrote about the misfortune of the 85-year-old Helen Rivas[2]:

"The most egregious case I saw [in Birmingham] was an 85-year-old woman who flushed her toilet only every other day," says Scott Douglas, executive director of Greater Birmingham Ministries, a social services group assisting more than a dozen religions. Water rates for another woman, Helen Rivas, a Birmingham grandmother of five, have increased to $480 a year from $120 two years ago.

In another article, William Selway and Martin Z. Braun continued to write about the plight that bankers at JPMorgan Chase and the corrupt politicians at the county council had brought to Birmingham, Alabama[3]:

As nighttime temperatures plunged in Birmingham, Alabama, last October, Dora Bonner had a choice: either pay the gas bill so she could heat the home she shares with four grandchildren, or send the Birmingham Water Works a $250 check for her water and sewer bill. Bonner, who is 73 and lives on social security decided to keep the

---

[2]Martin Z. Braun, Darrell Preston, and Liz Wilken, "The Banks that Fleeced Alabama. *Bloomberg* Markets," September 2005.

Retrieved from http://www.mobilebaytimes.com/alabama.pdf.

[3]William Selway and Martin Z. Braun, "JPMorgan Swap Deals Spur Probe as Default Stalks Alabama County." *Bloomberg*. May 22, 2008.

Retrieved from http://www.bloomberg.com/apps/news?pid=newsarchive&sid=aF_f8g LLNvn0.

house from freezing. "I couldn't afford the water, so they shut it off," she says.

As we shall see later, the impact of the scandalous conspiracy between policy makers in Jefferson County and two key executives at JPMorgan Chase was beyond the pale. The two executives from JPMorgan Chase — Charles E. LeCroy and Douglas MacFaddin — had orchestrated selling variable rate bonds and swap contracts to Jefferson County in such a quantity and processes that led to disastrous outcomes, defying the worst stories of the Wild, Wild West. When Jefferson County filed for bankruptcy in November 2011, its total debt was nearly $5.3 billion. Back then, and before the bankruptcy of the City of Detroit, Jefferson County's bankruptcy was the largest municipal bankruptcy in U.S. history. The impact of losing billions of dollars was chilling enough for the municipality to lay off employees, cancel hiring schoolteachers, defer work on roads and bridges, increase the cost of supplying water and sewer services to citizens, and eliminate many other services and essential activities that were planned for the community.

It All Started with the Sewer

The saga of Jefferson County started back in the mid-1990s when some citizens asked the attorney Bart Slawson to sue the county (*Kipp, et al. v. Jefferson County, Alabama*) for not complying with the Clean Water Act of 1972. The problem resulted from the overflow of sewage into the Cahaba River after heavy rains. The river is about 194 miles long and is a home to many rare species of fish and plants. More importantly, it is also the source of drinking water for hundreds of thousands of residents.

In 1996, Jefferson County accepted a consent decree issued by the Environmental Protection Agency to make extensive improvements to its sewer system.[4] For nearly 2,000 miles of pipes, repairing the sewer system was considered to be both extensive and expensive. The $250 million initial cost estimation was deemed inadequate, and the county retained the brokerage firm of Raymond James & Associates to underwrite the sale of

---

[4] A consent decree is a legal mechanism of resolving disputes in which the defendant does not admit or deny guilt but agrees to perform some action at a future date.

An Impossible Choice

$555 million of revenue bonds dedicated to repairing the sewer.[5] Raymond James & Associates assigned Charles E. LeCroy to be the executive in charge of interacting with the commissioners of Jefferson County. LeCroy was later hired by JPMorgan Chase and took his client, Jefferson County, with him.

Assigning LeCroy to deal with officials at Jefferson County was the first error of many that JPMorgan Chase had committed. To see how the multi-billion dollars disaster shaped up, we need to keep in mind the names and roles of the cast of characters:

- *Larry Langford.* He was a member of the county commission and finance committee, then became the president of the commission and later the mayor of Birmingham, the administrative seat of Jefferson County, Alabama. Currently Mr. Langford is completing a prison sentence of 15 years.
- *Charles E. LeCroy.* He was managing director of J.P. Morgan Securities' southeast regional office in Orlando and was responsible for J.P. Morgan Securities' entire municipal-bond business.
- *Douglas MacFaddin.* He was a managing director and head of J.P. Morgan Securities' Municipal Derivatives Department from 2001 until March 2008. He worked closely with LeCroy to orchestrate JPMorgan Chase swap deals with the county.
- *Anonymous Associate.* Unidentified employee of JPMorgan Chase.
- *William Blount.* He was the senior partner in Blount Parish & Company but acted more as a wheeler-dealer, freelance agent who could best be described as a connector. He was a close friend of Langford.
- *Albert LaPiere:* A lobbyist and a close friend of Blount and Langford.
- *Jeff Germany.* A county commissioner who had interest in giving two local financing houses, Gardnyr Michael and ABI Capital, a piece of the action in recognition of their support for his election campaign.
- *Gardnyr Michael* and *ABI Capital.* Two local financial firms that have friends and supporters on the county commission.

---

[5]The term *revenue bonds* here means that the county will borrow money to fix the public work project and collect earmarked fees from the residents to pay off that debt.

- *Mary Buckelew*. A member of the county commission and the finance committee.
- *Rice Financial Products*. A financial consulting firm based in New York.
- *Goldman Sachs*. One of the five largest banks in the USA.
- *James White*. The president of Birmingham financial advisory services of Porter White & Co. who investigated the excess fees that JPMorgan Chase had charged the county.

Between 2002 and 2007, LeCroy privately (secretly) agreed with Larry Langford, the president of the county commission, and a local businessman by the name of William Blount to load this relatively financially poor county with over $3 billion of adjustable-rate debt in addition to swap contracts on $5.6 billion notional amounts.[6] At that time, interest-rate-exchange contracts with Jefferson County constituted the largest swap portfolio at JPMorgan Chase — a portfolio larger than the swap portfolio of any government entity or public corporation back then. To prepare the groundwork for dancing with the swaps, JPMorgan Chase sent trainers in risk management to Alabama to make presentations at numerous times and, additionally, cosponsored a high-profile statewide conference on risk management. The county commissioner, Larry Langford, was the lead organizer and promoter of the conference and actively brought participants from all over the state and adjacent regions.

In 2002, the county commission elected Larry Langford as the president of the commission. That was also the time when Charles E. LeCroy of JPMorgan Chase approached Langford to offer the services of JPMorgan Securities. These services included (a) underwriting new bond issues that would pay variable (adjustable or floating) rates, (b) using the proceeds from these variable-rate bonds to refund the outstanding fixed-rate bonds, and (c) at the same time, entering into interest-rate-swap agreements with JPMorgan Chase, requiring the county to pay interest at

---

[6]The notional amount is the face value upon which the two parties to the swap contract agree. Notional amounts don't change hands but are used to determine the payoff. What one party owes to the other party is roughly measured by the change in the benchmark interest rate times the notional amount. Thus, the role of designating a notional amount is for the purpose of making this calculation.

pre-specified fixed rates and receive interest at variable (adjustable) rates. LeCroy and MacFaddin promoted abandoning the conventional "plain" fixed-rate municipal bonds and extolled the virtues of synthetic-rate financing resulting from a package of adjustable rate bonds and interest-rate-swap contracts.

New Contracts and Deception

Before the legal proceedings of the bankruptcy of Jefferson County began, no one outside a closed circle knew of the extent to which JPMorgan Chase executives had bribed their way through. Without obtaining that knowledge from litigation records, it would have been perplexing to understand why county officials relied on the advice of the completely self-interested employees of JPMorgan Chase and agreed to a more complex financing structure. Namely, to switch their financing from a conventional fixed-rate bonds to a series of contracts that were so complex and beyond the ability of anyone in the county to comprehend. In 2004, the county had 18 swap agreements having notional amounts adding up to $5.6 billion; a large portfolio and long-term noncancelable commitments — up to 35 years! This behavior did not escape the attention of Judge Thomas B. Bennett, the bankruptcy judge at the US Bankruptcy Court Northern District of Alabama. In the judgment dated January 6, 2012, Judge Bennett noted, "Some of what failed was the structure the so-called experts sold to the county as being able to counteract the impact of an increase in interest rates."[7]

There is no evidence to show that all of the $3 billion borrowings were needed for the sewer repair and renovation. Issuing new debt seems to have been cooked up between LeCroy and Langford, who was authorized to sign on behalf of the county commission. LeCroy had to worry about the fees from underwriting the bond issues and interest-rate-exchange contracts, and Langford had a possible generous gift and fame in sight. LeCroy used the setting of a dinner engagement with Langford to emphasize the lower cost

---

[7] United States Bankruptcy Court, Northern District of Alabama, Southern Division. *In Re: Jefferson County, Alabama, Alabama, a political subdivision of the State of Alabama. Case No.: 11-05736-TBB*, January 6, 2012.

   Retrieved from http://www.gpo.gov/fdsys/pkg/USCOURTS-alnb-2_11-bk-05736/pdf/USCOURTS-alnb-2_11-bk-05736-0.pdf.

of debt financing that could be attained by using the combination of adjustable-rate bonds and interest-rate-exchange contracts. The bank solicitation was direct and self-serving, but Langford wanted to include two of his protégés in the deals. These were the self-appointed intermediaries, William Blount of Blount Parrish & Company and the lobbyist Albert LaPiere.

A tape-recorded conversation between LeCroy and MacFaddin reveals the dynamics of that interaction[8]:

> The day the 2003-B bond transaction closed, LeCroy had dinner with Langford in Birmingham, during which he solicited a new bond and swap transaction. The next day, May 2, 2003, LeCroy called MacFaddin and told him Langford responded "Let's go for it." However, LeCroy told MacFaddin that Langford had specific requirements for JPMorgan to win the county's business:
>
> - LeCroy: This time the advice we're getting is to get with Bill Blount early, bring him in by bringing him on our team, so he doesn't go to a competitor. So, "Larry," I said.
> - MacFaddin: That sounds fine.
> - LeCroy: I said, "Commissioner Langford, I'll do that because that's your suggestion, but you gotta help us keep him under control. Because when you give that guy a hand, he takes your arm." You know?
> - MacFaddin: [Laughing] Yeah, you end up in the wood-chipper.
> - LeCroy: Yeah, that's right. So he said, "Don't worry, I can control him. Just get him on board." And he says he might have a couple of other little local minority firms to take care of, but he said, "Let's see if we can get it done."

William Blount had a local financial company, Blount Parrish & Company, and he constantly sought to have the county retain his company for underwriting different bond offerings. He was given that opportunity for underwriting small bond issues. But when it came to large bond offerings such as 2003-B ($1.01 billion) and 2003-C ($1.05 billion), Blount

---

[8] U. S. Securities and Exchange Commission. Securities Act of 1933 Release No. 9078 and Securities Exchange Act of 1934 Release No., 60928/ November 4, 2009 Administrative Proceeding file No. 3-13673 *in the Matter of J. P. Morgan Securities Inc. Respondent. Order Instituting Administrative and Cease-and-Desist Proceedings.* November 4, 2009. Retrieved from https://www.sec.gov/litigation/admin/2009/33-9078.pdf.

Parrish & Company did not meet the regulatory threshold to be the underwriter because of having capitalization below the required level. Nevertheless, Blount got himself involved as a self-appointed adviser to two competing financial institutions from New York: Goldman Sachs & Co. and Rice Financial Products.

Blount pushed for using these two firms to underwrite the county's bonds and interest-rate-exchange contracts. But LeCroy and MacFaddin over staged him by agreeing to pay $3 million to Goldman Sachs and $1.4 million to Rice Financial Products to get them out of the way and not compete with JPMorgan Chase. The payment to Goldman Sachs was made by structuring another swap agreement to guarantee a credit of $3 million to go Goldman Sachs' way. The conspiracy that took place was noted in a letter to LeCroy in which MacFaddin presented the need to pay these companies the "requested fees" so that they would not be in competition. In the letter dated March 28, 2003, MacFaddin wrote the following[9]:

> [T]he County [a.k.a., Langford] has requested, as a condition to entering into the Transaction with JPMorgan "that JPMorgan include Goldman Sachs and Rice Financial" in the Transaction, directly or indirectly, such that Goldman and Rice Financial receive a specified percentage of JPMorgan's net economic "benefit from the Transaction."

And that was exactly what JPMorgan Chase did. The court records reveal that LeCroy and MacFaddin, in negotiations with Langford, agreed to pay $3 million to Goldman Sachs and $1.4 million to Rice Financial. (Starting item 53 on page 18 of the SEC document)[10]:

> To justify these payments, MacFaddin and LeCroy attempted to create a role for both Goldman Sachs and Rice Financial in the 2003-B swap transaction. Yet, neither firm entered into a swap agreement with the county, or served as an advisor to the county on the transaction.

In other words, the contract between JPMorgan Chase and Goldman Sachs was a make-believe swap agreement constructed for the purpose of allowing JPMorgan Chase to funnel $3 million to Goldman Sachs & Co.

---

[9] Securities and Exchange Commission, November 4, 2009.
[10] https://www.sec.gov/litigation/complaints/2009/comp21280.pdf.
p. 18

and make it appear as a legitimate business transaction. Even to the unsophisticated legal eye, this was clearly anticompetitive and is likely to be in violation of antitrust law. Goldman Sachs & Co. showed its appreciation to William Blount by paying him $300,000 (10% of the $3 million, take) as a commission.

Additionally, JPMorgan Chase paid Rice Financial Products a "fee" of $1.4 million, also for doing nothing other than ceasing competition with the bank for the business of Jefferson County transactions. The total of $4.4 million in bribes was labeled "fees" but was never disclosed to investors in the bond-offering documents, which was a violation of the SEC regulation, as noted in the commission's complaint[11]:

> In its role as managing underwriter, J.P. Morgan Securities offered and sold the 2003-B bonds to investors. In doing so, J. P. Morgan Securities transmitted the official statement to investors. The official statement did not disclose to bond investors the material information concerning the payment scheme or the conflict of interest raised by the agreement with Langford to pay $4.4 million to firms on Langford's behalf to secure the county Business.

As another way of persuasion, LeCroy and MacFaddin resorted to injecting fear of facing high borrowing costs into the minds of selected county commissioners. They alerted county officials that about 95% of the sewer-related bond issues were paying fixed rates of interest at slightly above 5%, which they said subjected the county to interest-rate risk. They then introduced a scenario portraying market interest rates to be on the decline, and the county could benefit if it refunded the fixed-rate bonds by issuing other bonds having floating (adjustable) rates.

In 2002, municipal-bond interest rates were near a 34-year low, and LeCroy persuaded county officials with the promise of lowering the county's cost of debt by switching from plain fixed-rate bonds to a structure that generates synthetic fixed-rate bonds. Based on this recommendation, the commission voted to issue $3 billion of adjustable rate bonds using the most risky type, auction-rate (all were weekly variable rates) bonds. The commission simplified its burden and fiduciary responsibility

---

[11] Securities and Exchange Commission, November 4, 2009, p. 20.

by authorizing Langford to sign for the commission.[12] By the end of 2003, the bond portfolio of the county had switched from 95% fixed-rate bonds to about 93% variable-rate bonds.

Although JPMC was the underwriter for both the bond and the swap contracts, selling bonds at *auction rates* that change every week was a very bad advice. For one thing, every week the county had to seek investors who would bid on how much interest rate they wish the county to pay them to become bondholders. Determination of the new rates depended on many factors including market liquidity, market credit risk and the credit rating of the county. It is costly to have this adjustment made once a week; the county needed administrative unit to manage the process and the banks making the ARS market demanded a remarketing fee varying between 0.3% and 0.7%. Nevertheless, concluding their counsel at this point would not have been as bad as when they took the next step. LeCroy and MacFaddin went on and presented the commission with swap contracts originated by JPMorgan Chase. However, like the vast majority of the US population, Jefferson County officials had no idea what interest-rate-exchange contracts were, what risk they might add, or the formulas used in calculating the termination penalty. Yet, when a hint of possible lack of knowledge came his way, Larry Langford was rather indignant and was quoted as saying[13]:

> You know, I get the impression that people think a bunch of rubes in Alabama shouldn't be smart enough to utilize these interest-rate-exchange contracts…And let there one understanding: as long as this is a legal

---

[12]For an auction-rate bond, interest rates are set every week, two weeks, or 35 days. A remarketing agent places the bond issue back in the marketplace seeking bids on interest rates. The remarketing could be set for periods from one week to 35 days. A weekly auction-rate bond requires remarketing and resetting interest rates on the bond weekly. The use of auction-rate bonds began in the mid-1980s with the dawn of the Swap Mania but collapsed in 2008. See The Securities and Exchange Commission, Auction Rate Securities.
   Retrieved from https://www.investor.gov/introduction-investing/basics/investment-products/auction-rate-securities.

[13]William Selway, "Jefferson County, Alabama's Path from Scandal to Settlement: Timeline," *BloombergBusiness*, September 16, 2011.
   Retrieved from http://www.bloomberg.com/news/articles/2011-09-16/jefferson-county-alabama-s-path-from-scandal-to-debt-settlement-timeline.

instrument, and it drives down costs, if we have to have one tomorrow, I will do it again.

Sharing the Loot

In the end, the negotiation led to agreeing to two types of interest-rate-exchange contracts. One type required the county to pay fixed and receive adjustable (fixed payer or plain vanilla), and the other type was variable-for-variable contracts. In these Basis Swap contracts, the county was required to pay the banks 67% of LIBOR and receive from the bank 56% of LIBOR plus 0.49% points. Entering into "Basis Swaps" has nothing to do with managing risk but has all things to do with gambling. To incentivize the county to enter into these swap agreements, JPMorgan Chase paid the county upfront money of $23 million.[14] As usual, the upfront money was intended to bind and oblige Jefferson County to enter into the swap agreements.

In these contracts, the bank bundled additional fees that were never adequately disclosed to the county.[15] The bankruptcy court brought in the financial advisory firm of Porter White & Company to examine the financing mess of the county's dealing with JPMorgan Chase. The firm calculated about $100 million of fees overcharged by the bank and another $7.3 million of money paid for various bribes.[16]

Nevertheless, even after having the county commission to agree to the swap arrangements, the work of JPMorgan Chase representatives was not done; they had to respond to Blount's request for 15% of the bank's fee on the swap contracts related to the 2003-C bond issue. Blount, who

---

[14]As discussed earlier, LIBOR is an unofficial rate of interest representing the average of the rates of interest at which a designated set of large banks could have borrowed money from one another

[15]Were never disclosed to anyone until the litigation of fraud and conspiracy. We shall see in the chapter related to the Commodity Futures Modernization Act (CFMA) how our elected officials had maneuvered to keep the derivatives market a "dark market" without any disclosure or transparency to the public or to any government agency. The government knew nothing about that market, including the swap transactions between JPMorgan Chase and Jefferson County, Alabama.

[16]William Selway and Martin Z. Braun, "JPMorgan Swap Deals Spur Probe as Default Stalks Alabama County," *Bloomberg*, May 22, 2008.

Retrieved from http://www.bloomberg.com/apps/news?pid=newsarchive&sid=aF_f8g LLNvn0.

blessed the negotiation meetings only by his silent presence, thought he deserved to be paid fees for maneuvering to keep Goldman Sachs and Rice Financial out of the competition.[17]

> Blount submitted a three-line invoice to JP Morgan for $2.6 million stating "Directed Fee payment pursuant to instructions from Jefferson County, Alabama Commission related to Interest Rate Swap executed between JP Morgan and Jefferson County, Alabama as part of the 2003C [bonds]." JP Morgan promptly paid the invoice. The $2.6 million was more than seven times as large as fees the county paid to any other consultant or advisor in the swap agreement, including its swap and financial advisors and legal counsel.

When an associate of LeCroy, who was not involved in the case, asked for Blount's justification for making such a request, LeCroy said that this would be Blount's fee "for not messing with us."

From the Securities and Exchange Commission records[18]:

> In [a] conversation, LeCroy described a meeting he had with Blount in Birmingham on the evening of June 10, in which Blount was insisting on being paid 15 percent of JPMorgan's fees on the 2003-C swap. The Associate [at JPMorgan Chase] expressed disbelief:

> Associate: How does he get 15%? For doing what?
>
> LeCroy: For, basically, his role in this deal—
>
> Associate: For not messing with us?
>
> LeCroy: — not messing with us and, I said [to Blount], look the only way I'm willing to even entertain this is if you're successful in keeping every other firm out of this deal. That's right. I said, so, because you know, we've got a lot more latitude dealing with him than Goldman Sachs. And I've

---

[17] United States District Court for the Northern District of Alabama, Southern Division. Securities and Exchange Commission v. Larry P. Langford, William B. Blount, Blount Parrish & Co., Inc. and Albert W. LaPiere. Case CV-08-B-0761-S, filed on April 30, 2008.

Retrieved from https://www.sec.gov/litigation/complaints/2008/comp20545.pdf.

[18] SEC 2009, p. 24

got to pay him some on the bonds. But, it's a lot of money, but in the end it's worth it on a Billion dollar deal.

LeCroy and MacFaddin referred to this request not as a bribe but as a basis for sarcasm in a conversation, they themselves had recorded[19]:

MacFaddin:	Now we have, what was termed a swap adviser.
LeCroy:	*Yeah, we had a swap adviser.*
MacFaddin:	And we had a structuring agent.
LeCroy:	*And we had a structuring agent.*
MacFaddin:	Right. So we've got to be careful there because he was neither of those.
LeCroy:	*Right, exctly.*
MacFaddin:	He was a broker dealer that did not participate in an underwriting because it went from fixed rate to floating rate.
LeCroy:	*Can we put — I mean would swap advisory, I mean an advisor to us, swap advisory services? Urn swap —*
MacFaddin:	Well, I want to be careful about describing him as a swap advisor. I'd rather just, you know, term something related or associated with the swap versus advisor —
LeCroy:	*Advisory.*
MacFaddin:	Because in the end, he really didn't advise us on the swap.
LeCroy:	*Right.*
MacFaddin:	Or the structure.
LeCroy:	*Right.*
MacFaddin:	Or anything like that.

Another employee of JPMorgan Chase was troubled by the payments the bank had made under the table to facilitate taking the sole role in the swap dance. The unknown associate said the following:

"But to just randomly pay off people that have nothing to do with the deal just doesn't sit well" LeCroy responded, "That's the deal — that is the price of doing business."[20]

---

[19] Securities and Exchange Commission, November 4, 2009, p. 14–15.
[20] Securities and Exchange Commission, November 4, 2009, p. 30.

Blount followed the plan, however, and in turn shared the money he had received from JPMorgan Chase with Langford and LaPiere. LeCroy and Langford had agreed to funnel the bribe money to Langford through William Blount and Andrew LaPiere. They paid Langford by helping him to borrow money from Colonial Bank then they themselves paid the loan back to the bank on his behalf. They also used Blount to help pay Langford's large credit-card debt and take him to New York on expensive shopping trips.

Two other county commissioners came into the swap play circle, one of whom was identified as Jeff Germany. Both of these two commissioners had lost reelection and wanted JPMorgan Chase to pay money to Gardnyr Michael and ABI Capital, two other local financial firms run by their friends who supported their campaigns. The money requested was intended to compensate these small companies for denying them participation in underwriting the bonds and the related interest-rate-exchange contracts. To avoid unwanted publicity, Commissioner Germany wanted to see JPMorgan Chase pay his friends the "fees" the bank should have paid to them if they were retained as underwriters.[21]

> And we kind of co-opted their — the minority firms they teamed up with because, the two black commissioners said, "Look if we support the synthetic refunding, you guys have to take care of our firms [Gardnyr Michael and ABI Capital]." And I said, "Whatever you want — if that's what you need, that's what you get — just tell us how much."

In the end, JPMorgan Chase paid $500,000 for the so-called fees to be split equally between Gardnyr Michael and ABI Capital.

That was not all, though. To entice other county commissioners to follow the lead of Larry Langford, LeCroy and MacFaddin arranged for JPMorgan Chase to spend $1,122 for a spa trip to New York City on July 26, 2003, for Commissioner Mary Buckelew; she was also a member of the commission's finance committee with Langford.[22]

---

[21] Securities and Exchange Commission, November 4, 2009, p. 11.
[22] Securities and Exchange Commission, November 4, 2009, p. 26.

However, neither Charles LeCroy nor Douglas MacFaddin had informed the county commission about the various added risks and costs to which the county was exposed as a result of entering into these agreements. The first added risk arose from the difference between the credit risk of the county and the credit risk of JPMorgan Chase. Because the county had a much higher credit risk (lower credit rating) than the bank, the weekly reset Auction Interest Rates on bonds were a problem for the county. *Weekly reset* meant that the adjustable interest rates the county paid to bondholders on its debt were governed by the credit ratings of the county and the quality of the surety companies that insured the bonds and the swaps. Payable interest rates, therefore, soared high when Moody's and Standard & Poor's downgraded the credit ratings of the two surety companies (Guaranty Insurance Company [FGIC] and the XL Capital Assurance Corporation [XLCA]) that insured the county's debt and swap contracts. The county's risk increased further when one of its auction-rate bonds failed and there was no taker even at the highest auction interest rate.[23] Following this failure, the adjustable interest rate on

---

[23] Auction-rate bonds are one type of floating-rate securities, but the floating rate is determined periodically every week or every month by placing the bonds back in the market for repricing. In his ruling of January 6, 2012, Judge Bennett noted the following:

> A fundamental, yet terrible error made by the county's experts in municipal finance is not paying attention to the fact that markets fail. This is the process that commenced in what is called the auction rate securities market in late 2007: purchasers of auction rate securities stopped purchasing them. There was no market for these and other types of securities. Once this occurred, the county's sewer system debt's fate was sealed and default was likely to follow with respect to the warrants. Despite being a simplistic explanation, the county's use of auction rate warrants was essentially taking advantage of short term interest rates to finance long term debt. To do this requires the existence of a market for short term debt refinancing, and when it became nonexistent, a critical part of the scheme collapsed. (footnote 1, page 7)

United States Bankruptcy Court, Northern District of Alabama, Southern Division. *In Re: Jefferson County, Alabama, Alabama, a political subdivision of the State of Alabama.* Case No.: 11-05736-TBB, January 6, 2012.

Retrieved from http://www.gpo.gov/fdsys/pkg/USCOURTS-alnb-2_11-bk-05736/pdf/ USCOURTS-alnb-2_11-bk-05736-0.pdf.

bonds skyrocketed from about 3% to levels close to 10%. In the meantime, the variable interest rate on the swap contracts was benchmarked either to either London Average Interest Rate (LIBOR) or the Municipal Bond Average Interest Rate (SIFMA).[24] With more than $3 billion of outstanding bonds paying an adjustable rate and $5.6 billion (notional amounts) of interest-rate-exchange contracts, the cash going out to service the bonds exceeded the cash coming in from the swap contracts many times over. Moreover, by December 2008, Jefferson County had accumulated $735 million of additional debt for unpaid interest and penalties for late payments.[25]

Clearly, "the transactions were complex but the scheme was simple, Senior JPMorgan bankers made unlawful payments to win business and earn fees."[26]

Additionally, in a bilateral swap contract there can be only one winner. Had JPMorgan Chase disclosed that feature of interest-rate-exchange (swap) contracts to the entire commission of Jefferson County, a commissioner like Betty White Collins, would have found ways to prevent the county from entering into them. Long before the county became entangled with JPMorgan Chase, Collins smelled a bad deal as far back as 1997 and

---

[24] In the meantime, the variable interest rate on the swap contracts was benchmarked either to LIBOR (London Interbank Offered Rate) or the SIFMA Municipal Swap Index. The SIFMA Municipal Swap Index is the benchmark compiled by the securities industry and Financial Markets Association. It consists of a seven-day high-grade market index comprised of tax-exempt variable-rate demand obligations with certain characteristics. The SIFMA Swap Index is used as the benchmark for floating rates in swap transactions. The index is based on averages of the rates submitted and specified remarketing agents who met the compliance criteria after excluding the rates above +1 and those below −1 standard deviation. Each participating remarketing agent is limited to a maximum of 15% of the number of securities selected in the index. The index is calculated and published by *Bloomberg*.

Retrieved from http://www.sifma.org/research/item.aspx?id=1690.

[25] The cash outflow is for paying the high interest rate on the bonds and for paying the swap fixed rate to JPMorgan Chase. The cash inflow is the collection of the significantly lower floating or adjustable rate from JPMorgan Chase for the swap. The difference should represent the cost of financing the debt, and that difference was higher than what the county could have paid if it elected to issue plain-vanilla fixed-rate bonds instead of resorting to the two-steps to obtain a synthetic fixed rate.

[26] US Securities and Exchange Commission. November 4, 2009.

alerted the Securities and Exchange Commission. However, at that time, it appears that the Securities and Exchange Commission had no basis to intervene.

The Jefferson County commission could not cancel these swap contracts without paying JPMorgan Chase all the obligations that represented the accumulated losses expected to accrue all the way to contractual maturities.[27] In general, it is illegal to sell swap contracts to the public and it was near impossible to enter into offsetting swaps. These obligations amounted to $647 million in 2008 when the case of Jefferson County finally reached the Administrative Judge at the Securities and Exchange Commission. However, the administrative judge at the SEC compelled JPMorgan Chase to forfeit the cancelation penalty because of the deception and promotion of corruption involved in both the bond offering and swap contracts. Additionally, Charles LeCroy and Douglas MacFaddin got away with paying financial penalties: $326,000 each.

In a 10-year period, the sewer and water rates quadrupled, and right before filing for Chapter 9 bankruptcy in November 2011, the county commission was discussing raising the sewer rates once more. The contract between Jefferson County and bondholders (i.e., the bond indentures) stated clearly that the bonds would be serviced from the sewer user fees. By the time the county filed for bankruptcy, the sewer fees were too high for many citizens to afford, especially since many households had lost their means of support. Yet the fees might continue to increase even more because the bankruptcy court had ruled that the sewer warrants (bonds) must be serviced by fees from the sewer and water taxes as stated in the bond indentures. The final estimate of the cost of the sewer debt repayment was at $6.7 billion and is likely to last until the year 2053.[28]

---

[27] Typically, the formulas for calculating the termination fees follow the structure of the master-agreement model issued by the International Swap and Derivatives Association (ISDA). See a quick summary in Prateek Shah and Michael Sadler, "Watch Your Swaps And Derivatives Termination Payments," *Law 360*, June 10, 2013.

Retrieved from https://www.law360.com/articles/448512/watch-your-swaps-and-derivatives-termination-payments.

[28] Katy Stech, "Judge Approves Jefferson County, Ala., Bankruptcy-Restructuring Plan. Residents to Shoulder Repayment Burden for Decades," *The Wall Street Journal*,

The SEC court counselors offered three conclusions to its complaint against Commissioner Larry Langford and the local businessman William Blount, stating they[29]

i. "knowingly, willfully or recklessly employed devices, schemes or artifices to defraud;

ii. obtained money or property by means of untrue statements of material facts and omissions to state material facts necessary to make the statements made, in the light of the circumstances under which they were made, not misleading; and/or

iii. engaged in transactions, practices and courses of business which are now operating and will operate as a fraud or deceit upon purchasers and prospective purchasers of such Securities in violation of Securities and Exchange Commission ion 17(a) of the Securities and Exchange Commission Act, 15 U.S.C. §77q(a)."

The Aftermath

In December 2008, the Securities and Exchange Commission charged Larry Langford; William Blount; and Albert LaPiere, a registered political lobbyist, with 101 counts of

> Conspiracy, bribery, and money laundering in an alleged long-running bribery scheme related to Jefferson County, Alabama bond transactions and swap agreements. According to the indictment, between 2002 and 2006, Langford used his position as president of the county Commission to generate $7.1 million in fees for Blount and Blount Parrish in

---

November 21, 2013.

    Retrieved from http://www.wsj.com/articles/SB1000142405270230433740457921255 3163071992.

[29] United States Securities and Exchange Commission. Northern District of Alabama, Southern Division. Case No. CV-09-~-2238-S. Securities and Exchange Commission (Plaintiff) v. Charles E. LeCroy and Douglass McFaddin, (Defendants), November 4, 2009, pp. 33–34.

    Retrieved from https://www.sec.gov/litigation/complaints/2009/comp21280.pdf.

connection with these Jefferson County, Alabama financial transactions. Blount, in turn, paid LaPiere approximately $219,500. In return, the indictment alleges that Blount and LaPiere gave Langford approximately $235,000 in expensive clothes, jewelry and cash to pay off his personal debts as part of a conspiracy to funnel Jefferson County, Alabama financial business to them.[30]

Soon thereafter, the judicial system, characteristically, ended up in a schizophrenic mode as it has always been — the bank and bankers were charged monetary fines, but others were sent to jail.

For Jefferson County:

- Larry Langford, the president of the county commission (15 years in prison)
- William Blount, the financier wheeler-dealer (52 months in prison)
- Albert LaPiere, the lobbyist (48 months in prison)

For JPMorgan Chase:

The Bank:

The Securities and Exchange Commission found JPMorgan Chase guilty of violating specific legal provisions of the 1933 Securities Act and the 1934 Securities Exchange Act.[31] Yet, in the same order, the SEC

---

[30] United States Securities and Exchange Commission. December 5, 2008. *United States of America v. Larry P. Langford, William B. Blount, and Albert W. LaPiere*, (United States District Court for the Northern District of Alabama, Case No. 2:08-CR-00245-LSC PWG). Retrieved from http://www.Securities and Exchange Commission.gov/litigation/litreleases/2008/lr20821.htm.

[31] "As a result of the conduct described above, JPMorgan Securities willfully violated Section 17(a)(2) and 17(a)(3) of the Securities Act, which prohibit any person from obtaining money "by means of any untrue statement of a material fact or any omission to state a material fact necessary in order to make the statements made, in light of the circumstances under which they were made, not misleading" or engaging "in any transaction, practice, or

ruled that JPMorgan Chase could get away free at a cost of $723 million:

i. $50 million to Jefferson County for compensation,
ii. disgorgement of $1,
iii. civil monetary penalty in the amount of $25 million,
iv. forfeiture of swap termination penalty of $648 million.

The Bankers:

After holding numerous hearings and investigations for nearly three years, the Securities and Exchange Commission decided on the punishment for the actions of JPMorgan Chase's main players in the case:

- Charles E. LeCroy, the maestro of the Jefferson County debt/swap scandal
  → Paid $326,373 civil penalty and walked free.[32]
- Douglas MacFaddin, the head of municipal derivatives
  → Paid $326,373 civil penalty and walked free.

---

course of business which operates or would operate as a fraud or deceit upon the purchaser" in the offer or sale of securities or security-based swap agreements.

Also as a result of the conduct described above, JPMorgan Securities willfully violated Section 15B(c)(1) of the Exchange Act, which makes it unlawful for any broker, dealer, or municipal securities dealer to "make use of the mails or any means or instrumentality of interstate commerce to effect any transaction in, or to induce or attempt to induce the purchase or sale of, any municipal security in contravention of any rule of" the Municipal Securities Rulemaking Board."

Securities Act of 1933 Release No. 9078/November 4, 2009 and Securities Exchange Act of 1934 Release No. 60928/ November 4, 2009 Administrative Proceeding file No. 3-13673 in the Matter of J. P. Morgan Securities Inc. Respondent. Order Instituting Administrative, and Cease-and-Desist Proceedings, page 9.

Retrieved from https://www.sec.gov/litigation/admin/2009/33-9078.pdf.

[32] LeCroy was sentenced to six months in jail by a court in Philadelphia for an incident unrelated to Jefferson County.

Alabama journalist Kyle Whitmire was clearly incensed about the settlement. In his report "SEC settlement with JPMorgan bankers just one more rotten deal for Jefferson County," he noted the following[33]:

Oh, and they have to promise never to do those bad things again, even if under the court settlement, they don't even have to admit they did anything wrong to start with...The Justice Department was fine with charging Birmingham Mayor Larry Langford, but these other guys never got to feel the cold cuffs around their wrists.

---

[33] Kyle Whitmire. SEC settlement with JPMorgan bankers just one more rotten deal for Jefferson County, December 2, 2015.

Retrieved from http://www.al.com/opinion/index.ssf/2015/12/sec_settlement_with_jpmorgan_b.html.

Paper Chasing Paper

Derivatives is "a fancy name for a ... contract in which two parties agree that they will bet on the future value of some market activity...

Is there money out there in these international markets for the procurement of goods, for firing the engines of manufacturing and production?

No. It is paper chasing paper."

From a speech by Congressman Henry Gonzalez in June 1993. Quoted in "Finding Cure for Financial Derivatives: The Market Cancer." The American Almanac. 1993

Retrieved from http://american_almanac.tripod.com/derivs. htm.

CHAPTER 4

Big Banks Took Nearly $900 million from Detroit for Terminating Swaps & Gave back Nothing

Detroit Exhibit 1
Water Shutoff Protest

Water shutoff protest in Detroit, July 18, 2014.

Based on an image by Marty Townsend, "Detroit Cuts Off Water To Poor People BUT
Not Delinquent Businesses!" *Liberal America,* June 1, 2014.

http://liberalamerica.s3.amazonaws.com/wp-content/uploads/2014/06/detroit-water-shut-off.gif.

The City of Detroit had acquired and consolidated the water and sewer
services of much of the surrounding areas. The Detroit water and sewer
systems consist of more than 3,400 miles of local water mains; 3,000
miles of local sewer pipes; 27,000 fire hydrants; and an extensive billing
and collection system. The water system covers 1,079 square miles and
serves about 40% of the State of Michigan residents. The system is, therefore, extremely vital to the entire state. However, most of the facilities of
the acquired local systems needed significant investments because they
were old and not well maintained.

As expansion continued, the city administration recognized the need for
better management of the Detroit Water and Sewer Department (DWSD). It
established DWSD as a quasi-independent corporation that was able to
issue its own revenue bonds, manage its operations, and produce its own
audited financial statements (KPMG is the auditor.) In addition, the city's

administration allocated a significant portion of the cost of financing the pension system to DWSD, which included the debt issued for that purpose and the related interest-rate-swap contracts. The decline in the city's economy and the steady annual loss of thousands of its population for more than 30 years reduced the tax base and caused the city to teeter on the verge of bankruptcy even during the good days of Mayor Colman Young (1974–1994). However, the administration of Mayor Kwame Kilpatrick made it happen.

But how?

The city's adventure into variable rate bonds and swaps began in 1998 under the leadership of Mayor Dennis Archer (1994–2001) but, for a variety of reasons, matters related to the city's finances got worse under his successor Mayor Kwame Kilpatrick (2002–2008). Kilpatrick started his mayoral term with an ambitious program to rejuvenate the city, and he initially made some noticeable progress. In order to undertake more projects, the city needed to borrow money but ran against the State of Michigan constraint on limiting the borrowed funds to a maximum of 10% of the assets owned. In what might have appeared to be an ingenious move, Mayor Kilpatrick divided the city's activities into three groups and incorporated each of them as a quasi-independent company. In that fashion, he and his administration reasoned that, as corporations, these units were not subject to the state limits on borrowing funds. The three corporations are:

(1) The Detroit Water and Sewer Department Corporation (DWSD),
(2) The General Retirement System Service Corporation (GRSSC), and
(3) The Police and Fire Retirement System Corporation (PFRSC).

Each "corporation" had a reasonable degree of autonomy and could sell its own bonds and manage much of its own financial affairs as if it were an autonomous entity. That was how the Detroit Water and Sewer Department was able to issue variable-rate bonds and follow the big banks' untested strategy for lowering the cost of borrowing. The strategy consisted of the same ballyhoo that big banks used across the country:

(a) Switch bonds from fixed rate to adjustable rate.
(b) Enter into interest-rate-exchange (swap) contracts with the same banks to pay them at fixed rates and receive interest at adjustable rates.

(c) Write these contracts for terms consistent with the lives of the issued bonds — usually several decades.

To implement this strategy, big banks from the USA, Canada, the United Kingdom, Germany and Switzerland dispatched their swap representatives to visit DWSD. They convinced the administration that the cash receivable from the adjustable leg of the swap would cover the variable payments for the bonds. In this loop, the residual cost to the city would be the fixed rate payable to banks for the swaps. The dreamt-up hope was for achieving a synthetic fixed rate lower than the interest rate payable on a conventional fixed rate bond. Fixing the cost of debt through this process is artificially constructed and is, therefore, called synthetic fixed rate. As in most other cases, the management of DWSD was more fanatical about the apparent "fixity" of interest rate rather than about the cost and inherent risk of a bundle of variable rate bonds and swap contracts.

Like the vast majority of people around the country, the administrators at DWSD could not have had any familiarity with the newly developed contracts called interest-rate swaps. Instead, they had to trust the presentations of swap dealers and incompetent consultants who claimed to know the stuff and hold the interest of DWSD dear to their hearts! Public documentations, however, do not reveal any information about considering the hidden and obscure cost of the synthetic fixed rate (see "Detroit Exhibit 2"). Nor was there any concern about writing non-cancelable contracts for long terms extending 30 or 40 years.

Every year the city accrued, without explanation, some fees for termination, which averaged 33 million a year since 2005.[1] That pattern continued until 2012 when the city had to respond to the banks demand to terminate most of the swap contracts with DWSD. The call for termination had actually begun in early 2009 when the city's credit rating was downgraded (credit risk increased) and thus triggered a qualifying termination event. Termination of long-term swaps meant that the city had to pay at once the "fair" market values of all expected future obligations on the swap.

---

[1] It is never clear from the annual reports why these fees were accrued specifically under the title "termination fees."

Detroit Exhibit 2
Basic Components of the Hidden Cost
of the Synthetic Fixed Interest Rate

This hidden transaction cost of the synthetic fixed interest rate includes

a. The swap underwriting fees, which could be substantial.

b. The requirement to pay periodic premium to surety companies to insure the swaps.

c. The variable rate payable on the bonds was an "auction rate," which means the bonds are put back to the market every week or every month and for new bondholders to bet on the interest rate they would accept a new rate is set with each remarketing. The direct fees for remarketing auction rate bonds, which ranged between 0.3% and 0.7% annually.

d. Exposure to Basis Risk, which means the variable rate payable on the bond is greater the variable rate received from the swaps.

e. Lost income from posting collateral and letting the collateral money sit idle.

f. All swap contracts have what is known as "triggering credit events," which are situations the occurrence of any of them would give the bank the right to terminate the contracts and seek the payment of termination fees.

> "Potential termination events in the original Swap Agreements included cases where the POCs ratings were withdrawn, suspended, or downgraded below "Baa3" (or equivalent) or if the Swap Insurers' ratings fell below an "A3" (or equivalent) rating." (CAFR 2012, P. 119).

g. Termination fees consist of the present value of the amounts of money that the city would have had to pay the banks for the entire life of the swap agreement. The terms of the swap extended for more than 30 years. Some of these triggering events were (a) defaulting — if the required quarterly payments are not met, and (b) credit downgrading — if the ratings of the city's debt were withdrawn, suspended or downgraded below Ba3 or equivalent.

Soon after the crisis of 2008, all of the big banks that had sold swaps to the city stood at the city's doorsteps asking for huge amounts of money to terminate their swap contracts.[2]

---

[2] Darrell Preston and Steven Church. "Detroit Swap Banks Go First as Bankruptcy Looms: Muni Credit." *Bloomberg*. June 20, 2013.

Retrieved from https://www.bloomberg.com/news/articles/2013-06-21/detroit-swap-banks-go-first-as-bankruptcy-looms-muni-credit.

What happened in Detroit, "the city," was a replay of the black comedy described in every case in this book.

- Swap dealers (bankers) knocked on the doors of city halls wearing big smiles and dressed up in expensive Italian-tailored suits.
- Bankers make sales presentations full of good promises engraved with jargon and unfamiliar financial-engineering terminology that border on being an exotic foreign language.
- Officials make decisions for their cities and municipalities to follow a well-traveled path: to switch from fixed rate bonds to a bundle of adjustable rate bonds and interest rate swap contracts.
- Bankers leave after securing a source that would bring them tons of money.
- Officials scramble to replace the losses by eliminating jobs, cutting off support to schools, reducing municipal services and raising water and sewer taxes.
- The poor cannot pay.
- The poor have running water no more.

This black comedy proved infectious; it traveled from Jefferson County to the cities of Detroit, Baltimore, and Pittsburgh among others.[3]

On July 8, 2013, the City of Detroit filed for Chapter 9 bankruptcy. The $18 billion bankruptcy filing gave the city the dubious honor of being the largest municipal bankruptcy in the history of the USA.[4]

---

[3] Carrie Sloan, "The Unexpected Cause of Water Crises in American Cities," *Talk Poverty.* March 9, 2016.

Retrieved from https://talkpoverty.org/2016/03/09/unexpected-cause-water-crises-american-cities/.

- Carrie Sloan, *The Nation*. March 11, 2016.
- Luke Broadwater, "City shuts off water to delinquent residents; hits Baltimore Co. homes hardest," *The Baltimore Sun,* May 15, 2015.

Retrieved from http://www.baltimoresun.com/news/maryland/baltimore-city/bs-md-ci-water-shutoffs-20150515-story.html.

[4] In 1994, the dubious distinction of being the largest municipal bankruptcy in the USA was bestowed on Orange County, California ($1.6 billion) but that was overtaken in 2011 by Jefferson County ($5.6 billion). Less than two years later, the city of Detroit assumed that space.

The City of Detroit entered into debt and swap contracts with Citigroup, JPMorgan Chase Bank, Morgan Stanley Capital Services, Bank of America, and UBS AG starting in 1998, but did not inform the public until 2005. As was the case with Jefferson County, the city's water and sewer systems figured prominently in this crisis as well.

In the Comprehensive Annual Financial Report of 2005, p. 102

> The City is party to derivative financial instruments consisting of interest rate swaps that are intended to effectively convert variable-rate financings to fixed-rate financing. These are not reported at fair value on the Statement of Net Assets at June 30, 2005.

> **Objective of the swaps.**
> In order to better manage its interest rate exposure and to reduce the overall costs of its financings the City has entered into 31 separate fixed-payor interest rate swaps.

It is important to notice the focus was on the goal of "fixity" of interest rates, not on the cost of borrowing. This was followed by a listing of 31 swap contract agreements on notional (reference face) amounts of $1.987 billion. Without further detail, the 2005 report noted that $11 million were paid in cash for terminating some swaps and the expected noncurrent, long-term liabilities for swaps were $20 million. These were not large amounts of losses but it did not take long before these amounts increased by a multiple of 40. In trying to explain the liability, the report had the following footnote (p. 103).

> Fair Value: Because interest rates have generally declined since the time the swaps were negotiated, many of the City's swaps have a negative fair value as of June 30, 2005. The negative fair values may be countered by lower total interest payments required under the variable-rate financing, creating lower synthetic interest rates.[5]

This footnote conveys three thoughts. First, a decrease in interest rate will decrease the synthetic fixed rate. This may be true if the interest rate

---

[5]The implication of lower synthetic rate does not follow.

payable to the related bond declines less than the interest rate receivable from the swap. Otherwise this conclusion does not make sense. Second, city officials became aware that changes in market-wide interest rates could increase the city's obligations for swaps. Finally, with this awareness, it is a mystery to figure out or understand the motives of city officials to aggressively double the size of the portfolio of swap contracts shortly before making this observation.

In the Comprehensive Annual Financial Report (CAFR) of 2007, the city reported about having received letters in March 2009 (the 2007 CAFR was issued in 2009) from counterparties of swap contracts (big banks) notifying the city of having a "Termination Event" that will require cancelation of the swap agreements and paying the present values to the counterparties (the banks). CAFR noted that termination of all swap contracts at that time would cost the city about $400 million as determined by the valuation provided by the very same beneficiaries — the banks who are also the counterparties.

By June 30, 2009, the number and composition of swap contracts increased to have total notional (reference face) amounts of $4.27 billion of which $1.096 billion were for swaptions.[6] The total amounts of long-term swap liabilities (the present value of expected future losses) at that time were $535 million but within one year these liabilities increased to $701 million.

Termination Penalties and Fees

- In 2011, the city paid a termination fee (penalty) of $222 million.[7] "In December 2011, the City's Water Fund issued $500,675,000 in revenue bonds. A portion of the proceeds were used to refund several outstanding revenue bonds as well as terminate all the Water Fund's interest rate swaps. The amount paid to terminate the interest rate swaps for the water system was $221,921,429." (p. 29)

---

[6]A swaption is a compound contract consists of an contract giving the buyer (the bank) the choice (option) to require the counterparty to buy an interest rate swap.

[7]http://www.detroitmi.gov/Portals/0/docs/finance/CAFR/2011%20Detroit%20CAFR%20Final.pdf.

- In 2012, the termination payment (penalty) was $547 million split between the Water and the Sewage systems.[8]
  In the year ended June 30, 2012, the Sewage Disposal and Water Funds issued $659.8 million and $500.7 million of revenue bonds, for sewage and water funds, respectively. A portion of the proceeds were used to refund several outstanding revenue bonds as well as terminate all the Water Fund's non-POC interest rate swaps. The amount paid to terminate the non-POC swaps was $321.6 million and $225.6 million for the Sewage Disposal and Water Funds, respectively. However, the termination fee for the swaps of the Water Fund should not be counted twice in 2011 and 2012.
  (p. 32 in CAFR and is in "Detroit Exhibit 3.")

In addition, the city paid an average of $33 million a year as termination "fees," which was an item appearing in every year's Comprehensive Annual Financial Report for which the city provided the most opaque

Detroit Exhibit 3
Use of Proceeds of the Bonds Issued in FY 2012
Use of $1.16 Billion Borrowed by the
Water and Sewer Departments

	Water Fund	Sewer Fund
Construction Fund (Cash out)	$163,088,241	$196,202,869
Swap-Termination Payments and Interest[a] (Cash out)	$225,620,525	$321,598,001
Redemption, Escrow, and Bond Reserve Funds (Cash out)	$116,059,121	$152,394,188
Par Amount of Bonds Issued Cash in	$500,675,000	$659,780,000[b]

Note:
(a) Comprehensive Annual Financial Report, 2012, p. 120.
(b) At 5.5% (p. 106).
Source: This is Figure 4 in the 2012 Comprehensive Annual Financial Report of 2012. http://citymobiletest.detroitmi.gov/How-Do-I/City-of-Detroit-CAFR-Find-How-Do-I-City-of-Detroit-MI.

---

[8] http://www.detroitmi.gov/Portals/0/docs/finance/CAFR/Final%202012%20Detroit%20Financial%20Statements.pdf.

explanation. The total amount since disclosures began in 2005 added up to about 264 million. Thus the total termination fees up to 2012 amounted to $811 million. In the hope of reducing the cost of borrowing and exposure to risk, the financing arrangement that involved swaps backfired and, between 2005 and 2012, the city paid a staggering sum of nearly $900 million in termination fees in different years.[9]

Yet, That Was Not All!

In addition, the city's two retirement systems, the general retirement system (GRSSC) and the police and fire departments' retirement system (PFRSC), joined forces to work through a third financial unit called the Detroit Retirement System Fund Trust. This Trust dealt with financial markets for borrowing, hedging using swaps, and settling contracts. To outside observers, this was a strange arrangement that allowed the Trust to borrow $1.44 billion for bonds the city sold under the label *pension obligation certificates* (POCs). The city issued POCs to fund certain unfunded pension liabilities and the obligations were distributed proportionately to different service functions. Of the funds collected by issuing these POCs, $640 million were paying a fixed interest rate, and $800 million were paying adjustable interest rates. By that time, the city administration was in the habit of buying swap contracts under the guise of lowering the cost of borrowing at variable rates.

By June 30, 2006, the city (through the Trust) entered into eight additional swap contracts, having total notional amounts of $800 million, in the hope of lowering the cost of the $800 million of variable rate money borrowed for the program of POCs. The swap contracts related to POCs required the city to pay a fixed rate of interest at 6.35% and receive 130% of the London Average Interest Rate (LIBOR). All of the eight swap contracts were purchased from UBS AG and Bank of America on June 12, 2006, for two groups of maturities consistent with the maturities of POCs:

- Group A (23 years): four swap contracts terminate in the year 2029.
- Group B (28 years): four swap contracts terminate in 2034.

---

[9]These amounts do not include any item of the relatively high transaction cost, including the lost resources by pledging the Casino tax and the revenues from the water and sewer systems.

Moreover, if the banks were to terminate any of these contracts earlier, the city would be required to pay all of the expected obligations (the "fair" market value of swap liabilities) for the entire life of the contract.

In addition to the information noted above, two aspects of Detroit's swap contracts and financial conditions need to be highlighted:

- The swap contracts lost money from the start. The change in fair-market values of total interest-rate swaps as of June 30, 2006, before the inception of the Financial Crisis, were in the negative, reflecting increased losses and liabilities. But the prevailing applicable accounting standards for nonprofit entities at that time allowed the city to conceal relevant information until after June 30, 2008, when the relevant accounting standard (Governmental Accounting Standard No. 53, 2008) became effective. Up until making that disclosure, the city's financial position looked to outsiders more creditworthy than it really was.[10]

- As other big banks had done earlier with bonds issued by the Detroit Water and Sewer Department, the swap contracts written by UBS AG and Merrill Lynch (Bank of America) required the city to purchase insurance policies for the swaps related to the $800 million POCs. The city obtained this insurance from two vendors, Syncora and Financial Guaranty. When the city's credit risk increased (i.e., credit rating was downgraded), the interest rate on borrowed POCs also increased. Additionally, the credit rating of the surety companies (Syncora and Financial Guaranty) became impaired. Moody's lowered the credit rating of Syncora to a "*Ca*" and the credit rating of Financial Guaranty Insurance to a "*Caaa*." Lowering the credit rating of the insurers increased the risk and cost of the swap contracts. In

---

[10]The swap-termination fee is actually a penalty because it payment for services not rendered and will not be rendered consisting of the following: calculate all the amounts that the city would have owed big banks until the end of the swap contract, which could be 30 years or longer, and use the zero-coupon rate to calculate the present values of these payments. Apply a few other adjustments according to the formula of the termination clause stated in the contracts, and you will be at close proximity of the termination fees. Big banks would be telling the city (or any other swap counterparty), "We do not trust that you could and would pay us the money you owe us for the remainder of the swap if the current conditions continue. So pay all of it now even if you bleed to death."

addition, cutting the credit ratings of the insurers attracted more financial scrutiny from regulators. Both conditions increased the weight of
the credit events that triggered swap sellers' action, which caused
UBS and Merrill Lynch to terminate the related swap contracts.

The Comprehensive Annual Financial Report of the City of Detroit
for 2012 presents a brief statement of these events[11]:

On January 8, 2009, due to POC (Pension Obligation Certificates) debt
rating and Swap Insurer's rating decline, the City received formal notice
from the Swap Counterparty (the banks) to four of the eight Swap agreements stating that an [a credit] event had occurred, which if not cured by
the City, would constitute an Additional Termination Event. On January
14, 2009, the City also received formal notice from the Swap Counterparty [the counterparty from the city's standpoint are the banks] to the
four remaining Swap Agreements. In June 2009, the City and the
Counterparties agreed to an amendment to the Swap Agreements,
thereby eliminating the Additional Termination Event... The termination events under the amended Swap Agreement include a provision for
the Counterparties [the banks] to terminate the amended Swap Agreement
and demand a termination payment if POCs ratings are downgraded
below "Ba3" or equivalent. (33)

When termination events were triggered in 2009, almost three years
before filing for bankruptcy, the city did not have the funds to pay the
required huge termination penalties and entered into negotiation with the
swaps' counterparties. Instead of canceling the contracts and try to find
ways to pay the termination fees, the city and the banks renegotiated to
restructure some of the terms of the contracts. First, the city pledged the
revenues from taxes on the Motor City Casino for up to $50 million a year
to service these swap contracts. Additionally, the city increased the fixed
rate it was paying to big banks on the swap agreements by 10 basis
points.[12]

---

[11] http://www.detroitmi.gov/Portals/0/docs/finance/CAFR/Final%202012%20Detroit%20
Financial%20Statements.pdf.
[12] Comprehensive Annual Financial Report, 2012, p. 120.

The pledged casino-tax revenue (called Casino hold back) went into a "lockbox" arrangement and could not be spent by the city for anything other than making swap payments. But this strange twist of events meant that the city itself became the insurer of the swap payments to Bank of America and UBS AG. With these arrangements, the banks had succeeded in converting the city's obligations related to swap contracts into a "secured" debt.[13] But Syncora, one of the two insurers retained by the city, went to the courts claiming ownership of the casino tax money in the lockbox. In the meantime, the liabilities related to swaps increased to an unprecedented level. The listing of the eight swap contracts in the 2012 Comprehensive Annual Financial Report (p. 118) shows two relevant pieces of information:

(a) The interest-rate-exchange (swap) contracts had been losing money every year and had a $439 million negative fair-market value. This was the amount of money the city would have had to pay to UBS and Merrill Lynch if the eight swap contracts were terminated on June 30, 2012.

(b) Having an additional indebtedness amounting to $439 million debt for the swaps was equivalent to having borrowed $1.239 billion instead of borrowing only $800 million. In this alternative scenario, the $439 million would have represented cash resources the city could have used for any function of value like shoring up its deteriorating public schools and infrastructure. Because of having made bad decisions to enter into swap contracts, the banks required the city to pay that much money to simply terminate the swaps in exchange for nothing. Yes, nothing!

Adding the $439 million termination payment to the total of $811 million the city had already paid to terminate swaps related to the bonds of the water and sewer systems up to that point in time meant that the

---

[13] Since then, the city has been paying for this approach to secure swap payments of about $50 million a year, with $878.7 million of expected payments through 2035, according to Orr's (the city's emergency manager) report. Amazingly, the city announced that it had budgeted about $57 million for public lighting that year. Much more could have been done with the payments for swaps.

city's termination payments would have been $1.239 billion. While there was no specific information provided, it is estimated that the city had paid more than $400 million for the recurring annual obligations from the start of entering into swaps contract up to 2012. By all accounts, chasing a hypothetical and illusionary reduction in the cost of borrowing left the city in a far worse financial shape.

After having paid $542 million in 2011 and 2012 to terminate swap contracts for the water and sewer funds (DWSD), filing for bankruptcy was the ultimate credit event that caused swap counterparties, UBS AG and Merrill Lynch (Bank of America), to demand terminating the other swaps related to the $800 million floating-rate pension obligation certificates. The two banks asked for an additional termination penalty of $345 million. Once again, the city did not have the funds to pay these penalties. After some negotiation, Kevyn Orr, the emergency manager overseeing the city's ways to extricate itself from bankruptcy, proposed lowering the penalties payable to UBS AG and Bank of America to $230 million but the bankruptcy court judge, Judge Steven W. Rhodes, refused to grant that request, saying, "This is too much." Subsequent negotiations between the city's emergency manager and the two banks lowered this number to about $85 million.[14]

The banks agreed to the settlement not only because it was acted upon at the bankruptcy judge's request but also because these banks knew fairly well that the city was in a dire financial condition and might not be able to pay the banks all the termination fees they would like to have. Even the lower settlement amount of $85 million, the city had borrowed from Barclays Bank to pay to UBS AG and Bank of America. By the end of 2014, the total penalties and fees for terminating most of the swaps amounted to $896 million, a high cost for betting on interest-rate movements under the semblance of lowering the cost of debt and managing risk. In exchange for making swap-termination payments of more than one billion dollars, the city received nothing. Absolutely nothing!

---

[14]Details of the negotiation are on pages 28 and 29 of the 2013 CAFR, http://citymobiletest.detroitmi.gov/How-Do-I/City-of-Detroit-CAFR-Find-How-Do-I-City-of-Detroit-MI.

THE CLAWS OF A BIG BANK:

For the swaps associated with the Sewage 2001 C-2 and Sewage 2001 C-2 Offsetting (mirror) issuances, the City pays a lower fixed rate in exchange for granting the counterparty a special termination option. Under this option, the counterparty can terminate the swap without payment if SIFMA averages 7 percent or higher for a consecutive 180-day period. The termination provision for the both swaps is effective after January 1, 2010.

(CAFR 2009, p. 104)

Interpretation: If the variable interest rate the bank pays the city on the swap increases to 7%, the bank has the right to terminate the swap without making any payment.

The Real Human and Social Cost of Swaps

The City of Detroit is about 700 miles away from Birmingham, Alabama, but big banks stationed their representatives on the front door steps of city hall just the same. They brought with them the same song and dance as well as the same virus that plagued Jefferson County. Armed with an unsubstantiated promise of lowering the cost of borrowing, swap dealers bombarded officials and financial officers in the municipality with presentations and special visits suggesting they had a magic wand to reduce the city's cost of debt. To help achieve this wonderful mythical goal, bankers followed the same strategy as they did in Jefferson County: persuaded the City to switch from financing by fixed-rate bonds to financing by variable-rate bonds, and then enter into noncancelable swap contracts requiring the city to pay banks a fixed rate and receive from banks a variable (adjustable) rate. However, implementation of that financing strategy turned out to be highly costly and requiring making significant adjustments to the cash outflow of the city.

Like Jefferson County, AL, the City of Detroit took some measures to reduce its operating cost and increase its revenues. Most impactful was raising the water and sewer rates and expecting the poor, including those whom the city had terminated their employment, to pay for their usage promptly. This expectation was necessary for the city to adopt because the city had pledged *all* water fund revenues for the swaps related to the water system and *all* sewage disposal fund operating revenues for the swaps related to the sewage. When the residents were late in making payments, the city copied Jefferson County once more and shut off running water supply to their homes.

Early in 2014, the city announced that one-half of its 323,000 water-service accounts were delinquent and threatened to shut off the water of any account having more than $150 past-due balance. Oddly enough, there is water everywhere around Detroit, the largest city in the State of Michigan. The city has a total area of 143 square miles, of which 4.12 square miles is water. The Detroit River connects the Great Lakes to Saint Lawrence Seaway all the way up to the Atlantic Ocean. Additionally, the best-kept secret is that the Great Lakes of North America contain 20% of freshwater in the entire world. While water is all around Detroit, it was not in the homes of tens of thousands of its citizens who claimed that the city had raised the cost of water and sewer services to levels beyond their abilities to pay. In July 17, 2014, Rose Hackman of *The Atlantic* estimated that the shut offs will affect 100,000 residents.[15] Marty Townsend estimated that number to be as high as 120,000, almost all are the poor residents who were delinquent on the payment of their water bills.[16] The numbers are large no matter how one looks at it and each one has a human face behind it.

The city management compounded this problem in at least two ways. The first complicating factor was the dismissal of 2,227 municipal employees in 2012–2013, reducing the salaries of those remaining on the job by 10%, and cutting down the support for a host of social programs. In essence, the city took actions to reduce the ability of the

---

[15] Rose Hackman. "What Happens When Detroit Shuts Off the Water of 100,000 People." The Atlantic. July 17, 2014. https://www.theatlantic.com/business/archive/2014/07/what-happens-when-detroit-shuts-off-the-water-of-100000-people/374548/.

[16] Marty Townsend, "Detroit Cuts Off Water To Poor People BUT Not Delinquent Businesses!" *Liberal America*, June 1, 2014.

Retrieved from http://liberalamerica.s3.amazonaws.com/wp-content/uploads/2014/06/detroit-water-shut-off.gif.

underprivileged to sustain their livelihood. "Detroit Exhibit 4" is a repro-duction of the 2012–2013 budget announcement by the city concerning this item in the budget. From that exhibit it is possible to estimate the cost savings of 10 selected programs to add up to $471 million. It is a matter of simple calculation to show that the swap-termination fees of $547 million the city paid to big banks in 2012 alone could have been used to avoid making these socially dysfunctional budgetary cuts and, furthermore, leave about $76 million to fix the infrastructure of the water and sewer systems.

The second complicating factor was retaining a demolition, recycling and remediation company by the name of Homrich to shut off the water supply at residential homes as directed by the city. The city paid Homrich more than $6 million to perform the task for a period of two years. Nine of the citizens demonstrating against the city shut offs were incensed and blocked the entrance to the parking lot of Homrich while holding a banner reading "Stop the Water Shut offs." The photo of their stand against the shut off is in "Detroit Exhibit 5." While thousands of citizens demon-strated in the streets (Detroit Exhibit 1), the city administration became highly agitated against these nine demonstrators who became known as the "Homrich 9." The city put them on trial. Their case continued in the courts for three years until Chief Judge Robert Colombo intervened to stop it as a senseless trial. In June 2017, Lee DeVito reported,

"After nearly three years of *dragged-out legal proceedings*, all charges have been dropped against Detroit's 'Homrich 9' water rights activists."[17] [Emphasis is in original source.

The United Nations Coming to Detroit

As was the case in the Deep South, bad fiscal management, big banks' greed and indifference to the vulnerability of the underprivileged became

---

[17]Lee DeVito, "All charges dismissed against the 'Homrich 9' Detroit water shutoff protes-tors," *Detroit MetroTimes*, June 20, 2017.

Retrieved from https://www.metrotimes.com/news-hits/archives/2017/06/20/all-charges-dismissed-against-the-homrich-9-detroit-water-shutoff-protestors.

Detroit Exhibit 4
A Partial List of the True Human Cost
of Paying Nearly $900 Million to Big Banks
to Terminate Swap Contracts

Next Year's Budget

The 2012–2013 budget includes

- Appropriations totaling $211.0 million to reduce the accumulated deficit.
- Reduction of $90.1 million in salaries and wages and a net decrease of 2,227 positions from the 2011–2012 budget.
- A 10% wage reduction for all employees.
- Net reduction of $79.1 million for employee benefits. Increased premium cost sharing by employees for all medical plans. Increases in co-pays and deductibles. Changes to the prescription plan.
- Airport subsidy reduced to $275,000 and transition to independent authority.
- Reductions totaling $11.2 million in the Solid Waste Fund.
- Net decrease of $62.8 million in federal grant appropriations for the Human Services Department. Funding for Head Start and Weatherization programs are not included in the Budget. The Community Services Block Grant (CSBG) will transition to an independent community agency.
- Net decrease $4.0 million for the Community Development Block Grants (CDBG).
- DDOT subsidy reduced $9.4 million to $43.0 million. Route rationalization for efficient and cost effective service delivery. Improved management of overtime. Improved risk management.
- Department of Health and Wellness Promotion $2.0 million net cost to the City. The department will be transferred to the Institute for Population Health.
- Increase in property tax rate for debt service due to decline in property valuation and increase in delinquency rate.
- Office of the Inspector General created with $0.6 million budget.
- The Public Lighting Department is transitioning street lights to an independent authority, transitioning the City's electricity customers to a third party, and beginning the replacement of the electricity grid.
- $1 million subsidy for the Charles H. Wright Museum of African American History.
- $0.6 million subsidy for the Detroit Zoo.
- $0.3 million subsidy to the Historical Museum Detroit Institute of Arts will no longer receive a subsidy.

Source: Comprehensive Annual Financial Report. For the Year Ended June 30, 2012. The City of Detroit Michigan, pp. 4–35.
Retrieved from http://www.detroitmi.gov/Portals/0/docs/finance/CAFR/Final%202012%20 Detroit%20Financial%20Statements.pdf.

Detroit Exhibit 5
Prosecuting the Homrich 9 Was a Disaster,
Says Chief Judge Robert Colombo

Source: Lee DeVito, "All charges dismissed against the 'Homrich 9' Detroit water shutoff protestors," *Detroit Metro Times*, June 20, 2017.

Retrieved from https://www.metrotimes.com/news-hits/archives/2017/06/20/all-charges-dismissed-against-the-homrich-9-detroit-water-shutoff-protestors. Reproduced with permission from Detroit Metro Times.

the rallying call of the citizens of the City of Detroit. Still, the rather unfortunate treatment of the "Homrich 9" protesters was not the highlight of the massive demonstrations in the city. Instead, it was the appeal of Detroit citizens to the United Nations' human rights commissioner, which in turn dispatched a delegation to the city expediently. To my knowledge, this was the first time a United Nations human rights group descended on a city or region in the USA to investigate human rights violation. The delegation consisted of three experts: Leilani Farha, the UN special rapporteur on adequate housing, Philip Alston, the UN special rapporteur on extreme poverty and human rights, and Catarina de Albuquerque, the first UN special rapporteur on the right to safe drinking water and sanitation.

In a news report, the High Commissioner of the United Nations' human rights said the following[18]:

> [T]he experts said the "most vulnerable and poorest" of the city's population were being disproportionately affected, including a predominant number of African Americans.
>
> "It is contrary to human rights to disconnect water from people who simply do not have the means to pay their bills," said Ms. de Albuquerque in a press release at the end of the experts' two-day visit to the city.
>
> "I heard testimonies from poor, African American residents of Detroit who were forced to make impossible choices — to pay the water bill or to pay their rent."

From Geneva, Switzerland, the UN made the following announcement.[19]

> GENEVA (25 June 2014) — Three UN experts on the human rights to water and sanitation, adequate housing, and extreme poverty and human rights expressed concern Wednesday about reports of widespread water disconnections in the US city of Detroit of households unable to pay water bills. "Disconnection of water services because of failure to pay due to lack of means constitutes a violation of the human right to water and other international human rights," the experts said.

---

[18] Office of High Commissioner "Detroit: Disconnecting water from people who cannot pay — an affront to human rights, say UN experts," United Nations Human Rights, June 24, 2014.

Retrieved from http://www.ohchr.org/EN/NewsEvents/Pages/DisplayNews.aspx?NewsID=14777.

Allison Kwesell, "In Detroit, city-backed water shut-offs 'contrary to human rights,' say UN experts," *UN News Center*, October 20, 2014.

Retrieved from http://www.un.org/apps/news/story.asp?NewsID=49127#.WdjTx2hSyUk.

[19] United Nations. Office of High Commissioner. "Detroit: Disconnecting water from people who cannot pay — an affront to human rights, say UN experts, United Nations Human Rights," June 24, 2014.

Retrieved from http://www.ohchr.org/EN/NewsEvents/Pages/DisplayNews.aspx?NewsID=14777.

Emily Badger also reported on this story for the *Washington Post*[20]:

And their conclusion reinforces what concerned on-lookers have been
saying since this summer: "When people are genuinely unable to pay the
bill," the U.N. says, the state is obligated to step up with financial assistance and subsidies. "Not doing so amounts to a human rights
violation."

However, it is a source of anguish that only few people had understood the swap dance between the City of Detroit and big banks well
enough to contrast the abundant resources handed out to big banks and the
deprivation of the city's residents. One of the banners held by the demonstrators in "Detroit Exhibit 1" has a written statement reading, "Paid $537
million to banks but shut the poor's water."

The city administration made bad decisions and ended up paying
big banks nearly $1.5 billion in payments for annual losses plus swap-
termination penalties and fees. In fact, total amounts of swap termination payments in 2012 *alone* were more than the cost of providing free
water for every man, woman, and child in the city for three full years
plus paying the full estimated cost of fixing the city's shamefully deteriorating public school buildings and infrastructure.[21]

Lessons Learned

From all the publicly known evidence, it appears that the swap contracting
between the City of Detroit and big banks suffered from three of the Four
Derivatives' Sins described by Carol Loomis: arrogance, ignorance, and

---

[20] Emily Badger, "The U.N. says water is a fundamental human right in Detroit,"
The Washington Post, October 23, 2014.

Retrieved from https://www.washingtonpost.com/news/wonk/wp/2014/10/23/the-u-n-
says-water-is-a-fundamental-human-right-in-detroit/?utm_term=.4a10302d2db6.

[21] Nadia Prupis, "Detroit Teachers Hold Sick-Out to Demand Fixes to School's
"Abominable" Problems," *Common Dreams,* January 15, 2015.

Retrieved from http://www.commondreams.org/news/2016/01/11/detroit-teachers-
hold-sick-out-demand-fixes-schools-abominable-problems.

lies. When the banks' favored financing strategy failed, the city felt the burn and switched back, though slowly, to the traditional municipal fixed-rate bond.[22]

> The Financial Recovery Income Tax Revenue and Refunding Bonds, Series 2014-A and Series 2014-B total $134,725,000 and $140,275,000, respectively. The bonds' interest rate at issuance was variable but was converted to a fixed rate in September 2015 when it was reoffered to the public.

Lessons Not Learned

Some recent actions by the city suggest that its administration still thinks that dancing with interest rate swaps was not as bad as dancing with snakes and, in 2016 the City of Detroit did it again! The 2016 Comprehensive Annual Financial Report shows that Detroit entered into one forward-starting swap contract on $200 million notional (reference face) amount. The swap would be effective in 2018 and would terminate in 2045. For this swap contract, the city agreed to pay 5.41% and receive three-month LIBOR plus 2.75%. While these terms might have a smaller interest rate spread than prior swap agreements, in a one-year span, the city's obligation for swap losses amounted to $26.3 million, or more than 13% of the notional amount of the swap.[23]

---

[22] City of Detroit, Comprehensive Annual Financial Report, 2015, p. 81.
[23] City of Detroit, Comprehensive Annual Financial Report, 2016, p. 68.
   file:///G:/DETROIT%202/FY16%20City%20of%20Detroit%20CAFR.pdf.

Paying for Nothing

Premature termination of swap contracts also terminates

- *Hedging*
- *Managing Interest Rate Risk*
- *Gambling*

Therefore, Paying termination penalty or fees is "paying for services not provided, and will never be, rendered."

CHAPTER 5

The City of Brotherly Love Drowned in the Eastern Swap Sinkhole

On July 29, 2013, the City of Philadelphia filed a class action suit against some of the largest banks in the world.[1] The suit claims that big banks have conspired and colluded to manipulate a key interest rate benchmark, LIBOR, which cost the City of Philadelphia mightily in both periodic settlements as well as the penalties of terminating interest rate swap contracts. The case was consolidated with numerous other class action suits making the same claim and all are currently moving in the halls of justice.

Only one decade earlier, the City of Philadelphia was minding the usual mundane duties of managing the water system, running the airport and doing all other mundane functions typical for a large city. Then dealers from big banks knocked on the doors of city hall and offered new products in the form of intangible contracts that could save the city some money. The new product was the interest rate exchange or swap agreement, which is a contract requiring the city to pay big banks interest at fixed rates and

---

[1]The parent banks named in the Philadelphia complaint are Bank of America Corp, Barclays Bank Plc, Citigroup Inc, Credit Suisse Group AG, Deutsche Bank AG, J.P. Morgan Chase & Co, Royal Bank of Canada, Royal Bank of Scotland and UBS AG.

receive from banks interest at adjustable rates. Lowering the cost of borrowing was the theme that swap dealers kept on emphasizing in their unprecedented campaign to draw nonprofit organizations into the net of the Swap Mania. Unfortunately, the city could not benefit by the history and experience of other cities or government agencies because most were in the same boat — beginning to listen to the same bankers who roamed the country looking for the unwary just as nomadic hunters did in the past.

There is no reason to believe that anyone on the staff of the city was well versed or had knowledge useful for assessing the risks and benefits of the proposed contracts that never existed until early 1980s. In the meantime, the financial advisors the city hired did not show signs that they really understood these contracts either. As in other regions, the financial advisors who dealt with buying and selling stocks and bonds were suddenly self-ordained swap advisors while knowing little about the risks, rewards and valuation of interest rate swaps. In this kind of environment, officials at the Philadelphia city hall had only the marketing shows of swap dealers and bankers to inform them of the benefits of swap contracts, even though such benefits were not tested and were based on unverifiable expectations.

The term "swap" could not be found anywhere in the 2001 Comprehensive Annual Financial Report (CAFR) of the City of Philadelphia. The city began to dance with interest rate swaps in a significant way in 2002 even before the Pennsylvania legislature permitted government agencies to do so. In a short time, dealing with swaps appeared to become a main function of the city; the word "swap" appeared 109 times in the 2003 CAFR. So many changes took place over time and whoever prepared the city's CAFR was taken by anything has to do with "swap" contracts. In the Comprehensive Annual Financial Report of 2008, the word "swap" was cited 356 times, many more times than the number of citations of words related to the city's essential functions. The accumulation of losses over the years lessened the enthusiasm about swaps and the word "swap" was cited only 231 time in the 2016 CAFR.

Two historic congressional acts had contributed to the eruption of the Swap Mania in the late 1990s. The first was the Gramm–Leach–Bliley Act in 1999 that repealed major sections of the 1933 Glass–Steagall Act allowing commercial banks to acquire and affiliate with investment banks. The second was the Commodity Futures Modernization Act, which President Clinton signed on December 20, 2000. A very important section of that Act

(Section 117) pre-empts all state and local laws and regulations against gambling using securities and prices. Both of these Acts gave big banks a license to sell interest rate swaps aggressively to nonprofit entities irrespective of the goal of doing so — hedging, speculating or simply gambling. The combination of these two Acts gave birth to the phenomenon of the Swap Mania in which the city became an important player. Just like many other cities, the novelty and acclaimed rewards of swap contracts appear to have given officials in the City of Philadelphia an insatiable appetite to enter into the rather dark halls of exotic high finance. To show the extent of being taken by the Swap Mania, we could compare the number of citations of the word "swap" in CAFR against the number of citations of a necessary function of the city such as the word "water." One of the city's responsibilities is managing the supply of fresh water to homes and businesses and disposing of wastewater. Looking at CAFR one gets the impression that the city's concern about these essential functions was much less than the attention given to swap contracts. For example, CAFR of 2016 repeated the word "water" 109 times but the word "swap" had 231 citations!

Starting in 2002, swap dealers paid the city more than $100 million in upfront money to persuade officials to enter into swaps and swaption contracts on more than $1.25 billion notional amounts. A swaption is a contract consisting of two steps: In the first step, the city sells an option contract to a bank. This option gives the bank the right to require the city to sign an interest rate swap contract to pay fixed and receive variable according to pre-specified terms and maturity stated in the contract. Combining the two steps into one contract generated the name "swaption." For the Airport Authority, for example, to give the bank the right to choose is a valuable feature for which the bank should pay a price — called option premium.[2] The bank has the right to exercise the option after a pre-specified period of time lapses by requiring the Airport Authority to enter into an interest rate (exchange) swap contract.

While accepting the upfront money from big banks binds the City to sign the swap contract when requested by the counterparty bank, the upfront money was a welcome relief from the standpoint of liquidity. However, the

---

[2] Although the official reports of the City claim that the upfront money represents "savings from refunding." The current accounting standards treat the upfront money as a loan that should be amortized during the term of the swap.

amount of losses on the swaps the City recorded in the first year was much higher than all of the upfront money it had received. For example, the 2003 CAFR reported the following information for the Water & Sewer swaption that was written to mature in 20 years.[3]

- **City of Philadelphia 1993 Water & Sewer Swaption/2003 Water and Sewer Swap**

  In December 2002, the City entered into a swaption that provided the City with an *up-front payment of $24,989,926.* .... The swaption gave Citigroup formerly Salomon Brothers Holding Company, Inc. the option to enter into an interest rate swap to receive fixed amounts and pay variable amounts. .....Under the swap, the City pays a fixed payment of 4.52% and receives a variable payment computed as the actual bond rate through March 1, 2005 and thereafter computed as the lesser of the actual bond rate or 68.5% of the London Interbank Offered Rate (LIBOR). .... The swap has a notional amount of $376,165,000 ...... The bonds and the related swap agreement mature on June 15, 2023. ... As of June 30, 2003, *the swap had a negative fair value [a loss] of $66,819,104.* [Emphasis added].

On June 30, 2003, the variable rate the City received from the swap contract with Citigroup was 0.75%. Thus, the difference between the payable fixed rate of 4.52% and receivable rate was 3.77%. On notional amount of $376 million, the city had to pay Citigroup $14 million for interest rate difference in 2003 alone ($376 million × 3.77%) and accruing a long-term liability for anticipated future losses. As we see from the above passage, Citigroup estimated that liability at $66 million. Thus, the total loss, realized and unrealized in one year, for the city from this one swaption contract was $80 million, while the upfront money received was $24 million only. Still, the city entered into three more swaption contracts on smaller undisclosed notional amounts for water and sewer bonds and accrued an additional $10 million for long-term losses. Two other units of the city's administration, the Airport Authority and Pennsylvania Interagency Cooperation Authority had similar fates as displayed in "Philadelphia Exhibit 1." Incidentally, while the

---

[3] Comprehensive Annual Financial Report, 2003, p. 67–68.
  Retrieved from http://www.phila.gov/reports/pdfs/cafr2003.pdf.

Philadelphia Exhibit 1
Swap Losses (Long-Term Liabilities) of Component Units
as of June 30, 2003

	Up-Front Money	Notional Amount	Fair-Value Losses on June 30, 2003
Airport Authority	$6.5	$189.5	($31)
Water and Sewer	$29	$453 plus?	($77)
PICA 1993, '96, '99*	$28	$467	($36)
PICA 2003	$10	$163	($33)
Total	$73.5	$1,273	($177)

Note: *PICA stands for Pennsylvania Intergovernmental Cooperation Authority, which is one component unit of the City of Philadelphia.
Source: Retrieved from http://www.phila.gov/reports/pdfs/cafr2003.pdf.

city purchased these swaptions in 2002, these contracts continue to trouble the city because they had contractual maturity in 2028 or 2033.

All of these losses were in addition to the cost of remarketing the bonds (at least 0.3% annually), the cost of underwriting and insurance. In simple words, the city lost money left and right on the swaps (and swaptions) and received nothing in exchange; nothing more than the satisfaction of using the new high finance instruments and the attendant jargon.

The Illusion of Lowering the Cost of Borrowing

Other than paying money upfront, the most important sales incentive that swap dealers adopted was the claim of "potential" lowering of the cost of borrowing from the bond market and, in passing, managing interest rate risk. The intensive campaign that big banks took to almost every substantive nonprofit entity in the country has actually led to a change of culture in financial management. Instead of working to economize and reduce the cost of debt, swap dealers persuaded the buyers of interest rate swaps to change their approach by taking steps having the presumed potential of greater savings. They were aggressive and city officials were eager to join others who were intoxicated by using the lingo of exotic swap contracts.

How else could the City move from no engagement with swaps whatsoever to suddenly gulp seven interest rate swaps and swaption contracts on notional amounts of $1.25 billion in 2002, its first year of entering into a totally unknown territory? The fact that the City had entered into seven large swap contracts in 2002, before the State legislature had approved PA 23 Act in 2003 permitting government agencies to deal with derivatives, is ample evidence of the success of swap dealers in affecting speedy indoctrination of City officials.

The indoctrination and change of culture focused on interest rate fixity to foster the perception of stability as long as the City kept on paying big banks annually the large amounts of money representing the difference between the payable and receivable interest rates times the notional amounts. The concern for "fixity" of interest rates was well displayed in all Comprehensive Annual Financial Reports from 2002 to 2016. "Philadelphia Exhibit 2" presents an example of how the city had, implicitly, announced the view of irrelevance of swap contracts in affecting the interest rate payable on the related bonds.

Moreover, the behavior of City officials seemed to bear the assumption that the economic environment will remain stable such that the apparent fixity of interest rate will also be maintained. As everyone knew or should have known back then that making such an assumption does not benefit by looking at the history of economic instability. For a maturity period as long as 20 or 30 years, anything could happen. In fact, it did happen that the synthetic interest rate skyrocketed to over 9.844% in 2008. "Philadelphia

Philadelphia Exhibit 2
A Display of "Fixity" of a Useless Synthetic Rate

	Terms	Rates
Interest Rate Swap		
Fixed payment to Citigroup	Fixed	4.52%
Variable payment from Citigroup	Actual Bond Rate	(0.75%)
Net interest rate swap payments		3.77%
Variable Rate bond coupon payments	Market driven	0.75%
Synthetic interest rate on bonds		4.52%

Philadelphia Exhibit 3
For Philadelphia Airport Swap (2008)
(A Very High Synthetic Fixed Rate for Airport Swaption!)

As of June 30, 2008, the rates were:

	Terms	Rates
Interest Rate Swap		
Fixed payment to JPMorgan under swap	Fixed	6.04400%
Variable payment from JPMorgan under swap	SIFMA	(1.55000)%
Net interest rate swap payments		4.49400%
Variable Rate bond coupon payments	Weekly resets	5.35%
Synthetic interest rate on bonds		9.844%

Source: Reproduced from CAFR 2008, p. 70.
Retrieved from http://www.phila.gov/investor/pdfs/Financial%20Statements/FY%202008%20
Financial%20Statements/FY%202008%20Phila%20CAFR.pdf.
Bring here 2009.

Exhibit 3" shows the components of the 9.844% and, thus, providing evidence that issuing the bundle of variable rate bond coupled with interest rate swaps does not ensure lowering the cost of borrowing.

Once again, if the city had not entered into swaps, its interest rate on the bonds would have been much lower. It looks as if the city administrators implicitly preferred to pay 4.5% to JPMorgan Chase than staying with the market. No wonder the swap pushers reportedly refer to these clients as the "muppets."[4]

In 2004, the City of Philadelphia expanded its portfolio of swaps to include Basis Swaps (swapping a variable rate based on one benchmark for another variable rate based on another benchmark). The city also entered into knock-in swap contracts (swaps that would be activated only after the interest rate reaches a specified level). By June 30, 2009, the city expanded its swap portfolio even more.

---

[4] Greg Smith, "Why I am leaving Goldman Sachs," *The New York Times*, March 14, 2012.
Retrieved from http://www.nytimes.com/2012/03/14/opinion/why-i-am-leaving-goldman-sachs.html?_r=0.

Why did city officials enter into so many and different swap contracts? This remains a mystery even for the former mayor of Philadelphia. The *Philadelphia Inquirer*'s Joseph DiStefano reports the following[5]:

> "We found it very difficult to find the documentation I would like to have seen, about why the city entered into swaps," said Winkler, a Mayor Nutter appointee who previously worked for Philadelphia-based Public Financial Management (PFM), financial adviser to Philadelphia under Nutter and to other communities across the U.S.
>
> Where are the people who recommended that Philadelphia buy swaps? *"The city's prior swaps advisers, the principals, were convicted and are mostly either in prison or awaiting sentence,"* Winkler said. [Emphasis added]

Covering up the Mess

Starting 2003, the Comprehensive Annual Financial Reports of the City of Philadelphia were written in such a way that no reasonably educated or even highly educated reader could understand the true financial picture. Compared to any other financial reports of other cities, the information in the city's Comprehensive Annual Financial Reports are opaque and scattered throughout. It would actually take a long time of specialists to study the reports to be able to patch up different elements and have a full picture of the cost of swaps and swaptions, if that is even feasible.

Like many other states, public entities in Pennsylvania were not permitted to enter into financial derivatives contracts including interest rate swaps before 2003. Under pressure from different sources, the legislature reversed that prohibition and enacted PA 23 Act in 2003 (almost at the same time as similar laws were enacted in Illinois and elsewhere), permitting public agencies to use interest-rate swaps and other derivatives without further authorization from any other state agency. As it happened in California and Illinois, legislations similar to the 2003 PA23 Act opened the floodgates for both swap pushers and swap buyers. The ensuing rush

---

[5]Joseph N. DiStefano, "Philly Deals: Interest-rate swap strategy backfires, costs city $186M," *The Philadelphia Inquirer,* October 24, 2012.

Retrieved from http://www.philly.com/philly/columnists/joseph-distefano/20121024_ PhillyDeals__Interest-rate_swap_strategy_backfires__costs_city__186M.html.

generated obligations that placed severe constraints on the use of Philadelphia's economic resources that is expected to continue until 2033 and beyond, when these contracts are scheduled to mature.

However, the threat to repeal PA 23 Act of 2003 and reinstate the prohibition on dealing with derivative contracts had fallen on deaf ears, and the attention shifted to proposing half measures. For example, after watching the city facing huge amounts of losses from being a party to swap contracts, city councilman James Kenney (who is the current mayor) offered a bill in July 2015 to ban depositing city funds into either Bank of America or Citigroup[6]:

> "Based on what these banks have done with swaps and misleading investors, why should we have any city deposits there?" he asked. "We shouldn't be doing business with our financial enemies."

Evidence of Cover Up

Accounting standards require reporting the value of an interest rate swap contract at the amount the entity could obtain (when the entity is in a gain position) or pay (when the entity is in a loss position) to get rid of the contract. For that purpose, the accounting and finance professions coined the term "fair market value." However, fair market values of most interest rate swap contracts are not readily available because these contracts are typically traded over-the-counter — i.e., privately in the dark. As a result, the reporting entity must select from among various methods to estimate the amount at which the swap contract could be traded or settled. This amount represents the non-current asset or non-current liability.

The Comprehensive Annual Financial Report of the City of Philadelphia gave us three methods the city had used to value swaps. The wording of each of the three methods is a perfect example of the needless complexity that begs the questions of both the incentive and knowledge of those who authorized the release of these reports and those who opined on them.

---

[6]Erin Arvedlund, "Kenney bill seeks to ban city deposits with Citigroup, Bank of America," The *Inquirer,* January 22, 2015.

Retrieved from http://www.philly.com/philly/news/breaking/20150123_Kenney_bill_seeks_to_ban_city_deposits_with_Citigroup__Bank_of_America.html.

1. Reporting a Complex Method of Valuation

CAFR Statement about the Fair Value of the Swap Related to the Bonds of the Airport:

> *Fair Value*: As of June 30, 2003, the swap had a negative fair value of $31,142,072 [a loss]. *Its fair value was estimated using the BDT option-pricing model. This model takes into consideration probabilities, volatilities, time and underlying prices.* [Emphasis added]
>
> (CAFR 2003, 67)

A Comment:

This statement was all the information the city had offered about the BDT option-pricing model and it is simply useless to all users of the annual report. Nothing is said about how the model incorporates probabilities and volatilities or about the limitations of the resulting values. The BDT option-pricing model was developed by Fisher Black, Emmanuel Derman, and William Toy in 1990.[7] It is a complex and highly technical model and is not the most frequently used or referenced option valuation model in finance. It will be very surprising if any of the financial administrators at Philadelphia city hall as well as the auditors who signed the annual reports knew anything about BDT model back in 2003 or even nowadays in 2017! This raises the question of the reasons for the brief mention of such a model in annual financial reports aimed to inform the public. Perhaps there was a different message embedded in the report. Both the finance administrators at city hall and the CPA who opined on the financial statements might be saying, "We play with big boys in Wall Street, and we speak their language of science and financial engineering. Trust us; we use a highly sophisticated model to price our swaptions and it does not really matter if you do or do not understand the disclosure."

---

[7]Fisher Black is the same author of the Black–Scholes model commonly used on Wall Street and academia. Black, Fisher, Emanuel Derman, and William Toy, "A one-factor model of interest rates and its application to Treasury bond options." *Financial Analysts Journal*, January-February 1990. Pp. 33-39. Retrieved from http://www.emanuelderman. com/media/faj-one_factor_model.pdf

2. Reporting the Second Method of Valuation

CAFR statement about the fair value of interest rate swap contracts related to the bonds issued for the water and sewer systems:

> *The fair value was estimated using the zero-coupon method. This method calculates the future net settlement payments required by the swap, assuming that the current forward rated[s] implied by the yield curve correctly anticipate future spot interest rates. The payments are then discounted using the spot rates implied by the current yield curve for hypothetical zero-coupon bonds due on the date of each future net settlement of the swap.* [Emphasis added]
>
> (CAFR 2003, 68)

A Comment:

To the non-specialist, this paragraph might sound like a meaningless collection of highly technical financial gibberish. That is not the case, however. The general approach to the valuation method noted is correct and should be known to specialists in that market. In all likelihood, it was copied from a finance source, and we shall see shortly the evidence for making this assertion.

However, the definition could not be deciphered by anyone other than specialists in financial economics and, more specifically, in financial derivatives. How could any reader wrap her/his head around buzzwords glued together in such a way that would not make any sense to most people? Lumping together in two sentences the technical terms of *zero-coupon curve, zero-coupon bond, yield curve, spot rates,* and *forward rates* is not particularly helpful in conveying confidence in the reporter's knowledge or ability. As a result, no one could assess whether the fair-market values presented in CAFR were accurate, too high, or too low because those who said they had calculated the numbers did not even understand the method used. One could not dispel the feeling that dumping a highly complex paragraph as is typically written in a specialized finance book without any attempt to provide further explanation is a signal of being overwhelmed.

Who Else Reported the Same exact Method?

As with all jurisdictions, many local government agencies operate in the State of Pennsylvania, and each agency has an auditor signing the annual financial statements (CAFR). If two different government agencies had two different auditors who were independent of one another and whose opinions were temporally separated by twelve years, *what would be the chances that the financial reports signed by both auditors use the same exact words and sentence structure to describe the determination of fair value?* A priori, one would argue, the chances for this coincident to occur without a common causal linkage are nil. But that was exactly the case when comparing the 2003 annual financial statements of the City of Philadelphia (reported above) and the 2015 annual financial statements of North Penn Water Authority (reported below). Except for five introductory words, both descriptions were identical!

North Penn Water had the same wording in 2015 as Philly had in 2003:

Fair Market Value Determination — The fair value of the interest rate swap was estimated using the zero-coupon method. This method calculates the future net settlement payments required by the swap, assuming that the current forward rates implied by the yield curve correctly anticipate future spot interest rates. These payments are then discounted using the spot rates implied by the current yield curve for hypothetical zero-coupon bonds due on the date of each future net settlement on the swap.

North Penn Water Annual Report 2015, p. 33

Retrieved from http://northpennwater.org/uploads/Annual%20 Financial%20Report.pdf.

How could anyone explain this uncanny similarity of the two uninformative disclosures? Neither the auditors in charge of these audits nor the audit firms employing them were related. Furthermore, the two entities were separated by thirty miles physical distance and twelve years time difference. This rather strange coincidence suggests that both groups were given the same boilerplate description by swap dealers who most likely copied it from finance books, and none of the CAFR signatories gave us any reason to believe they understood it.

It should also be noted that being located in the same State has nothing to do with this coincident.[8] For example, the financial statements of Arizona State University for 2016 report the same exact paragraph (on page 45). Additionally, the 2016 CAFR of the Dormitory Authority of the State of New York (DASNY) used the same exact wording as discussed in Chapter 10. Once more, this practice begs the general question: Do these types of financial reports really inform the public of anything other than showing off complexity?

Translation:

It appears that all of those who were connected with preparing and distributing the annual reports (CAFR) had achieved some goals unrelated to the main mission of the annual reports' disclosure. These are the goals of informing others that they speak the language of Wall Street; they knew what they were doing, but it is just too complicated to explain it to others who should simply trust them!

3. Reporting the Third Method of Valuation

Fair Market Value. This is the simplest of all methods reported, but also the least credible: "We do not know and left the complexity to big Banks."

> **Fair value**: As of June 30, 2003, the 1996 swaption had a negative fair value [i.e., loss] of approximately $12,000,000 and the 1999 swaption had a negative fair value of approximately $26,000,000. *The fair value was determined by the counterparty using its proprietary methodology.* [Emphasis added]
>
> (CAFR 2003, 69)

---

[8] Arizona State University. Comprehensive Annual Financial Report. Year ended June 30, 2016.

Retrieved from http://www.asu.edu/fs/documents/annual_reports/ASU-2016-CAFR.pdf.

The counterparty banks informed the city of the amounts of money the city owed them on two swaption contracts. They calculated these amounts using their own proprietary (secret) methodology and, although neither city officials nor the auditor had any idea how they did that calculation, they accepted the numbers as "true."

Looking at these three methods of presenting numbers for fair market values of interest rate swaps that were supposed to measure settlement or termination values, no one could claim that any of these methods is comprehensible by anyone other than finance specialists. The practice of using specialized financial terms in the city's Comprehensive Annual Financial Reports continued for many years without any attempt to explain what any of these terms mean or how interest-rate-exchange contracts had benefited the city. Even explaining the nature of some of the contracts signed by the City of Philadelphia is unsatisfactory. For example, the following information was provided for the swaption contract related the bonds/swaps issued for Airport bonds. These annual reports convey some hidden desire to overload the readers so that they could be intimidated enough not to ask questions.

Objective of swaption: In April 2002, the Airport entered into a swaption that provided the Airport with an up-front payment of $6,536,836. As a synthetic refunding of its 1995 Bonds, this payment represents the present value savings as of April, 2002, of refunding on June 15, 2005, without issuing refunding bonds as of April, 2002. The swaption gives JPMorgan Chase Bank–New York the option to enter into an interest rate swap to receive fixed amounts and pay variable amounts. If the option is exercised, the Airport would then expect to issue variable-rate refunding bonds.

(2003 CAFR, 67)

A Comment:

This transaction is quite strange and was most definitely costly. The interpretation of this short paragraph is as follows:

- The City of Philadelphia wrote (sold) a contract with JPMorgan Chase and collected an option premium of $6,536,836. This was not savings from any deal.
- The contract gives JPMorgan Chase the right to require the City of Philadelphia to enter into an interest-rate-exchange (swap) contract at a future date of the bank's own choosing.
- Once the bank exercises the option, the swap contract would require the city to pay interest to JPMorgan Chase at a fixed rate and receive interest from JPMorgan Chase at an adjustable rate.
- Initiating this last step gives the city the green light to issue bonds at an adjustable rate.

This case is an example of a decision made with little forethought for several reasons:

- JPMorgan Chase will force the city to enter into a swap contract only when it is highly beneficial to the bank. This would be the case when the adjustable rate is expected to be much lower than the fixed rate so that the bank pays interest to the city at a low rate but the city pays the bank the predetermined fixed interest rate.
- The purported relationship assumes that the swap transaction is undertaken to artificially fix a variable rate on a bond issue that has already been sold. But in this case we see the reverse. The swap contract was completed, then the variable rate bond issue was sold to fit the swap.
- There was absolutely no economic justification to enter into a swap agreement in order to issue adjustable or floating interest rate bonds.[9]

---

[9]This was the order issued by the attorney general of the State of Texas in relationship to another case. Please see the entry "A Word of Prudence from the South."

- Both the swap contract and the bond issue require paying up-front underwriting and legal fees as well as paying for insurance and maintenance continually.

In addition, the term *synthetic refunding* is a highly specialized term, but like all other terms, no further explanation was ever provided in CAFR. We provide the definition as reported by the Municipal Securities Board Rules in a footnote for the interested reader.[10]

In Summary

Once more, the thought the preparers of the annual report (CAFR) appeared to convey to the public was "we do not care if you, the reader, understands what we say because we also do not know enough to explain it any better."

So, what do all these issues mean to the people of Philadelphia? There are several issues of relevance, actually:

(a) The City of Philadelphia received upfront money with the initiation of swap and swaption contracts. The Comprehensive Annual Financial Report claims that the up-front money is a form of savings. Such a claim is, of course, false because (i) the upfront money for

---

[10] *Synthetic refunding* as defined by the Municipal Securities Rules Board is as follows:

> An arrangement that allows an issuer to generate debt service savings that it would realize if it were permitted to advance refund the outstanding bonds. This agreement is generally used by issuers that either choose not to or are not permitted under the Internal Revenue Code to advance refund outstanding bonds on a tax-exempt basis. Such arrangements generally an issuer to enter into an agreement with a counter-party and receive an up-front payment from the counter-party in return for a specified action of the issuer or a right to take a specified action by the counter-party at a future date, typically a date on which the issuer can call the outstanding bonds and effect a current refunding. For example, on the future call date, the counter-party may have the right to require the issuer to issue refunding bonds with certain specified terms for purchase by the counter-party. Alternatively, the issuer may issue variable rate refunding bonds and have the right to require the counter-party to enter into an interest rate swap on specified terms.

Synthetic Refunding. MSRB Glossary of Municipal Securities Terms. Retrieved from https://www.definedterm.com/a/definition/97780.

the swaption is the premium collected for selling an option to the bank, and (ii) the upfront money collected for the swap contracts were essentially loans in disguise. It is more convenient for the city to have a loan linked to the swap so that the city would not need to go to the debt market to borrow money. Nevertheless, providing short-term liquidity may have come at a high price. The amounts of money the city owed on the swaps *in a single year* were twice as large as all of the upfront money it had received. More precisely, for easing up short-term liquidity, the city took on a higher long-term risk.

(b) In 2003, interest-rate-exchange (swap) contracts were unknown at most universities at any level; they were new betting instruments that came on the scene after 1982. So it is highly unlikely that anyone at city hall had vetted and carefully understood the terms and implications of any of the swap contracts banks had offered to them and which they signed. Actually, starting in 2003 soon after the city got entangled in the net of the Swap Mania, the communication reported in the Comprehensive Annual Financial Report of any year since then conveyed a total lack of understanding of the rewards and risks of these contracts.

(c) Only a few months after entering into swap contracts, the city accumulated huge debt obligations reflecting the long-term debt owed to the banks, the swap counterparties. By June 30, 2003, the City of Philadelphia owed big banks more than $177 million for interest rate swap contracts they had just signed on to only one year earlier. This rather poor early performance of increasing indebtedness for exchanging fixed for variable interest rates did not seem to give anyone at city hall a hint of having embarked on a losing venture. Instead of suspending the chase of paper contracts that have real financial consequences, subsequent annual reports show that the city continued to acquire more swaps until the burden of paying high annual settlements became arduous.

More on the City of Philadelphia is included in Chapter 12 and Chapter 34.

Wealth Transfer

Interest Rate Swaps are instruments
⇨ *For wealth transfer,*
⇨ *Not for wealth creation.*

CHAPTER 6

The Heart of America and Windy City Handed Its Compass to the Banking Cartel

The Big Picture

City of Chicago Exhibit 1
Reported Losses (Realized and Unrealized) from Swap
Contracts Including Termination Penalties (In Million Dollars)

City Of Chicago Liabilities for Swaps

Sources: City of Chicago, Comprehensive Annual Financial Report, 2004–2016.

141

Feeling the pain of giving money away while facing financial difficulties, the City of Chicago officials became convinced of having committed a blunder by following the directives of swap pushers to switch from fixed-rate bond financing to variable-rate bonds plus entering into swap contracts. It took more than two decades of consistently paying out money to big banks before the city took three major actions in 2015 (see Exhibit 1):

(a) Borrowing money at high fixed rates of interest to terminate some interest rate exchange (swap) contracts.
(b) Paying very high prices to terminate other swap contracts.
(c) Negotiating with, and seeking forbearance of, some lenders to turn full circle and convert variable-rate bonds into fixed-rate debt.

In recent years, the City of Chicago decided to terminate a large number of its swap contracts and slow down the annual bleeding of cash it had been paying to settle claims made by swap counterparties. In a span of 18 months between January 2015 and May 2016, the City of Chicago (excluding the public school system which is discussed separately in Chapter 14) handed big banks $357 million to terminate some of its outstanding swap (interest rate exchange) contracts. These funds had to be borrowed because the city did not have that much money available to give away. As usual, these termination amounts were in addition to the amounts the city had already paid for the recurring annual settlement of swap obligations.

Like all state agencies in the State of Illinois, the City of Chicago was prohibited from transacting in financial-derivatives until the Illinois legislature passed Public Act 093-0009 in May 2003, which removed that prohibition. However, somehow the City of Chicago was able to enter into interest-rate-swap agreements starting in 1997, and by the time the legislature took action in 2003, the city had already entered into five swap contracts on total notional amounts of $403 million. Yet, those swaps were already losing money, and the net liability arising from these losses amounted to about $20 million in 2003, which was a relatively small amount in comparison to what was in store for the future.[1] It appears that this much loss did not provide city-hall officials a strong enough signal

---

[1] City of Chicago, Comprehensive Annual Financial Reports, 2004, p. 70.
    Retrieved from https://www.cityofchicago.org/content/dam/city/depts/fin/supp_info/CAFR/2004/CAFR_2004.pdf.

to make the administration of Mayor Richard M. Daley (1989–2011) pause and think of the economic viability of these contracts. Instead, in 2003 and 2004, the city entered into four more swap contracts on $1.2 billion notional amounts, bringing total notional amounts of the swap portfolio to $1.6 billion. These contracts were poorly conceived and contained contingencies favoring big banks all the way. Almost immediately, these new swaps accumulated losses and added to the city's swap liabilities. By the end of 2004, the city's total liability for its nine swap contracts was more than $70 million. It appears that the learning curve at City Hall continued to be so steep that no one realized that the city was moving into a disastrous trap. In 2005, the city entered into more swap contracts, increasing the total notional amounts of its swap portfolio to $1.9 billion, accompanied by increasing the swap debt for expected losses to $74 million.

Falling for the Weekly Auction Rate

More of the story of Chicago's attraction to the Swap Mania will follow in this chapter as well as in Chapter 14 and Chapter 34, but we must pause and ask the question of how poorly these interest rate exchange (swap) contracts were designed. We could consider, for example, the swap contracts related to the Midway Airport Revenue Bond Series 2004C-D, the same bond series noted in Chapter 1:[2]

> The Series 2004C-D bonds were sold in December with an initial *auction rate* of 1.55 percent and 1.45 percent and maturity dates ranging from January 1, 2012 to January 1, 2035. [Emphasis added]
>
> ......
>
> At the discretion of the City, the Series 2004C-D bonds may *bear interest at a weekly, flexible, adjustable long, auction rate or fixed rate. The City issued the bonds in the auction rate mode for a seven-day auction period.* [Emphasis added]

It is important to note that the interest rate on the bond was the Auction Rate that was adjustable every week and reset according to market conditions and changes in the credit risk of the city. Concurrent with the sale of these bond series, the city entered into swap contracts having

---

[2]City of Chicago, Comprehensive Annual Financial Reports, 2004, p. 69.

notional amounts and terms to maturity set to match the bond series. These swap contracts required the city to pay a fixed interest rate at 4.14% and receive a variable rate at the Municipal Bond Average Interest Rate (SIFMA, the acronym for the Securities Industry Financial Markets Association swap rate). The contracts mature in 30 years. The city's 2004 Comprehensive Annual Financial Report explains some of the terms and objective of entering into swap contracts:

> In connection with the issuance of the Series 2004C-D bonds, the City entered into three interest-rate swap agreements to obtain a [synthetic] fixed interest rate.

Unfortunately, this quote asserts a false relationship. In a system requiring the interest rates on bonds to be reset weekly, the synthetic rate could not be fixed for more than one week at a time. To make some sense of the inaccuracy of the above quoted statement, let us look at the "City of Chicago Exhibit 2," which shows why the weekly adjustable auction rate for a swap converts the related bond to a weekly floating rate.

This picture is very much disconcerting for several reasons:

- The City of Chicago agreed to sell bonds at Auction Rate, which requires resetting the interest rate on the bonds once a week and, thus, exposing the city to short-term market credit risk. When the auction rate market collapsed in 2008, coupled with downgrading the city's credit rating, the bond's related interest rate was reset at the default interest rate of 9%.
- The interest cost was actually understated by the 0.7%, the annual cost of remarketing bonds to reset the rate.
- The actual cost of the swap also includes fees for underwriting, insurance, legal and financial advisors and other components of unrecognized transaction cost.

Although each swap contract requires making a payment for underwriting fees (typically payable to the same bank involved in underwriting the related bonds) and for the insurance required for the banks' benefit, the city kept on signing more swap contracts as if they were costless. When the financial crisis hit in 2008, the notional amounts of all swaps (and

City of Chicago Exhibit 2
The Not-So-Fixed Synthetic Rate*

Fixed Interest Rate Payable for the Swaps	4.14%
Less Variable Interest Rate Receivable from the Swaps (SIFMA Changes Weekly) but May Be Reset for the Swap at Different Periods.	−0.65%
Net Cash Payment to Big Banks	= 3.49%
Variable Interest Rate Payable on the Bonds (the component "xx" was Reset Weekly by Means of Dutch Auctions)	+1.55% + "unknown change, xx"
Remarketing Fee	Between 0.3% and 0.7%
The Effective Floating Synthetic Rate on Debt (This rate could be fixed for one week at a time; it is in effect a floating rate.)	5.04% + "xx"+ remarketing fees ("xx" Could Be Any Number)

Note: * This is the rate the CAFR erroneously called "synthetic fixed."
Source: City of Chicago, Comprehensive Annual Financial Report 2008. Retrieved from https://www.cityofchicago.org/dam/city/depts/fin/supp_info/CAFR/2008/CAFR2008.pdf.

swaptions)[3] in the city's portfolio totaled $2.83 billion. In the same year, the city owed $467 million because of the swap trap of paying a fixed interest rate ranging between 3.56% and 6.89% but receiving either the Municipal

---

[3] A swaption is a complex contract consisting of an (a) option and (b) a swap. The nonprofit entity, in this case the City of Chicago, sells the swaption contract to a bank for three functions. (i) To collect a premium in advance; (ii) to give the bank the option to decide, i.e., the right to choose, on entering into a swap agreement with the city; and (iii) to obligate the city to accept the bank's decision. The terms of exercising the options are typically limited to a time frame during which the bank could make that decision, the fixed rate the city would pay on the swap, the formula for the variable rate the bank would have to pay the city, and the duration of the contract. The bank will make the decision when it is highly convenient and profitable to it. When the bank makes the decision to sell a swap contract to the city, the city cannot refuse; it is locked into a noncancelable and enforceable contract for two or three decades, depending on the life term of the related bond.

Bond Average Interest Rate (SIFMA) or 0.67% of one-month of London Average Interest Rate (LIBOR) for fourteen swap contracts.

The table enumerating swap contracts in "Chicago Exhibit 3" is a reproduction of page 73 of the 2008 Comprehensive Annual Financial Report. The information in this table includes interest rate swaps only but there was also another chart (on page 75) covering five swaption contracts. In combination, the notional amounts of swaps and swaptions in 2008 add up to $2.83 billion and the combined fair value liabilities for the estimated long-term losses added up to $467 million. An equally disturbing feature is the very long time to maturity — up to 35 years. Given that these interest rate exchange (swap) contracts are noncancelable (without paying huge fees) and enforceable under the law, it is simply inscrutable to think of the incentives of city officials who committed the city to gambling contracts on $2.83 billion for periods ranging between 20 and 35 years ahead. All the contracts were losers requiring the city to pay big banks annual amounts of money equal to the notional amounts ($2.83 billion) times the difference between the fixed and variable rates for the entire tenor of the contract. That difference averaged 3.3% in 2008 but future percentage differences will depend on the pattern of the economy-wide yield curve. In addition to paying about $92 million annually for recurring losses, the city and big banks had to agree on the expected losses from 2008 to the end of contractual maturity. These expected losses are the negative fair values reported in "Chicago Exhibit 4" for the swaps (but excluding swaptions and obligations for related transaction cost).

It is perhaps necessary to reiterate that big banks sold these swaps as means to reduce the cost of borrowing but had consistently achieved the opposite. The city received absolutely no benefit from these contracts — the money given to big banks was the price of overconfidence and playing in the big league of financial engineering while being totally not cognizant of the negative shocks lurking in the dark. In fact, the information presented in "Chicago Exhibit 3" implies that the cost of borrowing has more than doubled based on some reasonable estimates. The estimation approach presented in "Chicago Exhibit 4" shows the effective rate of interest on the swap related debt of the City of Chicago in 2008 was nearly 6.5%. Thus, the combination of issuing

City of Chicago Exhibit 3
Interest-Rate-Exchange Contracts on June 30, 2008
(In Thousand Dollars)
(As Reported)

Bond Issue	Notional Amounts	Date	Pay	Receive	Fair Value	Maturity
GO VRDB (Series 2007EFG).	$ 200,000	11/08/2007	3.998%	SIFMA	$ (41,116)	01/01/2042
GO VRDB (Series 2005D).	222,790	08/17/2005	4.104	SIFMA	(50,034)	01/01/2040
Chicago Midway International Airport Revenue Bonds (Series 2004C&D)	152,150	12/14/2004	4.174	SIFMA Plus .05%	(25,216)	01/01/2035
Wastewater Transmission Variable Rate Revenue Bonds (Series 2004A).	332,230	07/29/2004	3.886	67% of 1 Mo. LIBOR	(81,112)	01/01/2039
Water Variable Rate Revenue Refunding Bonds (Series 2004)	197,970	08/05/2004	3.8669	SIFMA	(46,813)	11/01/2031
Water Variable Rate Revenue Refunding Bonds (Series 2004)	196,955	04/16/2008	3.8694	SIFMA	(37,013)	11/01/2025
Second Lien Water Revenue Refunding Bonds (Series 2000).	100,000	04/16/2008	3.8694	SIFMA	(29,107)	11/01/2030
GO VRDB (Series 2003B).	202,500	08/07/2003	4.052	66.91% of 10 Yr LIBOR	(42,666)	01/01/2034
GO VRDB (Neighborhoods Alive 21 Program, Series 2002B).	206,700	10/03/2002	3.575	70% of 1 Mo. LIBOR	(49,224)	01/01/2037
Sales Tax Revenue Refunding Bonds (VRDB Series 2002).	114,980	06/27/2002	4.230	SIFMA Plus .13%	(24,619)	01/01/2034
Tax Increment Allocation Bonds (Near North TIF, Series 1999A)	44,900	09/01/1999	5.084	67% 1 Mo. LIBOR	(10,219)	01/01/2019
Others to mature before 2014					(5,088)	
Total	$ 1,983,835				$ (442,227)	

Average Maturity = 29 Years	Pay	Receive

Question:

   What incentives would any rational person or group have to pay
   money to enter into contracts having these features?

Answer:

   That remains a mystery, but we just did what others have done!

Source: City of Chicago, Comprehensive Annual Financial Report 2008.
Retrieved from https://www.cityofchicago.org/dam/city/depts/fin/supp_info/CAFR/2008/CAFR2008.
pdf.

bonds at adjustable rates and coupling them with interest rate swaps had increased, not lowered, both the cost of debt and risk exposure. The sales ballyhoo of swap dealers that such a combination of instruments will lower the cost of borrowing was unattainable lofty mirage-like promise. The problem was further complicated by city officials acceding to signing swap contracts that were noncancelable for 30-year maturities as if they have the know-how to manage interest rate risk for three decades.

Furthermore, agreeing to have bonds sold at <u>auction rate</u> is also bewildering. Having auction rates required hiring a remarketing agent (and staff support) to remarket the debt once a week. Additionally, the banks performing the remarketing charge between 0.3% and 0.7%, depending on

City of Chicago Exhibit 4
Estimating the Effective Interest Rate on
Variable Rate Bonds having Related Swaps
(For Year Ended December 31, 2008)

Description	Dollar Amounts	%
Total long-term losses expected till maturity	$442 million	
Assume borrowing a total amount of $1.98 billion for 15 years (the remaining time to expiry), which is equal to the notional amounts of swaps		
The required <u>increase</u> in interest rate that would produce lifetime interest payments of $442		1.48%
+ The average interest rate difference between the payable fixed rate and receivable variable rate on swap contracts		3.3%
+ The interest payment on the related (hedged) debt		1.0%
+ Bond remarketing fee		0.7%
= Total (effective) interest rate on the swaps and related bonds (excluding insurance and underwriting fees)*		6.48%

* Excluding transaction cost.

the credit rating of the borrower, in addition to the stated interest rate. Furthermore, the reset rates, under most scenarios, will be sensitive to changes in the credit rating and credit risk of both the city and financial markets. In fact, the city hired a remarketing agent (and staff) for that purpose in 2004:

> The City has appointed a remarketing agent for the Series 2004A bonds in other than the fixed rate mode. The remarketing agent will use its best efforts to resell the bonds at favorable rates following either an optional or a mandatory tender. In the event the remarketing agent is unable to resell the bonds, the City has obtained a reimbursement and standby bond purchase agreement, which may be drawn upon for the purchase of the bonds until the remarketing agent, is able to resell the Series 2004A bonds.[4]

Between 2012 and 2014, the city terminated all the swaption contracts and one swap agreement and paid termination penalties totaling $50 million. During 2015, the City terminated six swap contracts having notional amounts of $1.1 billion and paid termination penalties totaling $257 million itemized as follows[5]

	In Thousand Dollars
Termination Payments Associated Bond Issue:	
• Amount Series 2003B General Obligation Variable Rate Demand Bonds	$30,951.5
• Series 2005D General Obligation Variable Rate Demand Bonds	62,815.5
• Series 2007EFG General Obligation Variable Rate Demand Bonds	62,007.0

(Continued)

---

[4] City of Chicago, Comprehensive Annual Financial Report 2004, p. 68.
[5] City of Chicago. Comprehensive Annual Financial Statements, Year Ended December 31, 2015. https://www.cityofchicago.org/content/dam/city/depts/fin/supp_info/CAFR/2015 CAFR/2015CityCAFR.pdf.

(*Continued*)

• Series 2002 Sales Tax Revenue Refunding Variable Rate Bonds	28,968.0
• Series 2008C Second Lien Wastewater Transmission Variable Rate Revenue Refunding Bonds	70,243.0
• Series 1999A Near North Tax Increment Financing Bonds	2,240.0

In 2016, the city terminated more swap contracts and paid a penalty of $101 million dollars. As far as one could discern from public disclosures, total disclosed termination penalties between 2012 and 2016 amounted to $408 million — money paid out for nothing received.[6] However, by 2016, the city's portfolio of swaps dwindled to two contracts and the fair value of long-term loss declined to $26 million. Thus, as compared to the City of Philadelphia, the City of Chicago seems to have been able to get from under the burden of swap contracts although at a high cost in terms of termination penalties and high interest rate on the debt.

Obsession with Swaps

Given the novelty and complexity of interest-rate swaps and financial derivatives in general, it is a safe bet — a very safe bet — to note that city officials had no clue about the risks and rewards of interest-rate swaps but listened to the fancily dressed and well-spoken swap peddlers and believed their polished presentations. Even more disturbing, they became both impressed and bamboozled by the magic these swap sellers had sewn together using financial-engineering terms: swaps, swaptions, notional

---

[6]The annual reports do not provide specific information to calculate the amounts paid for annual settlements, but Saqib Bhatti and Carrie Sloan, in their report titled *Turned Around: How the Swaps that Were Supposed to Save Illinois Millions Became Toxic*, provide an estimate of $537 million for the amount of money the city paid for the swaps through 2015, excluding any termination fees.

Saqib Bhatti and Carrie Sloan, *Turned Around: How the Swaps that were Supposed to Save Illinois Millions Became Toxic*, The Roosevelt Institute Refund America Project, January 2016, p. 20.

Retrieved from http://rooseveltinstitute.org/wp-content/uploads/2016/01/Turned-Around-Jan-2016.pdf.

amounts, knock-in swaps, knock-out limits, and synthetic fixed. A casual evidence of this observation may be gleaned from the frequency of citing the word *swap* in annual reports, as shown in "City of Chicago Exhibit 5."

City of Chicago Exhibit 5
Obsession with Swaps: The Frequency
of Repeating the Word *Swap* in Comprehensive
Annual Financial Reports, City of Chicago

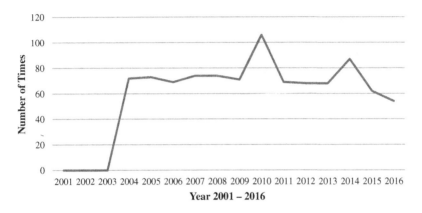

Sources: Comprehensive Annual Financial Reports, 2001–2014.

CHAPTER 7

Tales of Two Small Cities

(a) The City of Gainesville, Florida: Pays for Swaps and Raises Electricity Rates

The City of Gainesville is located in north-central Florida and is a home to the University of Florida and Shands Hospital. The city owns and operates Gainesville Regional Utility (GRU), which supplies electricity, water, gas, and sewer services to the metropolitan area of Gainesville.

The city began a journey to get entangled in the net of the Swap Mania in July 2002 when it entered into a fixed-payer contract with Merrill Lynch on a reference face (notional) amount of $37 million. The goal of entering into swaps is reported as protecting "against the potential of rising interest rate." For a brand new complex subject like interest rate swaps, there is no reason to expect the City of Gainesville to have a skilled financial advisor who understood interest rate swaps, structure and valuation. For example, protecting against rising interest rates may be better served by a financial instrument known as an interest-rate cap, which would be like an insurance policy requiring quarterly payments of premiums. Compared to interest-rate swaps, interest-rate caps have no downside risk (the possibility of losing) other than the commitment to pay premiums.

In 2004, the city reported a liability of $2.1 million for the long-term loss arising from this single swap contract, but that loss was reported off the balance sheet. The applicable governmental accounting standards (for nonprofit entities) did not come on the scene or become effective until 2008. Up until that point in time, every public agency had adopted either the accounting standards for the corporate world (issued by the Financial Accounting Standards Board) or its own homemade form of presentation. The first adequate disclosure about derivatives by GRU appeared in the financial report of 2007, which presented seven swap contracts having total notional amounts of $888 million. For a city of nearly 160,000 inhabitants, the officials at city hall were displaying their high risk-taking aptitude by betting on the unpredictable changes in interest rates for nearly $1 billion. To any reasonable person, this was simply misguided, especially since swap contracts having notional amounts of $535 million were related to a single bond issue, Bond Series 2006A. Over the years, the city appeared to reconsider the appeal of interest-rate swaps, and the reference face (notional) amounts on the swaps related to Bond Series 2006A dwindled to $38 million only by 2015. However, there was no explanation of whether this change was the result of a voluntary or scheduled termination and, in addition, the report provides no information on the amounts of penalties paid, if any.

Six of the seven interest-rate-swap contracts were fixed-payer (plain vanilla) swaps requiring the city to pay fixed rates varying between 3.2% and 4.22% and receive a fraction of London Average Interest Rate (LIBOR). The one Basis Swap contract in the portfolio was written on $45 million notional amounts, requiring the city to pay Municipal Bond Average Interest Rate (SIFMA) and receive a fraction of London Average Interest Rate (LIBOR). As noted earlier in other cases, a basis swap is simply a bet on the spread between two benchmark rates and has nothing to do with good financial management. In 2008, the seven contracts had expected long-term losses equal to $9.8 million. In the span of one year, the expected long-term losses of all interest rate exchange (swap) contracts increased to $36.5 million, and increased further to $85 million by the year 2012 and again in 2016. These reported swap liabilities represented the present values of expected future loss payments because contract losses for each year were settled in cash in the same year. Therefore, the present values of long-term liabilities arising from the swaps represented the expected obligations that belong to future periods. "City of Gainesville Exhibit 1" presents these obligations, showing an increase of

City of Gainesville Exhibit 1
Reported Expected Long-term Losses of Swaps

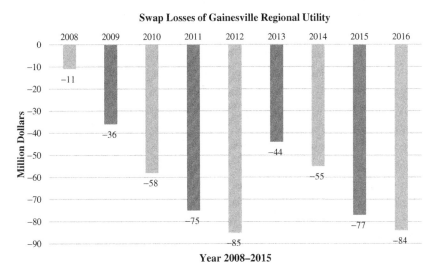

Swap Losses of Gainesville Regional Utility

Year 2008–2015

Sources: City of Gainesville, FL, Comprehensive Annual Financial Reports for the period 1996–2016.

Retrieved from http://www.cityofgainesville.org/GOVERNMENT/CityDepartmentsAM/Budget Finance/CAFR/tabid/189/Default.aspx.

up to $85 million in 2012. The Comprehensive Annual Financial Reports of the City of Gainesville did not have sufficient information to determine the amounts of cash paid to swap counterparties annually. Nevertheless, neither the amounts paid for annual settlements nor the present value of expected future obligations is consistent with the promise of lowering the cost of borrowing, which swap dealers had promoted aggressively.

The utilities arm of the City of Gainesville (GRU) entered into these swap agreements, but there were no known budgetary allocations made to cover the losses on the swaps. Therefore, GRU must recover these losses from the rate-paying consumers of electricity, water, and sanitation by raising the rates of different services. Without additional information, it is difficult to know the average share of the burden of this unproductive cost to individual households.

As an indicator, however, GRU electricity rates are high compared to similar operations in the State of Florida. Reporting on the commissioners' meeting about the new budget, Andrew Caplan of *Gainesville Sun* noted, in July 2017, "according to June residential rates, provided by GRU, the utility will remain second highest in average electric rates in the state out of all municipal-owned utilities." This is essentially the same sentiment that Chelsea Hazlett reported two years back.[1]

Interestingly, in all the debates about raising utility rates, public records do not show that anyone highlighted the subject of interest-rate-exchange (swap) contracts and the losses they impose on the system. Moreover, it is not clear or known if city commissioners had asked anyone to make an analysis of how much these losses had contributed to budgetary constraints. Absent knowledge of this debate or analysis, it is very difficult to comprehend the rationale that led the officials in the administration of this small city to enter into these complex bilateral swap contracts for which there can be only one winner. It was not a secret that the first swap contract was losing money from the start, although this fact did not seem to make a difference in abating their appetite to enter into more swap contracts.

(b) The City of Oakland: Got Stuck with Goldman Sachs and is Getting Nothing

In 1997, the City of Oakland, California, signed a plain-vanilla interest-rate-exchange (swap) contract with Goldman Sachs requiring the city to pay a fixed rate at 5.6% and receive from Goldman Sachs an adjustable rate equal to 65% of London Average Interest Rate (LIBOR). The

---

[1] Andrew Caplan, "City Sets Budget, Bumps Up GRU Rates," *The Gainesville Sun*, Jul 18, 2017.

Retrieved from http://www.gainesville.com/news/20170718/city-sets-budgets-bumps-up-gru-rates.

Chelsea Hazlett, "The Scandalous Baseline of Your Utility Bill." *Gainesville Scene*, July 6, 2015.

Retrieved from http://gainesvillescene.com/2015/07/06/the-scandalous-baseline-of-your-utility-bill/.

contract was intended to hedge the cost of $187 million outstanding debt that would terminate in 2021. The city paid off all the related debt by 2008, but the swap contract will remain outstanding until it matures in 2021, even though its presumed usefulness as an economic hedge was long gone. After the Financial Crisis hit the world in 2008, Oakland was paying Goldman Sachs relatively large sums of money for the difference between the high fixed rate, which the city had agreed to pay, and the few cents on the dollar that Goldman Sachs was paying for the swaps. While the difference between these two rates was not very large to begin with, the increase came to being through the actions of the Federal Reserve Bank and other regulatory agencies to lower the benchmark interest rate to less than 0.5% a year following the Financial Crisis. Oakland was caught in the same swap trap as many participants in the swap market — pay 5.6% and receive nearly 0.5% for many years. For this totally unbalanced relationship, it is estimated that the city has been paying Goldman Sachs an average of $4 million a year for this one swap agreement since 2008. According to local officials, the city has paid Goldman Sachs roughly $32 million more than it has received and will keep on losing money on the swap until 2021.

The citizens of Oakland understood the burden that the swap contract with Goldman Sachs was placing on the city's modest resources. Civic and religious figures in the city formed groups of activists like "Decolonize Oakland" and the "Oakland Coalition for Social Justice" and took the case to the city council and to the public in the streets, demanding that the city stop doing business with Goldman Sachs if the swap contract was not terminated without penalty. Reverend Daniel Buford, head of the Prophetic Justice Ministry at Allen Temple Baptist Church in East Oakland, said the interest-rate-swap deal with Goldman Sachs is an injustice. "Oakland should end its relationship with Goldman Sachs … and Goldman Sachs should give back the money that's been paid to them by our city."[2]

---

[2] Darwin BondGraham, "Oakland Toxic Deal with Wall Street," *East Bay Express*, February 15, 2012.

Retrieved from http://www.eastbayexpress.com/oakland/oaklands-toxic-deal-with-wall-street/Content?oid=3125660.

The irony of this entire episode is that the swap contracts with Goldman Sachs provided no service of any kind, and the City of Oakland managed to pay the related debt 16 years before its stated maturity date (see Exhibit 1). The function of using the swap as a hedge of the interest rate on the bond issue no longer existed after paying off the debt. Instead, the swap had been adding to the city's risk burden. Oakland is not a rich city and would have to make sacrifices to pay Goldman Sachs for swaps, and get nothing. Unless something happens to rule against the unjust nature of the contract or the Federal Reserve Bank magically raises the Fed interest rate ten folds, the City of Oakland will continue to pay more

Oakland Exhibit 1
Street Protest of Swaps

SEIU Local 1021, Local 1021 Members Visit Goldman Sachs to Demand
a Fair Deal for Oakland, Tag *Archives: City of Oakland*, August 6, 2012.

Based on an image retrieved from http://www.seiu1021.org/tag/city-of-oakland/page/2/.

than $4 million a year to Goldman Sachs until 2021. The annual average payment of $4 million might not seem like a large amount for many other cities, but it is a relatively heavy burden for a city that is not rich and that had not received any benefits from the deal.[3] To the contrary, to pay for the swap agreement with Goldman Sachs, the city has suffered, relatively speaking, cuts in public service. Members of Service Employee International Union (SEIU), Local 1021 visited the offices of Goldman Sachs to raise the citizens concern about the swap contract that lost providing any benefit to the city. They had a demonstration in the streets while holding a banner stating "Oakland. Drop the Swap! Swap Meet."

---

[3] John W Schoen, "Damage to city budgets: Self-inflicted with help from Wall Street," *NBC News*, November 18, 2013.

    Retrieved from http://www.nbcnews.com/business/damage-city-budgets-self-inflicted-help-wall-street-2D11603593.

Cases in Wealth Transfer from State Government Entities to Big Banks:

All the Four Sins of Derivatives Described by Loomis Were at Play Here

CHAPTER 8

The State of Illinois and Other Swap Gorillas

Many state governments have entered into interest-rate-swap-contracts and suffered huge losses. The sates of Texas, Illinois, New Jersey, New York and Massachusetts have the largest portfolios of derivatives among all 50 states. This chapter provides an elaboration of the case of the State of Illinois. The next two chapters present the cases of New York and New Jersey. However, because of space limitations, I provide a limited exposé of derivatives in the sates of Texas and Massachusetts in Appendixes 10 and 11 at the end of this book. Adding the information in Appendix 8 to the information for the State of Illinois completes the picture suggesting that the officials in these three states appear to be trying to mimic the operations of hedge funds.

The State of Illinois is not as rich as the other two states and should not have been in the business of dealing with derivatives whether it is for hedging or simply gaming. At the center of governance in the state, financial managers in Springfield offices should not enter into a financial derivatives race with the more skilled and self-centered swap dealers and bankers. Simply put, no matter how they try, government bureaucrats cannot outfox the bankers in dealing with contracts for which there can be only one winner.

For example, "State of Illinois Exhibit 1" below is bad enough to scare the devil away from dealing in derivatives. After paying and settling

The State of Illinois Exhibit 1
The State of Illinois's Expected Swap Losses after
Making Annual Settlements

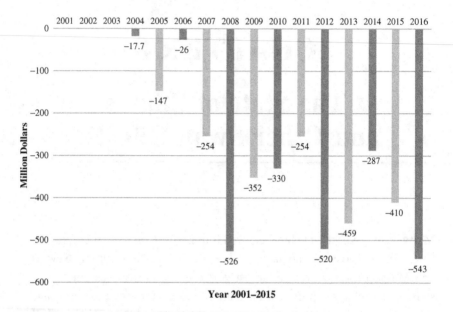

Source: The Ledger, the State of Illinois. Comprehensive Annual Financial Reports, 1981–2016.

Retrieved from https://ledger.illinoiscomptroller.com/find-reports/comprehensive-reporting/comprehensive-annual-financial-report-cafr/.

the annual differences between the variable and fixed interest rates, the State of Illinois reported estimates of long-term liability for expected future differences in interest rates to be above $500 million in several years — the years of 2008, 2012 and 2016. These are the amounts of payments (or rather penalties), the state would have had to pay to terminate these swap contracts at the end of any one of those years.

The Comprehensive Annual Financial Report (CAFR) of the Illinois state government suggests that the state turned itself into a small hedge fund-like entity starting in 2010. For example, page 125 of the Comprehensive Annual Financial Report for 2015 shows the extent to which an administrative unit of the state government (the Teachers' Retirement System) got involved in all kinds of financial derivatives (reproduced here in Appendix 8). These include rights; warrants; futures, both written and purchased; options, both written and purchased; currency forwards, both sold and purchased; credit-default swaps, both written and purchased...all related to commodities, inflation, fixed-rate instruments, variable-rate instruments, and more.[1] It does not seem that the officials knew that all these instruments are merely bets not backed by any real fundamentals or resources.

Although the State of Illinois' table in Appendix 8 is for the Teachers Retirement System, it is descriptive of the entire derivatives portfolio of the state government and its operating units. Raising special curiosity is the item related to selling "fixed income futures" for a total amount of $2.43 billion. This profile raises questions of who and how many people in the state administrative offices in Springfield, Illinois, had the expertise or the knowledge to manage that size of hedge fund-like operations. More curiously, why do state officials confuse gambling with investing? Actually, the State of Illinois seems to be fond of all derivatives just the same — buying and selling — just as much as the state of Texas, except that the latter is much richer and had a much larger portfolio. We should leave this question for another book, perhaps, and turn to the simpler but disturbing feature of interest-rate swaps, especially swaps aimed at hedging interest rate risk of the so-called governor's bonds. The presentation below reveals that Governor Blagovich's (2003–2009) untold mishap will continue to haunt the state until the year 2033, the year when the swaps are scheduled to terminate.

After passing a legislation in 2003, giving the state and its agencies the right to enter into derivatives contracts, the State of Illinois under Governor Rod Blagovich got deep into interest rate swaps. In fact, the Illinois' Comprehensive Annual Financial Report of 2003 does not have any reference to swaps because there was no room in traditional finance to handle them. But shortly after the end of the fiscal year on June 30, 2003, the state sold $963 million of tax-exempt general obligations for new and refunding bonds in two series:

 (i) 2003A bonds — $363 million fixed-rate bonds.
(ii) 2003B bonds — $600 million variable-rate demand bonds scheduled for refunding in 2033.

---

[1] See Appendix 8, "Illinois appendix."

The 2003B bonds became known, perhaps not for good reasons, as the governor's bonds. Simultaneously, the state entered into interest-rate-swap contracts with different banks with the stated intention of achieving a synthetic fixed rate and lowering the cost of debt on the governor's bonds[2]:

> Pursuant to Public Act 93-9, the State simultaneously entered into Interest-rate-exchange Agreements ("Agreements") with five counter-parties under substantially identical terms, to create a net fixed rate debt service obligation on the 2003B bonds. All are considered to be cash flow hedges. The Agreements together with the issuance of the 2003B bonds as variable rate debt produced a synthetic fixed rate on the bonds that was expected to provide a lower rate than what was available in the primary market, if the State issued traditional fixed rate bonds.

This particular paragraph from the annual report is misleading because it implies that the Public Act 93-9 required a simultaneous entry into contracts for interest rate exchange (swap) agreements and a bond issue. The Act was about removing the restrictions on transacting in financial derivatives, not about requiring or even recommending them.

For that bond issue, the state acquired a liquidity facility from *Depfa Bank at a cost of* 0.32% of the principal amount of the outstanding 2003B bonds plus interest for 35 days. A liquidity facility is like a line of credit available to draw on if needed and, therefore, offers assurance to the counterparties of swap contracts. However, in 2013, Depfa Bank *was replaced with a syndicate of five banks that cost more than seven times as much,* 2.35% *of the outstanding par amount of the bonds.* Thus, the synthetic fixed rate payable for the bonds would be higher than the rate specified in the contract by 2.35% a year plus renarketing fees and other transaction cost.

"State of Illinois Exhibit 2" presents data about the swaps of the governor's bonds. Total notional amounts and the termination date of 2033 correspond to the terms of the bonds. For swaps with notional amounts of $600 million, the state reported $165 million total fair value (expected long-term loss) reflecting long-term debt as of 2016. This long-term loss

---

[2] State of Illinois, Comptroller. Comprehensive Annual Financial Report for the Year Ended June 30, 2016, February 28, 2017, p. 121.
  Retrieved from http://illinoiscomptroller.gov/ioc-pdf/CAFR_2016.pdf.

State of Illinois Exhibit 2
The Losses on the Swaps Related to the Governor's Bonds

Associated Bond Issue (1)	Notional Amounts	Effective Date	Fixed Rate Pa d i	Variable Rate Received	Fair Values (2)	Change in Fair Value	Swap Termination Date	Counterparty Credit Rating (3)
Series 2003B	$ 384,000	10/03	3.890%	67% of 1 mo. LIBOR^^	$ (105,474)		10/33	BBB+/Baa2/A-
General Obligation Bonds	54,000	10/03	3.890%	when 1 mo. LIBOR^^	(14,786)		10/33	A-/Baa1/BBB+
	54,000	10/03	3.890%	is > 2.5%, or	(15,077)		10/33	A/A1/A+
	54,000	10/03	3.890%	SIFMA^, when 1 mo.	(15,077)		10/33	BBB+/Baa1/A
	54,000	10/03	3.890%	LIBOR^^ is < 2.5%	(15,009)		10/33	A+/Aa3/AA-
	$ 600,000				$ (165,423)	$ (34,964)		

^ Securities Industry and Financial Market Association
^^ London Interbank Offered Rate
(1) All bond issues are tax-exempt debt instruments.
(2) Includes accrued interest.
Credit rating companies: Standard and Poor's (S&P)/Moody's Investors Services/Fitch Rating

Mark-to-Market valuations shown above are received by the State from each of the counterparties. Each firm has its own proprietary method of deriving valuations and there are no guarantees that actual trades could be terminated at such values. At the end of the fiscal year, the variable rate received by the State was the SIFMA rate (0.41% was in effect on June 30, 2016) as the LIBOR rate was below 2.5%.

: Average Maturity = 30 Years : : Pay : : Receive :

Question:

> What incentives did the State of Illinois have to pay money to enter into contracts having these features?

Answer:

> That remains a mystery, but others did it too!

Source: Comprehensive Annual Financial Report 2016, p. 121.

Retrieved from https://illinoiscomptroller.gov/financial-data/find-a-report/comprehensive-reporting/comprehensive-annual-financial-report-cafr/fiscal-year-2016/

26% of the reference notional amounts of the swaps, a rather prohibitive premium to "insure" against rising interest rate. Additionally, the $165 million was over and above annual payments of recurring losses, which were $35 million in 2016, the recurring transaction cost and the increased cost of the liquidity facility from 0.32% to 2.35%. Moreover, entering into these swap contracts has led to a jump in the synthetic rate on the bond from 3.89% to 6.24%. That was indeed increasing, not lowering, the cost of debt.

At the foot of the table on the Governor's bonds, a note about the valuation method is worth recalling.

"Mark-to-Market valuations shown above are received by the State from each of the counterparties. Each firm has its own proprietary [secret] method of deriving valuations and there are no guarantees that actual trades could be terminated at such values. At the end of the fiscal year, the variable rate received by the State was the SIFMA rate (0.41% was in effect on June 30, 2016) as the LIBOR rate was below 2.5%."

This quote is misleading and raises two serious issues:

1. The state was paying a fixed rate of 3.69% on the swap, but receiving only 0.41%, leaving interest rate spread (burden) of 3.28%. Paying this spread was in addition to the interest rate payable on the bond issue plus other fees for obtaining the liquidity facility, underwriting and insurance. Thus, the state was paying more than $34 million a year of which $14 million were for the liquidity facility and $20 million (3.28% times $600 million) were for the difference between the fixed rate and the variable rate on the swap. All of this was in addition to the interest rate paid on the bond and all other transaction costs. That cannot be considered a cost reduction; it was simply a waste of money for which the state received nothing in exchange. Furthermore, the "mark-to-market" or fair values were negative reflecting losses and liabilities that the State would have to pay to, not collect from, counterparties.

2. The State relied on the five big banks (the counterparties) to value the swap contracts using their secret (proprietary) methods and inform the state of its debt to them. This is the same problem we saw in the City of Philadelphia among others. There is obviously a conflict of interest because the state obligations to the banks are the banks gains and the higher the estimated liabilities means higher termination cost if and when either party wishes to terminate swap contracts. Just as in the case of the City of Philadelphia, nothing in the report suggests that anyone had verified the validity of the noted "proprietary methods of valuation." Similarly, accepting the debt calculated in secret by counterparties using secret methods that were invented by the beneficiaries

Illinois Exhibit 3
Payments on the Governor's Interest-Rate
Swaps on a Monthly Basis*

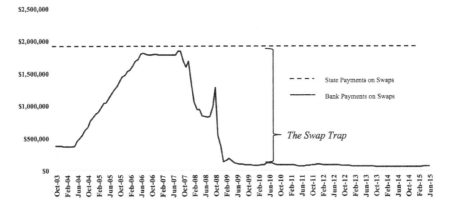

Notes: *Interest-rate-swap payments are not necessarily made on a monthly schedule. Instead, the payment dates for each party are specified in the swap agreement. We chose to represent the payments on a monthly basis to allow for an easy comparison. This provides an approximate representation of the costs of the deals [11].

Source: Adapted from Saqib Bhatti and Carrie Sloan, *Turned Around: How the Swaps that were Supposed to Save Illinois Millions Became Toxic*," The Roosevelt Institute Refund America Project, January 2016, p. 11.

Retrieved from http://rooseveltinstitute.org/wp-content/uploads/2016/01/Turned-Around-Jan-2016. pdf.

is like screaming out loud "we could not understand what the banks are doing, but they asked us to trust them and we do."

Saqib Bhatti and Carrie Sloan of the Roosevelt Institute Refund America Project also discuss understating the reported amounts of the state's obligations and the troubles arising from entering into Series 2003B bonds and related swaps. Bhatti and Sloan authored an interesting study called *Turned Around: How the Swaps that Were Supposed to Save Illinois Millions Became Toxic*.[3] "Illinois Exhibit 3" was adapted from the

---

[3] Saqib Bhatti and Carrie Sloan, *Turned Around*, January 2016.

"*Turned Around*" study and depicts the difference between the state's monthly payments of $2 million (the dotted line) and the much lower amounts receivable by the state (the solid curve). At no time since 2003 have the amounts of interest the state received from big banks in connection with swap contracts exceeded the amounts of interest it paid.

Nonetheless, we cannot blame the governor's bonds solely for all the financial mess the State of Illinois had and continues to have with financial derivatives. The state entered into 19 plain vanilla swap contracts (pay fixed and receive variable) of which only five contracts were related to the $600 million variable rate debt of the governor's bonds. But in 2004, the state officials were either persuaded or got the idea of hedging interest rate risk of other debt using interest-rate swaps. Then, some sort of madness took over. The state acquired another 14 swap contracts related to the debt issued to fund the various administrative components as if no one had informed the finance officers in Springfield that buying swaps is not needed to sell bonds at variable rates. Total notional amounts of interest-rate swaps increased to $2.53 billion in 2010, and more swap losses began to accumulate. Every year, the state paid the recurring losses in cash and reported the unrealized balance as swap liabilities.

"Illinois Exhibit 1" presents the expected long-term losses of interest-rate swaps at the end of each year for all the components of the state government together with a picture of long-term losses related to the governor's bonds. It is overwhelming to see the state's liabilities for swaps' expected long-term losses had reached more than $520 million in 2008 and 2012, then $543 million in 2016. This exhibit elicits three observations:

1. The losses began to appear soon after signing these swap agreements.
2. There was not a single year in which the net impact of the swap contracts was positive (gain) even long before the Financial Crisis came ashore in 2008.

It appears that financial administrators in Springfield, Illinois, were not aware that they were playing a game of ruin by committing to enforceable and noncancelable contracts for 30 years! Repeating the word "swap" 145 time in the 2016 CAFR is a further indication of the mind set prevailing in Springfield, Illinois.

CHAPTER 9

The State of New Jersey: The Pandora's Box of Interest Rate Swaps Cost Nearly $1.5 Billion

Changing the Landscape

Enter the Garden State and marvel at the many beautiful plants, flowers, beaches, and other gifts of nature. If you continue, you might hit the State Capitol, and there you could picture a gambler who kept on losing money but also kept on doubling down and increasing the stakes until it almost emptied the reserves kept in all the state accounts. That big gambler is none other than the top administration of the State of New Jersey in its struggle to manage interest-rate swaps acquired under the predecessors of Governor Chris Christie. Ever since the start of the Swap Mania in late 1990s, the State of New Jersey has been a loyal customer of big banks, providing them with lots of cash for receiving literally nothing tangible. The state entered into swap contracts related to bond issues for large segments of its own infrastructure: the New Jersey Sports Exposition Authority, the New Jersey Transportation Trust Authority, the New Jersey Economic Development Authority, the New Jersey Building Authority, and the School Facilities Construction Program.

Total notional amounts of swaps increased to a high of $4 billion, and long before the 2008 Financial Crisis, the fair value of long-term losses on the swaps went up as high as $460 million then increased to more than $700 million after the Financial Crisis. These liabilities were for expected future losses up to contractual maturity of the swaps. In addition, the state was paying in cash the recurring annual losses of nearly $50 million a year. The state always settled the short-term (current) portions by paying cash while the long-term portion remained as a noncurrent liability to be carried forward. Starting in 2002, all financial-derivative instruments had been a steady source of draining the state's resources year after year. In 2003, the state had 16 interest-rate-swap agreements to pay fixed interest rates and receive variable interest rates on large notional amounts with maturities of nearly 30 years, extending up to the year 2032.

While the state administrators were not diligent in avoiding interest-rate-swap contracts about which they did not know much, they were sly in reporting the information to the public. The state told the readers of its annual reports that the swaps were losing propositions, having negative values, but "due to the fact that interest rates have slightly declined since the execution of the swap agreements, the swap agreements have an esti-mated negative fair value equal to their termination value at March 1, 2032."[1] Naturally, with this confounding and incorrect statement, no reader of the report would have any idea of these amounts because termination values at the end of the swap term would be the loss of the last year while the "fair" value in 2003 would be the expected present value of losses for the 30 years remaining in the life of the contract. The present value of losses for 30 years could not be approximated by the fair value of the last year of the same contract. Furthermore, the reader would not know the magnitudes of these values because the state did not provide either number.

Rational decision-makers would have taken the large negative fair val-ues of 16 interest-rate-swap contracts as a warning signal of a rough road ahead. However, that was not the thought at the State of New Jersey admin-istration when big banks were banging on their doors to sell more swaps to them. It could also have been a case of "swap envy" as the State of New York continued to deny having failed in managing swaps, as we shall see in the next chapter. To the contrary, the State of New York compiled and

---

[1] State of New Jersey, Comprehensive Annual Financial Report, 2003, p. 69.

published reports claiming success in its engagement in interest rate swaps, which we shall see to be simply false. In 2004, the state had "30 active swap agreements with elven swap providers for a combined notional amount of $4.4 billion," having a negative fair value of $99.3 million.[2]

Accelerating Losses

However, swap losses continued to accelerate until the expected long-term swap liabilities reached a high of $711 million following the 2008 financial crisis. That was the time when the forces of reason appeared to scramble seeking an exit from the commitments to swaps, and the state decided at the beginning of 2010 to whittle down the swap portfolio. Terminating swap contracts in these circumstances was not a simple process because the state would have had to pay big banks almost all of the expected long-term liabilities attributable to these swap contracts. In 2008, the state paid $21 million to terminate one swap contract. Subsequently, the Christie administration took an active role in getting rid of all swaps. In 2010, the state hired the firm of Lamont Investment Advisors Corporation to estimate the termination values of all outstanding swaps. In a letter from the president, Robert Lamb, to the state officer James Petrino, Lamont concluded the following:

> As of November 30, 2010, the mark-to-market value of the swaps is $(695.825) million compared to a $(765.206) million mark-to-market value on October 31, 2010. This value represents the total amount the State would pay to the counterparties in the event all of the swaps were terminated at mid-market rates, excluding any dealer spread. Refer to the attached valuation report for key detailed information regarding the value of each of the outstanding swaps.[3]

This letter must have provided the shock needed to do away with all swap contracts. In 2010, the state began to speed up liquidating its swap portfolio. The following five paragraphs are excerpted from the annual

---

[2]CAFR 2004, p. 75 and p. 78.
[3]Lamont Investment Advisory Corporation, "State of New Jersey Interest Rate Swap Valuation-Portfolio Summary," November 30, 2010.
  Retrieved from http://www.nj.gov/transparency/bond/pdf/20100531_swap_portfolio.pdf.

reports of 2010–2015, showing the gradual termination of swaps and the related termination fees (text is as reported):

o   On June 8, 2010, the State terminated one of these swaps having notional amount of $250 million. The swap that remained outstanding leaving the State with a net fixed rate of interest on the related agreement through September 1, 2015. [The amounts of penalties and fees were not disclosed.]

o   On January 20, 2011, the State terminated various outstanding New Jersey Economic Development Authority swap agreements. That notional amount of the swap agreements was $784.8 million and the **termination payment** amount paid to the swap providers was **$122.6** million.[4]

o   On February 22, 2011, the State terminated additional outstanding New Jersey Economic Development Authority swap agreements. That notional amount of the swap agreements was $488.4 million and the **termination payment** amount paid to the swap providers **was $63.2** million.[5]

o   On January 31, 2013, the State terminated additional outstanding New Jersey Economic Development Authority swap agreements. The notional amount of the terminated swap agreements was $1.13 billion. The **termination payment** made to certain swap providers was **$186.8 million**. The State also received $21.6 million from one swap provider.[6]

o   On June 24, 2015, the State terminated the outstanding New Jersey Economic Development Authority swap agreements. The notional amount of the terminated swap agreements was $1.15 billion. The **termination payment** made to the swap providers was **$351.6 million**, or 30% of the notional amount.[7]

---

[4]Basic Financial Statements, New Jersey, p. 76.
   http://www.state.nj.us/treasury/omb/publications/11cafr/pdf/finstats.pdf.
[5]Basic Financial Statements, New Jersey, 2011. p. 76
[6]Basic Financial Statements, New Jersey, 2013, p. 82.
   http://www.state.nj.us/treasury/omb/publications/13cafr/pdf/finstats.pdf.
[7]Notes to Basic Financial Statements, State of New Jersey, 2015, p. 84.
   http://www.state.nj.us/treasury/omb/publications/15cafr/pdf/finstats.pdf.

Adding up all the termination fees starting in 2008, the State of New Jersey has paid at least a total of $749 million in termination payments and penalties in addition to the undisclosed amount of termination in 2010 — money given up for *nothing* received or receivable. The $749 million termination cost was paid in addition to the annual cash payments made to settle the respective year's current portions and other undisclosed termination payments. Adding up the amounts of termination penalties, estimates of the losses the state paid annually and the cost of underwriting and insurance is very likely to bring the total amount of money the State had paid for the swaps close to $1.5 billion. This was a total waste of large sums of money, especially since the state did not need the swaps to sell bonds at variable rates and big banks sold these swaps as means of cost reduction.

Where else might the State of New Jersey have used the $749 million? There is no shortage of possibilities here: public schools, public health, hospitals, roads, and so on. In fact, the 2016 budget for the New Jersey Department of Transportation and Turnpike has the following item:

- $720 million for the Route 278, Goethals Bridge Replacement in Union County. The Goethals Bridge Replacement budget of $1.5 billion was shared with the State of New York.[8]

More to the Story

The state also paid $23 million termination fee to Bank of Montreal for swaps related to hedging interest rate on debt that was never issued.[9] On December 4, 2009, *NJ Internet Marketing* published an article titled "New Jersey Losing $22,000-a-Day With Swap for Bonds Never Sold."[10] This

---

[8] Bill Hutchinson. "New $1.5 billion Goethals Bridge will provide pedestrian, bike paths to N.J." *New York Daily News*. April 25, 2013.

Retrieved from http://www.nydailynews.com/new-york/1-5b-goethals-bridge-provide-bike-route-n-article-1.1326769.

[9] Cited in Ryan Chittum, "Bloomberg Covers Yet Another Swap Flop," *Columbia Journalism Review*, December 4, 2009.

Retrieved from http://archives.cjr.org/the_audit/bloomberg_covers_yet_another_s.php.

[10] David Lazar, "New Jersey Losing $22,000-a-Day With Swap for Bonds Never Sold," *NJ Internet Marketing*, December 4, 2009.

article was about a forward-starting swap contract that the State of New Jersey had entered into with Bank of Montreal.[11] Specifically, the article notes the high cost and points out the extent of the sacrifice:

> New Jersey taxpayers are being saddled with a bill of about $657,000 a month from Bank of Montreal for an interest-rate swap approved by state officials and linked to bonds that were never sold. The 11th-largest U.S. state by population, which is cutting expenses to close a $1 billion budget deficit, will pay Canada's oldest lender $23.5 million. *The sum, about the same as the salaries for 113 teachers over three years,* will allow it to avoid a $50 million penalty for canceling the contract, which was tied to planned sales of school-construction bonds. [Emphasis added]
>
> "This is a classic case of a strategic error," said Robert Brooks, a finance professor at the University of Alabama–Tuscaloosa and author of a book on derivatives. "It's arrogant to believe that you have such a command of the future that you know with certainty what is going to happen."
>
> *The cost would cover the $23.6 million price of a typical elementary school,* according to New Jersey Schools Development Authority reports. [Emphasis added]

---

[11] A forward-starting swap contract is an agreement to exchange interest rates at some future dates signed in advance of selling the bonds to which the swap would be related, sometimes many years in advance.

Paying for Nothing

Premature termination of swap contracts also terminates

- *Hedging*
- *Managing Interest Rate Risk*
- *Gambling*

Therefore, Paying termination penalty or fee is paying for services not received or receivable.

CHAPTER 10

The Empire State Doctored Interest Rate Swap Gains Artfully

Beating Own Drums

Like the neighboring states, the State of New York administration entered into numerous interest-rate-swap contracts starting at the dawn of the Swap Mania. This was in 2002 when the state legislature permitted state agencies to enter into derivatives contracts. Since then the swap portfolio of the state government has gone through many changes, having contracts with notional amounts varying between $1.9 billion and $6.5 billion.

However, unlike the State of New Jersey, the financial officials in the State of New York not only denied that entering into swap contracts was an egregious mistake, but they instead extolled their virtues and even suggested having gone beyond cost savings and made profits.

In October 2015, the state published a 77-page report titled "Annual Performance Report: Interest-rate-exchange and Similar Agreements: Fiscal Year 2015" under the name of Mary Beth Labate, the state Budget Director. The aim of this elaborate report was to convince the readers that the performance of interest-rate swaps had done wonders for the State of New York. The report boasts that these swap contracts saved the state $130 million.

After reading this report, I had the distinct impression that it was probably issued with the expectation that the readers of the report will either skip the details and go straight to the conclusions, or have a low level of intelligence such that he or she could not see through the lubricated untruth. In several cases, the report chose and presented hypothetical calculations as if they were reflections of the true economics of the transactions, then followed up by providing an analysis in an articulate financial obfuscation.

Let us take some examples[1]:
(Page 6)

> Overall, the State's swap portfolio generated savings of approximately $131 million since inception, as shown in the chart below. This consists of a cumulative $143 million of savings from existing swaps, with approximately $133 million produced from synthetic fixed rate swaps and $10 million from synthetic variable rate swaps before they were fully terminated in FY 2011. The total savings of the swap portfolio also includes a $43 million payment received from terminating variable rate swaps, offset by $55 million of present value termination costs associated with fixed rate swaps.

Superficially speaking, all of this sounds fine, but only if they were true. This paragraph is profoundly confusing and erroneous enough to raise a number of questions.

First, why would the state terminate swap contracts that had been generating savings? If the contracts generated savings, why would the State pay termination fees or penalties? Normally, these termination penalties are the present values of expected future losses based on many assumptions. Moreover, how did the budget office calculate the $131 million savings? The report does not provide answers to the first two questions but attempts to answer the last one starting with page 6:

> Based on this analysis, the State saved approximately $130 million through March 31, 2015, compared to the estimated cost of traditional fixed rate bonds. This subsection explains the composition of the synthetic fixed rate portfolio and the process for calculating savings.

---

[1] State of New York. *Annual Performance Report Interest Rate Exchange and Similar Agreements Fiscal Year 2016. New York State of Opportunity*, October 2016, p. 6.

Retrieved from https://www.budget.ny.gov/investor/bond/SwapsPerformanceReport.pdf.

In other words, compared to the hypothetical rates the state would have paid had it issued traditional fixed-rate bonds, the office of the budget believes that paying fixed rates for the swaps saved about $131 million. These presumed savings are based on decisions not made and information not known or disclosed. If instead we talk about reality, we should look at the decisions the state did make. To begin with, the interest-rate-swap contracts into which the state had entered were not needed for issuing bonds at variable rates. That was the state's choice, and the costs or benefits attributable to making that choice are real. Therefore, the appropriate yardstick for comparison should be the actual realization of cost or benefit from decisions already made, not from the hypothetical of what could have been. If this alternative comparison were made, there would be no way the state could claim cost savings because the state actually paid big banks significant amounts of money for the difference between the received variable rate and the fixed rate it paid.

Second, where did the $55 million "present value of termination fees" come from?

The Shrinking Present Value

Well, this is another make-believe story. The state terminated some swaps and paid $270 million to big banks for termination fees, but some wise person in some office told the budget office of a method that could "shrink" that number and report a much lower cost. This method is capable of calculating the fair value of $270 million paid today as $55 million also today! However, other than the voodoo magic of shrinking skulls, such a method of shrinking a cash price to lower present values does not exist simply because it is an impossibility. Here is the text of this creative and miraculous financial gibberish[2]:

Mark-to-Market Discussion

"The State's swap agreements were terminated at their mark-to-market values, which is a defined calculation prescribed in related swap documents. Based on this calculation, the State **paid $270 million** to its

---

[2] State of New York, Annual Performance, pp. 18–19.

counterparties (investment banks) to terminate $3.8 billion of synthetic fixed rate swaps. In the performance analysis, however, *the termination costs were normalized using a present value approach, which was recommended by the State's financial advisor, Public Resources Advisory Group (PRAG).* The recommended approach analyzes the present value benefit/costs of swap terminations, assuming the swaps remained in place through their original term. Conceptually, the analysis measures the cost of using non-callable fixed rate bonds initially as compared to the actual cost of the alternative used, i.e., a synthetic prod- uct. **Several factors contribute to the present value cost of the swap terminations ($55 million) being less than the cash payment made to terminate the swaps ($270 million)."** (18–19, Emphasis added)

Also, on page 19, the report repeats the same vacuous and erroneous claims:

"Measuring Performance of Terminated Swaps[3]
To analyze the performance of the terminated swaps, a present value calculation was used to compare the debt service costs of: (1) **a hypo- thetical non-callable fixed rate bond issue,** to (2) **the actual debt service cost of the associated terminated swap.** Using this analysis, the State concluded that the "all in" present value cost of terminating its $3.8 billion in swaps was **$55 million."** [Emphasis is in original]

These statements seem to follow the dictum "If you repeat it, they may believe it." The issues of concern are:

(a) If the state had truly saved $130 million by entering into swap con- tracts, why did the state voluntarily terminate more than two-thirds of its swap portfolio?

---

[3]The state had the choice from among several alternatives.
    Alternative I: issuing bonds at variable rates and never entering into swap contracts.
    Alternative II: issuing bonds at fixed rates and never entering into swap contracts.
    Alternative III: issuing bonds at variable rates and entering into swaps to convert these variable rates into synthetic fixed rates.
    The state selected Alternative III, in reality, but the report chose to compare the results of this action with what could have been under Alternative II, while the proper benchmark should be Alternative I.

(b) How could the state pay $270 million in cash but claim its present value could be shrunk to $55 million on the same day and at the same exact moment?

(c) Assuming for a moment that the State's calculations of saving $130 million were correct. Paying termination fee of $270 million means that the State had lost at least $140 million if the actual termination penalty is combined with the hypothetical cost savings.

In fact, the *State of New York Monthly Swaps Report of September 2016* also shows (a) $1.74 billion total notional amounts of outstanding swaps and (b) total liabilities arising from these outstanding swap contracts were as much as $288 million. These long-term liabilities were the amounts of money the State would have had to pay if it decided to terminate the contracts at the end of the fiscal year of 2016. Indeed, the State of New York counterparties, the big banks, were realizing their goals. In all of these swap contracts, the banks knew fairly well that swap agreements are zero-sum games, and for them to win, the State must lose, and that was exactly what happened.[4]

More about the State of New York Swap Contracts

In 1944, the State of New York established the Dormitory Authority of the State of New York (DASNY) as a conduit to borrow money to finance construction of dormitories for public universities in the state. In addition, DASNY provides other services by leasing and managing the dormitories it builds. As part of its financing activity, DASNY announced its policy of entering into swap contracts. However, DASNY arranged to recoup its losses on the swaps from the lease and financing agreements.

> The related lease and financing agreements between DASNY and the State or the City include provisions that obligate the State or the City, subject to annual appropriation, to pay to DASNY all amounts due in connection with the swap agreements."

---

[4]The counterparties in these swap contracts are the usual suspects of big banks: JPMorgan Chase, Goldman Sachs, Morgan Stanley, UBS AG, Merrill Lynch (Bank of America), and Société Générale.

According to this arrangement, the $144 million loss on interest rate swaps in 2016, were passed on to the lessees (the State of New York and other cities) in accordance with the arrangement.

The Irony

While the contracting arrangement to recover the swap losses from the lessees is clever, the description of how the fair value of expected future losses were calculated does not live up to the perceived degree of managerial competence. That description is a perfect copy of what is in finance books, which was also copied in the various annual reports of the City of Philadelphia (Chapter 5, pages 131 & 134), Arizona State University and many others. Given the complexity of how all the noted technical items relate to one another to arrive at fair value, one must ponder some questions: Did the managers and the CPAs involved in the audited financial report really understand a thing from that description? To whom were these entities aiming the annual report? It could not be the bureaucrats in Albany. Or, could it?

> *Fair value* — The fair values of the swap agreements and the swap repayment terms in the lease and financing agreements were estimated using the zero-coupon method. This method calculates the future net settlement payments required by the agreements, assuming that the current forward rates implied by the yield curve correctly anticipate future spot interest rates. These payments are them discounted using the spot rates implied by the current yield for hypothetical zero-coupon bonds due on the date of each future net settlement on the agreements.

Cases in Wealth Transfer from Public Schools to Big Banks

CHAPTER 11

Jack Wagner's Mission to Rescue Pennsylvania from the $17.4 Billion Derivatives Mess

The Pennsylvania Department of Community and Economic Development (DCED) reported that a shocking 21% of all school districts — or 108 of 500 school districts in the state — and 105 local government agencies in the commonwealth of Pennsylvania had a total of $17.4 billion (notional amounts) in interest-rate swaps tied to public debt between October 2003 and September 2012.[1] No one showed more alarm about the magnitude and spread of these swap contracts than Jack Wagner, the former Auditor General (2005–2009) of the State of Pennsylvania. Unlike any other official, Wagner distinguished himself by taking keen interest in public schools' use and misuse of financial derivatives, which consisted almost totally of interest-rate-exchange (swap) contracts. The public outcry about swap-related losses surfaced after Wagner's office discovered how swap pushers from big banks had exploited public school officials'

---

[1] Cate Long, "Pennsylvania's worthy debate over swaps," *Reuters*, September 10, 2013.
  Retrieved from http://blogs.reuters.com/muniland/2013/09/10/pennsylvanias-worthy-debate-over-swaps/.

lack of knowledge about swaps and sold to them large numbers of these complex contracts. In one of his testimonies, Wagner asked the question, "Do the local elected officials who wrote to enter into these transactions really understand them?"

Wagner examined in more detail two of the Bethlehem Area School District's swap contracts in 2009. The school district was advised to sell bonds at floating rates and enter into swap contracts to pay fixed and receive adjustable rates to reach the promised land of lower artificial (synthetic) fixed rates for the bonds using the entire bundle.[2] Between April 29, 2003, and June 27, 2006, the Bethlehem Area School District entered into 13 different swap contracts having total notional amounts of $272.9 million for school construction projects.[3]

> Wagner reviewed just two of the district's swaps because those were the only two that had concluded by the time of his investigation. The two swaps cost district taxpayers $10.2 million *more than if the district had issued a standard fixed-rate bond or note.* Ironically, the swaps cost taxpayers $15.5 million more than if the district had simply paid the interest on the variable-rate note without any swaps at all. The district's losses were largely due to excessive fees and other charges and the termination payment. "Because the district has many other swaps still in effect, the ultimate financial impact on the taxpayers remains to be seen," explained Wagner.

In 2008, the Bethlehem Area School District had a portfolio of swaps that rivals the portfolios of most profit-making corporations: it had only $280 million in debt but had interest-rate-exchange (swap) contracts on total notional amounts of $445 million. Of these contracts, $224 million were plain-vanilla swaps that pay fixed and receive variable, whereas

---

[2]The resulting interest rate from the combination of these transactions is referred to as the synthetic fixed rate and will be discussed further in the following chapters because it has become one of the main tricks that banks use with nonprofit agencies.

[3]Jack Wagner, "A Special Investigation of the Bethlehem School District Leigh/North Hampton Counties." Pennsylvania Department of the Auditor General. November 2009.

Retrieved from http://www.cftc.gov/idc/groups/public/@swaps/documents/dfsubmission/dfsubmission3_080910-afl-cio.pdf.

$221 million were Basis Swaps paying and receiving variable rates based on different benchmarks.[4] The second group of contracts (Basis Swaps) had nothing to do with education or responsible financing; it was simply wagering on the spread between two different benchmark interest rates, the London Average Interest Rate (LIBOR) and the Municipal Bond Average Interest Rate (SIFMA). It is totally dysfunctional, however, for any public service agency to have Basis Swaps on $221 million. Basis Swaps are not instruments of hedging any risk. Instead, they are instruments of adding risk — the risk of gambling on the spread between two variable benchmarks.

For every one of these contracts, the Bethlehem Area School District must pay underwriting fees, insurance, and all other processing costs. Reporters Tim Darragh and Steve Esack of the local newspaper *The Morning Call* wrote about the decision making process of acquiring swaps, including the cost of making totally uninformed decisions. For example, they estimated the cost of swaps to Bethlehem Area School District for the first six years between 2003 and 2009 to be more than $35 million.[5]

> Subtract the cash receipts and the deals have cost taxpayers about $28 [$35] million between 2003 and last April [2009], a Morning Call investigation has found. That includes $25.5 million in scheduled fees to financial advisers, lawyers and banks. Taxpayers also have paid $9.9 million in monthly swap payments to JP Morgan Chase and Morgan Stanley for the interest rate gambles.

Interestingly, there is no evidence that any of the officials at Bethlehem Area School District Board had understood the contracts to which they had agreed. Tim Darragh and Steve Esack note that the Board approved a swap plan jointly submitted by Stanley J. Majewski, Jr., the assistant superintendent for finance and administration, and the

---

[4]Cate Long, Pennsylvania's Worthy Debate, 2013.
[5]Tim Darragh and Steve Esack, "Firms Reap Millions from Interest Rate Swap Deals," *The Morning Call*, June 7, 2009.

Retrieved from http://www.mcall.com/news/local/swaps/all-news-swaps-060709-pt2-story.html.

district's external swap advisor, Les Bear, "even though board members later said in interviews with *The Morning Call* that they didn't understand it."

The district was essentially betting on outfoxing big banks: the spread between the two interest rate benchmarks would go in its favor and the amounts gained would be higher than the amounts lost. As most people would agree, this gaming had nothing to do with financing education, but it had everything to do with betting and abusing the freedom given to the school district starting 2003 when the legislature allowed local and state governments to enter into derivatives contracts. One of the complicating problems was the $3.46 million upfront payment had received from JPMorgan Chase to enter into a swap contract. As noted in Chapter 1, the upfront payment may be seen as a gift to ease up short-term liquidity concerns, but it is not a free gift. Rather it is essentially a conditional loan binding the school district to the bank selling the swap contract.

Sharon Ward, the head of the nonprofit organization Pennsylvania Budget and Policy was equally concerned about school districts burning money by entering into interest-rate-exchange (swap) agreements. She authored a study titled *Too Big to Trust?* (January 2012) supporting the findings of the investigation of Auditor General Jack Wagner and concluding that the net loss to the Bethlehem Area School District alone from dealing with swap contracts up to 2010 was nearly $72 million.[6]

> The first swaps agreements to undergo major scrutiny was that of the Bethlehem School District, which entered into at least 13 swaps agreements between 2003 and 2009 on principal of $273 million in debt. Auditor General Jack Wagner found that a single swap agreement undertaken by the district cost taxpayers between $10.2 million and $15.5 million more than if the swap had not been authorized.
>   ....
> Based on analysis of historical bond and swap interest rates and information obtained through Comprehensive Annual Financial

---

[6] Sharon Ward, *Too Big to Trust? Banks, Schools and the Ongoing Problem with Interest Rate Swaps.* Pennsylvania Budget and Policy Center • 412 North 3rd Street, Harrisburg, PA 17101, January 17, 2012. p. 2.

Retrieved from http://pennbpc.org/sites/pennbpc.org/files/TooBigSwaps.pdf.

Reports (CAFRs) and bond official statements, we estimate the [Bethlehem] school district has paid approximately $157,965,000 to the banks and received $86,098,000 in exchange over the entire life of the 10 swaps — a net loss of $71,867,000.

In recent years, the Pennsylvania legislature has been debating whether to repeal Act 23 and return to the pre-2003 prohibition on public entities from entering into derivatives contracts. One of the proponents of this move was state senator Mike Folmer.[7]

"They may have (seen) it as an opportunity, as a creative way for local governments to raise revenues without having to raise taxes," Folmer said. "As it turned out, it wasn't a very good idea. We found out about them, now we need to ban them."

Senator Folmer and the former Auditor General Jack Wagner warned that entering into interest-rate-exchange contracts was like gambling with taxpayers' money. In 2010, state senator Lisa Boscola sponsored a bill to repeal Act 23 and end the use of derivatives by cities, towns, school districts, and local authorities. She noted that the consequences of local agencies' entering into derivative contracts may be shifted to individual taxpayers by increasing taxes to offset the soaring amounts of derivative losses. In reality, she was not far off track if we think of the episodes of many schools and agencies in the State of Pennsylvania or if we venture into the details of other cases like those of public schools in the City of Chicago or in the City of Philadelphia. During a meeting of the Senate Finance Committee about this bill, Senator Boscola said, "We must put an end to all this…The goal of my legislative package is solely to protect taxpayer dollars. Taxpayer dollars should never, ever be compromised again with financial swaps in my school district, or in any municipality,

---

[7]Melissa Daniels, "In Pennsylvania, swaps are a $17.2 Billion problem." *Pennsylvania Watchdog*. May 29, 2013.

Retrieved from http://watchdog.org/217204/paindy-in-pennsylvania-swaps-are-a-17-2-billion-problem/.

or by any other municipal authority."[8] She was not the only one in the legislature who believed that paying big banks for nothing was like burning money in a bonfire.

Did anyone listen?

Well, not really!

As recent as July 2014, the commissioners of Dauphin County approved an ordinance authorizing a deal called a prepaid swaption, typically a combination of an option and a swap. The county sold the swaption to Royal Bank of Canada (RBC), collecting a premium and giving the bank the right, but not the obligation, to enter into a swap contract with the county on a specified date in the future. If the bank decides to exercise the option and complete the swap agreement, the county would be obliged to accept the swap and the stated terms and maturity. The nonnegotiable terms of the contract include the flow of cash: the school district pays interest at a fixed rate, while the counterparty (RBC) pays interest at a variable, floating rate. As a prepaid derivative, the signals were out there loud and clear: the county accepts quick cash to ease up short-term liquidity concerns even if that creates long-term exposure to risk and damage of a much greater magnitude. Indeed, this behavior is consistent with psychological theories: a threat of pain in the far horizon is not fully evaluated or felt as much as the threat of a much lesser pain at the present time.

The bank involved in this transaction, Royal Bank of Canada (RBC), retained the right to compel the county at a future date to sign an interest-rate-exchange (swap) agreement. The bank also had the choice of timing that move, and no one should expect anything other than the bank choosing the time when changes in interest-rate are more advantageous to the bank. The swap contract is enforceable and noncancelable until 2033. The city and the county were low on cash to meet their short-term needs, and RBC offered to help by promising a bag full of money and snakes. Ironically, Royal Bank of Canada had few offices for retail service in the

---

[8]Michelle Kaske, "Keystone State Talks Swaps," *The Bond Buyer*, May 5, 2010.

Retrieved from http://www.bondbuyer.com/issues/119_335/pennsylvania_prohibit_local_governments_derivatives-1011756-1.html.

USA, the but bank managers seemed to know how to hunt for money using derivatives across the country. It should be noted that, unlike losing money to a U.S. bank, losing betting money to Royal Bank of Canada or any other foreign-domiciled bank is giving away U.S. resources for ever.

By entering into the swaption agreement with Royal Bank of Canada, Dauphin County had access to some cash upfront, which would essentially represent a loan borrowed from the future and increase the effective swap rates to levels above those prevailing in the debt market. It is a unique way of bait-and-switch that big banks had practiced throughout.

Entering into a new swaption contract with Royal Bank of Canada when all the news about swap contracts in the State of Pennsylvania were bad might just be a reflection of how Dauphin County officials made decisions. Dauphin County is the home of the city of Harrisburg, the capital of the State of Pennsylvania. The city suffered massive losses by entering into interest-rate-exchange contracts (also with RBC), coupled with the poor engineering of renovating its incinerator. The capital city declared bankruptcy in 2011, owing the banks more than $350 million, $105 million of which were penalties for terminating swap contracts. The banks do not want to use the term *penalty* for this termination cost, but that is exactly what it was because of paying for services not rendered, as elaborated on throughout this book and highlighted in the Epilogue.

CHAPTER 12

The School District of Philadelphia Dismissed Staff to Save Money to Pay for Swaps

Philadelphia Public Schools Exhibit 1

Philadelphia protests against school closings and "doomsday" budget (AP photo)

Based on an image by Valerie Strauss, "Philadelphia School District Laying Off 3,783 Employees," *The Washington Post*, June 8, 2013.

https://www.washingtonpost.com/news/answer-sheet/wp/2013/06/08/philadelphia-school-district-laying-off-3783-employees/?utm_term=.80c30f57bdb8.

The Commonwealth (State) of Pennsylvania gave public schools mixed signals in connection with financing policies. In 2002, the state took over the management of the School District of Philadelphia, but in 2003, Pennsylvania's Act 23 gave the school district the authority and the freedom to issue debt and enter into derivative contracts with insignificant oversight. On March 25, 2004, the School District of Philadelphia (SDP) entered into three qualified interest-rate-management agreements for notional amounts of $55.7 million (see Exhibit 1). However, no money changed hands at the start. Shortly thereafter, with the issuance of its general obligation refunding bonds, Series B of 2004, SDP terminated these interest-rate-agreements and settled for paying a *termination loss of $39.1 million.*[1] This termination fee amounted to 71% of the notional amount and it is difficult to think of any good reason that would compel SDP to terminate the contract and pay that much termination fee or penalty.

In 2006, the School District of Philadelphia entered into two basis-swap contracts — i.e., interest-rate-exchange contracts to pay variable rates based on one benchmark interest rate (London Average Interest Rate, LIBOR) and receive variable rates based on another benchmark (Municipal Bond Average Interest Rate, SIFMA) — on notional amounts of $500 million. As was discussed in cases like Bethlehem Area School District among others, the variable-for-variable swaps (Basis Swaps) have nothing to do with education, students, or school infrastructure. It is not an investment because no money changed hands at the start, and each party bears the risk of either winning or losing. In other words, a Basis Swap is simply a bet or a gamble on the spread between two variable interest-rate benchmarks, which is a function that should never be part of the activities of any school system.

But in June 2008, the school district officials became like youngsters who just got inside a candy store for the first time. During that month, the school district entered into 10 plain-vanilla swap contracts to pay fixed rates and receive variable rates on notional amounts of $690 million, all

---

[1] The district also entered into five swaption contracts that it terminated on June 28, 2004, resulting in a net gain of $11.3 million. A swaption contract is an agreement the city sold to big banks giving them the right to enter into a swap contract with the city at a specified time in the future.

having very long durations. June 2008 was very bad timing; a severe drop in interest-rate benchmarks followed, and as we shall see in Chapters 33 and 34, large banks colluded and conspired to depress London Average Interest Rate (LIBOR) even more. All that information was, perhaps, unknown to SDP. By the end of 2008, losses on all the swap contracts added $30.7 million to the school district's debt. While SDP was paying the annual losses as they occurred, expected future losses had also increased over time. By 2009, these obligations for expected long-term losses had increased to $124 million, which was also the amount of money the school district would have had to pay to terminate the contracts at that time.

SDP was one of the 108 public school districts in the State of Pennsylvania that fell for the myth of benefitting by swap contracts. It was actually more than a myth in 2008 because big banks were actively manipulating LIBOR, as we shall see in Chapter 32, to benefit themselves and their compiled economic projections which they did not disclose to SDP. As in many large cities, the policies of the city itself heavily influenced the policies of the city's school district. In 2006, for example, the city had active plain-vanilla swaps (pay fixed, receive variable) on notional amounts of $1.9 billion, of which $690 million were for the school district.

By 2008, the liabilities for the losses of the school district's interest-rate-exchange (swap) contracts increased to $113 million, in addition to settling the recurring annual losses as they occurred. Shortly thereafter, the school district began to feel the dysfunctional effects of its interest-rate-swap policy and engagement. In 2010, for example, the district *paid $63 million* to terminate five interest-rate-exchange contracts. This was $14 million higher than what the district had spent on schoolbooks and supplies during that year. If not canceled, these contracts would have continued to drain annual cash from the district until 2030, the contractual maturity date of the contract.[2] The amounts of payable cash were likely to increase, especially when the school district was paying interest rates at 3.8% and receiving interest at a mere 0.42%.[3]

---

[2]This is calculated as 3.4% times $690 million, but in reality, the interest differential will fluctuate.

[3]Marcia Merry Baker. "Swaps'/Gambling Slams School Districts," *EIR*. September 6, 2013.

Philadelphia schools paid the banks fixed rates of about 3.8 percent and received in return a variable rate equal to 58.5% of the one-month London interbank offered rate, plus 0.27 percent, bond documents show. As recent as 2016 that amounted to *Philadelphia receiving 0.42 percent on the $350 million of debt related swaps.*

It does not take much intelligence to know that one would be following a disastrous path by paying 3.8% but receiving only 0.42%, even with the knowledge that the receivable variable rate fluctuates and might increase. By then, the increases would not be adequate to repair the severe financial drain that would have taken place. The School District of Philadelphia was faced with the need to find money somewhere to pay what was owed to the banks in relation to the swaps. One way of finding some of the needed cash was to reduce the cost of operation by cutting down the size of labor force. Most surprisingly, that was one path that SDP followed; more than 3,783 schoolteachers and supporting staff employees lost their jobs in 2012 and 2013. "Philadelphia Schools Exhibit 2" presents some facts disclosed by the ABC local station "Action News" detailing the composition of the duties of those employees who were let go.

However, the connection between dismissing about 20% of the staff of the School District of Philadelphia and losing money to big banks for interest-rate-exchange contracts was depressing to many citizens, especially when Daniel Denvir reported that the district had paid $63 million to terminate some of its swap contracts[4]:

That month, the *district paid out $63 million* to Morgan Stanley Capital Services, Goldman Sachs Capital Markets and Wells Fargo Bank to cancel a budgetary gamble gone horribly wrong. In 2004, at the height of the pre-recession financial deregulation adventure, the district took out something called "interest-rate swaps" on a number of bonds. The swaps were supposed to protect the district from high interest rates. But interest rates crashed, and the district lost an astonishing $71.87 million,

---

Retrieved from http://larouchepub.com/eiw/public/2013/eirv40n35-20130906/44-47_4035.pdf.

[4] Daniel Denvir, "Who's killing Philly public schools?" *My City Paper*, May 2, 2012. Retrieved from https://mycitypaper.com/cover/whos-killing-philly-public-schools/.

Philadelphia Schools Exhibit 2
Sacrificing Skilled Labor to Save
Money to Pay for Interest-Rate Swaps

ABC Action News

PHILADELPHIA - June 7, 2013 –

The Philadelphia School District announced Friday it is laying off 3,783 people across entire range of district employees, from senior administrators to support staff.

Superintendent of Schools William Hite made the dramatic announcement Friday afternoon at school district headquarters.

"The layoff notices that will be issued today are nothing less than catastrophic for our schools and our students," he said.

Those being laid off include:
- 127 assistant principals
- 676 teachers
- 283 counselors
- 1,202 noontime aides
- 307 secretaries
- 769 supportive service assistants
- 89 teacher assistants (early childhood)
- 53 school operations officers
- 45 school improvement support liaisons
- 25 community relations liaisons
- 25 food service workers
- 22 special ed classroom assistants
- 21 conflict resolution specialists
- 18 nonteaching assistants

In all, the district is reducing its total workforce of 19,530 by nearly 20%. Unless the district gets money from the state or city, the layoffs will take effect June 30th.

Source: Retrieved from http://6abc.com/archive/9130566/.

---

according to the liberal Pennsylvania Budget and Policy Center. [Emphasis added]

By 2014, the school district (SDP) terminated all of its plain-vanilla swap contracts that paid fixed and received variable. However, Basis-Swap contracts (the contracts betting on interest-rate spread) that paid variable rates linked to one benchmark and received variable rates linked to another benchmark remained in SDP's portfolio of swaps. The fair value of losses related to these two swap contracts in 2014 created a liability of $23 million. This liability declined to $9 million in 2015. Nevertheless, SDP claimed, "From the date of execution of the two basis swaps through June 30, 2014, the net benefit to the School District has been $11,417,796."[5]

Having been conditioned to the experience of laying off teachers and sending money to big banks, it was a pleasant turnaround for many residents when the school district announced in 2015 that it was hiring new teachers again.

---

[5] School District of Philadelphia, Comprehensive Annual Financial Report 2014, p. 65.
Retrieved from https://www.philasd.org/accounting/wp-content/uploads/sites/125/2017/07/cafr_2014_ADA.pdf.

CHAPTER 13

Two Other Special Cases in Pennsylvania Schools

The two cases of Bethlehem Area School District (presented in Chapter 11) and the School District of Philadelphia (presented in Chapter 12) represent examples of the conditions that prevailed at some of the 108 school districts in the State of Pennsylvania that ventured into the uncharted territory of interest-rate-exchange (swap) contracts. However, two additional cases of school districts got entangled into the net of the Swap Mania and were more revealing of the consequences of the Four Derivatives Sins described by Carol Loomis than any other case in the State of Pennsylvania. The two cases are for the Erie City School District and the State College Area School District.

(a) Erie City School District

In early 2000, the Erie City School District was nearly 150 years old and had 18 schools serving about 12,000 students. In addition to paying upfront money of a loan for $785,000, somehow, JPMorgan Chase convinced the school district board to be a counterparty in an interest-rate-exchange (swap) contract. In a short time, this contract cost the district about 370% of the upfront payment the bank had made. The reporters Martin Braun and William Selway of *Bloomberg* chronicled the story in

March 2008.[1] Back in 2003, James Barker, the school superintendent, was searching for a way to raise funds to renovate an 81-year-old school building. That was the time when almost no one outside the banks and a very small circle of Wall Street professionals knew anything about interest-rate-exchange (swap) contracts, and it was, therefore, not difficult for people from JPMorgan Chase & Co. to get the Erie City School District to sign a contract taking the district right between the shark's jaws.

> In September 2003, [James Barker] the superintendent of the Erie City School District in Pennsylvania watched helplessly as his buildings began to crumble. The 81-year-old Roosevelt Middle School was on the verge of being condemned. The district was running out of money to buy new textbooks. And the school board had determined that the 100,000-resident community 125 miles north of Pittsburgh couldn't afford a tax increase. Then JPMorgan Chase & Co., the third-largest bank in the U.S., made Barker an offer that seemed too good to be true.
>
> David DiCarlo, an Erie-based JPMorgan Chase banker, told Barker and the school board on September 4, 2003, that all they had to do was sign papers he said would benefit them if interest rates increased in the future, and the bank would give the district $750,000, a transcript of the board meeting shows. *"You have severe building needs; you have serious academic needs," Barker, 58, says. "It's very hard to ignore the fact that the bank says it will give you cash."* So Barker and the board members agreed to the deal. [Emphasis added]
>
> What New York-based JPMorgan Chase didn't tell them, the transcript shows, was that the bank would get more in fees than the school district would get in cash: $1 million? The complex deal, which placed taxpayer money at risk, was linked to four variables involving interest rates. Three years later, as interest rate benchmarks went the wrong way for the school district, the Erie board paid $2.9 million to JPMorgan to get out of the deal, which officials now say they didn't understand.

---

[1] Martin Z. Braun and William Selway, "Schools Flunk Finance," *Bloomberg Markets.* March 2008.

Retrieved from http://www.bloomberg.com/apps/news?pid=nw&pname=mm_0308_story2.html.

"That was like a sucker punch," Barker says. "It's not about the district and the superintendent. It's about resources being sucked out of the classroom. If it's happening here, it's happening in other places."

When asked about the bank's fee or the cost to the school, DiCarlo, the banker, said, "Everybody has asked, and it's a reasonable question. What does JPMorgan, what do we get on this transaction? *I can't quantify that to you.*"[2] Such a response was reminiscent of the statement that Bankers Trust of New York made to Procter & Gamble back in 1993, stating[3]

"We did not and could not represent in advance the cost to end these [swap] transactions prematurely," said Douglas Kidd, a spokesman for Bankers Trust. That, he said, "necessarily would have to be based on the market when such a request is made."

While evasive and alarming, this lack of response was more direct than the advice of the pretend–swap adviser firm Investment Management Advisory Group (IMAGE) which the district had retained to help fill in the gaps of knowledge and experience. IMAGE charged the school district a $50,000 fee for the service, and when James Barker asked the consultants at IMAGE a similar question about the cost of entering into the interest rate exchange (swap) contract with JPMorgan Chase, the swap advisor entwined an array of financial gibberish offering a masterful obfuscation:

The net swaption premium to the district was adjusted to reflect the forward starting and option-adjusted nature of the swaption, a reasonable hedging spread in the *LIBOR* (London Interbank Offered Rate of Interest for the U.S. Dollar) markets and a fee to JPMCB reflective of its

---

[2] Martin Z. Braun and William Selway, "Hidden Swap Fees by JPMorgan, Morgan Stanley Hit School Boards," *Bazaarmodel Posts*, February 1, 2008.

Retrieved from http://bazaarmodel.net/phorum/read.php?1,5487. Martin Z. Braun and William Selway, "Schools Flunk Finance," *Bloomberg Markets,*. March 2008.

Retrieved from http://www.bloomberg.com/apps/news?pid=nw&pname=mm_0308_story2.html.

[3] Hansell, October 28, 1994.

time and effort dedicated to the district as well as the inherent credit, operational and market underwriting hedging risk of the transaction.[4]

This type of response seems to reflect one thing: the financial advisers at IMAGE did not show much more knowledge about swaps than did the members of the school district board. In fact, legal authorities implicated IMAGE in other schemes, and on March 15, 2006, the FBI raided the firm's offices as part of an ongoing investigation. That response to a simple question reflects three of Carol Loomis's Four Derivatives' Sins: ignorance, arrogance, and lies. To this, Eva Tucker, a board member and retired professor of geoscience at Penn State University's Erie campus, said that <u>the board trusted IMAGE and did not fully understand the deal but nonetheless recommended the transaction</u>. Indeed, the behavior of IMAGE's consulting advisory service is consistent with the proposition that swap advisors must close the deal; otherwise they would not get paid.[5]

Looking at the balance sheet of the deal uncovers a costly mishap. The swap transaction with JPMorgan Chase brought into the school district $785,000 and cost the school district $2.9 million to get rid of the contract. The $2.9 million included the swap-termination payment plus the following:

- ○ ($1,000,000) swap underwriting fee paid to JPMorgan Chase,
- ○ ($50,000) consulting fees paid to IMAGE,
- ○ ($57,585) a premium paid to Financial Security Assurance, Inc., and
- ○ ($206,000) lawyers' fees

To raise funds to finance this high cost of the school's first and perhaps last adventure into swap contracts, the district was dragged into two other swap contracts with PNC Bank, adding to a total burden of

---

[4] Braun and Selway, "Hidden Swap Fees....February 1, 2008.

[5] Andrew Kalotay, "*SEC Hearing on The State of Municipal Securities Market Birmingham, AL*," Securities and Exchange Commission, July 29, 2011.

Retrieved from https://www.sec.gov/spotlight/municipalsecurities/statements072911/kalotay.pdf. & Tim Darragh and Steve Esack, "Firms Reap Millions...", 2009.

$2.9 million. Perhaps this case more than any other brings us into the realm of "unconscionable contracts" because the buyer (the school district, in this case) not only had much less knowledge and bargaining power than the seller–agent of JPMorgan Chase, but the buyer was also denied any fair disclosure — the very same features of an unconscionable contract, defined as follows[6]:

> [O]ne that is so one-sided that it is unfair to one party and therefore unenforceable under law. It is a type of contract that leaves one party with no real, meaningful choice, usually due to major differences in bargaining power between the parties.

(b) State College Area School District

Back in 2004, the State College Area School District received authorization from the Pennsylvania Department of Community and Economic Development to issue $58 million in variable-rate bonds to fund planned renovations and expansion to its high school buildings. The project was scheduled to begin in 2007, one year after authorization. The uncertainty about interest-rate markets brought the fear of facing higher interest rates just as the district was planning to sell the bonds. While the plans were uncertain, the district wanted to avoid the potential of paying higher cost of borrowing if benchmark interest rates increase. The school district sought financial advice, and Royal Bank of Canada (RBC) was happy to oblige. RBC made the district a proposal to lock in the interest rate it might pay on the bonds by entering into an interest-rate-exchange (swap) contract to pay a fixed rate and receive variable rate. Knowing nothing about this type of contract, the district superintendent and board did not doubt the veracity of RBC or the advice of the swap advisor, Public Financial Management, and the legal advisors; the board unanimously approved a financial derivative contract with RBC in April 2006. The agreement obligated the district to make

---

[6] Kourosh Akhbari, "What is an Unconscionable Contract?" *Legal Match*, March 9, 2013.
Retrieved from http://www.legalmatch.com/law-library/article/what-is-an-unconscionable-contract.html.

semiannual payments to RBC at a fixed annual interest rate of 3.884% on a notional amount (principal amount) of $58 million for 20 years. In exchange, RBC would make monthly adjustable-rate payments to the district based on a fraction of the London Average Interest Rate (LIBOR). The exchange of payments of interest was set to begin in December 2007.[7]

In May 2007, the school district board canceled the project after bids for the proposed high school building came in at $17 million above budget. By that time, the district had not begun the process of selling the $58 million bond series. Nor was there any exchange of money with RBC for the swap contract. These conditions were comforting enough for the school district board to come to the belief that canceling the swap agreement with RBC should be costless but necessary. At that time, RBC informed the school district that canceling the swap contract would cost the school a penalty of $168,000 (only). The school district board was stunned because the school had not received any money or service from the bank to justify the audacity of its officials in asking for $168,000 in fees or penalties! That was in June 2007, and the school district board members, who had never studied financial derivatives in college and had no reason to get practical training and build knowledge in it, did not appreciate the dilemma they were facing.[8] They had no idea that such a penalty was insignificant in the new high finance world of swaps and swaptions, leading to the transfer of large amounts of money to big banks whether it was a cost of service or a price for not knowing the risks involved.

Nonetheless, the fast drop in global interest rates at the inception of the Financial Crisis in 2007–2008 led to increasing the difference between

---

[7]"State College Area School District Agrees to $9 Million Payment in Interest Rate Swap Agreement with Royal Bank of Canada." *StateCollege.com.*

Retrieved from http://www.statecollege.com/news/local-news/state-college-area-school-district-agrees-to-9-million-payment-in-interest-rate-swap-agreement-with-royal-bank-of-canada,1222044/.

[8]As noted in numerous places, as derivative contracts, interest-rate swaps were accidentally invented in 1982 and did not catch the attention of Wall Street market makers until a few years later. Colleges and universities lagged further behind in incorporating this material in their curricula.

(a) the payable fixed rate, which the school district would have been obligated to make, and (b) the adjustable rate potentially receivable from RBC. The distance between these two rates widened significantly between June and October 2007, raising the termination fees from $168,000 to $3 million. In the meantime, global benchmark interest rates continued their sharp decline. The district felt the impact of this monetary policy when RBC reported an increase in the (payment) penalty of termination to $10 million — an increase of 60 folds from the initial estimate only a few months earlier. Based on the same logic of "no tangible service, no pay," the school district board continued to refuse paying the termination fee.

By September 2010, the school district board had realized the possibility of not having received the correct advice from either the swap adviser or the legal counsel. The board then took a corrective action by appointing "a new bond counsel and financial adviser — distancing themselves from the legal and financial experts who helped the district enter into its controversial, and potentially costly, interest rate swap deal with RBC. In separate votes, the board voted unanimously to replace the Harrisburg law firm Rhoads and Sinon and Public Financial Management, whose website says it represents more than 200 Pennsylvania school districts."[9]

Having false confidence in its own assessment, the school district board took RBC to court, claiming that the swap contract with the bank was invalid "because they didn't follow all of the provisions of the Pennsylvania Local Government Unit Debt Act — a state law the General Assembly amended in 2003. The swaps contracts with RBC were considered enforceable "naked" swaps, because they do not relate to bonds issued or to be issued."[10]

However, the court saw the case as a matter of executing the terms of a contract into which the school district had entered voluntarily and not under duress. Later on it became clear that members of the board had no idea of the impact of the terms of the contract they had signed. In the end,

---

[9]Ed Mahon, "The Swap. State Swap College goes National," *Ed Mahon Sample of Journalism,* May 21, 2011.

Retrieved from https://edmahon.wordpress.com/clips/enterpriseinvestigative/the-money-swap/.

[10]Ed Mahon, *Ibid.*

the school district and RBC negotiated a settlement agreement requiring the school district to pay $9 million to RBC. Of that amount, the school district wired $6 million to RBC at the time of settlement and agreed to pay the balance in installments.[11]

After reaching a settlement with RBC, the State College Area School District board issued a statement of apology to the public: "We profoundly regret that from inception to termination, many millions of dollars will have been spent on this transaction with no benefit to public education."[12] The case of the State College Area School District and Royal Bank of Canada was truly a perfect example of the gullibility and ignorance about which Carol Loomis had written one decade earlier. As we shall see in Chapter 34, the case of State College Area School District is also another case of unconscionable contracting.

---

[11] Mike Dawson, "State College Area school board agrees to pay $9 million in swap settlement with Royal Bank of Canada," *Central Daily Times*, January 14, 2013.

Retrieved from http://www.centredaily.com/2013/01/14/3465128_state-college-area-school-board.html?rh=1.

[12] "Auditor General Jack Wagner Calls on General Assembly to Ban Risky "Swap" Contracts by Schools, Local Governments," *Cision, PR Newswire*, November 18, 2009.

Retrieved from http://www.prnewswire.com/news-releases/auditor-general-jack-wagner-calls-on-general-assembly-to-ban-risky-swap-contracts-by-schools-local-governments-70388252.html.

CHAPTER 14

Chicago Public Schools Dismissed Staff and Borrowed at High Interest Rates to Pay for Interest-Rate Swaps

The Chicago Public Schools system (CPS) serves nearly 400,000 students attending more than 600 schools. It was May 2003 when the state legislature voted on granting every public entity, large and small, the authority and right to deal in derivatives without any serious constraints.[1] By that time, bankers and swap pushers had been already on the doorsteps of different state and city agencies offering their magical snakes, called interest-rate swaps, coupled with the highly risky variable rate called <u>auction rate</u> that would reset variable (adjustable) rates on the bonds based on weekly remarketing.[2]

---

[1] There was a lower bound. Any entity that qualifies for selling at least $10 million in bonds should also qualify for getting engaged in financial derivatives.

[2] Jason Grotto and Heather Gillers, "Risky Bonds Prove Costly for Chicago Public Schools," *Chicago Tribune*, November 7, 2014.

Retrieved from http://www.chicagotribune.com/news/watchdog/cpsbonds/ct-chicago-public-schools-bond-deals-met-20141107-story.html.

Chicago Public Schools Exhibit 1
Demonstrators Carrying Petitions to the Local SEC Office

Chicago community activists and local elected officials 88,000 petition signatures to the US Securities and Exchange Commission's (SEC) regional office Thursday morning, urging the agency to investigate complex financial agreements called interest-rate swaps.

Source: Based on the article by Ellyn Fortino, "Chicago Activists, Lawmakers Deliver Petitions To SEC For Action On 'Toxic' Interest-rate swaps," *Illinois Progress*, July 7, 2016.

http://progressillinois.com/quick-hits/content/2016/07/07/chicago-activists-lawmakers-deliver-petitions-sec-action-toxic-swaps.

As early as 2000, *a vice president of municipal finance at Goldman Sachs* asked to meet with CPS officials about the possibility of *issuing auction-rate bonds* in a letter circulated to Cepeda (the financial advisor to the Chicago Public Schools Board) and school and city officials. The letter highlighted the potential cost savings, and accompanying materials quoted an *anonymous financial adviser as saying the product had "no downside."* [Emphasis added]

Issuing debt at weekly auction rates meant that the debt had to be remarketed, and new interest rates were to be *reset weekly*. In addition to the high uncertainty involved in that type of arrangement, as discussed previously, it was also costly. The remarketing service added between 0.3% and 0.7% annually to the cost of debt in addition to the administrative costs incurred in carrying out the process of remarketing. But both types of cost, just like all transaction cost, were always obscured and were left out from any comparative cost analysis against the cost of a hypothetical fixed-rate bond. However, big banks continued their intensive lobbying until the state legislature passed Public Act 093-0009 in May 2003, allowing public schools to deal with derivatives.

At Chicago City Hall, Mayor Richard M. Daley took advantage of the newly granted freedom of governance and the newly minted financial derivatives — the city sold bonds at floating interest rates and coupled that sale with entering into interest-rate-exchange (swap) contracts. These were contracts about which no one either at city hall (see Chapter 6) or the Chicago Public Schools board understood more than what they had heard from swap sellers. Even then, it is highly unlikely that any banker disclosed the fact that a swap contract has only one winner. Disclosing this fact would have given rise to the thought that banks had no interest in writing contracts that would make them lose money. At that time, no one had experienced or understood the nuances of swaps and derivative contracts because they were brand-new on the scene (only one decade old), and anyone claiming otherwise would be making a false representation. Nevertheless, that did not stop the so-called expert financial advisers from touting their lengthy, though clearly irrelevant, experience in finance and financial services. All post-crisis evidence suggests that the financial advisory firm of Adela Cepeda hired by the Chicago Public Schools fell in that category[3]:

> The district's longest-serving financial adviser, Adela Cepeda of A.C. Advisory, consulted on the deals before CPS signed off, but an examination of public records raises questions about whether her presentations detailed the full scope of the risks. The school board, meanwhile, unanimously approved complex debt contracts with blanket measures that didn't even specify the exact costs involved, records show.

---

[3] Grotto and Gillers, November 7, 2014.

In general, when it came to financial derivatives, the experience with traditional capital markets and corporate finance was not of much help. Bankers emphasized lowering the cost of debt by following the strategy of issuing variable-rate debt coupled with an interest-rate-exchange agreement to pay fixed and receive adjustable rates. Other than faith and repeated promises, they provided no evidence to substantiate the effectiveness of such a process in reducing the cost of borrowing. The message seemed to be, "Just trust us; we know this stuff."

Almost immediately following the enactment of Public Act 093-0009 in 2003,[4]

> CPS [Chicago Public Schools] entered into two interest rate [exchange] swaps [with Goldman Sachs and Bank of America] associated with the issuance of the Series 2003B bonds in February 2003 as a *means of lowering its borrowing costs* when compared against fixed-rate bonds at the time of issuance. *The intention of entering into the swaps was to effectively change the variable interest rate on the auction-rate bonds to a fixed interest rate* of 3.782%. [Emphasis added]

Shortly we shall see why this statement is a representation of falsehood. First, it appears that the school board had accepted Goldman Sachs's assertion that entering into such types of contracts would reduce the cost of borrowing. Second, any thinking person should have known there can be no synthetic fixed rate in a system using a *weekly adjustable rate* for the bond. In such a system, the synthetic rate will be "fixed" for one week at a time only. Finally, no one, even the so-called financial advisors, seemed to be concerned about locking the school district into a new and untested contract for 30 full years. That decision was based on the totally false assumption that the world of variable interest rates would not change. In September 2007, CPS issued Bond Series 2007A ($262,785,000) at auction-rate securities (variable rate adjustable weekly) and coupled it with interest-rate swaps to pay fixed rates and receive variable. This

---

[4]Chicago Public School. Comprehensive Annual Financial Reports for the year ended June 30, 2007.

Retrieved from http://cps.edu/About_CPS/Financial_information/Documents/FY07_CAFR.pdf.

cycle was repeated in 2008 and again in 2011 and 2013 when CPS sold bonds for $498 million at floating variable rates indexed to LIBOR but mimicked the auction rate because they were to be reset weekly or monthly as LIBOR changes. This was what CPS called floating rate. In essence, after 2008, when the auction-rate market failed, big banks invented a rate-setting process not too much different from the original Auction Rate Securities market but does not require the support of banks.

To show the downside risk of using weekly auction rate for the issued bonds and a different benchmark for the related swaps, let us look at one case of the terms of the bond/swap combination.

- Total notional amounts were $183 million.
- Chicago Public Schools District pays fixed at 3.782% and receives variable at Municipal Bond Average Interest Rate (SIFMA) or 70% of one-month London Average Interest Rate (LIBOR).
- The contract terminates in 30 years on March 1, 2033 — a full 30 years before expiry.

The comparison with alternative financing methods was made by reference to the time of issuance, which was hypothetical. Moreover, no one was willing to say anything about the risk assumed down the road for making an enforceable and noncancelable commitment to bet on interest rate movement for 30 years. Evidently, the majority of the Chicago Public Schools board members were either gullible or arrogant enough to believe that they could manage interest-rate spread over *three decades*. This was totally unrealistic and wishful thinking. Yet, the CPS board felt the thrill of a gold-rush-like and entered into all kinds of swaps, whether needed or not. By 2007, just as the Financial Crisis was ringing the doorbell, CPS had entered into several interest-rate-exchange contracts on notional amounts totaling $1.78 billion.[5]

Up until that year, just one year before the advent of the Financial Crisis, CPS administrators must have thought that getting into derivative contracts was a good deal because they were netting some gains, though

---

[5]These include $1.138 billion of fixed-payer swaps, $379 million basis swaps, and $263 million swaptions. In the same year, CPS had debt totaling $4.58 billion.

relatively small amounts, from most contracts. Nevertheless, that blessing was short-lived and drastically reversed course in less than one year. By 2015, CPS had paid more than $200 million to terminate some swap contracts and reported $117 million of expected losses. All of that was in addition to paying the recurring annual losses. "Chicago Public Schools Exhibit 2" shows the extent of this reversal:

Two factors exacerbated the inability to maintain positive fair-market values for most of the interest-rate-exchange contracts.

(1) The interest rates on almost all variable-rate bonds were auction rate. In an auction-rate setting, the bonds were remarketed once a week, and new bondholders bid on the interest rate they would accept. The auction-rate system involved charging a remarketing fee between 0.3% and 0.7% and bears the risk of morphing into the default interest rate. Thus, when the system of auction rate disappeared in 2008 after

Chicago Public Schools Exhibit 2
Reversal of Fortune: Assets and Liabilities (for Swap Losses) For the Chicago Public Schools District for a Sample of Four Years

Bank Name	Notional Amount	Fair-Market Value Asset (Liability) in Million Dollars			
		2007	2008	2014	2015
Lehman Brothers (Followed by Goldman Sachs)	$269	$ 2.2	($10)	($35)	($38)
Loop Financial	$319	$13.6	($10)	($48)	($48) Deutsche Bank
Royal Bank of Canada	$347	($14)	($61)	($94)	($31)
Bank of America	$100	—*	($21)	($37)	—
Total	$1,035	1.8	($102)	($214)	($117)

Notes: *Swaption contracts not yet exercised
**Termination fees are the fair-market values of terminated swaps and are paid over and above the payments made to settle the current year's liability.

the Securities and Exchange Commission sued the big banks involved in Auction Rate Securities for fraud, the transaction cost and risk exposure increased. Both factors have significantly penalized the borrower for any minor downgrading of its credit rating. *Chicago Tribune* reporters Jason Grotto and Heather Gillers note:[6]

CPS' contracts specified that if there weren't enough bids to cover all the available bonds, then the auctions failed and interest rates owed on the bonds would go as high as 9 percent, an outcome that could obliterate any projected savings.

(2) Exposure to Basis Risk, the risk of paying higher interest due to the difference between the interest rate payable on the bond and the interest rate receivable from the swap contract.

Grotto and Gillers also quote Kathleen Hagerty, the chair of the Finance Department at Northwestern University back then, saying that "the pitfalls of CPS's auction-rate deals should have been evident at the time officials signed off…The investment banks are smart, and they aren't doing you any favor." She was, of course, correct — there is no free lunch. Clearly, no one in her/his right mind should take the unfiltered advice of self-interested bankers and issue bonds using auction rates. On the other hand, to this day, no one is willing to admit having erred in accepting this type of financial arrangement, and officials at Chicago City Hall and CPS point to others as the responsible party. With rampant corruption, there is no transparency to help know how banks got their way and essentially got CPS to accept a clearly inferior financing packages.[7] Perhaps all of that and more will come out in time when the class-action suits filed by the Chicago Teachers Union against a number of big banks come to conclusion and what is now private information would become public.

---

[6]Grotto and Gillers, *Chicago Tribune,* November 7, 2014.

[7]Heather Gillers and Jason Grotto, "Banks kept CPS in shaky bond market," *Chicago Tribune,* November 10, 2014.

Retrieved from http://www.chicagotribune.com/news/watchdog/cpsbonds/ct-chicago-public-schools-bonds-banks-met-20141107-story.html.

When the Financial Crisis hit the economy in 2008, the federal government bailed big banks out using taxpayers' money, and concurrently, all benchmark rates, including London Average Interest Rate (LIBOR), the Municipal Bond Average Interest Rate (SIFMA), and the Fed Rate, dropped to unprecedented levels as low as 0.05%. Since interest-rate-exchange contracts were mostly plain vanilla swaps (pay fixed and receive variable), the interest payment of CPS remained unchanged, but the variable rates CPS was receiving from the banks dropped sharply.

The effect of these events was to drain money from Chicago Public Schools equal to the excess of the fixed rate that CPS was paying over the adjustable rate it was receiving on interest-rate-exchange contracts. These amounts were in addition to the usually ignored transaction cost — recurring fees for remarketing, insurance, and for legal and swap advisers. Feeling the negative effect of the sudden shift in the economy in 2008, CPS board terminated six swap contracts and paid a penalty of $20 million. "Chicago Public Schools Exhibit 2" displays the reversal of fortune from profiting small amounts to losing much larger amounts. The effect of this reversal continues to this day. In 2015 alone, Chicago Public Schools paid $109 million to terminate four interest-rate-exchange contracts and continued to owe $117 million long-term liability, representing the fair value of expected losses on the remaining contracts.[8] This fair value was a close approximation of the amount of money that Chicago Public Schools board would have to pay to terminate these swaps at that time — money for which it received only phantom promises.

Heather Gillers and Jason Grotto of the *Chicago Tribune* presented the Chicago Public Schools saga with respect to financial derivatives in a series of articles. The articles are excellent investigative reports for readers who are interested in the political maneuvering that surrounded the unsteady decision-making machine of the Chicago Public Schools.[9]

---

[8]Chicago Public Schools. Comprehensive Annual Financial Report for the Year Ended June 30, 2015.

Retrieved from http://www.cps.edu/About_CPS/Financial_information/Documents/FY15_CAFR.pdf.

[9]Jason Grotto and Heather Gillers. November 7, 2014.

Watch Dog, Borrowing Troubles. *Chicago Tribune*, Multiple reports.

The Infeasibility of Attaining Synthetic Fixed Rates

After the realization of having made poor decisions, the administration of Chicago Public Schools toned down its recurring public pronouncements about the benefits of interest-rate-exchange contracts into which it had entered. In addition, the annual report presented the relevant information in a scattered way, making it difficult for most people to connect and interpret various pieces of information. For example, the 2014 Comprehensive Annual Financial Report presents the following information (page 59) for the swaps and related bonds separately. It is not difficult for our purposes to establish connections, by taking two bonds and the related swaps as examples.

Interest dollar amounts for two swap contracts:

Series 2008A — (5.250% −0.38614%) × swap principal amounts
[Interpretation: pay 5.25% and receive 0.38614%]
Series 2013A-3 — (3.6617% — 0.10614%) × swap principal amounts
[Interpretation: pay 3.6617% and receive 0.10614%]

Interest dollars for the two related bonds:

Series 2008A — 0.90100% × outstanding principal   [pay 0.901%]
Series 2013A-3 — 0.89000% × outstanding principal   [pay 0.89%]

Connecting these two sets of data was expected to give a picture of the synthetic "fixed" rate as shown in "Chicago Public Schools Exhibit 3." This exhibit is a simplification of the contents of several long and tedious misguided presentations. In particular, the exhibit shows netting the two variable rates — the rate payable on the bond and the rate receivable from the swap — then adding the fixed rate payable for the swap to measure the synthetic (artificially constructed) rate. However, the synthetic rate of interest in this case cannot be fixed for any period longer than one week because the bonds' rates of interest were "floating" and changed every week. Thus, the rate of 5.765% for Bond Series 2008A was fixed only for one week, the week of the fiscal year's end. Similarly, the rate of 4.4457% for Bond Series 2013A-3 was fixed only for that same week. The proper

---

Retrieved from http://www.chicagotribune.com/news/watchdog/cpsbonds/.

Chicago Public Schools Exhibit 3
The Presumed True Interest Rate Charged to Bonds:
Two Examples of CPS Wanted the Public to See
(A Wishful but Inaccurate Description of Synthetic Fixed Rate)

The Interest Cost of Bond Series 2008A	
Pay Variable Interest Rate on the Bond	(0.901%)
Receive Variable Interest Rate from the Swap	0.386%
Net Variable Payment	(0.515%)
Pay Fixed Rate on the Swap	(5.25%)
Remarketing Fee	(0.3%)
Net Cost of Borrowing Series 2008A	(6.28%)
(this synthetic rate was fixed for one week only)*	
The Interest Cost of Bond Series 2013A-3	
Pay Interest Rate on the Debt	(0.89%)
Receive Interest Rate from the Swap	0.106%
Net Variable Payment	(0.784%)
Pay Fixed Rate on the Swap	(3.6617%)
Remarketing Fee	(0.3%)
Net Cost of Borrowing Series 2013A-3	(5.5297%)
(this synthetic rate was fixed for one week only)*	

*This is because the interest rates on the debt change weekly.

description of the synthetic rate is presented in Chicago Public Schools Exhibit 3A. Accordingly, it is easy to see that the promise of achieving a synthetic fixed rate below the rate that CPS would have paid on a tradi-tional fixed-rate bond was simply a charade. The reality, however, is that the specific combination of a floating auction-rate bond and a swap to pay fixed and receive variable actually results in another type of floating syn-thetic rate. This is truly incredible; plain vanilla swaps that require paying fixed and receive variable had converted the auction rate bonds into a synthetic floating-rate bonds! Yet, public documents continue to refer to the synthetic rate as a synthetic fixed rate. Clearly, the factors and incentives that led CPS's administration to make these rather costly decisions are of essence but will not likely be unearthed until the pending litigation concludes. Nevertheless, for the Chicago Public Schools board to believe the representations made by big banks and take them at face value tells a lot about their lack of financial sophistication and knowledge of the risk that swap contracts create.

Chicago Public Schools Exhibit 3A
The True Interest Rate Charged to Bonds:
Two Examples of the Impact of Resetting the
Interest Rate on the Bonds Weekly
(A more accurate Description of Synthetic Rate When Bonds Have a Weekly — Adjustable Rate)

The Interest Cost of Bond Series 2008A	
Pay Interest Rate on the Bond	("???," changes weekly)
	Plus the remarketing fee of 0.3%
Receive Interest Rate from the Swap	0.386%
Net Variable Payment	("???" Plus 0.3% remarketing fee minus 0.386%)
Pay Fixed Rate on the Swap	(5.25%)
Net Cost of Borrowing	(5.25% plus "???" plus 0.3% and minus 0.386%).
(This rate could never be considered a synthetic fixed rate for more than a week.)	= Another floating rate.
The Interest Cost of Bond Series 2013A-3	
Pay Interest Rate on the Debt	("???" Changes weekly) + 0.3% remarketing fee.
Receive Interest Rate from the Swap	0.106%
Net Variable Payment	("???" plus 0.3% less 0.106%)
Pay Fixed Rate on the Swap	(3.6617%)
Net Cost of Borrowing	3.6617% plus "???" & 0.3% and minus 0.106%.
(This rate could never be considered a synthetic fixed rate for more than a week.)	= Another floating rate!

Given that information, the appropriate presentation of the synthetic rate structure should look like the information in "Chicago Public Schools Exhibit 3A."

To this day, officials at CPS continue to squabble about assigning responsibility and blame for the financial fiascos coming out of involvement with big banks in purchasing interest-rate swaps. Gillers and Grotto wrote about the last CPS bond issue, marketed and swapped by Bank of America and Royal Bank of Canada that ended up costing CPS large amounts of money for swap losses. For those deals, CPS hired the advisory service of Adela Cepeda of A.C. Advisory. In addition to the allegation of incomplete and primitive analysis of the deals, the banks offered upfront money if CPS would agree to contracts that gave the banks the right to require Chicago Public Schools to enter into swaps (swaptions). Bank of America began this track by paying CPS $18 million upfront, and Royal Bank of Canada followed by paying $25 million upfront for a similar arrangement. Gillers and Grotto note that the lure of quick cash was irresistible. Yet, when the deals backfired and CPS was drowning in red ink, no one wanted to take responsibility[10]:

> Exactly how the district decided to enter the swaption deals is unclear. CPS officials could not explain who raised the idea of swaptions with the public school system.
>
> The former treasurer who oversaw the transactions, David Bryant, says he doesn't recall the details of the swaptions. The chief financial officer whose signature appears on the contracts, John Maiorca, did not return calls.
>
> School Board President David Vitale, who oversaw the finance department as chief administration officer from 2003 to 2006 and served as chief operating officer from 2006 through 2008, declined to answer questions about the swaptions. But the deals incorporated the kinds of new-market solutions that Vitale, a former banker, had championed.
>
> In an interview, Vitale said that in general he had tried to save money over traditional borrowing methods by taking advantage of floating-rate debt options and derivative products.

---

[10] Heather Gillers and Jason Grotto, "Banks kept CPS in shaky bond market," *Chicago Tribune*, November 10, 2014.

Retrieved from http://www.chicagotribune.com/news/watchdog/cpsbonds/ct-chicago-public-schools-bonds-banks-met-20141107-story.html.

It is dumbfounding to see that the CPS board took an optimistic view of the world and locked the school system into 30-year-long agreements that

(a) are noncancelable,
(b) are nonchangeable, and
(c) legally enforceable.

Further issues related to the decision-making process of CPS raise other distressing questions[11]:

- After suffering significant losses from prior swap contracts, why would the Chicago Public Schools board purchase more swap contracts in 2011, and then again in 2013?
- What made CPS's board members muster the overconfidence that led them to write enforceable and noncancelable long-term contracts that had the potential of bleeding money for three decades in exchange for mirage (synthetic) fixed rates?

Shortly after the Financial Crisis, the impact of the damage arising from entering into swap agreements began to hit the essential functions of the public school system. On July 7, 2015, Chris Fusco of the *Chicago Sun-Times* reported about some of these actions:

> Struggling to make payments for pensions and pay down Billions of dollars in debt, the Chicago Public Schools last week announced 1,050 layoffs and $200 million in spending cuts to keep the school system afloat.[12]

---

[11]Chicago Public Schools, Comprehensive Annual Report for the year ended June 30, 2015.

Retrieved from http://www.cps.edu/About_CPS/Financial_information/Documents/FY15_CAFR.pdf.

[12]Chris Fusco. "The Watchdogs: CPS' pain is these firms' gain," *Sun Times*, July 4, 2015.

Retrieved from http://chicago.suntimes.com/the-watchdogs/7/71/740413/watchdogs-cps-bond-fee.

A year later, on August 2016, Matt Masterson of the *Chicago Tribune* wrote:

> The district announced its plan to inform 508 teachers — more than half of whom are tenured — and 521 support personnel they will be laid off as part of annual staffing changes it says are brought on by declining enrollment and available positions at other schools.[13]

On the same day, Juan Perez Jr. provided the breakdown of the specialties of the personnel who had lost their employment:

> The layoffs broke down this way: 314 elementary school teachers and 194 high school teachers for a total of 508, and 378 elementary personnel and 143 high school support staff, for a total of 521.[14]

The Chicago Teachers Union (CTU) did not take these actions lightly because many of the swap contracts were related to bonds that CPS had issued to fund teachers' pensions. The CTU took actions of its own. First, the members of CTU led a public demonstration to the office of Bank of America on LaSalle Street to close the union's checking account at the bank. The account did not have a large balance, but the action conveyed the symbolism of the protest and hurt of the entire community. Second, CTU engaged the community to collect over 88,000 petitions to take to the regional office of the Securities and Exchange Commission and City Hall pleading to cancel or litigate the swap contracts. The picture in "Chicago Public Schools Exhibit 1" shows some of the demonstrators carrying boxes of all these petitions with a writing on one box stating, "Stop Swapping Our Schools for Profits." The demonstrators would have

---

[13] Matt Masterson, "CPS to Cut More Than 1,000 Teaching, Support Staff Positions," *WTTW*, August 5, 2016.

   Retrieved from http://chicagotonight.wttw.com/2016/08/05/cps-cut-more-1000-teaching-support-staff-positions.

[14] Juan Perez, Jr., "CPS lays off more than 500 teachers, another 500 school-based workers," *Chicago Tribune*, August 5, 2016.

   Retrieved from http://www.chicagotribune.com/news/local/breaking/ct-chicago-schools-teacher-layoffs-0806-20160805-story.html.

been much more outraged had they known that CPS was losing money and all the profits belonged to big banks.

Third, when none of the actions had any noticeable impact, CTU joined the City of Baltimore on February 25, 2016, in filing a class-action suit in the US District Court, Southern District of New York, alleging that big banks had conspired to restrain trade and control the market for swaps. The big banks named as defendants in the suit are Bank of America, Barclays, BNP Paribas, Citigroup, Credit Suisse, Deutsche Bank, Goldman Sachs, HSBC, JPMorgan Chase, Morgan Stanley, Royal Bank of Scotland, and UBS AG.[15] The complaint alleges that the defendants had conspired to prevent the evolution of an exchange-like trading system that would have made the CTU benefit by the effects of transparency and competition[16]:

> The Dealer Defendants have historically acted as market makers (or "dealers") in the OTC market, meaning one of them was typically on one side of every IRS [interest-rate swaps] trade with end users. In the OTC market, investors must request a quote from one or more of the Dealer Defendants. While investors could obtain quotes from more than one dealer, they could only negotiate a final actionable price — which, due to market volatility, often has to be accepted on the spot — typically with one dealer at a time. This inefficient form of trading does not allow for competitive price shopping by customers, and it denies the buy-side immediate execution and access to real-time price information.

To cope with budgetary shortfalls and make the payments for the losses on interest-rate-exchange (swap) contracts, CPS sold $725 million in fixed-rate bonds in February 2016 to keep afloat (Exhibit 4). Issuing

---

[15]Royal Bank of Canada was heavily involved in the swap market in the USA and in Chicago, but the antitrust litigation did not include it.

[16]United States District Court Southern District of New York. *Amended Class Action Complaint. Jury Demanded. Public Schools Teachers' Pension and Retirement Fund of Chicago and Mayor and City Council of Baltimore on behalf of themselves and all others similarly situated, Plaintiffs, — against — Bank of America Corporation; etc.* Case No. No. 15 Civ. 9319 (SAS) February 25, 2016.

Retrieved from https://www.cohenmilstein.com/sites/default/files/IRS%20Amended%20Complaint.pdf.

Chicago Public Schools Exhibit 4
Chicago Teachers Union Cannot Take It Anymore

CTU Closes Bank of America Account Over "Toxic" Interest Rate Swaps

One day after Chicago Public Schools officials announced $100 million in proposed budget cuts, the Chicago Teachers Union closed its Bank of America account on Wednesday in protest over the controversial interest rate swap agreements held between the bank and school district.

CTU says cash-strapped CPS, which is facing a $480 million budget hole this fiscal year, has lost more than $502 million to "predatory" swap deals with financial institutions, including Bank of America. According to the union, Bank of America has collected $77 million in profits off of its interest rate swaps with CPS. (Emphasis added).

"What we hope is that our withdrawal of funds will spark people all over this city, all over this state and all over the country to start withdrawing funds from Bank of America until they give back some of the ill-gotten gains they've made off the backs of our students," CTU Vice President Jesse Sharkey said outside the Bank of America at 135 S. LaSalle St.

Source: Based on an image reported at http://www.progressillinois.com/quick-hits/content/2016/02/03/ctu-closes-its-account-bank-america-over-toxic-interest-rate-swaps.

these bonds at a fixed rate was in effect an admission of having committed errors by taking the earlier actions of issuing bonds at variable rates and fixing them synthetically by entering into swap agreements.

However, the credit rating of Chicago and its school system was a problem. In spite of pledging real-estate taxes to guarantee the bond issue, the interest rate on these new bonds was set at 8.5%, which was quite high in a market having the Fed Rate and London Average Interest Rate (LIBOR) below the 1% level. In addition, the $725 million fell short of the budgeted need by $100 million. Neither the City of Chicago nor the State of Illinois was in any sound fiscal shape to assist; both had their large shares of swap losses. Resorting to more service cuts and layoffs to save enough resources to cover this shortfall might just be the next act in this saga.

CHAPTER 15

Denver Public Schools: Paid High Price for the Advice of Unwitting Experts

The Denver Public Schools District (DPS District) consists of 162 schools serving about 80,000 students and had a high-cost experience with interest-rate-exchange (swap) contracts. Until 2008, DPS District was swap free. In 2008, it had $300 million of fixed-rate bonds outstanding and $400 million deficit in public schools' pension fund. Closing that pension deficit was of concern to DPS District. In 2008, JPMorgan Chase went to the district jointly with Bank of America and Royal Bank of Canada (RBC) with a proposal to help manage this financial difficulty. The plan had two prongs:

- To issue corporate bonds under the name of *certificates of participation* (COP) at adjustable (variable) rates. These were Certificates 2008A and 2008B. The total amount of borrowing was $750 million subscribed to by the three banks: $450 million sold to JPMorgan Chase, $200 million sold to Bank of America, and $100 million sold to RBC. The designated variable rate was the worst kind of all from the perspective of the Denver Public Schools District; it was the *dreaded auction rate that requires remarketing the COP certificates and resetting the interest rate once a week.* All certificates were noncancelable and have 30-year terms extending to 2037. Incidentally, it is very difficult to believe that the three banks were not strategic in timing their move since signs of the Financial Crises were evident by the time they approached DPS.

- While DPS District could have issued variable rate bonds without adding swap contracts, the banks either requested COPs to be coupled with writing interest-rate-exchange (swap) contracts or simply took DPS Board to trips on a trail illuminated by mystical financial engineering jargon. The swap contracts required DPS District to pay to each of these three participating banks interest at a fixed rate of 4.859% or higher and receive from them interest based on London Average Interest Rate (LIBOR). At that time, LIBOR was 2.785%.

Obsession with swaps is evident in all reports until the end of 2015. For example, the 2008 Comprehensive Annual Financial Report of Denver Public Schools cites the word *swap* 103 times, but the word *education* was repeated 63 times only.

Denver Public Schools District followed the path of others and sold bonds at the totally disastrous auction rate. As was the case with many others, using the weekly adjustable auction rate generated high uncertainty about the cost of financing. At any point in time, the district would not have had any idea or prediction of the cost of debt for periods longer than one week. "Denver Schools Exhibit 1" depicts that uncertainty as of April 2008.

DPS District was supposed to benefit by the financial expertise of two officials: Thomas Boasberg and Michael Bennet. Both of them had worked with financial institutions before coming to Denver Public Schools, and both have endorsed the refinancing packages of issuing variable-rate bonds at auction rate plus swap contracts. Thomas Boasberg was the DPS superintendent, and Michael Bennet was the head of the Denver Public Schools Board.[1] Bennet and Boasberg worked for a number of years in different financial advisory firms dealing with structured finance and were the pretend-swap-experts in residence. Others, however, did not know much about the expertise of these two local stars, especially when it came

---

[1] Michael Bennett is the US senator from Colorado.

Denver Schools Exhibit 1
The Cost of the Financing Package of Selling
Variable-Rate Bonds and Buying Plain-Vanilla Swaps

The initial picture of this financing arrangement in April 2008 looked like the following. (All contracts terminate in 2037):	
○ Pay fixed rate on interest-rate-exchange contracts	4.859%
○ Receive adjustable rate from interest-rate-exchange contracts**	(2.785%)**
○ Net interest payment on swap contracts	2.074%
○ Pay adjustable rate of interest on debt certificates (weekly auction rate)	??? (changes weekly)
○ Pay remarketing fees	Between 0.3% and 0.7%
= Net cost of debt (a phantom synthetic fixed!) (??? could be any number)	2.074% + ??? Unknown Percentage?? + remarketing fee

Notes: **This data is based on LIBOR in early 2008. But LIBOR kept on decreasing from 2008 onward until it reached 0.15% in 2014 and 0.56% in December 2015.

An assessment of this package should shock anyone in two respects: the open-ended cost of debt and the 30 years' duration of noncancelable contracts.

Source: Denver Public Schools. Comprehensive Annual Financial Report for the Year Ended June 30, 2012.

Retrieved from http://static.dpsk12.org/gems/generalaccounting/CAFR2012.pdf. Retrieved from https://www.denvergov.org/content/denvergov/en/denver-department-of-finance/financial-reports/comprehensive-annual-financial-reports-cafr-.html.

to dealing with financial derivatives. "There was not one person on that board who understands bonds," said Andrew Kalotay, president of Andrew Kalotay Associates Inc., who has studied the costs of the earlier swaps.[2]

A symptom of the lack of understanding and perhaps the credulity that Kalotay noted, DPS District hired one of its own lenders, Royal Bank of Canada, as its swap advisor. It appears that DPS District did not

---

[2] Quoted in Darrell Preston, "Denver Pays Wall Street $216 Million as Swaps Fail: Muni Credit," *Bloomberg*, May 10, 2013.

Retrieved from http://www.bloomberg.com/news/articles/2013-05-10/denver-pays-wall-street-216-million-as-swaps-fail-muni-credit.

notice or care about the conflict of interest of having the same bond buyer and counterparty on the related swaps to also act as the swap adviser. This is simply like hiring a wolf to guard the henhouse and was a signal of gullibility and lack of skill in managing interest rate swaps. In a case like this, when goals conflict, who in his/her right mind would think that RBC would provide DPS District any type of advice other than what benefits RBC?

Nevertheless, the sales pitch swap sellers from big banks made to DPS District contained the same promises they had made throughout, namely that the combined package of refinancing using variable-rate bonds and a swap to pay fixed rate and receive variable rate would lower the cost of borrowing and help manage interest-rate risk. As has been the story throughout, all such promises turned out to be untrue. *In less than two years, DPS paid $25 million more in interest cost on this financing package than the interest cost the school district would have paid on conventional fixed-rate municipal bonds.*

In 2011, the DPS District reversed direction and went back to conventional municipal-bond financing — selling bonds at fixed rates. DPS District issued $597 million traditional municipal bonds at a 4.24% fixed rate and used the proceeds in refunding the bonds with JPMorgan Chase and paying the *swap-termination penalty of $36 million.* The 2012 Comprehensive Annual Financial Report (CAFR) shows DPS District having three swap contracts with Wells Fargo, Bank of America, and RBC on total notional amounts of $396 million. Shortly thereafter, *DPS District terminated all three swaps at a penalty of $216 million* — amazingly, the termination fee was equal to 55% of the notional amounts! It must be noted that this termination cost was paid in addition to the annual payments of due amounts and the significant hidden transaction costs — remarketing fees, underwriting fees, insurance, and others. By the end of 2016, DPS became swap free again. In the meantime, the pension liability gap had increased to over $600 million.[3]

---

[3] Gretchen Morgenstern, "Exotic Deals Put Denver Schools Deeper in Debt," *The New York Times*, August 5, 2010.

   Retrieved from http://www.nytimes.com/2010/08/06/business/06denver.html.

In total, DPS District paid more than \$252 million to terminate interest-rate-exchange contracts, which were initially intended to save the district money.[4] It was also surprising to know that the total termination fees were equal to 77% of the entire instructional budget of Denver Public Schools in 2012–2013, which totaled \$327 million.

Even with these disturbing facts, Thomas Boasberg, the initial supporter of the mixed funding plans, did not ponder the issue of waste. Instead, he claimed that the transactions had accomplished the goal by saving DPS about \$78 million. From all publicly available information, it appears that Boasberg needed a new calculator.

However, the real human cost was deferred and began to show in later years. For example, in spite of growth in revenues from legalizing the sale of marijuana, the Denver Public Schools District had to dismiss 170 teachers and staff in 2016 to free up funds to meet other needs.[5]

> "This deal hasn't done much for anyone — except the bankers, who are dancing in the streets," said MacPherson_(Darrell Preston, May 9, 2013)

---

[4]This sum consists of \$36 million to JPMorgan Chase, \$10 million to Wells Fargo, and \$216 million to terminate the remaining swaps.

[5]Matt Stannard, "What Wall Street Cost Denver's Schools. Public Banking Institute," March 28, 2016.

Retrieved from http://www.publicbankinginstitute.org/what_wall_street_cost_denver_s_schools.

Cases in Wealth Transfer from Colleges and Universities to Big Banks:

Paying Big Banks Huge Sums of Money for Ill-Advised Interest-Rate-Exchange Contracts

The Missed Opportunities

With the fall semester underway at American University in Washington, D.C., students are starting new classes, making new friends, and joining new clubs. Most of these students will pay over $43,000 this year in tuition and fees, and collectively their payments will account for nearly four-fifths of the school's operating budget. But a sizable portion of that budget isn't going toward better instruction, new classrooms, or even new dormitories and amenities: It's going to Wall Street institutions that convinced American to enter into risky financial deals.

Over the last decade and a half, toxic interest rate swaps have cost American $91 million, enough to pay the full annual tuition and fees of more than 2,100 students. And it's not over yet: American will likely pay another $76 million on these swaps in the coming years. The presence of current or former executives of these financial firms on American's Board of Trustee raises serious questions about potential conflicts of interest. [Emphasis added]

Source: Dominic Russell, Carrie Sloan, Aman Banerji, and Alan Smith, "It's Time for Universities to Pick Students over Swaps," Roosevelt Forward: Rewrite the Rules, September 20. 2016.

Retrieved from http://rooseveltforward.org/its-time-our-universities-pick-students-over-swaps/.

CHAPTER 16

The Flagship of the Tar Heel State Kept Dipping into the Same Losing Swap Well

University of North Carolina at Chapel Hill — Exhibit 1
Expected Long-term Losses of the Contract
with Lehman over Fourteen Years

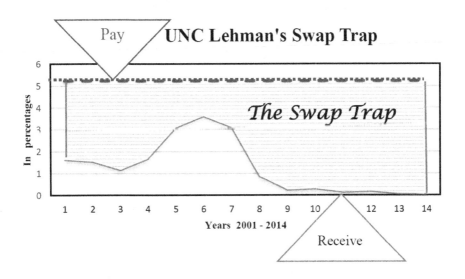

Like many others, this story could make many people question their rationality. The University of North Carolina joined the swap train at the start of the Swap Mania in 2000 by signing an agreement to swap interest rates on a small notional amount of $22 million. The contract generated losses every year, but the university continued on the dreaded path and signed into other swap contracts on notional amounts of $250 million.

On October 3, 2000, Lehman Brothers convinced the officials at the University of North Carolina–Chapel Hill to adopt a financing strategy that would presumably lower the cost of borrowing and help to manage interest-rate risk. The strategy made use of interest rate swap contracts, which were new on the scene, and no one at the university administration had any chance of studying the nature, risk and valuation of these contracts. Other than the publicly disclosed promise of being better able to manage interest-rate risk, there is no way of knowing the methods by which Lehman Brothers persuaded the university officials to accept its proposed strategy. All the details of the negotiation that preceded signing the contracts remain private, and no information could be currently obtained from Lehman Brothers because it went out of business in 2008. A combination of gullibility, lack of knowledge, and overconfidence led these officials to get entrapped into the Swap Mania and make very costly decisions.

The university had variable-rate bonds outstanding back then with interest rates indexed to common benchmarks. These bonds were scheduled to terminate sometime between 2010 and 2018, which was 10 to 18 years down the road. Somehow, by some obscure logic or magic, the university refunded the six outstanding variable-rate bond issues and replaced them with two other variable rate bond issues (2001 B & C) also paying variable rates based on the most risky system: the <u>weekly adjustable auction rate</u>.[1] Moreover, the university entered into an interest-rate-swap

---

[1] University of North Carolina, Comprehensive Annual Financial Report, 2009, p. 53.
    Retrieved from http://finance.unc.edu/about/reports-data/.
In 2001, the university issued two series of variable-rate demand bonds in the amounts of $54,970,000 (2001B) and $54,970,000 (2001C), with each having a final maturity date of December 1, 2025. The bonds are subject to mandatory sinking fund *redemption* on the interest-payment date on or immediately preceding each December throughout the term of the bonds. *The proceeds of these issuances were used to provide funds to refund in advance of their maturity the following issues*: Ambulatory Care Clinic, Series 1990; Athletic

contract with the same bond underwriter, Lehman Brothers Financial Services, on $22 million notional amounts, which was one-half of the face amount of Bond Series 2001B. The contract required the university to pay Lehman a fixed interest rate at 5.24% and receive a variable (floating) rate based on the swap index of the municipal-bond market. (The index was called BMA and is now called SIFMA reflecting for Municipal Bond Average Interest Rate compiled by the Securities Industry and Financial Markets Association.) The swap contract had the same life term as the bond (Series 2001B) that will terminate in 2025. One must wonder about the connection between the bond issue and the swap contract if the university pays weekly adjustable auction rates on the bonds and receive variable rate adjusted less frequently by the movement of the municipal bond interest rate.

In its Comprehensive Annual Financial Report, the university informed the public of what the officials had thought to be the goal of the swap contract with Lehman:

Lehman Brothers Special Financing, Inc.

> **Objective** *In order to protect against the risk of interest rate changes,* effective October 3, 2000, the University entered into an interest rate swap agreement with Lehman Brothers Special Financing, Inc. (Lehman Brothers) related to $22,000,000 of The University of North Carolina at Chapel Hill Variable Rate Housing System Revenue Bonds, Series 2000. This series of bonds was refunded in its entirety by the issuance of the University's Variable Rate General Revenue Demand Bonds, Series 2001B (2001B Bonds), and the interest rate swap agreement was amended to reflect the refunding.

This disclosure is misleading; it refers to the interest rate on the newly issued bonds as "Variable Rate General Revenue Demand Bonds, Series

---

Facilities, Series 1998; Carolina Inn, Series 1994; School of Dentistry, Series 1995; Kenan Stadium, Series 1996; and Parking System, Series 1997C. While bearing interest at a weekly rate, the bonds are subject to purchase on demand with seven days' notice and delivery to the university's remarketing agents, JPMorgan Chase (2001B) and Bank of America, LLC (2001C). Effective September 23, 2008, JPMorgan Chase replaced Lehman Brothers, Inc. (emphasis added).

The bonds that were refunded prematurely had termination dates ranging between 2010 and 2027.

University of North Carolina Exhibit 2
The Annual Report Description of the Relationship
between the Bond and Swap Interest Rates

Under this amended agreement, Lehman Brothers pays the university interest on the notational amount based on the Bond Market Association (BMA) Municipal Bond Index on a quarterly basis. For the fiscal year ended June 30, 2003, Lehman Brothers paid the university $285,962 under this agreement. On a semiannual basis, the university pays Lehman Brothers interest at the fixed rate of 5.24%. For the fiscal year ended June 30, 2003, the university paid Lehman Brothers $1,147,167 under this agreement. The notional amount of the swap reduces annually; the reductions began in November 2002 and end in November 2025. The swap agreement matures November 1, 2025. As of June 30, 2003, rates were as follows:

	Terms	Rates
Fixed payment to Lehman	Fixed	5.24
Variable payment from Lehman	BMA	1.13
Net interest rate swap payments		4.11
Variable-rate bond coupon payments		1.00
Synthetic interest rate on bonds		5.11

As of June 30, 2003, the swap had a negative fair value of $5,505,094.

Source: Reproduced from Financial statement Audit Report of the University of North Carolina At Chapel Hill for the year ended June 30, 2003 (pp. 60–61).
Retrieved from http://www.ncauditor.net/EPSWeb/Reports/Financial/FIN-2003-6020.pdf.

2001B" without noting that the adopted variable rate was the worst most risky type, the auction rate that changes *weekly*. Moreover, to justify their decisions, the officials reported the connection between the issued bonds (Series 2001) and the swap contract with Lehman in a table reproduced here as "University of North Carolina Exhibit 2."

This paragraph provides four pieces of information:

(a) The university retained Lehman to underwrite issuing variable-rate bonds and used the collected proceeds to refund some of its outstanding variable-rate bonds prematurely and for no other compelling reason.

(b) The variable rates of the newly issued bonds were auction rates and were truly *floating* because *they must be reset weekly.* For a fee, Lehman was the remarketing agent placing the bonds back in the market every week and using the interest rate the new bondholders were willing to accept.[2]

(c) Concurrently, Lehman wrote an interest-rate-swap contract with the university requiring it to pay interest at a 5.24% fixed rate and receive a variable (floating) rate based on the swap index of the municipal-bond market.

(d) In addition to making net payment of $861,205 to Lehman Brothers to settle swap differences in 2003, Lehman Brothers told the university it owes Lehman $5,505,094 for expected future differences in cash payments.

The proclaimed motivations for this type of arrangement were (a) to avail the university of an artificially generated fixed interest rate (synthetic fixed rate), and (b) to lower the cost of borrowing. As it turned out, the structure of the contract had all the reasons to guarantee that both aims could not be accomplished: there can be no "fixed" synthetic rate in a system of weekly changeable rates, and the cost of borrowing had in fact increased significantly from the moment the contract was signed. In each annual report of the first three years, the university described this contract as follows:

- For the fiscal year ended June 30, 2001, the university paid Lehman Brothers $188,000 under this agreement.[3]
- For the fiscal year ended June 30, 2002, Lehman Brothers paid the university $431,597, and the university paid Lehman Brothers

---

[2] While bearing interest at a weekly rate, the bonds are subject to purchase on demand with seven days' notice and delivery to the university's remarketing agents, Lehman Brothers, Inc. (2001B) and UBS Paine Webber Incorporated (2001C). UNC Comprehensive Annual Financial Report, 2001.

Retrieved from http://finance.unc.edu/files/2015/12/2001_cafr.pdf.

[3] University of North Carolina, Comprehensive Annual Financial Report, 2001, p. 65.

Retrieved from http://finance.unc.edu/about/reports-data/.

$1,152,800 under this agreement (i.e., net payment of $721.203 to Lehman).[4]

- For the fiscal year ended June 30, 2003, Lehman Brothers paid the university $285,962, and the university paid Lehman Brothers $1,147,167 under this agreement. The notional amount of the swap reduces annually; the reductions began in November 2002 and end in November 2025 (i.e., net payment of $861,205 to Lehman).[5]

In 2004, there was a different form of disclosure:

As of June 30, 2004, the swap had a negative fair value of $3,513,801. *The fair value was developed by Lehman Brothers.* Its method calculates the future net settlement payments required by the swap assuming that the current forward rates implied by the yield curve correctly anticipate future-spot interest rates.[6]

This was an admission that all along Lehman Brothers was in control of remarketing the debt weekly and calculating the amount of money the university owed it for the swap agreement. The generic name of the method of calculation was stated, but it does not appear that anyone knew the structure and relationships that Lehman Brothers had used to calculate the obligations of the university. The university trusted Lehman to estimate its liability, oblivious to the fact that Lehman was the fox counting the chicken in the henhouse.

Three additional points should be emphasized. (a) The reported cost excludes any transaction cost — the cost of underwriting, insuring, and handling the swap contract. (b) The calculation of the synthetic rate

---

[4]University of North Carolina, Comprehensive Annual Financial Report, 2002, p. 54.
   Retrieved from http://finance.unc.edu/about/reports-data/; http://finance.unc.edu/files/2015/12/2002_cafr.pdf.
[5]University of North Carolina, Comprehensive Annual Financial Report, 2003, p. 61.
   Retrieved from http://finance.unc.edu/about/reports-data/; http://finance.unc.edu/files/2015/12/2003_cafr.pdf.
[6]University of North Carolina, Comprehensive Annual Financial Report, 2004, p. 67.
   Retrieved from http://finance.unc.edu/about/reports-data/; http://finance.unc.edu/files/2015/12/2004_cafr.pdf.

ignored the cost of remarketing the bond, which added to interest rate a fraction between 0.3% and 0.7%. (c) The two contracts (the bond issue and the swap) exposed the University of North Carolina at Chapel Hill to a particular form of interest-rate risk called "basis risk", which arises in this case when the variable rate payable on the bond issue is higher than the variable rate receivable from the swap.

This disclosure suggests what has been happening — confusion! As "University of North Carolina Exhibit 1" shows, the university has been losing money on the contract that started with Lehman and remained in effect all the way until this day.[7] However, the interest-rate-exchange contract with Lehman could not be a fair-swap agreement for two reasons:

(a) There was no way the present market value of the two sides of the contract, the fixed leg and the floating leg, could have been equal at the time of initiating the transaction if all items of transaction cost were taken into account.
(b) The difference between the fixed and variable rates was so huge that it was highly unlikely the forward yield curve would become steep enough to overtake that difference.

Nevertheless, of more importance is the misleading nature of the disclosure that continued year after year. As "University of North Carolina Exhibit 2" reveals, bundling the bond issue and the swap contracts resulted in a synthetic rate of 5.11% for the week ended June 30, 2003. It is critical to notice that the disclosure did not say "synthetic fixed rate" because that synthetic rate was highly volatile and floating. The interest rate on the bond was presented as 1%. However, that rate was to be in effect for one week only, most likely the week of June 30, 2003; the bond had a weekly auction rate. Therefore, an accurate representation of the data should not be as reported in "University of North Carolina Exhibit 2." Instead, the report in "University of North Carolina Exhibit 2A." reflects the inherent high risk and uncertainty associated with a weekly changeable auction rate on the

---

[7]In 2008, JPMorgan Chase took over Lehman Brothers' assets, obligations, and contracts.

University of North Carolina Exhibit 2A
The Correct Disclosure of the
Nature of the Synthetic Rate*

	Terms	Rates
Fixed payment to Lehman	Fixed	5.24
Variable payment from Lehman	BMA	1.13
Net interest rate swap payments		4.11
Variable-rate bond coupon payments		???
(Changes weekly and could rate on bonds)		
Synthetic interest rate on bonds		4.11 plus ???
(??? Could be any number)		

Note: *Plus 0.3% for remarketing fee. All numbers ignore transaction cost.

bonds. Under that system, the synthetic rate could never be fixed for more than one week.

In a later paragraph, the university acknowledged the possibility of having an effective interest rate on the bonds greater than the fixed rate payable on the swap[8]:

> With the alternative tax structure of the swap, a change in tax law would trigger the swap being converted from a BMA swap (nontaxable) to a percentage of LIBOR swap (taxable). This would introduce basis risk. If the relationship of the University's bonds trade to a percentage of LIBOR greater than 65%, the *University will experience an increase in debt service above the fixed rate on the swap.* [Emphasis added]

The presumed goals of the bundle of bonds and swaps were (a) to lock in a fixed rate on the debt, even though that fixed rate was synthetic (as a combination of two contracts), and (b) to lower the cost of

---

[8] Financial statement audit report of the University of North Carolina at Chapel Hill for the year ended June 30, 2003, p. 62.

Retrieved from http://www.ncauditor.net/EPSWeb/Reports/Financial/FIN-2003-6020.pdf.

borrowing. As in other cases, however, neither goal was achieved. The locked-in interest rate was variable, truly floating and highly unpredictable. Thus, the cost of borrowing kept on increasing by the amounts of losses to Lehman in addition to other embedded costs, such as that of underwriting, insurance, fees for swap advisers, and the weekly cost of bond remarketing.

For an auction-rate bond, the university had to pay a remarketing fee, which typically ranged between 0.3% and 0.7% in addition to hiring supporting staff to oversee the process. Moreover, the university had to pay fees of 0.08% to acquire a letter of credit from JPMorgan Chase to use as collateral, as required by the contract with Lehman Brothers. On September 23, 2008, JPMorgan Chase replaced Lehman Brothers, and the university designated the swap contract as an "investment."

By 2013, the notional amount of the Lehman Brothers swap for one-half of Series 2001B had decreased to $18.5 million, but the liability arising from this particular swap contract had increased to $4.2 million. With piling up all types of cost, there can be only one winner, which was Lehman Brothers (JPMorgan Chase), and one loser, which was the University of North Carolina. The university had fallen into what appeared to be a bottomless swap trap, as shown in "University of North Carolina Exhibit 1."

Getting Deeper into the Swap Mania

The continual loss on the contract with Lehman did not seem to give university officials a red light warning them to have a different look at the new "high" finance. Instead, the university administration made other inexplicable moves by entering into two larger swap contracts on notional amounts of $250 million.

1. An interest-rate swap contract with Wachovia Bank to pay fixed at 3.34% and receive variable at 0.67% of LIBOR on a notional amount of $100 million. This contract was effective on December 1, 2007, and was supposed to be a hedge for the two bond series 2001B and 2001C. Three important pieces of information should reveal how the university officials were essentially seeking more pain for totally unknown reasons:

(a) The two bond issues 2001B and 2001C pay variable rates that change weekly — it was the *weekly auction rate*. Thus, there can be no such thing as a synthetic fixed rate when piling a swap contract on top of bonds that were issued at auction rates. Yet the 2010 annual report falsely states that the bond issue with a swap paid a "synthetic fixed rate."

2001B	0.180% – 5.170% *
2001C	0.150% – 2.969% *

* For variable-rate debt, interest rates in effect on June 30, 2010, are included. For variable-rate debt with interest-rate swaps, the *synthetic fixed* rates are included.[9]

In other words, by 2010, the officials at the University either changed or have a loss of memory or understanding that a weekly changeable interest rate cannot produce a "fixed" synthetic rate for more than one week at a time. By 2015, the swap with Wachovia had a loss of $29 million, $25 million of which was reported under long-term liability, and $4 million was charged to 2015 income statement alone.

(b) A segment of this report is reproduced in "University of North Carolina Exhibit 3." That exhibit refers to a synthetic rate but did not reveal that it was not a fixed rate. It was perhaps evident that such a revelation would have raised red flags about the incentives behind entering into these swap contracts.

(c) The swap contract with Wachovia was also generating losses for the university. The loss was in the amount of $10 million on June 20, 2009, and increased to $16 million in 2010, then to $25 million in 2015. Clearly, the university could have issued bonds at variable rates without the added burden of entering into swap contracts.

This information tells us that the bond issue related to the swap contract paid an annual rate of interest less than one-third of 1% (0.003%), at

---

[9]The University of North Carolina at Chapel Hill. Comprehensive Annual Financial Report 2010, p. 59.

Retrieved from http://www.unc.edu/finance/fd/c/docs/2010_cafr.pdf.

University of North Carolina Exhibit 3
The Interest-Rate-Exchange Contract with Wachovia
After Being Burned by Lehman's Losses

WACHOVIA

Objective The University entered into an interest rate swap agreement with Wachovia on December 5, 2006, based on a notional amount of $100,000,000, effective December 1, 2007, maturing on December 1, 2036. This transaction serves as a hedge of variable interest rates on a portion of the General Revenue 2001 B&C bonds and the outstanding commercial paper bonds.

Terms Under the agreement, Wachovia pays the University 67 percent of the one-month LIBOR index times the notional amount, payable monthly. The University pays Wachovia a fixed rate of 3.314 percent on the notional amount, payable monthly. The effective date of this swap was December 1, 2007. As of June 30, 2009 rates were as follows:

	Terms	Rate
Fixed payment to Wachovia	Fixed	3.314% ◀
Variable payment from Wachovia	LIBOR	0.213% ◀
Net interest rate swap payments		3.101%
Weighted Average Variable Rates		0.003%
Synthetic interest rate on bonds		3.104%

The Quandary:

Why would any rational person enter into contracts with these terms?

Fair value As of June 30, 2009, the swap had a fair negative value of $10,079,658. The fair value was developed by Wachovia. Market value represents the amount that would be paid to (or received from) another swap dealer to assume the payments under the swap.

Interpretation: The negative fair value is a liability representing the amount the university would have to pay to Wachovia to terminate the swap.

Source: Retrieved from http://www.unc.edu/finance/fd/c/docs/2009_cafr.pdf.

least in 2009. It also informs us that the university administration must have been fascinated by the sound of "synthetic rate" and entered into an interest-rate-exchange contract that would get them to pay a net interest rate on the bond more than one thousand times the actual contractual interest — a change from 0.003% to 3.14%. The stated logic behind that move raises more curiosity and questions about the misuse of the word "hedge." It is true that weighted average variable interest rates on issued bonds will likely increase, but for these statistics one must ask the difficult question. What type of hedge that would justify paying a cost of 3.3% a year with near certainty?[10]

> This transaction serves as a hedge of variable interest rates on a portion of the General Revenue 2001 B&C bonds and the outstanding commercial paper bonds.

2. An interest-rate swap with the Bank of New York was set to pay fixed rate at 3.78% and receive 0.67% of one-month LIBOR on a notional amount of $150 million. The data about this swap contract are scattered throughout the financial statements and provide little useful information. However, there is enough information for the reader to know that the swap contract with Bank of New York became effective in December 2011, and in the seven months up to June 30, 2012, the contract lost $89 million, adding up the total loss of swaps to $128 million.[11]

    Going over this saga of signing unneeded swap contracts at the University of North Carolina at Chapel Hill and losing lots of money, one cannot help but remember the questions raised by Jim Kenney about the City of Philadelphia swaps:

-   Who authorized these contracts?
-   Why?
-   Where are the people who signed them now without having access to privately written contracts?

---

[10] CAFR, 2009, p. 62.

[11] CAFR 2012, p. 60.

    Retrieved from http://www.unc.edu/finance/fd/c/docs/2012_cafr.pdf.

CHAPTER 17

The MSU Spartans
Kept On Swapping
Their Money for Nothing

Michigan State University Exhibit 1
Reported Expected Losses on Interest-Rate-Exchange Contracts

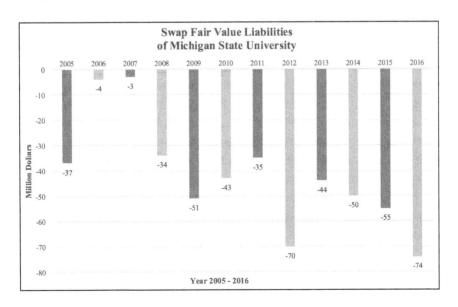

Michigan State University (MSU) ventured into the jungle of the Swap Mania on July 1, 1998. Ambac Financial Services wrote the first contract requiring MSU to pay interest at a fixed rate of 4.604% and receive the Municipal Bond Average Interest Rate (SIFMA).[1] The first annual report to disclose the status of swap contracts was in 2005 because the accounting rules adopted by MSU (Governmental Accounting Standards) did not require making such disclosures earlier. The disclosure reveals a costly experience with interest-rate-exchange (swap) contracts because in 2005, the termination (fair) value of this contract was a loss of $6.7 million, which was about 13% of the notional amount ($52 million). In simple terms, the only benefit the swap contract offered to MSU was the promise, not guarantee, to keep a ceiling of 4.074% for the interest rate on the related debt. MSU could not terminate that contract before its expiry date in 2022 without paying Ambac the entire fair-market value of $6.7 million, which is relatively low as compared to what will come. A losing enforceable, and noncancelable contract written to last one-quarter of a century could not be considered to favor MSU under any circumstances because Ambac did not write a contract to lose on average so that MSU would gain.

Yet, not seeing the dark clouds on the horizon, in 2002, MSU entered into five other swap contracts with Lehman Brothers and UBS Warburg on total reference face (notional) amounts of $163 million. The disclosed expected loss or termination amounts (long-term liabilities) that may result from these interest-rate-exchange contracts amounted to more than $16 million, suggesting no improvement over the contract with Ambac. Seeking more of the same pain, in 2003 and 2007, MSU entered into four other swap contracts, which also started as losers. By 2005, the notional amounts of the 10 contracts in the swap portfolio totaled $415 million, and the total expected future losses (termination amounts) totaled $36 million. These were the expected future losses remaining after paying the banks for the losses attributable to current periods.

In 2007, JPMorgan Chase joined the crowd of big banks selling interest-rate-exchange (swap) contracts to MSU, and the floodgate was wide

---

[1] The SIFMA rate is the weekly average of interest rates of high-grade, variable-rate, tax-exempt municipal bonds compiled and published by the securities industry and Financial Market Association.

open for more swap contracts and more losses. In that year, MSU had 15 swap contracts on notional amounts of $948 million divided almost equally between plain-vanilla, fixed-payer interest-rate-exchange contracts (pay fixed, receive variable) and Basis Swaps to pay an adjustable rate based on one benchmark, such as London Average Interest Rate (LIBOR), and receive an adjustable rate based on another benchmark, such as Municipal Bond Average Interest Rate (SIFMA). This was MSU's portfolio of swaps at the start of the Financial Crisis, and MSU's losses for that year were slightly above $3 million. However, the financial crisis hit MSU just as hard as any other organization, and the liabilities for expected future losses on the interest-rate-exchange (swap) contracts increased to $34 million in 2008 and to $70 million in 2012. From there on, as "MSU Exhibit 1" shows, swap losses got larger, and MSU funds went right down its own swap sinkhole. Clearly, MSU took on more risk by entering into swaps about which the administration knew little and the added risk caught up with them.

It is curious here, as it is elsewhere, to ponder several issues:

- Why would a university enter into Basis Swaps betting on the spread between two interest rates? This type of deal has nothing to do with education or responsible financial management.
- Why would a university of higher learning seem to never display learning from experience? First, it is not necessary to be party to swap contracts to issue variable rate debt. Second, when swap contracts were losing money, why have more of the same?
- Given the open ended uncertainty about the behavior of future interest rates, why would MSU officials enter into binding contracts through the year 2037?
- The form of variable rate used by Michigan State University for bonds was the worst of all; it was the auction rate, just as with the University of North Carolina, the City of Chicago, the Denver Public Schools District, the City of Philadelphia and numerous others. This type of variable rate requires remarketing the bonds once a week and seeking bids for the interest rate the new bondholders wish to earn. The annual fee of weekly remarketing of bonds adds between 0.3% and 0.7% to the stated interest rate in addition to the cost of maintaining a supporting staff.

- Given the constant variation in the auction rate of interest on the bonds, the resulting synthetic rate could not be fixed for more than one week at a time. When plain vanilla swaps are coupled with auction rate bonds, the resulting rate will be a synthetic floating rate.
- If the goal of entering into plain vanilla swaps was the theoretical "fixity" of interest rates, why not issue traditional municipal bonds and avoid (a) taking on more risk and (b) wasting resources on additional underwriting, insurance and legal fees.
- Also, like most others, MSU officials seem to have resisted thinking of the notion of interest rate swaps as "zero-sum" games. Whatever MSU gains would be the loss of the counterparties, big banks, and vice versa. Big banks do not offer free luncheons and are in the business to gain, at least, on average. That is, on average, as a counterparty, MSU will lose.
- Without having access to private information, we may never know what gave MSU officials the overconfidence to think they are capable of managing interest rate risk for three decade ahead?
- Furthermore, the variable rates the university collects from swap contracts could never be the same as the variable rates of interest paid on the bonds because these rates follow different processes and different bases. Under these circumstances, it would be very unlikely to have a match between the rates paid on the debt and the rates received from the related interest-rate-exchange contracts — i.e., the university is exposed to basis risk.
- Additionally, there was no educational mission or policy justification for entering into basis swaps (to pay a variable rate linked to one benchmark and receive a variable rate linked to another benchmark). By entering into these contracts, the university was betting (gambling) on changes in the spread between two benchmarks of interest rates and was committed to carry on that betting for long periods — up to 30 years. However, swapping and gaming have never been the task, role, or mission of any university; it is a job for hedge funds and gamblers.

Just as the cases with all other educational institutions, it is beyond the realm of rational thought to understand how the top officers at any university permitted these contracts to go through.

In fairness to MSU, the same exact issues are commonly shared with a large number of universities whose officials became enthralled by the Swap Mania.

Obsession with Swap Contracts

Like many other educational and nonprofit institutions, once it got into interest-rate-exchange contracts, MSU fell deeper into the swap trap, and the word *swap* became one of the most frequently used words in its audited annual financial statements, as shown in "Michigan State University Exhibit 2."

Michigan State University Exhibit 2
Frequency of Repeating the Word *Swap* in Annual Reports

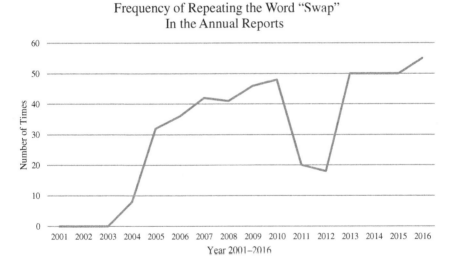

Frequency of Repeating the Word "Swap"
In the Annual Reports

CHAPTER 18

Interest-Rate Swaps Cost Harvard More Than $1.47 Billion

At Harvard you can find some of the most intelligent and skilled people in the institutions of higher learning. Among these highly regarded people are professors who invented and taught some of the mathematical models used for the valuation of financial derivatives. There are also professors who were actually active in affecting the federal government rules that governed, or more accurately failed to govern, Over-the-Counter (OTC) market for financial derivatives. Also at Harvard you find the largest university endowment. In 2008, the university's total endowment was valued at $36 billion, but for a variety of reasons, including the slump in the economy, the value of the endowment dropped to about $26.03 billion by the end of 2009. Of that drop, at least $1.176 billion was due to losses on swap contracts: $497 million of it was paid out in cash and $768 million was recorded as a liability representing the fair value of long-term obligations — the amount of money that must be paid at that time to terminate the swaps.

In December 2009, *Bloomberg* published an article titled "Harvard Interest-Rate-Exchange Contracts Are So Toxic Even Summers Won't Explain." The article was referring to Larry Summers, the president of Harvard University at the time of entering into these contracts, who was also a top academic scholar in financial economics before joining the federal government. However, unlike many academics, he had a unique history with financial derivatives, a history that he probably wishes to be forgotten. Curiously, Harvard University entered into these costly swap contracts when Summers was the president of the university and a member of the governing board of Harvard Management Corporation. In 1998, he became the Deputy Secretary of the Treasury and joined Robert Rubin, the Secretary of the Treasury; Alan Greenspan (chairman of the Federal Reserve Board); and Arthur Levitt (chairman of the Securities and Exchange Commission) to champion the fight against requiring any disclosure or oversight of OTC derivatives. The team fought hard to keep these OTC derivatives privately traded in the dark behind closed doors. He testified before Congress numerous times, and his testimonies reflected an attitude of challenging anyone who sought the slightest regulation of the OTC market, even for a trivial degree of transparency — none whatsoever. In one of his testimonies before Congress, Larry Summers declared that transparency of trades in the OTC market was unnecessary. As Deputy Secretary of the Treasury at the time, he explicitly spelled out his reasoning[1]:

> [T]he parties to these kinds of contract are largely sophisticated financial institutions that would appear to be eminently capable of protecting themselves from fraud and counterparty insolvencies and most of which are already subject to basic safety and soundness regulation under existing banking and Securities and Exchange Commission laws.
>
> [The] derivatives market has grown from nothing to become a highly lucrative industry of major international importance…American OTC derivatives market is second to none. In a few short years it has assumed a major role in our own economy and become a magnet for derivative business from around the world. The dramatic development of this market has occurred on the basis of complex and fragile legal and legislative understandings.

---

[1] U. S. Department of the Treasury, *"Treasury Deputy Secretary Lawrence H. Summers Testimony before the Senate Committee on Agriculture, Nutrition, and Forestry on the CFTC Concept Release*, Press Center, the July 30, 1998.

Ironically, this was the same ammunition that President Clinton had used to side with Greenspan, Levin, Rubin, and Summers in fighting Brooksley Born, the chair of the Commodity Futures Trading Commission (CFTC), to keep her agency totally uninvolved with the OTC market, a position that Clinton came to regret ten years later.[2]

Unlike the rest of the world, it would be a safe bet to say that Summers knew much more about swap contracts and financial derivatives than most people anywhere. However, after moving to the government, the same well-known and respected financial economist elected to ignore the cost of the externalities that these sophisticated OTC derivatives could heap on the unwary and uninvolved human beings. There can be no doubt that he knew that interest-rate-exchange contracts (swaps) are bets (gambles) on the direction of changes in interest rates, resulting in transferring wealth from one party to the counterparty. More specifically, the gains of one party would be exactly the losses of the counterparty and nothing added to the wealth of society; this is what social scientists refer to as a zero-sum game.

Nevertheless, under his leadership, Harvard Management Corporation entered into derivatives contracts on notional amounts over $7.0 billion that ended up costing the university at least $1.47 billion to settle and terminate. The rationale for making those decisions remains locked in private records and will not be known until they are made public. "Harvard Exhibits 1 and 2" show the details of this cost as obtained from the annual reports of Harvard University. It is of import to know that this listing ignores any and all transaction cost.

To reduce the negative impact of these large losses, the university took resource-preserving steps not too much different from the steps that would be taken by a public university facing a state-funding shortfall. In the annual report of 2009, President Faust, the president of

---

[2] James Kwak, "Clinton Confesses: Rubin and Summers Gave Bad (strike that) Excellent Advice on Derivatives," *The Baseline Scenario: What happened to the global economy and what we can do about it*, April 20, 2010.

Retrieved from https://baselinescenario.com/2010/04/20/clinton-rubin-summers-derivatives/.

Harvard Exhibit 1

Losses and Cost of Terminating Swaps: (Interest-Rate-Exchange Contracts)

All Dollar Amounts Are in Million Dollars
(Interest-Rate-Exchange Contracts Table)

Year	Total Notional Amounts	Terminated Interest-Rate-Exchange Contracts (Notional Amounts)	Termination Cost		Annual Cash Settlement of Interest-Rate-Exchange Contracts	Total Cash Payments for Interest-Rate-Exchange Contracts
			Paid in Cash	As a Ratio of Notional Amounts		
2006	$3,524	—	—	—	$18.7	$18.7
2007	$3,534	—	—	—	$7.9	$7.9
2008	$3,525	—	—	—	$15.6	$15.6
2009	$3,141	$1,138	$497	43.6%	$34	$531
2010	$3,823	—	—	—	$55	$55
2011	$2,039	$1,938	$277	14%	$45	$322
2012	$1,076	$756	$134	17.7%	$23	$157
2013	$125	$942	$345	36.6%	$14	$359
2014	?	—	—	—	$3.7	$3.7
Total		$4,772	$1,253	26%	$216.9	$1,469.9

Harvard Exhibit 2
Losses and Cost of Terminating Swaps:
(Interest-Rate-Exchange Contracts)

Harvard University Cash Payments
for Interest Rate Swaps

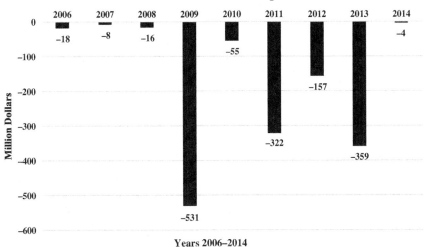

Years 2006–2014

Harvard University (2007–2018), noted the consequences of paying so much money for nothing[3]:

> We have aggressively slowed both new hiring and the filling of vacant positions; we offered voluntary retirement incentives for long-serving staff; we undertook a painful but important round of reductions in force, affecting more than 275 of our colleagues, many of whom had served Harvard ably for years; and we held salaries flat for both faculty and exempt staff. At the same time, we have slowed our ambitious capital plans — most obviously, with regard to our long-term aspirations in Allston. Overall, we expect to reduce by roughly half the capital spending we had originally anticipated for the next several years.

---

[3] Harvard University Financial Report, Fiscal Year 2009.
Retrieved from http://finance.harvard.edu/files/fad/files/2009fullreport.pdf?m=1389978230.

> In fiscal 2009, the University terminated interest-rate-exchange [swap] agreements with a notional value of $1,138.0 million, for which it realized a loss of $497.6 million. A portion of this loss was offset by $85.9 million in gains on the sale of U.S. Treasury bonds which had been purchased to hedge a portion of the liquidity risk associated with the interest-rate-exchange agreements. (36)[4]

That Harvard Management Corporation entered into interest-rate-swap contracts and lost big remains a case worthy of further study, especially since Larry Summers (President of Harvard, 2001–2006) and Robert Rubin, the former secretary of The Treasury, were members of the governing board that approved entering into these contracts. There was more damaging publicity when Peter F. Zhu, a student at Harvard back then, wrote an article in *The Harvard Crimson* about Harvard's engagement in derivatives and the connection with a former Harvard employee named Iris Mack. Having earned a PhD in mathematics from Harvard University and worked in Wall Street, Harvard Management Corporation (HMC) hired Mack as a quantitative analyst. A short period after she was hired, she wrote a letter to her boss displaying fear about the costly consequences of the HMC's risk exposure to the $7.3 billion of financial derivatives in its portfolio.[5] Zhu wrote the following:

> Mack, a derivatives researcher for Enron before coming to HMC, says she was "shocked" by the mishandling and ignorance of derivatives at the HMC international equities division where she worked.

The University fired Mack in July 2002 only a short period following her writing the letter, but all her fears came true in 2008–2009. So, what went wrong with the swap contracts at Harvard? It was not a case of conspiracy, and corruption as we saw with the case of Jefferson County. Nor was it the case of ignorance as we saw in many cases such as the City of

---

[4] Peter Zhu, "HMC Analyst Questions Dismissal: Analyst says she was fired for criticizing controversial investment practices," *The Harvard Crimson*, March 30, 2009.

Retrieved from http://www.thecrimson.com/article/2009/3/31/hmc-analyst-questions-dismissal-after-a/.

[5] Office of the Comptroller of the Currency, Quarterly Derivative Statistics.

Detroit (Chapter 4), the City of Philadelphia or Bay Area Tunnel Authority. Nor was it a case of gullibility and ignorance (although Mack's letter alleges such a qualification) as we saw in public school districts in Pennsylvania, Illinois, California, and Colorado among others around the country. Rather, it appeared to be a case of hubris blinding the governing board of Harvard Management Corporation. The board acted with high confidence, as if it could predict the unpredictable and knew better than to allow big banks and dealers to fool them or a derivatives analyst to criticize them. Both Larry Summers and Robert Rubin should have known that interest-rate-exchange (swap) contracts are bets or instruments of gambling, and one of the two parties to a gambling contract must lose. Yet they had fallen victim to the sales pitch of swap pushers from big banks just the same way as those who were much less informed. With all good intentions, Harvard Management Corporation had simply failed to outfox big banks.

CHAPTER 19

The University of Texas System: A Large State-Run Hedge-Fund-Like in Austin

When it comes to dealing with financial derivatives, the University of Texas System lives up to the mythical image of Texans in terms of pursuing grand and majestic sizes. For the entire University of Texas System,[1] total notional amounts of all financial derivatives in 2015 were over $18.85 billion, of which $3.05 billion were for interest-rate-exchange (swap) contracts alone. "Texas Exhibit 1" presents the notional amounts and fair-market values (termination values) of interest-rate-exchange contracts held by the University of Texas System between 2010 and 2016.[2]

As we know by now, as interest-rate benchmarks increase, the adjustable rates follow, resulting in

(a) The university system owing money to counterparty banks for interest-rate-exchange contracts that require the university system to pay a variable rate and receive a fixed rate,

---

[1]The system consists of UT Arlington, UT Austin, UT Dallas, UT El Paso, UT Permian Basin, UT Rio Grande Valley, UT San Antonio, and UT Tyler.
[2]I could not find active websites for annual reports of earlier periods.

Texas Exhibit 1
Data about Long-term Losses (liabilities) of
Interest-Rate-Exchange Contracts of the University
of Texas System

Year	Notional Amounts of Interest-Rate-Exchange Contracts (In Million Dollars)	Fair-Market Values (In Million Dollars)
2010	$1,968	($233)
2011	$1,989	($406)
2012	$2,394	($341)
2013	$2,534	($331)
2014	$2,704	($216)
2015	$3,052	($261)
2016	$2,892	($352)

Source: Comprehensive Annual Financial Reports.

(b) Banks would owe money to the university system for swap contracts that require the university system to pay a fixed rate and receive a variable rate.

The reverse, of course, would be true if interest rate benchmarks decline.

As "Texas Exhibit 1" reveals, the system had large amounts of expected net long-term loss every year represented by long-term liabilities. Nevertheless, there are other costs hidden from the public. Let us look at some of the sources of these costs.

The University of Texas System has three types of swap contracts. These types are as follows:

- *Type A*: Pay interest at fixed rate and receive interest at adjustable rate.
- *Type B*: Pay interest at adjustable rate and receive interest at fixed rate.
- *Type C*: Pay interest at an adjustable rate using one type of benchmark and receive interest at an adjustable rate based on a different benchmark i.e., Basis Swap.

As of August 31, 2015, the three types had large notional amounts — more than $2.9 billion, as shown in "Texas Exhibit 2."

Texas Exhibit 2
Types of Interest-Rate-Swap Contracts Held by The
University of Texas System

Swap Type	Segment	Pay	Receive	Notional Amounts	In Million Dollars CAFR 2016 Net Fair Value of Assets Minus (Liabilities) (Termination Value)
Type A	1	Fixed Rate	Variable Rate	$1,208	($338)
	2	Fixed Rate	Variable Rate	$504	($16)
Type B	—	Variable Rate	Fixed Rate	$412	($15)
Type C	—	Variable Rate	Variable Rate	$768	$17
Total	—	—	—	$2,892	($352)

Source: Comprehensive Annual Financial Report, 2016.
Retrieved from https://www.utsystem.edu/sites/default/files/documents/Consolidated%20Annual%20
Financial%20Report%3A%20FY%202016/consolidated-audit-afr-2016.pdf.

Typically each swap contract requires several costly arrangements, which constitute what is called "transaction cost," that are excluded from almost all reported comparative analyses of costs and are not disclosed to the public. The picture in Texas Exhibit 2 raises questions about efficiency, effectiveness, and competence. Most of these interest-rate-exchange contracts were claimed to be hedging cash-flow risk.[3]

> The System has entered into interest rate swap agreements with various counterparties, all of which are highly rated financial institutions, to manage various risks associated with the System's debt programs.
>
> **Interest rate**. interest-rate-exchange contracts determined to be hedging derivatives are designated as cash flow hedges. Hedging

---

[3]The University of Texas System Annual Financial Report — Primary Financial Statements Fiscal Year 2015, p. 29.
    Retrieved from https://www.utsystem.edu/sites/default/files/documents/Consolidated%
20Annual%20Financial%20Report%3A%20FY%202015/consolidatedafr15.pdf.

derivative assets and hedging derivative liabilities are recorded on the System's statement of net position. Under hedge accounting, for derivatives that are determined to be effective, changes in the fair value of hedging derivatives are considered to be deferred inflows and reported as hedging derivative assets (for hedging derivatives with positive termination values) or deferred outflows and reported as hedging derivative liabilities (for hedging derivatives with negative termination values).

Changes in the fair value of derivatives that are not effective are recorded as net increase (decrease) in the fair value of investments in the statement of revenues, expenses and changes in net position.

By examining the composition of interest-rate-exchange contracts, two basic questions arise:

- First, why did the university have both types — *Type A* (pay fixed, receive variable) and *Type B* (pay variable, receive fixed) — of interest-rate-swap contracts?

  In particular, when the interest rate increases, the system would "gain" with *Type A* but would be in a "loss" position with *Type B* and vice versa. The implications of this contrast are important because each *type of these two swap contracts is effectively hedging the cash-flow risk of the other type of swap* up to the notional amounts of $412 million. More specifically, the combined amounts of interest-rate-exchange contracts are not hedging any cash-flow risk inherent in the related bonds, securities, or any other activity of the university system. *Type A* and *Type B* swap contracts offset each other. That is, they are hedges of *the cash-flow risk of each other.* Why enter into offsetting contracts if each swap contract requires paying significant underwriting fee, insurance, fees for legal and financial advisers, and a host of other embedded costs? It looks like the university created risk exposure by entering into some contracts then followed years later by entering into other contracts to hedge the risk exposure of the first type. Having two large portfolios of interest-rate swaps where one hedges the risk of the other meant that all the related transaction cost and expenses were incurred for no benefit in managing other risks facing the university. This is the ultimate nightmare of efficiency experts, who would have the right to shout, "What a waste!" However, the University of Texas System is not alone; Shands Hospital of the University of Florida has a similar situation to a much lesser extent.

- Second, what does *Type C* of interest-rate-exchange contracts (pay variable, receive variable) offer for risk management?

To pay interest at Municipal Bond Average Interest Rate (SIFMA and receive interest at London Average interest Rate (LIBOR) is an expensive way of structuring what seems to be a Basis Swap betting against interest-rate spreads — the difference between two benchmark rates of interest.[4] Basis Swaps could serve as a way of modifying the cash flow of other types of interest-rate-exchange contracts (such as *Type A* in this case), and, if it was not for gambling, this might have been the incentive of administrators at the University of Texas System. Most of the swap contracts that required paying fixed and receiving variable (*Type A*) used the Municipal Bond Average Interest Rate (SIFMA) for the *variable leg*. If the system administrators wished to change the *variable leg* from Municipal Bond

---

[4] Same as "IU Health Exhibit 3," showing the spread between LIBOR and SIFMA.

Historical SIFMA vs. 67% of 6M LIBOR

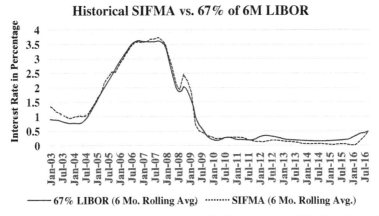

—— 67% LIBOR (6 Mo. Rolling Avg) ········ SIFMA (6 Mo. Rolling Avg.)

Note: The London Average Rate (LIBOR) is taxable, but the Average Municipal Bond Rate (SIFMA) is not. To have equivalence, SIFMA is compared with 65% or 67% of LIBOR.

Average Interest Rate (SIFMA) to London Average Interest Rate (LIBOR), they could take one of two actions: (a) terminate the existing interest-rate-exchange contracts or (b) enter into Basis Swaps to pay Municipal Bond Average Interest Rate (SIFMA) and receive London Average Interest Rate (LIBOR). Both approaches entail high transaction costs, but the university system administrators seem to have opted for the latter approach. Thus, the flow of cash payments would be as presented in "Texas Exhibit 3," showing the system receiving Municipal Bond Average Interest Rate (SIFMA) from one type of interest-rate-exchange contract (*Type A*) and paying it to another type of swap (*Type C*), ending up with London Average Interest Rate (LIBOR) as the net receivable variable rate.

Nevertheless, this behavior raises two questions:

(a) How much economic advantage could arise from this modification?
(b) Was that advantage large enough to justify the added transaction cost and risk of entering into one more swap contract?

It is doubtful that this circle of contracts was useful because any economic advantages that may be obtained from a Basis Swap are, by construction, uncertain. The dual-swap idea is interesting but costly and highly controversial for nonprofits. As we see in footnote 4, the spread between Municipal Bond Average Interest Rate (SIFMA) and 67% of London Average Interest Rate (LIBOR) is very small in terms of basis points and is not stable in one direction or another — sometimes SIFMA is greater than 67% of LIBOR, and the reverse occurs at other times.[5] Thus, in the dual swap, the only way the university system comes out on top would be if Municipal Bond Average Interest Rate (SIFMA) declines or if London Average Interest Rate (LIBOR) increases. In contrast, the university system would be penalized if SIFMA increases and LIBOR declines. In other words, the university system is simply gambling with the public's money.

---

[5] Note that SIFMA is a tax-free index, while LIBOR is a taxable rate, and the conventional wisdom found that 67% of LIBOR traces SIFMA almost exactly.

Texas Exhibit 3
Dual Interest-Rate-Exchange Contracts
of the University of Texas System

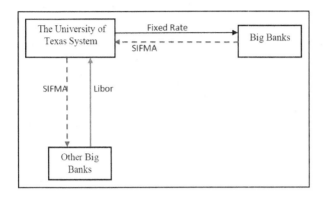

The net result:

(a) Paying and receiving Municipal Bond Average Interest Rate (SIFMA) is a wash
(b) Paying a fixed rate
(c) Receiving London Average Interest Rate (LIBOR)
(d) Paying three underwriting and related fees:
1. For the variable-rate bond
2. For the fixed-payer swap
3. For the basis swap

While the cost of entering into swap contracts are not discussed, evidence of the high cost of dealing with derivatives may shed some light on the system's policy. Consider, for example, the high costs and low benefits the university system reported for trading in two types of option contracts[6]:

The System has purchased options on ten-year constant maturity interest-rate-exchange contracts, with expiries ranging from five to seven

---

[6]The University of Texas System, Consolidated Financial Statements for the Years Ended August 31, 2015 and 2014, December 18, 2015, p. 40.

Retrieved from https://www.utsystem.edu/sites/default/files/documents/Consolidated%20Annual%20Financial%20Report%3A%20FY%202015/auditedafr15.pdf.

years, as insurance against possible future increases in inflation. As of August 31, 2015, these options had a notional value of $10,000,000,000 and a fair value [termination value] of $33,376. As of August 31, 2014, these options had a notional value of $10,000,000,000 and a fair value [termination value] of $1,371,292. The risk of loss on these options is limited to *the premiums paid by the System upon the purchase of the options, which totaled $57,013,750 as of August 31, 2015 and 2014.* [Emphasis added]

The System also purchased puts on the Japanese Yen, with expiries ranging from one to two years, as insurance against the possibility of a downturn in the Japanese economy. As of August 31, 2015, the puts had a notional value of $1,000,000,000 with a fair value [termination value] of $55,405. As of August 31, 2014, the puts had a notional value of $1,000,000,000 with a fair value [termination value] of $540,179. The risk of loss on these options is limited to *the premiums paid by the System upon the purchase of the options, which totaled $10,727,217 and $7,452,315 as of August 31, 2015 and 2014, respectively.*

To elaborate on this unusual relationship, the university system did the following:

(a) Purchased options[7] and paid $57 million for the premiums, but the options had fair (termination) values equal to $0.33 million in 2015 and $1.27 million in 2014. The net loss in 2014 was $55.73 million.
(b) Purchased options to sell Japanese yen and paid $18 million for premiums, but the fair value of these options was $0.54 million. The loss was $17.46 million. Because these options were written for two years, the observed data suggest the absence of hope in making profits high enough to cover the premium.

Both of these transactions are highly costly and perhaps speak volumes for the managerial talents at the system. Unfortunately, no

---

[7] A Swaption is a contract sold by one party (Party A) for a premium. The contract gives the counterparty (Party B) the option, i.e., the choice, to require the first party (Party A) to enter into a swap contract. If so, Party B would be obliged to enter into the swap agreement.

information was provided about the transaction cost of entering into interest rate swaps.

Obsession with Swaps and Other Derivatives

More than many other nonprofit entity, the University of Texas system's obsession with interest-rate-exchange contracts and other financial derivatives has made their annual financial statements resemble the financial statements of a hedge fund. We see all types of derivatives noted with high frequency in the annual reports. Furthermore, the signs of obsession with derivatives may be gleaned from the number of times related terms were repeated. As Texas Exhibit 4 shows, "derivatives were cited 283 in the 2015 report and 273 in the 2017 report, while the word *education* was repeated 46 and 28 times for these two years, respectively.

Texas Exhibit 4
Frequency of Using Derivatives Terms in the
Annual Reports of the University of Texas System

Repeated Financial Derivatives — Related Words in Annual Reports and the word *Education*	Sample of Annual Reports			
	2011	2014	2015	2016
Swap	119	106	110	111
Derivative	101	109	110	116
Option	48	62	63	46
Total Number of Times Mentioning Derivatives	**268**	**277**	**283**	**273**
Total Number of Times the word *Education was cited*	**25**	**53**	**46**	**28**

Cases in Wealth Transfer from Health-Care Organizations to Big Banks

On Auction Interest Rate

"Auction Rate Securities ("ARS") are clever creations of investment bankers that enable borrowers to incur long-term debt at short-term rates and lenders to obtain the safety and liquidity of money markets at a higher return. As could be expected with clever creations of investment bankers . . . the incredible benefits conferred on the issuers of, and investors in, these instruments turn out to be too good to be true."

Robin Smith. "Southern Discomfort: An Examination of the Financial Crisis in Jefferson County, Alabama, Alabama. Houston Business and Tax Law Journal. 2010.

The 2010–2011 final report of the civil grand jury of Alameda County, California, included the jury's opinion of the auction rate condition. It stated,

■ The use of Convertible Auction Rate Securities [bonds] exposed the district to poorly understood, complicated, and expensive financial risks.

Source: "The Civil Grand Jury of Alameda County CA, Final Report 2010–2011," June 27, 2011, pp. 147–148.

Retrieved from https://www.scribd.com/document/58911903/Alameda-County-Grand-Jury-Report-Final-2011.

CHAPTER 20

Indiana University Health: A Case of Derivatives Abuse from the Midwest

Indiana University health-related units were incorporated in 2011 as a non-profit private corporation named Indiana University Health, Inc. (IU Health). IU Health owns and is affiliated with more than 20 hospitals and health centers throughout the state of Indiana, including the Methodist Hospital, Indiana University Hospital, and Riley Hospital for Children. In addition, IU Health provides the teaching facilities for Indiana University's medical school. Like most nonprofit entities, IU Health obtains part of its funding from the municipal-bond market. It maintained the tradition of issuing bonds at fixed coupon rates until big banks promoted the presumed, and hopeful benefits of lowering the cost of borrowing when a variable-rate bond is coupled with swap contracts. Swap dealers and underwriters from big banks eagerly helped IU Health do both: issue variable-rate bonds and concurrently enter into swap contracts to pay fixed and receive adjustable.

Was it true that IU Health paid $8 million in cash to cover loss on the swap contract in its first year? Yes, this appears to be the case, but that was only a small start of a road to financial adversity. In connection with these interest-rate-exchange contracts, IU Health, Inc. paid in cash $19.9 million in 2010, $17.7 million in 2011, and $21.9 million in 2014, but collected $11.4 million in 2013 in connection with swap contracts. These amounts were the annual settlement of the cash flow difference between the payable fixed rate and the receivable variable rate. They also represented a harbinger of what to come.

IU Health began issuing bonds at <u>auction rates</u>, the highly risky type of variable rate. The interest rates for auction-rate bonds are reset either every week or every 35 days as the bonds are remarketed, and new bondholders bid on purchasing them at reset interest rates. This was a highly risky strategy because the issuer of the bonds, which was IU Health in this case, would constantly bear the cost of changes in both market risk and own credit risk. Further, remarketing of bonds weekly does not guarantee finding new bondholders who were willing to price the bonds.[1] When remarketing a bond issue does not result in a successful bid, typically the default interest rate is assigned to the bond. Internally, uncertainty must have filled the administration hall; it could not properly plan or budget for the money to be paid as interest on the related bonds.

More interestingly, financial institutions invented the auction rate to benefit themselves because big banks charged between 0.3% and 0.7% of the face amount of the bond as a remarketing fee. This process of using auction rates to set the bond's variable rates began in the 1980s before the Financial Crisis but collapsed with the crisis in 2008. However, weekly or even daily resetting of variable interest rates continues to this day, except that the reset would be indexed to a benchmark interest rate rather than being determined by Dutch auctions.

This is the story of adjustable interest rates from the bond side, but the story of adjustable interest rates receivable from the floating leg of swap contracts is different. The variable rates that IU Health received from big banks in connection with interest-rate-exchange contracts were typically indexed either to the London Average Interest Rate (LIBOR) or to the Municipal Bond Average Interest Rate (SIFMA). While LIBOR is determined daily by big banks, voting (see Chapter 32) and SIFMA is determined weekly (from market transactions), the index used to adjust the rates on the swaps is reset less frequently (quarterly or semiannually) than the

---

[1] The City of Chicago; Jefferson County, Alabama; and many others have faced this same problem. When the bonds could not be priced, the new interest rate was reset at the high default rate.

reset of the rates for the bonds. Accordingly, the processes and times of setting interest rates for swap contracts were different in frequency and timing of setting interest rates on the related bonds. This inconsistency between determining the receivable and payable variable rates exposed IU Health to another type of risk known as "basis risk", which is the risk of receiving less or paying more.[2] As a result, one of the conditions necessary to achieve lower borrowing costs could not be satisfied.

As of June 30, 2011, IU Health, Inc. had entered into two types of interest-rate-exchange (swap) contracts, and on December 31, 2014, the corporation reported having 19 interest-rate-exchange contracts on notional (face value or principal) amounts of $2.31 billion. These contracts were of two types:

A. *The first type is plain-vanilla interest-rate-exchange contracts to pay fixed and receive variable.* In a plain-vanilla swap, IU Health pays amounts of cash calculated based on a pre-specified fixed interest rate and receives other amounts of cash based on adjustable rates of interest. In the new finance jargon, the fixed payment is called the fixed leg, and the adjustable payment is called the floating leg. For this type of interest-rate-exchange contract (pay fixed and receive adjustable), financial engineers had devised a model that would calculate the starting rates such that the present values of the fixed and floating legs would be equal at the time of initiating (writing) the contract. Because of this initial equality in values, neither party invests money upfront.[3] Accordingly, the value of the swap contract at inception is zero.[4]

Up until 2011, IU Health had six plain vanilla (pay fixed and receive adjustable) swap contracts on total face (notional) amounts of $245 million. These contracts were losing money and had created an

---

[2]This risk is called basis risk, which means, in simple terms, that IU Health is facing the risk of receiving a lower interest rate than it is paying.

[3]This is the typical case for plain-vanilla swaps. Any money paid up front is in effect a loan and treated in accounting as such.

[4]This is the common case. However, as noted in chapter 1, big banks also pay up-front money to encourage officials of nonprofit entities to agree to the terms of the swap contract. That up-front money is an investment for the bank and a loan for the nonprofit entity. A swap contract that pays up-front money has two components: a loan and a derivative. At inception, the value of the derivative (swap) remains to be zero.

expected long-term liability of $156 million (about 64% of total notional amounts) by the end of the 2010 fiscal year. These amounts were the expected long-term losses, while the recurring short-term losses were settled every year. So far, other than being in a loss position, the most troublesome aspect was the complexity of the contracts themselves. However, in retrospect, the behavior of the officials at IU Health is inexplicable; in 2011 they became entangled in more losing transactions when IU Health entered into five more interest-rate-exchange (swap) contracts on total reference (notional, face) amounts of $240 million. At that time, all plain-vanilla swap contracts were losing big money, which raises a couple of questions:

o   Why did the officials sign on to more interest-rate-exchange contracts when IU Health was paying an average fixed rate of more than 4.15% and receiving only 0.73%, which was LIBOR interest rate at the time of signing the new contracts?

o   If the first six contracts were generating large losses, why commit to purchasing five more contracts of the same type?

Unfortunately, no one was willing to respond to these questions.

IU Health Exhibit 1
Expected Future Swap Losses Reported
as Long-term Liabilities

Year	Noncurrent Liability (losses) in Million Dollars
2010	$156
2011	$229
2012	$199
2013	$163
2014	$155
2015	$125

A Technical Note: These amounts are the reported noncurrent liability arising from swap contracts after making correction for the amounts reported by IU Health for the valuation allowance, which IU Health incorrectly called CVA.

"IU Health Exhibit 1" shows the size of reported expected long-term swap losses from 2010 ($156 million) to 2015 ($125 million) after terminating some contracts, as will be discussed later in this chapter. The year 2011 was unique: losses peaked to $229 million. Clearly there was no evidence that entering into swap contracts had lowered the cost of debt as promised. Furthermore, there was no evidence that such contracts had helped IU Health to better manage interest-rate risk one way or another.

B. *The second type of swaps is the variable-for-variable interest-rate-exchange contracts* (basis swap). In this type of contract, IU Health was required to pay an adjustable interest rate based on a specified index and receive another adjustable interest rate based on another index. The two indexes used in this case were the London Average Interest Rate (LIBOR) and the Municipal Bond Average Interest Rate (SIFMA). Although these two benchmarks are determined differently, both rates reflect the changes in market conditions and move together with small differences between them that could change from one direction to another. The financial community's name for that difference is *the spread*. "IU Health Exhibit 2" shows the movement of these two indexes for the period from 1990 to 2015; IU Health agreed to pay the interest rate shown by the blue curve and receive the interest rate shown by the red curve. IU Health was betting on having the spread move in its favor. The graphed pattern of these two indexes shows the spread was not always in one direction because different external forces set up the movements of the indexes differently. The benchmark LIBOR is set up by polling a designated panel of large banks every day as we discuss in Chapter 32, while the benchmark Municipal Bond Average Interest Rate (SIFMA) is determined by bond markets for a seven-day trading window. Typically the result of betting on the spread is not different from betting in a casino; it is gambling on the unknown and uncertain behavior. Just like a casino, IU Health won sometimes and lost at other times. Other than having cash-flow implications, basis-swap contracts have nothing to do with health care, education or risk management in any shape or form.

Of late, officials at IU Health took actions to suggest they may have realized that being on the losing side may not end before the contractual

IU Health Exhibit 2
The Movements of London Average Interest Rate (LIBOR) and Municipal Bond Average Interest Rate (SIFMA)

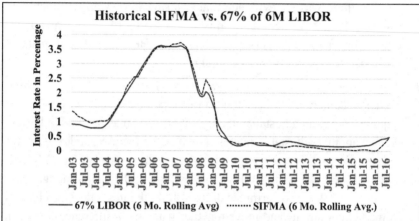

Historical SIFMA vs. 67% of 6M LIBOR

——— 67% LIBOR (6 Mo. Rolling Avg)   ········ SIFMA (6 Mo. Rolling Avg.)

Note: The London Average Interest Rate (LIBOR) is taxable, but the Municipal Bond Average Interest Rate (SIFMA) is generated from trading in tax-exempt securities. To have equivalence, SIFMA is compared with a fraction of LIBOR, which is 65% in this graph.

The IU Health Basis-Swap Gamble:

If *LIBOR* increases more than *SIFMA*, IU Health loses.

If *SIFMA* increases more than *LIBOR*, IU Health wins.

Note: The London Average Interest Rate (LIBOR) is taxable, but the Municipal Bond Average Interest Rate (SIFMA) is not. To have equivalence, SIFMA is compared with 65% or 70% of London Average Interest Rate (LIBOR).

maturities of all swap contracts in 2033. If nothing was done, IU Health could stay on the losing track for 20 more years, and officials began to take some actions to stem the tide of losses. In 2014, they terminated basis swaps on notional amounts of $309 million. The termination brought to IU Health a total gain of a mere $44 (forty four dollars). They also negotiated the deferral of payments on some contracts for three years. Nevertheless, IU Health exposure to interest rate risk remained high.

Obsessed with Swaps

With all the visible and painfully large amounts of losses, the annual reports of IU Health revealed what appears to be an obsession with interest-rate swaps. "IU Health Exhibit 3" shows that the word *swap* was repeated in annual reports more than the <u>total</u> number of repetitions of more functionally-relevant terms like *treatment*, *medicine*, and *education*.

IU Health Exhibit 3
Frequency of Disclosing the Word "*Swap*"

Terminology	Frequency of Repetition in the Financial Statements			
	Year			
	2011	2012	2014	2015
Swap	**40**	**46**	**44**	**54**
Treatment	5	6	1	1
Medicine	19	18	16	14
Education	18	16	19	17

A Word of Prudence from the Deep South

On June 15, 1999, John Cornyn, the attorney general of the State of Texas, argued against allowing government entities to be a party to swap contracts, reasoning that they would be facing both the upside and the downside risk and that "they do not need to have swaps to sell bonds." His specific ruling states:

> "A hospital district is not authorized to execute an interest rate hedge contract that entitles the district to receive a lump sum if market interest rates rise in relation to the interest rate on certain outstanding district bonds but that requires the district to pay out a lump sum if interest rates fall.
>
> ....
>
> Because execution of the interest rate hedge contract is unnecessary to effectuate issuance of bonds or refunding bonds, it is the opinion of this office that the district is not authorized to execute such a contract."
> (Opinion No. JC0068)

Source: John Cornyn, Office of the Attorney General of the State of Texas, "Opinion No. JC-0068.

Re: Whether a hospital district is authorized to execute a contract to hedge against interest rate fluctuations," June 15, 1999.

Retrieved from https://texasattorneygeneral.gov/opinions/opinions/49cornyn/op/1999/pdf/jc0068.pdf.

CHAPTER 21

The University of California Health System: A Case of Derivatives Abuse from the West

On November 15, 2012, the board of regents of the University of California convened as a "Committee of the Whole" in order to permit members of the public an opportunity to address university-related matters (see Exhibit 1). At that meeting, Charley Eaton (a graduate student at the University of California–Berkeley back then) referred to a report he had coauthored with five other graduate students in relationship to the amounts of money the University of California System (UC System) was paying to big banks for interest-rate swaps.[1] The report is titled *Swapping*

---

[1] Charley Eaton, Jacob Habinek, Mukul Kumar, Tamera Lee Stover, Alex Roehrkasse and Jeremy Thompson, "*Swapping Our Future: How Students and Taxpayers are Funding Risky UC Borrowing and Wall Street Profits,*" Department of Sociology at the University of California at Berkeley, 2012.

Retrieved from https://publicsociology.berkeley.edu/publications/swapping/swapping.pdf.

California Exhibit 1
University students' demonstration in 2012.
Wearing orange colored cloths and calling themselves
"Prisoners sentenced to debt."

Melody Petersen, "UC Lost Millions on Interest-Rate Bets," *The Orange County Register*, February 24, 2014.

Based on image at http://www.ocregister.com/2014/02/24/uc-lost-millions-on-interest-rate-bets/.

Our Future: How Students and Taxpayers Are Funding Risky UC Borrowing and Wall Street Profits. The minutes of the meeting report the concern raised by Eaton[2]:

> Mr. Charlie Eaton, UC Berkeley graduate student, expressed concern that, despite the passage of Proposition 30, the UC budget presumed a 24 percent tuition increase over the upcoming four years. He stated that a report he authored with other colleagues, "Swapping Our Future: How Students and Taxpayers Are Funding Risky UC Borrowing and

---

[2]The Regents of the University of California Meeting as a Committee of the Whole, November 15, 2012.

Retrieved from http://regents.universityofcalifornia.edu/minutes/2012/cw15.pdf.

Wall Street Profits," had recommended that the University renegotiate interest rate swaps or litigate against the banks holding the interest rate swaps. He expressed concern that the Board had not taken action. Mr. Eaton stated that the San Francisco Asian Art Museum saved $40 million by renegotiating its interest rate swaps [with JPMorgan Chase]. Mr. Eaton stated that several large banks were under investigation for illegally manipulating interest rates; he urged the Board to consider litigation against these institutions.

The report shows how the officials of the university had fallen for the lure of dancing with the swaps in a way not much different from the highly costly dance of the City of Detroit; the City of Chicago; the City of Philadelphia; Indiana University Health, Inc.; and many others. The baiting process followed the same well-orchestrated ritual: telling the officials at UC System to deviate from the tradition of issuing municipal bonds at fixed rates (plain-vanilla bonds) and issue adjustable-rate bonds instead, coupled with entering into interest-rate-exchange (swap) contracts to pay fixed and receive adjustable. The representatives of big banks made the same promises as they did elsewhere: the combination of the two contracts would result in synthetic (artificial) fixed rates that may lower the cost of borrowing and help manage interest-rate risk. However, such a mythical objective did not materialize. Melody Petersen, the certified public accountant and staff writer with the *Orange County Register*, noted in a 2014 article that the[3]

> University accountants estimate the 10-campus system will lose as much as $136 million over the next 34 years that it is locked into the deals. Those potential losses would be reduced only if interest rates start [were] to rise.
>
> Already officials have been forced to unwind a contract at UC Davis, requiring the university to pay $9 million in termination fees and

---

[3]Melody Petersen, "UC Lost Millions on Interest-Rate Bets," *The Orange County Register*, February 24, 2014.

Retrieved from http://www.ocregister.com/2014/02/24/uc-lost-millions-on-interest-rate-bets/.

other costs to several banks. *That sum would have covered the tuition and fees of 682 undergraduates for a year.* [Emphasis added]

The university is facing the losses at a time when it is under tremendous financial stress. Administrators have tripled the cost of tuition and fees in the past 10 years, but still can't cover escalating expenses. Class sizes have increased. Families have been angered by the rising price of attending the university, which has left students in deeper debt.

The Department of Sociology report "*Swapping Our Future*" directs attention to the compromising effect of using interest-rate swap contracts by diverting the funds from education to pay banks for these contracts. The authors write, "UC [University of California] management has more than doubled the university's debt burden from $6.9 Billion in May 2007 to $14.3 Billion at the end of 2011...Since 2003, UC's swap agreements have cost the university nearly $57 million and could cost another $200 million." The report is critical of the state government for allowing the university system to issue its own bonds starting in 2003 instead of continuing to go through the state system, as had been the practice in the past. The resulting autonomy, they claimed, eliminated the monitoring role of the state and removed the guardrails that protected the universities in the system from the aggressive sales force of big banks. The study goes on to say, "What is clear is that over this period, big banks marketed interest rates swaps to public organizations like UC as a safe way to borrow more money less expensively." (p. 5)

The accountant and Bay reporter Melody Petersen wrote in the *Orange County Register* a brief history of swap contracts at UC System.[4] She went on to describe a peculiar linkage between two senior employees at Lehman Brothers, John Augustine and Peter Taylor, and the UC System in 2003 when the state permitted individual agencies to issue its own bonds unchecked[5]:

The university began using interest-rate swaps in 2003 after John Augustine, a Lehman Bros. banker, advised officials of their potential advantages.

---

[4] Charley Eaton, *et al. Swapping Our Future.*
[5] Melody Petersen, "UC Lost Millions," February 24, 2014.

Augustine also told officials about "new variable rate borrowing products," according to the minutes, and how the use of interest-rate swaps could save the university money.

Later in 2009, the UC System hired Peter Taylor of Lehman Brothers as its chief financial officer, who then defended the decision to enter into interest-rate-exchange contracts with Lehman Brothers, his former employer. These were contracts of which he was keenly aware, if not involved, while being employed at Lehman.

> In interviews, Peter Taylor, the university's chief financial officer, defended the decisions. He said he was confident that interest rates will rise in coming years, reversing what the deals have lost.
> "We have a long-term view," he said.

In a hopelessly defensive move, Taylor went on further by writing a letter to the *Orange County Register* claiming that the *Register* was incorrect[6]:

> "To suggest that the university has made 'risky bets on the advice of Wall Street bankers' is unsubstantiated by the facts and portrays either ignorance or a willful disregard for the truth," Taylor wrote in the letter.
> Chris Knap, investigations editor for the OC Register, said Taylor's letter mischaracterized the story. He added that numbers came directly from financial statements that the reporter was trained to interpret. The reporter, Melody Petersen, is trained as a certified public accountant and audited companies, local governments and universities before becoming a journalist.

Taylor joined other defenders of big banks by noting that, if all went as planned, the net cost of funding debt to the university would be lower

---

[6]Fiona Kirby, "UC CFO refutes accusation of interest rate swap losses," *Daily Bruin*, February 28, 2014.

Retrieved from http://dailybruin.com/2014/02/28/uc-cfo-refutes-accusation-of-interest-rate-swap-losses/.

than the cost of traditional fixed-rate bonds. Also, like many others, Taylor's argument bypassed three major questions:

(i)   Would the cost of borrowing be higher if UC issued bonds at variable rates and never entered into swaps? Listen to the Word of Prudence from the Deep South: swap contracts are not needed to issue bonds at variable rates.
(ii) Would the cost of borrowing really drop by entering into interest-rate-exchange (swap) contracts if all the related transaction costs (such as underwriting fees, insurance cost, legal fees, advisers' fees and the cost of remarketing) were included in making the comparison?
(iii) Would entering into interest-rate swaps lower the cost of debt if the variable interest received from the swap contract was persistently lower than the variable interest payable to bondholders?

The document *"Swapping Our Future"* provides another glimpse of Taylor's connection[7]:

The UCLA medical center swap — which has already cost UC $23 million — was sold to UC in 2007 by Lehman's/Barclays during UC CFO [chief financial officer] Peter Taylor's tenure with that firm. At the time, Taylor also served on the board of the UCLA Foundation where he concluded his term as Board Chair just two years earlier. While Deutsche Bank took over the swap after the collapse of Lehman's, Taylor's ties to the swap's origination raise questions about what consideration has been given to renegotiation. This swap also deserves attention because Lehman's served both as the broker for the bond and the counterparty for the swap, a practice that was not allowed for mortgage derivatives until deregulation under the Glass–Steagall Act of 1999. (Glass–Steagal Act was enacted in 1933. The repeal of a significant part of the act was in 1999.)

In other words, *Swapping Our Future* hints at the presence of two of the Four Derivatives Sins described by Loomis: arrogance and lies. Or was it a hint of corruption? That remains to be seen; the class-action suits filed by the

---

[7] *Swapping Our Future*, p. 10.

UC board of regents against big banks are still running their course in the halls of justice. However, a former employee of the former swap king, Lehman Brothers, who later became an insider at the University of California System, seems to have pulled the shades over the eyes of the university's financial administrators. Apparently, all parties seem to have forgotten the fact that, in offering these deals, big banks were motivated solely by their own self-interest. Because in this bilateral contract only one party of the interest rate swaps wins and the counterparty loses,[8] the gains of big banks would equal the losses of the university and vice versa. It is, therefore, improbable that big banks would design such contracts with the expectation of losing. Just as with many others, the University of California and its medical centers joined the Swap Mania and fell into the big banks' swap trap.[9]

> Because of swap agreements, UC has missed out on refinancing opportunities, instead continuing to pay high fixed rates. Ironically, rock-bottom interest rates have greatly increased UC's relative debt servicing burden despite the fact that the cost of new borrowing remains at record lows. Losses on the swaps associated with the UC Davis medical center were so significant that UC paid $6.8 million in termination fees when it refinanced the underlying bonds. The swaps associated with medical centers at UCSF and UCLA are projected to create combined annual losses of $9 million. The projected total loss from UC's engagement in interest-rate swaps is more than $200 million.

In addition, it really does not matter what anyone asserts about hypothetical cost savings if we just look at the facts. The financial statements of the University of California provide information about the increased cost of debt after using swap contracts — the net payments of the combination of adjustable-rate bonds and the net interest cost of the swap. At the start of January 2007, an administrative entity of the medical centers of the UC System named "Pooled Revenue Bonds" issued $537.3 million in revenue bonds — $441.2 million of fixed interest rate and $96.2 million of variable interest rate. The fixed-rate bonds paid an

---

[8]This is what economists call a zero-sum game. In all cases however, the counterparty to the dealer bears most of the transaction cost.

[9]*Swapping Our Future*, pp. 5–6.

average of 4.6%. The variable-rate bonds were coupled with swap contracts aimed at achieving the lower net artificial (synthetic) fixed rate of 3.6%. The noncancelable swap contract was written to terminate after two decades. However, that relationship between interest rates did not last more than six months. In July of the same year, the fixed rate for the conventional municipal bond dropped from 4.6% to 4.3%, whereas the net artificial (synthetic) rate for the combination of variable-rate bond and interest-rate-exchange contract had increased from 3.6% to 4.7%.[10]

	Fixed interest rate of traditional municipal bonds	Synthetic fixed rate on the combination of variable-rate bonds and interest-rate swaps
In January 2007	4.6% (average rate)	3.6%
In June 2007	4.3%	4.7%

These transactions raise the question: If the University of California Medical Center could have borrowed money using conventional (plain-vanilla) bonds at a fixed interest rate of 4.3% or even 4.6%, why did it go through the two-step approach of issuing bonds at a variable rate and incur high transaction cost to fix the rate artificially? Each step costs a significant amount of money for underwriting and insuring and other items of irrecoverable transaction cost. In addition, the package of variable rate bond and plain vanilla swap exposed the university system to a combination of risks that were not well articulated or understood. For example, writing noncancelable swap agreements for 20 or 30 years deprives the system of the flexibility of responding to changing market conditions or terminating the swap contracts at the appropriate times.

Initially the plan intended to have the amounts of cash received from the floating leg of swap contracts match the amounts of cash payable to bondholders. However, as time passed, the situation got worse, and that

---

[10]The University of California Annual Financial Report 2007–2008.

Retrieved from http://finreports.universityofcalifornia.edu/index.php?file=07-08/pdf/fullreport_08.pdf.

was not to be because these hospital administrators forgot to factor in three critical issues: insurance, taxes, and remarketing fees for resetting interest rates. In particular,

(a) Municipal bonds are tax-free, and if they were taxable, the Treasury Department would provide a subsidy equal to about 25% of paid interest;
(b) The swap contracts are taxable;
(c) The adjustable-rate municipal bonds were issued at the highly risky Auction Rate, for which the variable rate was to be reset weekly; and
(d) The direct cost of resetting the auction rate varied between 0.3% and 0.7% a year, which was never factored into the elements of cost comparison. There is, in addition, the indirect cost of hiring staff and supporting personnel to oversee the process.

These conditions create disparity between the rates received from swap contracts and the variable rates paid to bondholders, exposing the university to basis risk — the risk of receiving less and paying more. The UC Medical Center appears to have recognized this risk exposure only one year after entering into swaps in 2007:[11]

Basis Risk There is a risk that the basis for the variable payment received on interest rate swaps will not match the variable payment on the bonds that exposes the University to basis risk whenever the interest rates on the bonds are reset. The interest rate on the bonds is a tax-exempt interest rate, while the basis of the variable receipt on the interest rate swaps is taxable. Tax-exempt interest rates can change without a corresponding change in the LIBOR rate due to factors affecting the tax-exempt market, which do not have a similar effect on the taxable market.

The fixed interest rate the University of California System had paid in connection with interest-rate-exchange contracts during the period between

---

[11] University of California. Annual Financial Report 2013–2014.
    Retrieved from http://finreports.universityofcalifornia.edu/index.php?file=13-14/pdf/fullreport-1314.pdf.

2007 and 2011 varied between 3.185% for the University of California at San Diego and 4.6873% for the medical center at UCLA. Meanwhile, the average adjustable rate the University of California had collected from the swaps was close to or less than 1%. The monthly dollar amount of the deficit in cash flow of the UCLA Medical Center kept on increasing and climbed from about $50,000 a month in early 2007 to an average of nearly $600,000 a month starting in 2009. "California Health System Exhibit 2" is adapted from *Swapping Our Future* and shows the swap trap in which the University of California–Los Angeles had fallen. The accumulated money in that trap was not going for medical care, education, buildings, infrastructure, or anything of value — it was going to pay gambling debt for which the university's infrastructure and education got nothing.

California Health System Exhibit 2
The Swap Trap of UCLA Medical School

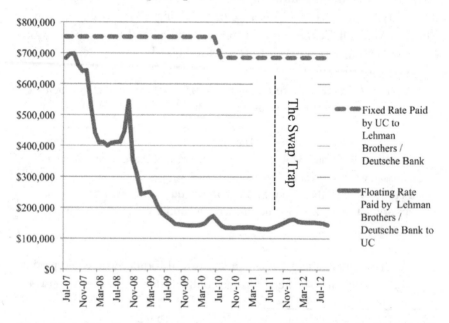

Source: Adapted from *Swapping Our Future: How Students and Taxpayers are Funding Risky UC Borrowing and Wall Street Profits*, Department of Sociology, UC Berkeley, 2012.

CHAPTER 22

Johns Hopkins Health System Corporation: A Case of Derivatives Abuse from the East

As was the case with some other universities, Johns Hopkins University had incorporated its health-service units into the Johns Hopkins Health System Corporation (JHHS). The corporation prepares and discloses its own annual reports of audited financial statements separately from the annual reports of the university. Much of the university-related contracts of swapping interest rates are concentrated at the Johns Hopkins Health System Corporation and Affiliates. In 2016, JHHS had 12 swap contracts on total notional amounts of $750 million while the rest of Johns Hopkins University, excluding the hospital and components of JHHS, had only three swap contracts with notional amounts of $154 million.[1]

For each interest-rate-exchange (swap) agreement, JHHS pays a fixed rate in exchange for the receipt of adjustable (floating) interest rate linked

[1]The JHH System consists of the Johns Hopkins Hospital; Johns Hopkins Bayview Medical Center, Inc.; Howard County General Hospital, Inc.; Suburban Hospital, Inc.; Sibley Memorial Hospital and other Affiliates; All Children's Hospital, Inc.; and Suburban Hospital Healthcare System, Inc.

to London Average Interest Rate (LIBOR).[2] The payable fixed rates range between 3.3265% and 3.946%, while the receivable variable rate (LIBOR) was 62% or 67% of one month LIBOR, which fell to levels as low as 0.16%. "Hopkins Health Exhibit 1" approximates the relationship between the fixed and adjustable rates of interest for the period 2004 through 2016.

"Hopkins Health Exhibit 1," chart is unique in that it shows that the first interest-rate-exchange contract started in 2004 while the last contract started in 2007. After 2007, JHHS did not enter into any new interest-rate-exchange (swap) contracts before this manuscript was completed in 2016. The existing swap contracts on $750 million (reference) notional amounts have long maturities, up to 35 years. The annual amounts of payable interest expense arising from interest-rate-exchange was about $24 million. In fact, the annual reports show these amounts to

Hopkins Health Exhibit 1
A Repeated Fall in the Swap Trap

The Swap Trap of Johns Hopkins Health System Corporation and Affiliates (JHHS)

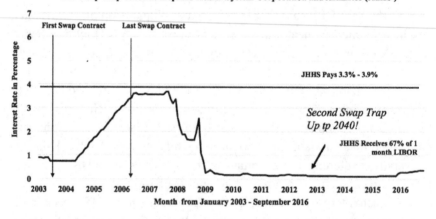

Month from January 2003 - September 2016

---

vary between 24 million and $27 million a year. Using this information and the relationships displayed in "Hopkins Health Exhibit 1," the sum of dollar amounts that JHHS paid annually to big banks since the beginning of playing this game in 2004 was very likely to be in the range of $250 million to $325 million. In addition, JHHS projected more than $387 million as noncurrent liabilities for the total losses it expected to owe banks (counterparties) until the contracts mature. These liabilities are the so-called "fair" market values that JHHS must pay to terminate or transfer these contracts to someone else.

All these interest-rate-swap contracts have two disturbing features:

- All contracts carry terms ranging between 17 and 40 years, with an average swap life of 31 years. In 2004, JHHS entered into three swap contracts with JPMorgan Chase and Bank of America for total notional amounts of $155 million having terms of 17 years. Nevertheless, other swap contracts have durations between 35 and 40 years. No one could attribute rationality, logic, or reason to signing uncertain contracts for that long.

- As "Hopkins Health Exhibit 1" shows, the adjustable rate that JHHS has been receiving from banks in connection with interest-rate-exchange (swap) contracts has fallen to fractions of 1% for several years, while JHHS continued to pay an average fixed rate of 3.63%. This is the same road to financial adversity traveled by other not-for-profit entities. Moreover, unlike the theoretical constructs, the variable rate receivable from big banks never exceeded or even came close to the fixed rate payable to the same banks, even when transaction cost is ignored.

Nonetheless, the problem at JHHS is much more complex than a simple explanation imputed from a graph. The case of interest rate swaps at JHHS is one of the most difficult cases to grasp. For example, it is not possible for the most educated person to comprehend the complexity of the information revealing the results of what appears to be a major blunder. Let us look at the facts as reported in *The Johns Hopkins Health System Corporation and Affiliates Combined Financial Statements and Supplementary Information June 30, 2016 and 2015.* Page 27 of these financial statements includes the information retrieved and reproduced as reported in "Hopkins Health Exhibit 2."

JHHS entered into 12 swap contracts between January 2004 and October 2007. "Part A" of "Hopkins Health Exhibit 2" outlines relevant information about these contracts, including expiry dates, which range between 2021 and 2042. That is, the maturity dates of some of these contracts extend to more than 35 years. All are noncancelable without paying huge termination fees. Additionally, Panel A of this exhibit provides two more observations:

i.   Payable fixed interest rate was greater than the receivable variable interest rate by an average of 3.3% every year for all these swap contracts.
ii. Total reference (notional) amounts did not exceed $758 million meaning that these swap contracts were acquired to hedge interest rate risk on a total of $758 million

These two observations also mean that JHHS was paying big banks about $25 million annually for the difference between the payable fixed and the receivable variable rates from the swaps ($758 million × 3.3%). Starting in 2004 and taking into consideration the volatility of benchmark rates, the total amounts of money that JHHS had paid in cash to big banks for interest rate swaps up to 2016 is estimated to range between a low of $250 million and a high of $325 million. This was "cash" given away to big banks for a quasi-insurance against volatility of interest rate on $758 million debt. By any measure or any calculation, this is an expensive insurance premium. But that was not all of it; JHHS will continue to pay every year up to expiry dates that drag on to 2042 unless benchmark interest rates reverse direction in a big way!

Because the swap drain on cash was expected to continue until the contractual termination or expiry of the swap contracts, JHHS and the counterparty banks estimated the present value of these expected long-term losses to be $300 million as of June 30, 3016 for the swap contracts used for hedging interest rate risk. This information is in Panel B "Hopkins Health Exhibit 2." There was also an additional expected long-term loss of $87.6 million for other undesignated interest rate swaps. This information is in Panel C of "Hopkins Health Exhibit 2." Thus, the

Hopkins Exhibit 2
Disclosure of Swap Contracts as of June 30, 2016

Disclosure of Swap Contracts as of June 30, 2016

Panel A (As reported)

The following table summarizes JHHS' interest rate swap agreements (in thousands):

Swap Type	Expiration Date	Counterparty	JHHS Pays	JHHS Receives	Notional Amount at June 30 2016	Notional Amount at June 30 2015
Fixed	2022	J.P. Morgan	3.3290%	67% of 1-Month LIBOR	$ 48,565	$ 49,500
Fixed	2025	Bank of America	3.3265%	67% of 1-Month LIBOR	63,870	69,500
Fixed	2021	J.P. Morgan	3.9190%	68% of 1-Month LIBOR	25,000	25,000
Fixed	2034	Royal Bank of Canada	3.6235%	62.2% of 1-Month LIBOR + 0.27%	14,410	14,500
Fixed	2034	Citibank, N.A.	3.6235%	62.2% of 1-Month LIBOR + 0.27%	24,040	24,200
Fixed	2039	Goldman Sachs Capital Markets, L.P.	3.9110%	67% of 1-Month LIBOR	150,000	150,000
Fixed	2040	Goldman Sachs Capital Markets, L.P.	3.9220%	67% of 1-Month LIBOR	150,000	150,000
Fixed	2039	Goldman Sachs Capital Markets, L.P.	3.9460%	67% of 1-Month LIBOR	40,000	40,000
Fixed	2038	Goldman Sachs Capital Markets, L.P.	3.8190%	67% of 1-Month LIBOR	82,475	82,900
Fixed	2038	Merrill Lynch Capital Services	3.8091%	67% of 1-Month LIBOR	82,875	83,800
Fixed	2025	Goldman Sachs Capital Markets, L.P.	3.6910%	67% of 1-Month LIBOR	8,325	9,500
Fixed	2047	Citibank, N.A.	3.8505%	61.8% of 1-Month LIBOR + 0.25%	60,000	60,000
					$ 749,560	$ 758,900

| Average Maturity = 31 Years | Pay | Receive |

Question:
   What incentives would any rational person or group have to enter into contracts having these features?

Answer:
   That remains a mystery, but others did it too!

Panel B (As reported)

Fair value of derivative instruments as of June 30 (in thousands):

	2016 Balance Sheet Caption Fair Value	2015 Balance Sheet Caption Fair Value
	Derivatives reported as liabilities	
Interest rate swaps not designated as hedging instruments (in thousand dollars)	Other long-term liabilities (losses)	Other long-term liabilities (losses)
	$ 300,883	$ 213,287

Panel C (As reported)

Derivatives not designated as hedging instruments as of June 30 (in thousands):

Amount of gain (loss) recognized in change in Classification of derivative loss in Statement of Operations unrestricted net assets

	2016	2015
Interest rate swaps: Nonoperating expense (in thousands)	$ (87,596)	$ (22,666)

Source: The Johns Hopkins Health System Corporation and Affiliates Combined Financial Statements and Supplementary Information June 30, 2016 and 2015, page 27.
Retrieved from: http://hscrc.maryland.gov/Documents/Hospitals/ReportsFinancial/Audited/FY-2016/JHHS_AFS_FY16.pdf.

sum of payments estimated from all three panels suggests that interest rate swaps were expected to cost JHHS a total of $637 million on the low side and $712 million on the high side — including past annual settlements and expected termination fees.

❖ But, wait.

These are too many numbers and most readers would have lost their track by now.
In this case, **here is a summary**:

- To hedge (i.e., insure against increasing) interest rate risk on debt amounting to $758 million, JHHS entered into 12 interest rate swap contracts.
- Estimates of the actual (past) and expected (future) losses on these swap contracts range between $637 million and $762 million.

❖ There is more!

- If these numbers could speak, what would they be saying?
- Would they be saying that JHHS will end up paying a total amount ranging between $637 million and $762 million as a quasi-insurance premium against increases in interest rates on the debt of $758 million?
- Surprisingly, and with total disbelief, this is the most obvious conclusion one could draw from the information published by JHHS in its annual financial statements. While JHHS is not unique in dumping lots of money in the swap sinkholes, this is simply a financial blunder irrespective of who caused it; paying more to save less!

❖ For the sake of understanding, how much would an <u>increase</u> in interest rate on the hedged debt have to be to cost the borrower an additional $637 million (on the low side) or $762 (on the high side) over the lives of the related bonds?

- Assuming bonds having an average time to expiry or maturity of 30 years, the interest rate would have to increase by 4.58% to have a $637 million increase in life-time interest cost, or by 5.33% to have a $762 million increase in interest cost over the entire lifetime of the debt.

➜ Implication:

The sales puffery that big banks enjoyed throwing around freely was that entering into swap contracts will "lower" the cost of borrowing. But the reality was precisely the opposite. Promises to lower the cost of debt with swaps were merely fish hooks being dangled from the sharks' mouths! And, once caught in-between their jaws, there can be no escape.

---

http://hscrc.maryland.gov/Documents/Hospitals/ReportsFinancial/Audited/FY-2016/JHHS_AFS_FY16.pdf.
2015–2016

CHAPTER 23

The University of Florida Shands Hospital: A Case of Derivatives Abuse from the South

In 2003, Shands Hospital of the University of Florida began entering into noncancelable interest-rate-exchange agreements with maturities extending to 2037 — a full 35 years! As of June 30, 2016, Shands Hospital had nine swap contracts of three different structures with total notional amounts of $453 million.[1] These contracts are of three types:

First Type:

> Five interest-rate contracts of plain-vanilla swaps. For these contracts, Shands was required to pay interest at fixed rates ranging between 3.175% and 4.249%. In exchange, Shands would receive interest at variable rates linked to the London Average Interest Rate (LIBOR). The amounts of interest changing hands were calculated on a total of $307 million reference notional amount. In the same year, expected losses

---

[1] Shands Teaching Hospital and Clinics, Inc. and Subsidiaries, "Consolidated Basic Financial Statements, Required Supplementary Information and Supplemental Consolidating Information June 30, 2016 and 2015."

Retrieved from https://ufhealth.org/sites/default/files/media/PDF/2016-shands-financial-statement.pdf.

from interest-rate-exchange contracts had generated noncurrent liabilities totaling $85 million. This amount represented the expected present value of future obligations of Shands Hospital for these swaps only assuming that the current economic conditions will not change. It was also the amount that Shands would have to pay to terminate the contracts at that time. In addition, the current obligations were paid when occurred.

Second Type:

Three variable-for-variable contracts (Basis Swaps) requiring Shands to pay the Municipal Bond Average Interest Rate (SIFMA) and receive a fraction of LIBOR. The same type of contracts as those used by IU Health, these Basis Swaps were simply betting on the spread between the two interest-rate indexes. In general, this form of swap contracts has nothing to do with health care, health education, or hospital finance; they are pure bets on interest-rate spread. The total notional amounts of Basis Swaps were $67 million, and fortunately for Shands, they had a positive termination value (fair value, asset) of $28 million, representing the estimated future gains if the current economic conditions continue until termination. This would be the amount of money Shands would demand from the counterparty should a termination event occurs.

Here is what this type of Basis-Swap contract in this setting means:

- If LIBOR increases more than SIFMA → Shands wins.
- If SIFMA increases more than LIBOR → Shands loses.

It is as much gaming as playing the machines in a casino; the outcome is dependent on forces totally outside the control of the hospital's administration.

Third Type:

One contract requiring Shands to pay a variable rate of interest at Municipal Bond Average Interest Rate (SIFMA) and receive interest at a 3.4% fixed rate. This contract is written on a notional amount of $75 million and, as of 2016, had a positive fair-market value of $10.9 million. But do not hold your breath; with the gains Shands had accrued on this contract, Shands had to pay losses for another swap contract of the first type having the same reference notional amount.

To avoid confusion, let us outline the two swap contracts related to bond issues 1996 A and B.

1. Swap One: A contract of the first type, pays fixed and receives variable on a notional amount of $75 million. This contract became effective in 2003 and had a (loss) negative fair-market value of $10,698,000 as of 2016, and the contractual maturity date is December 2026.
2. Swap Two: A contract of the third type, pays variable and receives fixed on a notional amount of $75 million. This contract became effective in 2009 and had a positive (gain) fair-market value of $10,902,000 as of June 30, 2016. The swap matures in December 2026.

With six years spread between the starting dates of these two swap contracts, it is likely that Shands entered into Swap Two to hedge the interest-rate risk of Swap One. While this move gives Shands a clever, though costly, way of undoing the potential damage of Swap One, it is the most inefficient way of hedging; each contract requires incurring high transaction cost for underwriting, insurance, and legal services.

"Florida Shands Exhibit 1" portrays the offsetting relationship between Swap One and Swap Two.

Florida Shands Exhibit 1
The Offsetting Nature of Two Swap Contracts

Related Bond Issue	Notional Amount	Effective Date	Termination Date	Pay	Receive	Termination (Fair) Value as of June 30, 2016 (Thousands)
1996B First Type (became effective in 2003)	$75 million	July 2003	December 2026	3.175% (Fixed)	67% of one-month LIBOR (Variable)	($10,689) Liability
1996B Third Type (became effective in 2009)	$75 million	June 2009	December 2026	SIFMA (Variable)	3.4% (Fixed)	$10,902 Asset

Note: Based on the data presented on page 40 of the 2016 annual report.

Even for plain-vanilla interest-rate-exchange (swap) contracts for which Shands pays fixed rates and receives variable, the hospital is exposed to basis risk when the cash receivable from the variable rates of the swap contract does not cover the cash payable for the variable rate on the debt. Exposure to basis risk is particularly acute when Shands, like many others, issues bonds at variable <u>auction rate</u> (continually changing) with the rates being reset periodically for periods ranging from one week to 35 days. Remarketing the debt and resetting interest rates so frequently create high exposure to basis risk because, given the difference in the structures of setting interest rates, the rates on the bonds will inevitably be more volatile than the rates on the swaps. As Shands's credit risk increases (credit rating downgraded), its weekly rate is reset higher, while neither Municipal Bond Average Interest Rate (SIFMA) nor LIBOR would be affected.

Losses and Collateral: Idle Cash

Expected long-term liabilities for swap losses amounted to $32 million in 2011, and counterparty banks required Shands to deposit cash collateral equal to $8 million. By 2014, the expected loss increased to $38 million, and the collateral increased to $14 million. This trend continued, and in 2016, expected swap losses added up to $57 million, and the collateral increased to $34 million. The amounts of the collateral were restricted cash that Shands Hospital could not use in its normal activities, which adds to the negative impact of entering into swap contracts. It is worth noting, however, that the last two swap contracts into which Shands entered were in 2008, one of which matures in 2028, and the second matures in 2037. Thus, the significant increases in swap losses and the required collateral since 2011 reflect, in part, the change in the credit worthiness of Shands Hospital.

Obsession with Swaps

In the financial statements of Shands Hospital, the term *swap* was repeated 69 times. As "Florida Shands Exhibit 2" shows, the word *swap*

Florida Shands Exhibit 2
Frequency of Citing Specific Terms
in Shands' Annual Report

	Terms Mentioned in the Annual Report	Frequency of Mentions in Shands's Annual Report
Financial Derivatives	*Swaps*	**69**
Medical	*Medical*	35
	Medicine	6
	Patients	17
	Treatment	5

was repeated more than the combined total citations of the words *medical, medicine, patients,* and *treatment.*[2]

---

[2] Shands Teaching Hospital and Clinics, Inc. and Subsidiaries, "Consolidated Basic Financial Statements, Required Supplementary Information and Supplemental Consolidating Information June 30, 2016 and 2015."

Retrieved from https://ufhealth.org/sites/default/files/media/PDF/2016-shands-financial-statement.pdf.

CHAPTER 24

The Sisters of Charity of Leavenworth Health System

Some people might argue with good reason that organizations like Johns Hopkins Health System and Affiliates or Shands hospital of the University of Florida have sources of funds and endowments that help them cope with losses from interest-rate swaps. However, it is difficult to make the same argument for charitable hospitals like the Sisters of Charity of Leavenworth Health System (SCL Health). The people involved in this type of organization derive satisfaction from providing services to the poor, the vulnerable, and the uninsured. As a result, the fees collected from the patients are typically much lower than the cost of providing them with medical services. To cover the excess of cost over revenues, SCL Health counts on raising funds from donations and grants to help support these charitable activities. In other words, SCL Health was not so flush with money to waste or hand over to big banks for nothing.

It is, therefore, most curious to ask why Merrill Lynch (Bank of America) and Deutsche Bank, among other big banks, went out of their way to persuade SCL Health to enter into interest-rate-exchange (swap) contracts. Members of the sales force and swap dealers in these two big banks must have known that these contracts had only one winner and one loser and that the ultimate result was preordained; neither bank had the intention of losing money consistently so that SCL Health could win.[1]

Furthermore, the managers who run and manage SCL Health are typically religious devotees who most definitely were not members of the financial-engineering clan. Moreover, it is highly unlikely they had chased the bankers urging them to write swap contracts for their organization. The only possible way the managers and sisters at SCL Health could have known about interest-rate swaps would have been through unsolicited presentations by the nomadic sales agents whose big banks had dispatched all around the country. It is indeed quite surprising to think of these sales agents rushing to a charity hospital to promote the sale of an instrument to bet on the movements of interest rates about which no one in the hospital could have known anything. It gets more infuriating to think that these sales agents knew they were selling gambling instruments with one winner only and when the charity hospital accumulates losses, some poor patients would be left without treatment.

SCL Health is a faith-based, nonprofit health-care system founded in 1864 in Leavenworth, Kansas (see "SCL Health Exhibit 1"). After the growth and expansion of the charity's activities, SCL Health moved its headquarters to Broomfield, Colorado. SCL Health operates nine acute-care hospitals, one community hospital, three safety-net clinics, one children's mental-health center, and more than 200 ambulatory service centers in three states — Colorado, Kansas, and Montana — with more than 15,000 associates and 700 employed providers (see "SCL Health Exhibit 1" for the service area). The mission of SCL Health is to improve the health of people in the communities served, especially the poor and vulnerable, and offer discounted health-care costs to the uninsured. In planning for the costs of charitable services, SCL Health typically establishes a charity-care allowance, which amounted to $181.9 million in 2014 and $152.7 million in 2015. Overall, SCL Health has provided more than $222 million a year in community benefits. To spread its mission, SCL Health formed partnerships with other organizations, including National Jewish Health in Colorado in 2015, to provide joint health care to a larger number of patients.

---

[1] I have contacted SCL Health and tried to obtain information about these contracts, but I was not given that opportunity.

SCL Health Exhibit 1
The Service Area of SCL Health

WHERE WE SERVE

St. James Healthcare
Butte

St. Vincent Healthcare
Billings

Holy Rosary Healthcare
Miles City

Platte Valley Medical Center
Brighton

Saint Vincent Clinic
Leavenworth

Duchesne Clinic
Kansas City

St. Mary's Medical Center
Grand Junction

St. Francis Health
Topeka

Good Samaritan Medical Center
Lafayette

Marian Clinic
Topeka

SCL Health Community Hospital – Westminster
(Emerus JV)

Saint Joseph Hospital

JOA – National Jewish Health/ Saint Joseph Hospital
Denver

Lutheran Medical Center
Wheat Ridge

● Hospital
● Clinic
○ Children's Mental Health Treatment Center

Mount Saint Vincent
Denver
(Children's Mental Health Treatment Center)

Source: Sisters of Charity of Leavenworth Health System, Inc. "Annual Financial Reporting Information for the Year Ended December 31, 2016," May 25, 2017, p. 4.

Retrieved from https://www.sclhealth.org/-/media/files/shared/about/financials/sclhealthannualdisclosure 2016final.pdf?la=en.

The structure and mission of SCL Health create two conflicting consequences:

- Supporting this organization would be a service to humanity.
- Taking money away from this organization would be a crime against humanity.

However, swap dealers either had never thought of the differences between these two consequences or elected to ignore them. In particular, bankers at Deutsche Bank and Merrill Lynch (now part of Bank of America) persuaded the leaders of SCL Health to sign contracts with the expectation of lowering the cost of borrowing. It is unclear whether the responsible personnel at Deutsche Bank and Merrill Lynch had fairly and fully presented the risks of interest-rate-exchange contracts as agreements of betting on the changes in interest rates. These two banks pushed and sold swap contracts that added $37 million of liabilities on the balance sheet of SCL Health by 2012 representing the expected future losses up to maturity. After paying losses for three years and facing changing economic conditions, this liability was reduced to $22.3 million in 2015 — $6 million owed to Bank of America and $16 million owed to Deutsche Bank, as the related segment of the annual report in "SCL Health Exhibit 2" shows.

After peeling off the fancy language, the substance of these contracts boils down to the following expectations:

○   If market interest rate increases, the banks pay SCL Health more money.
○   If market interest rate decreases, SCL Health pays the banks more money.

Thus, the nature of the gamble consists of betting on opposite movements: the banks were betting on decreasing rates, while SCL Health was betting on increasing rates. These interest-rate-exchange (swap) contracts were enforceable and noncancelable before the contractual terminal dates in 2023 and 2031. "SCL Health Exhibit 2" presents a segment from the balance sheet of 2015 showing the information about the three outstanding swap contracts. We may use the information in that section of the balance sheet to calculate the amount of cash payments SCL Health made to both Merrill Lynch and Deutsche Bank in 2015. An additional piece of information: in December 2015, London Average Interest Rate (LIBOR) was at 0.35%, and Average Municipal Rate (SIFMA) was at 0.01%. Both indexes presented bad news for SCL Health.

SCL Health Exhibit 2
Swap Contracts and Losses

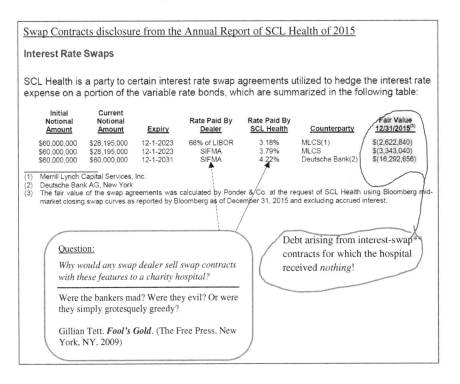

Swap Contracts disclosure from the Annual Report of SCL Health of 2015

Interest Rate Swaps

SCL Health is a party to certain interest rate swap agreements utilized to hedge the interest rate expense on a portion of the variable rate bonds, which are summarized in the following table:

Initial Notional Amount	Current Notional Amount	Expiry	Rate Paid By Dealer	Rate Paid By SCL Health	Counterparty	Fair Value 12/31/2015[3]
$60,000,000	$28,195,000	12-1-2023	68% of LIBOR	3.18%	MLCS(1)	$(2,622,840)
$60,000,000	$28,195,000	12-1-2023	SIFMA	3.79%	MLCS	$(3,343,040)
$60,000,000	$60,000,000	12-1-2031	SIFMA	4.22%	Deutsche Bank(2)	$(16,292,656)

(1) Merrill Lynch Capital Services, Inc.
(2) Deutsche Bank AG, New York
(3) The fair value of the swap agreements was calculated by Ponder & Co. at the request of SCL Health using Bloomberg mid-market closing swap curves as reported by Bloomberg as of December 31, 2015 and excluding accrued interest.

Debt arising from interest-swap** contracts for which the hospital received *nothing*!

Question:

Why would any swap dealer sell swap contracts with these features to a charity hospital?

Were the bankers mad? Were they evil? Or were they simply grotesquely greedy?

Gillian Tett. *Fool's Gold*. (The Free Press. New York, NY, 2009)

For the two contracts with Merrill Lynch on notional amounts of 56 million:

○ SCL Health paid fixed rates at 3.18% and 3.79%.

○ SCL Health received 0.23% on a $28 million notional amount and 0.01% on another $28 million notional amount.

○ The net cash payment to Merrill Lynch in 2015 alone amounted to about $1.88 million.

For the contract with Deutsche Bank on notional amounts of $60 million:

o   SCL Health paid 4.22%.
o   SCL Health received 0.01%.
o   The net cash payment to Deutsche Bank in 2015 alone was about $2.5 million.

In total, SCL Health paid both Merrill Lynch and Deutsche Bank $4.38 million in 2015 alone in exchange for nothing other than a promise of the possibility of lowering the cost of borrowing, which of course backfired. Future payments of similar losses were estimated to have total fair-market values of $22.6 million. This is the total expected losses of the three swap contracts presented as "Fair Values" on December 31, 2015, in "SCL Health Exhibit 2."

Remember, in each case, SCL Health had two different types of contracts: one contract is for a bond issue and the other is for exchanging interest rates — pay fixed and receive variable. Presumably these two contracts for the bond and for the swap of interest rates are independent of each other, but that is only in theory. In reality, the stated justification for entering into contracts to exchange interest rates was to manage interest-rate risk and lower the cost of borrowing. SCL Health is a party to both contracts and is subject to their combined effects on risk and cash flow. When combined, the result was not consistent with the promises big banks made — SCL Health was paying higher, not lower, interest rates. This is illustrated below using the interest-rate-exchange contract between SCL Health and Deutsche Bank. As "SCL Health Exhibit 3" shows, in 2013, the combination of the adjustable interest rate of the swap contract and the interest rate on the related bond shows the artificially calculated, synthetic fixed rate to be 4.565%.

As with most other cases, the sales promotion that big banks offered consisted of two main points:

(a) Sales Promotion 1: If SCL Health were to issue a traditional fixed-rate bond, the interest rate would be higher than the synthetic fixed rate it would pay for the combination of a variable rate and a swap contract.

SCL Health Exhibit 3
The Simple and Combined Effects of the Issued
Bond and Related Interest-Rate Exchange

	Contract 1	Contract 2	Sum of the Bond
	The Bond	The Swap	Plus the Swap
Fixed Rate Payable to Deutsche Bank for the Swap	—	4.215%	4.215%
Less Average Variable Rate Receivable from Deutsche Bank for the Swap	—	0.150%	0.150%
= Net Interest Rate Payable on the Swap		4.065%	4.065%
Plus Variable Rate Payable on the Bond	0.5%		0.5%
= Interest Cost of Borrowing *without* the Swap	0.5%		
= Net Interest Cost of Borrowing *with* the Swap (This is called the synthetic [or artificial] fixed rate.)			4.565%

(b) Sales Promotion 2: The swap contract protects SCL Health from increases in the cost of borrowing beyond the fixed rate payable on the swap, which was 4.215%.

However, these two premises were hypothetical, evolving from simplistic and somewhat optimistic assumptions. For the first argument, that relationship between the traditional fixed-rate bond and the synthetic fixed rate may be true at the start, in the very short run. However, the swap contract was noncancelable for a quarter of a century, and there were absolutely no evidential grounds for extending this argument for the entire term of the agreement. The second argument is tenuous because it assumes no basis risk or transaction cost — i.e., the variable rate receivable from the swap was assumed to cover the variable rate payable on the bond.

The information contained in "SCL Health Exhibit 4" suggests that, if SCL had issued bonds at adjustable rates and never entered into swap agreements, the interest cost of debt would have always been significantly lower than the 4% the SCL Health paid for the swaps.

In 2016, SCL Health reported a reduction in swap losses to $17.9 million, no new swaps were added, and a transfer of the swap contract on $60 million notional amount from Deutsche Bank to Wells Fargo.

SCL Health Exhibit 4
The Swap Trap of Sisters of Charity Health of Leavenworth

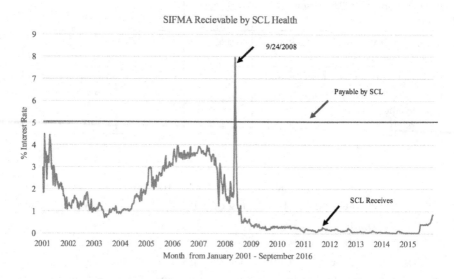

CHAPTER 25

Dignity Health Holds
A Bigger Bag of IOUs to the
Banking Cartel

The $22 million liability of SCL Health for swap contracts seemed to be a large amount relative to the organization's scale and size, but that judgment fades when compared to Dignity Health, another Catholic charity. In 2011, the noncurrent liability of Dignity Health arising from interest-rate-exchange (swap) contracts amounted to $249 million. Dignity Health is a California-based charitable health-care organization providing service throughout the states of California, Arizona, and Nevada. Dignity Health spells out its mission on its website[1]:

---

[1] Religious Sponsors. Dignity Health.
Retrieved from https://www.supportdhfglobalmissionprogram.org/about-us/religious-sponsors.

Dignity Health is a healing ministry. Our legacy of service to the poor and undeserved is deeply rooted in the founding of the organization by our religious sponsors in 1986. Today our sponsors continue to serve on our boards and in our hospitals, and include:

Sisters of Mercy of the Americas
Dominican Sisters of St. Catherine of Siena
Sisters of St. Dominic of the Most Holy Rosary
Sisters of Charity of the Incarnate Word
Sitters of Dominic of the Most Holy Name
Sisters of St. Francis of Penance and Christian Charity

Their healing work with the underprivileged extends throughout the United States as well as to communities abroad, in countries such as Latin America, Africa, Asia and Europe.

Additionally, Dignity Health has a Global Mission Program that awards grants to projects targeting certain diseases and serving low-income communities. The grants program depends on both employees' donations and budget allocations. Grant awards vary between $5,000 and $25,000. The total award allocation for 2014–2015 was $100,000.

The criteria for evaluation of award proposals center on projects that

o   Promote the health and status of women and children,
o   Contribute to clean water and food and sustainable agriculture,
o   Prevent human trafficking and offer care and rehabilitation for its victims,
o   Expand education and communication within rural communities, and
o   Promote education on the prevention of HIV and health care for its victims.

During 2015, Dignity Health awarded five Global Mission Program grants to the Dominican Republic, Haiti, South Sudan, Tanzania, and Romania.

Thus, most definitely, paying big banks for swap contracts took money away from making these awards. These payments for the swaps were and continue to be unrelated to any health care, education, treatment, or community service; they were obligations arising from bets on interest-rate movements. In its annual report of 2015, Dignity Health reported having 16 swap contracts, which require Dignity Health to pay a fixed interest rate to banks and receive variable interest rates in exchange on total reference notional (face) amounts of $940 million.[2] Under these interest-rate-exchange contracts, Dignity Health pays annual fixed rates averaging 3.3% but receives a fraction of the London Average Interest Rate (LIBOR), which has fallen to levels below 0.5%.

Big banks sold these interest-rate-exchange contracts with the promise to lower the cost of debt and to shelter Dignity Health from the volatility of interest rates on variable-rate bonds. However, the variable rates paid on the debt in 2015 (without adding swap contracts) ranged between 0.05% and 1.28%, as "Dignity Health Exhibit 1" reveals[3]:

The story was different for swap contracts. The fixed rates that Dignity Health paid to the banks for interest-rate-exchange contracts were much higher than the variable rates of interest that Dignity Health received from these banks in connection with the same contracts.[4] Every

Dignity Health Exhibit 1
Rates of Variable-Interest-Rate Debt as of 2015

Variable-Rate-Debt Face Amounts	The Ranges of Interest Rates Paid on Outstanding Adjustable-Rate Bonds	Terminal Date
$369 Million	1.06% to 1.28%	2020
$776.4 Million	0.05% to 0.16%	2047
$313.6 Million	0.1% to 0.6%	2042

---

[2] The annual reports were short on details.

[3] Extensive research to find annual reports on the web for other years was not successful.

[4] Dignity Health had a serious exposure to basis-risk. Without garbling the presentation one could think of basis risk of change in interest rate resulting in your receiving less and paying more.

Dignity Health Exhibit 2
Reported Long-term Losses from Interest-Rate-Swap Contracts

Fiscal Year	Notional Amounts of Interest-Rate-Exchange Contracts (In Million Dollars)	Losses = Fair Values = Noncurrent Liabilities = Termination Values (In Million Dollars)
2011	$944.5	($110)
2012	$940.5	($228)
2014	$940.5	($186)
2015	$940.4	($178)
2016	$937.7	($249)
		** These obligations relate to projected future payments after paying for current obligations in cash.

Source: Dignity Health and Subordinates Annual Financial Statements 2014–2015.
Retrieved from https://emma.msrb.org/ES730463-ES572510-.pdf.

year, Dignity Health would pay the current year's obligations in cash and report the projected future obligations arising from expected similar differences between the payable and receivable interest rates as noncurrent liabilities. The present-value balances of these liabilities (projected future losses expressed in current dollars) varied between $156 million and $249 million. To have an idea of the real cost of entering into interest-rate-exchange contracts, it suffices to note that this liability is more than twice the amount of money Dignity Health spent in 2015 for charitable activities.

The noncurrent liabilities presented in the third column of "Dignity Health Exhibit 2" show the different amounts that Dignity Health would have had to pay to big banks to terminate the contracts at the end of each respective year. These are not all the obligations that came about from failing in betting on interest-rate exchanges; the full amount should

Dignity Health Exhibit 3
Paying at Least 3.1% on Debt Instead of Only 0.4%

	Swap	bond	Total
Pay fixed interest to swaps (average)	3.3%		3.3%
Receive variable rate from the swaps (average)	– 0.6%		0.6%
Net average interest-rate cost of the swap (average)	= 2.7%		2.7%
Pay for the variable-rate bonds (average)		+ 0.4%	+ 0.4%
Net borrowing cost (debt + swap) (average)*			= 3.1%

*The annual current obligations related to interest-rate-exchange contracts are estimated at $29 million annually for the period 2011–2015. This is calculated as 3.1% times $940 million. This is also an estimate of the annual settlements paid for the same five-year period.

include the annual payments the hospital made to settle current liabilities.[5] While the details are missing from financial reports or other publicly available documentation, it is compelling to ask the following question: Why did the management of Dignity Health see the need to enter into interest-rate-exchange contracts requiring them to pay a fixed rate at about 3.3% and receive a lower interest rate that became as low as 0.6%? It is true that these numbers are *ex post*, but increasing cost is what happens when one takes on additional risk. If Dignity Health had not entered into these interest-rate-exchange contracts, it would have saved nearly $25 million annually — money that could be used in its health care, community service, and grants programs. A presentation of this calculation is in "Dignity Health Exhibit 3."

The excess of the payable fixed rates over the receivable variable rates for interest-rate-exchange contracts is estimated to be $25 million a year. The expected future losses on the swaps are the fair values reported in "Dignity Health Exhibit 2." Accordingly, without entering into swap

---

[5] For the years included in the above table, the current liabilities are estimated as follows: $940 million × 0.031 = $29 million annually. The 0.031 is the difference between the payable and the receivable interest rates. This difference is calculated in the next table. Unfortunately, the annual cash payments made were not disclosed separately.

agreements, the cost of debt issued at variable rate would have been only $3.7 million instead of $25 million a year.

During the year 2014–2015, Dignity Health awarded grants for worthy public-health causes. Normally grant awards varied between $5,000 and $25,000, and total award allocations for each year totaled $100,000. Thus, the interest-rate-exchange loss of $178 million in that year would have covered 7,120 grants of the highest award.

By the end of 2016, officials at Dignity Health had to choose between two alternatives:

○ To make one payment to big banks equal to $249 million (in addition to the recurring liability of about $29 million paid in cash) or
○ To continue making annual payments until 2047, the terminal date stated in the interest-rate-exchange contracts.

But Dignity Health did not choose to terminate the contracts and in one year, the noncurrent liabilities increased from $186 million to $249 million. Moreover, the terms of the swap contracts have added severe restrictions on Dignity Health. For example, Assured Guaranty Co. insured interest-rate-exchange contracts on notional amounts of $160 million, which had a loss liability (negative fair value) of $60 million in 2016. The counterparties to these swap contracts wanted to make sure any obligations by Dignity related to these interest-rate-exchange contracts were fully covered by having the insurance company maintain a high credit rating. Accordingly, they inserted the following contingency in these contracts[6]:

> In the event the insurer, Assured Guaranty, is downgraded below A2/A or A3/A — (Moody's/Standard and Poor's), the counterparties have the right to terminate the swaps if Dignity Health does not provide alternative credit support acceptable to them within 30 days of being notified of the downgrade. If the insurer is downgraded below the

---

[6] Dignity Health and Subordinate Corporations, Consolidated Financial Statements for and as of June 30, 2016 and 2015 and Independent Auditors Report, June 30, 2016, p. 40. Retrieved from https://emma.msrb.org/ES823341-ES646022-ES1041174.pdf.

thresholds noted above and Dignity Health is downgraded below Baa3/BBB — (Moody's/Standard and Poor's), the counterparties have the right to terminate the swaps.

In its reports of audited financial statements, Dignity states that it "has the right to terminate the swaps prior to maturity for any reason." However, the implication is that Dignity will still have to pay the termination penalty.

CHAPTER 26

Texas Methodist Hospitals Did Not Escape Big Banks' Vise

In the State of Texas, the Methodist Health System (MHS), consisting of Methodist Dallas Medical Center, Methodist Charlton Medical Center, Methodist Mansfield Medical Center, and Methodist Richardson Medical Center, has declared its charitable mission in its statement of policy:[1]

> As a part of its mission, Methodist Health System (MHS), *provides financial assistance to patients who lack the ability to pay for hospital services.* (Emphasis added)

Notwithstanding the implied call for donations to support this humanitarian cause, swap dealers did not hesitate to entrap MHS in their creation of interest-rate exchange (swap) contracts, just the same as they did with the Catholic charities SCL Health and Dignity Health. In its annual statements, MHS reported having entered into six swap transactions in 2007 to

---

[1] Methodist Health System, "Financial Assistance Policy," September 28, 2016.

Retrieved from http://www.methodisthealthsystem.org/workfiles/financial/Financial-Assistance.pdf.

fix the expected net-interest expenses associated with its bonds.[2] The three
large banks that sold these interest-rate-exchange contracts to MHS were
Goldman Sachs; Merrill Lynch (Bank of America); and the leading minor-
ity women–owned bank, Siebert Brandford Shank & Co. The declared
lofty goal of signing these interest-rate-exchange (swap) contracts was
simply a repeat of the same: namely "to lower the risks and costs associated with its financing activities." This was one goal that was never
achieved, as we shall see shortly.

Upon signing these agreements, the MHS Media Center hailed the
occasion as a victory in the fight to lower the cost of borrowing. On
January 10, 2008, the MHS Media Center distributed a glowing, puffed-
up and unsubstantiated news report presented in Methodist Hospitals
Exhibit 1:

Methodist Hospitals Exhibit 1
The Misleading Communication about
Interest-Rate-Exchange Contracts

Methodist Health System Uses Progressive Financing to Save Millions of Dollars

01/10/2008

> Methodist Health System recently used an innovative financing option to fund
> upcoming growth initiatives. Instead of issuing long-term fixed-rate bonds to
> investors, the hospital issued short-term bonds and fixed the long-term interest
> rate through municipal swap (interest-rate-exchange) market. It is estimated
> that [this approach] will save the organization millions of dollars over the next
> 35 years. The financial arrangement was facilitated by Methodist Health
> System Board Member Levi Davis.
>
> "I applaud the board members, finance staff and financial advisors of
> Methodist for using this progressive form of financing," says Anand Kesavan,
> vice president of SBS Financial Products Company, LLC. "This arrangement
> involves more work and expertise than traditional bond financing, but expands
> the organization's capacity for securing additional funding in the future and
> greatly lowers the hospital's interest costs."

Retrieved from https://www.methodisthealthsystem.org/body.cfm?id=93&action=detail&ref=59.

---

[2]The original text uses the term *swap* instead of *exchange*.

This news announcement was a piece of propaganda that turned out to serve the interest of big banks, not that of MHS. In this respect, the announcement is alarming for several reasons:

o The announcement writes about short-term financing, which was not exactly correct. It is a long-term financing at short-term rates. That feature increases the financing risk all the way up to expiry.
o The announcement writes about the tremendous savings of cost without giving any evidence or reasoning in support of this assertion. The reality was exactly the opposite, as the evidence will show shortly.
o The announcement totally ignores the risk inherent in the contracts of interest rate swaps.
o Frequent nonsynchronous changes of the adjustable rates for both the bonds and the interest-rate-exchange contracts exposed MHS to serious basis risk and additional cost, none of which was acknowledged in the propaganda piece.

The available public evidence suggests that MHS was a victim of misrepresentation and negative consequences of the moral hazard arising from the lack of independence between Siebert Brandford Shank & Co. and the derivatives adviser to MHS. Part of the interest-rate-exchange (swap) contracts was signed with Siebert Brandford Shank & Co., and in the meantime, an affiliate of the same bank served as the derivatives adviser to MHS. Ross Eisenbrey disclosed this information in connection with the role of the same bank, Siebert Brandford Shank & Co., in Detroit's disaster with interest-rate-exchange. Eisenbrey, report is reproduced below:

The company's website discloses the following relationship between itself and SBS Financial:

"In 2005 the principal owners of Siebert Brandford Shank created a separate single purpose corporate entity, SBS Financial Products

---

(Continued)

(Continued)

Company, LLC ('SBSFPC') to serve as a principal in interest rate swap [exchange] transactions with Siebert Brandford Shank municipal issuer clients. Since that time SBS Financial Products has executed swaps for numerous issuers across the nation. SBSFPC derivatives professionals work in conjunction with the Siebert Branford Shank advanced analytical investment banking staff to develop and implement comprehensive plans of finance that include a range of traditional fixed income and derivative products."

Ross Eisenbrey, "Detroit's Deals with Financial
Institutions Led to Disaster, *Economic Policy Institute*.
December 24, 2013.

Retrieved from http://www.epi.org/blog/detroits-deals-financial-institutions-led/.

Like all other hospitals, let alone charity hospitals, it is not likely that the staff at the Methodist Health System had insiders who had useful knowledge of the risks brought about by interest-rate-exchange contract. Instead, MHS relied on the advice of a financial-service advisor whose skills and independence were never ascertained. The consequences of making these decisions were costly to MHS. Publicly available reports show that interest-rate-exchange (swap) contracts were written on $200 million notional (face) amounts, which were reduced to $170.2 million in 2015:

- Pay 3.7% per annum on a notional amount of $85,100,000
- Pay 3.8% per annum on a notional amount of $85,100,000
- Receive 64% of the U.S. dollar one-month LIBOR rate reset weekly, plus 0.2%.

The "fair" market value of the swaps for the years 2012–2016 are reported in "Methodist Hospitals Exhibit 2."[3]

---

[3] http://www.dacbond.com/dacContent/doc.jsp?id=0900bbc780144e4e.

Methodist Hospitals Exhibit 2
Losses Arising from Interest-Rate Swaps

MHS obligations from swap contracts provided in the annual reports of the respective years:
2012 $57.0 million
2013 $34.1 million
2014 $38.0 million
2015 $55.2 million
2016 $68.3 million

The reported expected long-term obligations do not include current liabilities for any period because MHS settled them regularly each year as they occurred. Instead, "Methodist Hospitals Exhibit 2" represents the noncurrent, long-term liabilities related to what MHS expected to pay big banks for future losses on interest-rate-exchange contracts. These amounts are the estimated fair-market values of swap contracts. These are measures of the prices at which the counterparty could sell them to someone else in the marketplace, given the measurement guides following the Master Agreement of the International Swap and Derivatives Association (ISDA). Moreover, they represent the amounts that MHS was expected to pay to terminate the agreements on September 30 of the given year, even though terminating the contract also terminate the services these contracts are purported to provide. Just the same as in the cases of SCL Health and Dignity Health, the funds paid to big banks in relationship to interest-rate-exchange contracts had to be taken away from providing for health-care activities and out handed over to big banks for nothing in return.

Cases in Wealth Transfer from Transit Authorities to Big Banks:

Increasing Fares to Pay Big Banks for Swap Contracts

CHAPTER 27

With Swaps, Riding the Gravy Train Is Expensive

Transit authorities generate revenue by providing services to the public in addition to receiving public funding from state and local governments. These agencies also borrow money by issuing bonds (in the municipal-bond market) to help provide the funds needed to support their operations. At the start of the Swap Mania in the late 1990s, big banks dispatched their swap sellers to give the financial administrators of these agencies the same song and dance they had performed repeatedly. The same song and dance meant emphasizing the benefits of entering into swap contracts: promises to lower the cost of borrowing and to manage interest-rate risk. Having a healthy degree of naïveté and inexperience when it comes to financial engineering, managers of transit authorities believed the promises made and agreed to switch their bonds from the conventional fixed rates to variable (floating) rates and simultaneously enter into swap contracts with these same banks to pay fixed and receive variable.

In theory and wonderland, the money the transit agency expected to receive from swap contracts should have covered the money it had paid to bondholders. In addition, in theory, the net cost to the agency would be the fixed rate of interest paid on the swap — i.e., the synthetic fixed rate. The banks volunteered to do it all in one: underwriting the bonds, buying the bonds as investors, underwriting the swaps, and being the counterparties for the interest-rate swaps they wrote.

This all sounds straightforward, but the costly hidden factors are rarely disclosed, and financial administrators have overlooked their inability to predict and manage interest-rate changes over three to four decades in the future. Transit authorities across the nation fell into the same swap traps as other nonprofit agencies that shared the same destinies — transferring millions of dollars from these agencies to big banks on a regular basis. The transfer started with millions of dollars and, over time, added up to billions of dollars.

A group of labor unions called the Refund Transit Coalition wrote a report on the amounts of money a sample of transit authorities across the nation had been losing annually to big banks after joining the Swap Mania.[1] This report had a rather colorful title, *Riding the Gravy Train: How Wall Street Is Bankrupting Our Public Transit Agencies by Profiteering off of Toxic Swap Deals*. For a convenient sample of 13 transit authorities, the Refund Transit Coalition estimated total annual payments for interest-rate swaps for 2011 to be around $528 million (see "The Transit Gravy Train Exhibit"). However, other estimates of the costs from the information published in annual reports are much higher. For example, in the cases of the New York Metropolitan Transportation Authority (NY MTA), the Bay Area Toll Authority (BATA), and the Massachusetts Bay Transportation Authority (MBTA), the costs reported in the annual reports are higher than the costs reported by the Refund Transit Coalition. We shall look at these organizations in the next three chapters.

---

[1] Refund Transit Coalition, "Riding the Gravy Train: How Wall Street Is Bankrupting Our Public Transit Agencies by Profiteering off of Toxic Swap Deals," June 2012.

Retrieved from http://www.nowandfutures.com/large/GravyTrainWallStBanksRipOffTr ansitAuthoritiesVariousCities-Strat-Transitswaps.pdf.

The Transit Gravy Train Exhibit
Annual Losses of Selected Transit Authorities as of 2011, Reported by the Refund Transit Coalition

Region	Transportation Authority	Annual Swap Losses
1. Baton Rouge, LA	Central Area Transit Authority	$12.0 million
2. Boston, MA	Massachusetts Bay Transit Authority	$25.8 million
3. Charlotte, NC	Charlotte Area Transit Authority	$19.6 million
4. Chicago, IL	Chicago Transit Authority	$88.0 million
5. Detroit, MI	Detroit Department Transportation Authority	$84.0 million
6. Los Angeles, CA	Los Angeles County Metropolitan Transportation Authority	$20.0 million
7. New Jersey,	New Jersey Transit Authority	$83.0 million
8. New York, NY	New York Metropolitan Transit Authority	$113.9 million
9. Philadelphia, PA	Southeastern Pennsylvania Transportation Authority	$48.0 million
10. San Jose, CA	Santa Clara Valley Transportation Authority	$13.9 million
11. San Francisco, CA	Metropolitan Transportation Commission	$48.0 million
12. San Jose, CA	Santa Clara Valley Transportation Authority	$13.0 million
13. Washington, DC	District of Columbia	$11.0 million
Total Annual payments (losses)		**$528.6 million**

Source: Refund Transit Coalition, "Riding the Gravy Train: How Wall Street Is Bankrupting Our Public Transit Agencies by Profiteering off of Toxic Swap Deals," June 2012.
Retrieved from http://www.nowandfutures.com/large/GravyTrainWallStBanksRipOffTransitAuthorit icaVariousCities-3uat-Transitswaps.pdf.

CHAPTER 28

The New York Metropolitan Transportation Authority Fell into the Eastern Swap Sinkhole

In an article in the *New York Daily News* on April 28, 2015, Ginger Adam Otis noted that the New York Metropolitan Transportation Authority (NY MTA) was losing money fast: "As fast as the cash comes in, it gets paid out." She referred to the huge payroll amounts and the money required for capital improvement but she did not mention the hundreds of millions of dollars handed out to big banks annually in connection with interest-rate swaps, essentially for nothing.[1]

The New York Metropolitan Transportation Authority is one of those agencies that was taken by the novelty and enigmatic nature of the Swap Mania in a big way since its start in the late 1990s. But strangely enough, in spite of continuing to lose on swaps to this day, officials at

---

[1] Ginger Adams Otis, "MTA is losing money and headed to financial disaster, despite attempts to find revenue," *Daily News New York*, April 28, 2015.

Retrieved from http://www.nydailynews.com/new-york/mta-losing-money-headed-financial-ruin-article-1.2202720.

NY MTA continue to go back for more of the same. In 2000, NY MTA had only one interest-rate-swap contract on a notional amount of $93 million (for tunnels and bridge transportation). This contract was written by Ambac Financial and required NY MTA to pay a fixed interest rate at 5.634% and receive variable interest rates equal to the variable rates NY MTA was paying on the bonds. In 2001, NY MTA added two more swap contracts on $468 million notional amounts written by Citigroup. The terms of these contracts extend to 2019, enforceable and noncancelable. This transaction also signaled to other big banks that NY MTA was open for the business of transferring more money to banks through the interest-swaps sinkhole. In less than one year, NY MTA had 13 swap contracts, adding Bear Stearns, Lehman Brothers, Morgan Stanley, and JPMorgan Chase to the list of swap counterparties who were also potential claimants on any of NY MTA's resources. For some unknown reason, the NY MTA portfolio of swaps swelled to total notional amounts of $2.85 billion. Just like all other organizations, NY MTA could have issued bonds at floating interest rates and never entered into swaps; with bonds plus swaps, the authority began to lose large sums of money.

By the end of 2003 and after paying the annual settlements, NY MTA owed all these banks a total amount of $214 million for expected swap obligations. None of the swap contracts had made gains or had a positive position. In 2008, once again for no apparent or compelling economic reason, NY MTA augmented its swap portfolio by entering into four more swap contracts. By that time, right at the start of the Financial Crisis, the total notional (face or reference) amounts of all swap contracts purchased by NY MTA had swelled to $4.3 billion, and the total liabilities for swaps had increased to more than $741 million, or 17% of notional amounts. For the first eight years of dealing with swaps, none of the swap contracts was ever in a positive position (gain). Anyone who deals with financial matters would have known that this swap business was a road to financial ruin, but NY MTA kept on dipping into the same wasteful well. None of the financial reports has ever indicated the benefits of these swaps to NY MTA's current or future business activities. Believing in the promise of lowering the

NY MTA Exhibit 1
Expected Long-Term Losses Related to Interest-Rate Swaps
Reported as Long-term Liabilities

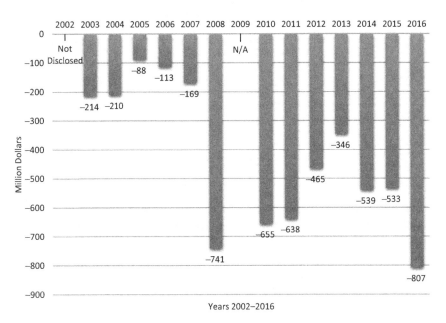

Years 2002–2016

cost of borrowing continued to be touted without any tangible evidence and continued to be more like chasing a ghost.

"NY MTA Exhibit 1" reports the long-term liabilities representing the anticipated losses on interest-rate-swap contracts for each of the 15 years, 2001–2015. As shown, these losses ranged between $88 million in 2005 and $807 million in 2016 — obligations for having received nothing tangible or intangible in exchange.

Continuing to enter into new interest-rate-swap contracts suggests that no one of influence at NY MTA had recognized the fact that the Authority did not need to enter into swap contracts to issue bonds at either fixed or variable rates. Furthermore, no one seem to have looked at the realized impact on the cost of debt. Has it declined? No, Not

NY MTA Exhibit 2
Word Citations in Comprehensive Annual Financial Reports: An Indicator of the MTA's Obsession with Swaps

	2002	2007	2015
Swap	**99**	**105**	**140**
Transportation	78	60	98
Passengers	27	30	43
Trains	8	11	21
Buses	37	20	103

really; it had actually increased, especially if all transaction cost are taken into consideration. Additionally, as we shall see in Chapter 34, the interest rates exchanged in these contracts represent contracting in an environment of imbalance in the information and bargaining power of counterparties that led to unjust enrichment of big banks. Instead of ceasing to deal with swaps, NY MTA's financial reports reveal a damning obsession with the mystique of interest-rate swaps although the benefits of such contracts appear to keep eluding the Authority. A look at the Comprehensive Annual Financial Reports (CAFR) suggests that such a mystique never seemed to go away. Why? That remains a mystery to this day. From 2002 to 2016, the word *swap* was repeated in each year's CAFR more than any other word of relevance to the functions of NY MTA. For example, the word *swap* was repeated 105 times in 2007 and 140 times in 2015, respectively. "NY MTA Exhibit 2" shows the word *swap* has been cited more frequently than the citation of any of four words relevant to the core functions of a transit authority: *transportation*, *passengers*, *trains*, and *buses*.

Draining financial resources to pay banks for losing interest-rate swaps angered activists in labor unions. A research document by Michael Stewart, titled *Money for Nothing: How interest rate swaps have become golden handcuff for New Yorkers*, published in 2011 displays that anger. In that document, Stewart writes about the following issues[2]:

- Since January 2000, the MTA has already paid out a net of $658 million to banks under these swap agreements.
- The MTA's net swap payments in 2010 alone would have been $40 million more than the amounts of money needed to head off cuts in services and layoff or termination of 1,764 positions.
- Furthermore, MTA has projected to pay banks in 2011 nearly $118 million in net swap payments.
- As of June 2011, terminating the swap portfolio would have cost the MTA $408 million. Three months later, at the end of September 2011, that termination fees increased to $714 million.

Michael Stewart illustrates the problem of swap losses by presenting a graph of the swap trap for one specific contract (the swap contract for Bond Series 2005B). The trap consists of the excess of the money that NY MTA had been paying annually to the banks for the swaps over the money it had been receiving from the banks for the same swaps. The swap trap was very much similar to the one presented for the Midway Airport (in Chapter 1) or for the Johns Hopkins Health System Corporation (Chapter 22). Toward the end of 2007, the trap widened as the amounts of interest based on floating rates that NY MTA was receiving from big banks dropped to levels below 0.5% — that is, one-half of 1% of the annual interest rate. NY MTA Exhibit 3 presents relevant information about five swap contracts. Total notional amounts of these contracts are $1.3 billion. They have 26 years average time to maturity and are expected to lose $381 million in future periods.

---

[2] Stewart, Michael, *"Money for Nothing: How interest rate swaps have become golden handcuffs for New Yorkers,"* December 14, 2011.

Retrieved from http://unitedny.org/files/2012/07/Money-For-Nothing-New-York-Interest-Rate-Swaps.pdf.

This site is currently inactive but the report may be retrieved from
https://www.coursehero.com/file/11150128/Report-on-New-York-Swaps1/.

NY MTA Exhibit 3
A Sample of NY MTA Portfolio of Swaps
(Values are in Thousand Dollars)

Metropolitan Transportation Authority						
Related Bonds	Notional Amount as of	Effective Date	Maturity Date	Terms	Counterparty and Ratings (S&P / Moody's / Fitch)	Fair Value as of 9/30/16
TRB 2002D-2	$200.000	01/01/07	11/01/32	Pay 4.45%; receive 69% 1M LIBOR	JPMorgan Chase Bank, NA (A+ / Aa3 / AA-)	$ (88.998)
TRB 2005D & 2005E	300.000	11/02/05	11/01/35	Pay 3.561%; receive 67% 1M LIBOR	UBS AG (A+ / A1 / A+)	(76.564)
TRB 2005E	100.000	11/02/05	11/01/35	Pay 3.561%; receive 67% 1M LIBOR	AIG Financial Products1 (A- / Baa1 / BBB+)	(25.522)
TRB 2012G	357.850	11/15/12	11/01/32	Pay 3.563%; receive 67% 1M LIBOR	JPMorgan Chase Bank, NA (A+ / Aa3 / AA-)	(117.606)
DTF 2008A	331.020	03/24/05	11/01/31	Pay 3.3156%; receive 67% 1M LIBOR	Bank of New York Mellon (AA- /	(71.968)

Average Time Remaining to Maturity = 26 years

Question 1:
Why would a rational decision maker enter into contracts with those terms?

Answer from the annual report: (a boiler plate!)

To achieve cash flow savings through a synthetic fixed rate, MTA and MTA Bridges and Tunnels have entered into separate pay-fixed, receive-variable interest rate swaps at a cost anticipated to be less than what MTA and MTA Bridges and Tunnels would have paid to issue fixed-rate debt, and in some cases where Federal tax law prohibits an advance refunding to synthetically refund debt on a forward basis (p. 98)

Source: http://web.mta.info/mta/investor/pdf/2016/2016-CAFR.pdf

Question 2: How does having a synthetic fixed rate save cash flow?

For these five contracts, the average fixed rate payable to banks was 3.688, while the average interest rate receivable is set at 67% of LIBOR.

For the cautious observer, Michael Stewart's portrayal of NY MTA in the *"Money for Nothing"* report actually understates the losses attributable to swaps. In his calculations, swap losses capture only the losses directly related to differences between the fixed rates that NY MTA was paying the banks and the variable rates that NY MTA was receiving from the banks. In reality, the cost of entering into swap contracts is much more egregious. A possible list of these (transaction) costs includes the following:

(a) Nearly doubling the underwriting fees by charging fees for underwriting both the bonds and the swaps.
(b) Nearly doubling the insurance cost by requiring the counterparty — i.e., NY MTA, in this case — to retain highly rated surety companies to insure both the bonds and the swaps.
(c) Adding between 0.3% and 0.7% (30 to 70 basis points) annually to the interest rate payable for remarketing auction-rate bonds.
(d) Increasing the processing cost for dealing with bondholders and for making periodical settlement of the swaps.
(e) Bearing a contingent liability for putting up money for collateral if the credit ratings of either the agency or its insurance companies fall below specified levels. Money used for collateral are resources not profitably employed.
(f) Exposing NY MTA to basis risk because the floating rates set for the bonds are usually different from the floating rates set for the swaps.
(g) Stipulating the conditions, events, or actions that would be considered "triggering events," causing the banks to terminate the swap agreement and ask for the expected high termination penalties.

After taking account of all these items in the cost comparison, achieving lower borrowing costs by entering into swaps would be only a metaphysical possibility acted upon by heavenly intervention. Clearly the focus of the swap sales pitch was on highlighting the possible benefits, although no rational person could really explain the behavior of financial decision-makers at NY MTA if the observed results were to be considered.

○ First, what incentives did the officials at NY MTA have to keep going back and adding swaps when the plan of coupling swaps with variable rate bonds has been ineffective use of money?

- ○ Second, how could the officials at NY MTA justify entering into more swaps when the expected loss is approaching one billion dollars?
- ○ Third, how do the officials at NY MTA explain spending and wasting so much money to accomplish a psychological fixation on the presumed "fixity" of interest rate? Did they not know that the chased synthetic rate cannot be fixed if the bond issue pays a <u>weekly adjustable interest rate</u>?

Transparency Questioned

It is actually difficult to retrieve "clean" information from the Comprehensive Annual Financial Reports of NY MTA. Consider for example, the following disclosure:

> *"Transportation Revenue Refunding Bonds, Series 2002D —* 4.45% per annum on SubSeries 2002D-2 taking into account the interest rate swap."

This seems to be a clever way of hiding information, though it is not possible to know if such an obfuscation was intentional. There is no direct way of knowing the fixed rate payable on the swap, the variable rate collectible from the swap, or the variable rate on the bond; one has to be an informed detective to find out the needed information.

This was not the only case, the Comprehensive Annual Financial Report is full of them. Here are other examples:

> *"Transportation Revenue Refunding Bonds, Series 2002G —* 3.542% per annum on SubSeries 2002G-1 taking into account the interest rate swap and 4.00% per annum on the unhedged portion."
>
> "It is assumed that the variable-rate bonds would bear interest at a rate of 4.0% per annum."
>
> "The net swap payments were calculated using the actual fixed interest rate on the swap agreements."

For some reason or another, NY MTA could not find a better way to be more transparent and communicate the needed information for the public to know what? and why? Instead, the Comprehensive Annual Financial Report is more like a collection of riddles.

CHAPTER 29

The Bay Area Toll Authority (BATA) Fell into the Western Swap Sinkhole

The Bay Area Toll Authority Exhibit 1
Gaines and Losses on Interest-Rate Swaps

Expected Long-term Gains and Losses of Swaps Reported as Long-term Debt

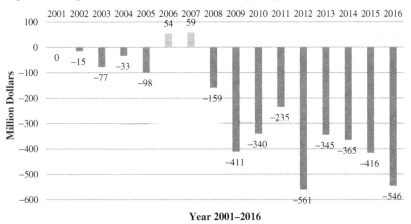

Year 2001–2016

Source: Comprehensive Annual Financial Reports.

The Metropolitan Transportation Commission of the State of California operates the Bay Area Toll Authority (BATA) and began its experience with interest-rate swaps in January 2002, shortly after the start of the Swap Mania. BATA started swap transactions with the intention of

> Controlling long-term debt costs while maintaining a hedge against increases in short-term rates. BATA is aware that swap transactions contain certain associated risks not traditionally associated with fixed-rate issues.[1]

As of June 2002, BATA had swaps on total notional amounts of $700 million: four fixed-payer contracts on $200 million notional amounts, $300 million Basis Swaps (variable for variable, $150 with AMBAC, and $150 with other banks), and a forward-starting swap contract on $200 million also with AMBAC. In a span of six months, the five swaps created additional liabilities of $15 million for expected losses as of June 30, 2002. In 2003, the same five contracts raised the liability for expected future losses to $77 million after having paid cash to settle the current portion due in 2003. "BATA Exhibit 1" shows the string of long term liabilities based on expected future losses for the period between 2002 and 2016. This Exhibit highlights the growth of long term losses from $15 million in 2002, to $561 million in 2012 and $516 million in 2013. In 2006 and 2007, BATA took a respite from losing and reported expected long term gains of $54 million and $59 million, respectively. These gains were, of course, transitory because they were washed away in 2008 and BATA reported long term losses in the amount of $159 million.

"BATA Exhibit 2" is reproduced from BATA's Comprehensive Annual Financial Report of 2003, detailing the composition of synthetic fixed rates, the net cost of borrowing when coupled with swaps.

As "BATA Exhibit 2" shows, BATA was paying a fixed rate of 4.139% for the swaps related to Bond Series 2003 and receiving a mere 0.858%, which meant that the Authority was giving away 3.281% (times the notional amounts) to big banks, essentially for nothing of value or guarantees. This was in addition to the 0.888% interest rate on the bond. BATA

---

[1] Metropolitan Transportation Commission Financial Statements for the year ended June 30, 2002, p. 69.
Retrieved from https://mtc.ca.gov/sites/default/files/MTC2002AR_Financials.pdf.

BATA Exhibit 2
Breakdown of the Components of the Synthetic Rate
(As Reported by BATA)

	Series 2001	Series 2003
	Bonds	Bonds
Interest Rate Swap		
Fixed payment counterparty*	4.105%	4.139%
65% Libor	−0.858%	−0.858%
Net interest rate swap payments***	3.247%	3.281%
Variable Rate bond coupon payments**	0.888%	0.888%
Synthetic interest rate on bonds	4.135%	4.169%
Remarketing/liquidity fee****	0.300%	0.300%
Total Cost	4.435%	4.469%

Source: Metropolitan Transportation Commission, Comprehensive Annual Financial Report, 2003. p. 57.
Retrieved from http://mtc.ca.gov/sites/default/files/Financial_Report_03.pdf.

also revealed making another mistake — the bonds were issued at the dreaded auction rate, requiring remarketing once a week. As most people know, nothing in Wall Street is free — the remarketing activity piled up an addition to the cost of debt. This presentation is one of the few that includes the cost of re-marketing auction-rate bonds, which was at its lower limit of 0.3%.

"BATA Exhibit 2" was reproduced from the annual report of the Metropolitan Transportation Commission. The net synthetic interest cost plus remarketing fees ended up being as high as 4.469% for Series 2003 bonds and 4.435% for Series 2001 (Excluding transaction cost). However, neither one of these items was a true measure of the synthetic "fixed" rate because an auction-rate bond violates all the assumptions of the pre-sumed "fixity." The rate was reset every week at levels acceptable to the new bondholders, who bid on the tendered bonds weekly. Furthermore, we shall see in BATA Exhibit 3 that the synthetic rates had increased to over 8% in 2007.

The management of BATA makes a distinction between short- and long-run effects of entering into swap contracts. The annual reports note that swaps may entail additional costs in the short run, but they were expected to become beneficial in the long run. We will shortly see that such an expectation is a dream that might require divine intervention to make it happen. Over a span of 15 years, the synthetic rates of the variable-rate bonds kept on increasing, and all the losses and money paid for the swaps, whether for annual settlement or for termination, were most definitely given away simply for nothing.

In 2004, BATA added one more swap contract with AMBAC on $200 million notional amount, and the losses from all six fixed-payer swap contracts increased to $98 million. Even with this increase in losses, the Metropolitan Transportation Commission explicitly stated that BATA intended to keep the swaps for the full duration of their terms — almost 30 years. Additionally, BATA continued shifting from conventional fixed-rate bonds to variable-rate bonds and simultaneously entering into new interest-rate swaps in order to artificially (synthetically) have a sought after fixed rate — rate that could not be fixed for more than one week at a time. BATA declared its intent to maintain the swap transactions steadily for the 35-year life of the contract. The years of 2005 and 2006 witnessed the largest and perhaps strangest activity: BATA entered into noncancelable swap contracts for a maturity of 39 years on notional amounts of $1 billion with four counterparties[2]:

> In November 2005, BATA approved a contract to swap variable-to-fixed rate bonds with a notional amount of $1 billion with an effective date of February 2006. At June 30, 2009, the counterparties to the transactions are Ambac for $315 million, JP Morgan AAA ISDA for $245 million, Citibank for $225 million and Bank of America for $30 million. During the 39 year-term of the swap, BATA will pay each respective counterparty based on a fixed rate ranging from 3.63 percent to 4.00 percent.
>
> In exchange, BATA will receive a variable rate payment based on varying percentages of LIBOR. BATA will receive from Ambac and Bank of America a variable rate payment based on 68 percent of the one-month LIBOR rate. BATA will receive from Citibank a variable rate

---

[2] Metropolitan Transportation Commission. Financial Statements for years ended June 30, 2009 and 2008, p. 65.

Retrieved from https://mtc.ca.gov/sites/default/files/CAFR_June30-2009.pdf.

payment based on 53.8 percent of the one-month LIBOR rate and 74 basis points. BATA will receive from JP Morgan a variable rate payment based on 67.8 percent of the 10 year LIBOR rate in years 1 through 30 (first leg) and a variable rate payment based on 75.105 percent of the one-month LIBOR in years 31 through 39 (second leg).

In 2006, before the financial crisis hit the market, LIBOR increased, and BATA entered into eight more fixed-payer swaps on notional amounts of $2 billion. These actions represented a total change of character and reversal of the financial structure; BATA went all the way from no swaps in 2000 to a swap portfolio of 13 contracts on total notional amounts of $2.8 billion. However, BATA ended fiscal year 2006 with $54 million profits on the swaps due to the combination of the increase in LIBOR and growth in the swap portfolio. But this good fortune lasted only one more year before all the reported gains were more than devoured in 2008, when the swap portfolio accrued net losses of more than $159 million.

Somehow and inexplicably, BATA administrators continued to have faith in financing by synthetic rates and added 11 new swap contracts: six fixed-payer (pay fixed, receive variable) and five fixed-receiver (receive fixed, pay variable). It remains a mystery why BATA entered into both types of swaps and incurring all the related transaction cost. Entering into these two types of swap contracts makes no sense because they are essentially hedging each other's cash-flow risk, just the same as the swaps of the University of Texas System and Shands Hospital of the University of Florida. It is, therefore, important to ask the following questions:

o   Why enter into swap contracts to add some form of risk and then enter into other complementary or offsetting swap contracts to hedge that risk? Unlike the case in the profit sector, entering into offsetting swaps does not relieve the entity of its legal and economic obligations.
o   Why? Who or what made BATA do it?

This seems to be very much inefficient use of resources because each swap contract entails paying high fees for underwriting, insurance, legal, and swap consulting fees among many other costs related to the contracting process. Moreover, both types together have no implication to the risk management of the core operation and financing of BATA.

The bankers' sales promotion has always emphasized that the synthetic fixed rate on a bundle that includes variable-rate bonds and swaps to pay fixed and receive variable will lower the cost of borrowing. If true, this would be a useful protection for the borrower in a financial crisis, but this was simply untrue using the data published by BATA itself. Consider the synthetic rates reported by BATA in 2008, as shown in "BATA Exhibit 3" (reproduced from the 2008 Comprehensive Annual Financial Report). It is evident that the synthetic fixed rate was nearly twice as much as the fixed rate payable on the swaps for every bond issued in the 2001–2007 bond series. The worst situation was for the transaction related to Bond Series 2001 for which the synthetic rate was 9.494% while the fixed rate payable on the swap was only 4.105%.

Additionally, with the financial crisis looming on the horizon, all of BATA's swap contracts backfired, and the total long-term losses from swaps added up to $561 million as of June 30, 2012. Yet, the administration at BATA was oblivious to the brewing disaster and held on to its own decisions to stay with the swaps to maturity, a decision that could lead only to financial death by swaps.[3]

> The termination value, or fair market value, BATA would pay to terminate all swaps on a voluntary basis is $546 million and $416 million on June 30, 2016 and June 30, 2015, respectively. The fair value was determined by an independent outside pricing service. *BATA's intent, however, is to maintain the swap transactions for the life of the related financings, notwithstanding market opportunities to restructure.* [Emphasis Added]

It appears that *restructuring* was an expression to suggest going back full circle to issue fixed-rate bonds for financing and give up some of the synthetic-rate financing. Subsequently, the restructuring began to take place only one month after the 2009 fiscal year's end[4]:

> In July 2009, BATA made a termination payment of $105 million to terminate the swaps with Ambac Financial Services. In August 2009,

---

[3] Metropolitan Transportation Commission. Comprehensive Annual Financial Report for r the Fiscal Years Ended June 30, 2016 and June 30, 2015, p. 76.

Retrieved from https://mtc.ca.gov/sites/default/files/FY_16_MTC_CAFR.pdf.
[4] CAFR. 2009, p. 80.

BATA Exhibit 3
Disastrous Synthetic Fixed Rates (As Reported)

Reproduced as in original source

	Series 2001	Series 2003	Series 2004	Series 2006	Series 2007
Interest Rate Swap					
Fixed payment to counter party	4.105%	4.139%	3.416%	3.731%	3.740%
LIBOR percentage of payments*****	−1.599%	−1.599%	−1.868%	−2.142%	−2.134%
Net interest rate swap payments***	2.506%	2.540%	1.548%	1.589%	1.606%
Variable rate bond coupon payments**	6.688%	5.369%	7.313%	3.482%	6.487%
Synthetic interest rate on bonds	9.194%	7.909%	8.861%	5.071%	8.093%
Remarketing/liquidity fee****	0.300%	0.300%	0.300%	0.500%	0.300%
Total Cost	9.494%	8.209%	9.161%	5.571%	8.393%

* Converted to 65% one month LIBOR on 1/1/06
** The ending average variable rate as of last June 2008 reset
*** Net receipt/(payment)
**** Remarketing/liquidity fees
***** LIBOR rates as of last June 30, 2008 reset

Source: Metropolitan Transportation Commission, Comprehensive Annual Financial Report for Fiscal Year Ended June 30, 2008, P. 66.
Retrieved from http://mtc.ca.gov/sites/default/files/CAFR-financials_07-08.pdf.

BATA restructured the variable rate bonds underlying the Ambac swaps by issuing $768.7 million in new fixed rate bonds and reissuing the balance of variable rate demand bonds.

By 2012, BATA terminated all the swaps with AMBAC and paid $200 *million for total termination costs up to that time.* Nevertheless, the losses of all the swaps remaining in the portfolio kept on increasing at an accelerated rate. In 2012 alone, total fair values of the expected losses on all swap contracts reached a high of $534 million.[5] Then, again in 2016 the total long-term loss expected from the swap portfolio was $546 million. BATA Exhibit 1 presents the history of long-term non-current losses as of the end of each year from 2002 to 2016. Indeed, it is incumbent upon the management to provide analysis or evidence showing that issuing municipal bonds in the traditional mode of paying a fixed rate would have cost BATA $546 million more! (See BATA Exhibit 1) Or else, the swap contracts should be terminated. Nevertheless, the management of the Metropolitan Transportation Commission (BATA), did not seem to falter and admit having taken the wrong turn. Instead, to this day, the management continues to insist on keeping the swap agreements for the contractual terms of maturity.

The pressure on BATA did not ease up, and the cost of the misguided decisions continued to waste both scarce resources and perhaps the toll money paid by travelers. Clearly this seems to be a reflection of the management's hubris to enter into a new arena in finance as complex as can be and to continue drowning deep in the swap sinkhole for more than 35 years.

---

[5] Metropolitan Transportation Commission. Financial Statements for years ended June 30, 2013 and 2012, p. 73.
   Retrieved from https://mtc.ca.gov/sites/default/files/CAFR_2013.pdf.

CHAPTER 30

The Massachusetts Bay Transportation Authority Joined the Eastern Swap Sinkhole

Did financial managers at nonprofits have second thoughts about the risk of committing to a 30- or 40-years noncancelable swap contract? Unlike the case with BATA, there is some evidence that such reflection was the case of Massachusetts Bay Transportation Authority (MBTA), but only 15 years after they got entangled in the net of the Swap Mania. In general many entities rushed to find an exit by terminating or changing the terms of the swap agreements after they suffered huge losses.[1] The publicly available evidence so far suggests that some nonprofits took notice of the difference after bleeding large sums of cash every year to pay big banks... for nothing tangible. A case in point is the effort of the officials at the Massachusetts Bay Transportation Authority (MBTA) in January 2017 to convince JPMorgan Chase to renegotiate the swap contracts they had signed in 2002. It took 15 years after joining the Swap Mania before MBTA discovered the long-term high cost of falling into swap traps. After paying $70 million to terminate five swap agreements, in January 2017, the authority began considering ways to reduce its losses on the remaining

---

[1] "Novation" is the term financial engineers call for replacing a contract by another.

three swap contracts. The three remaining contracts are displayed in a special document that MBTA issued and is partially reproduced here as "Massachusetts Bay Transportation Authority Exhibit 1."

If the authority were to follow through and terminate the three contracts noted in that document, it would have to pay nearly $39 million more. Instead, MBTA began to speculate on the amounts of loss decrease that would accrue if the banks were to agree to reduce the required fixed rate. The two contracts of concern were the swap agreements with JPMorgan Chase that had accumulated losses of about $37.5 million.

Additionally, in its report "Interest-Rate-Swap Agreements — Amendments Opportunities," MBTA speculated on the loss reduction that could accrue from lowering the required fixed rate to 2%. The authority

Massachusetts Bay Transportation Authority Exhibit 1
MBTA Interest-Rate Swap — Amendment
Opportunities Position in January 2017

Current Swap Profile

After terminating five interest rate swaps in May 2016, three remain in place

Maturity	Counterparty	Current Mark-to-Market*	Pay	Receive
2020	Morgan Stanley	($1,677,000)	4.13%	CPI + 79 bps
2022	JP Morgan	($8,218,000)	5.20%	SIFMA
2030	JP Morgan	($29,332,000)	5.61%	SIFMA

- Since the MBTA is not posting collateral to JP Morgan or Morgan Stanley, both banks are exposed to MBTA nonrepayment (i.e., credit) risk
- Due to the size of its Mark-to-Markets and related risk, JP Morgan has the largest incentive to terminate or amend the contracts
- There are two ways in which the MBTA can capitalize on this:

   (1) **Terminate the swaps at a discount**
   (2) **Pay down the fixed rate at a discount (recommended)**

Source: Retrieved from https://www.mbta.com/uploadedfiles/About_the_T/Board_Meetings/K. Interest Rate Swap Amendments.pdf.

presented that option in "Massachusetts Bay Transportation Authority Exhibit 2." The exhibit refers to the two relatively large swaps: "swap 1" is the contract with JPMorgan Chase for which MBTA pays a 5.2% fixed rate, while "swap 2" is the contract with JPMorgan Chase for which MBTA pays a 5.6% fixed rate. If JPMorgan Chase were to agree to reduce the fixed rate to 2%, MBTA would save 3.2% and 3.6% on these two contracts, respectively. Nonetheless, there is no apparent or obvious incentive for JPMorgan Chase to agree to such a deal; as always, the bank is in the position of controlling the steering wheel.

Massachusetts Bay Transportation Authority Exhibit 2
The Wishful Thought of Renegotiating the Swaps' Fixed Rates

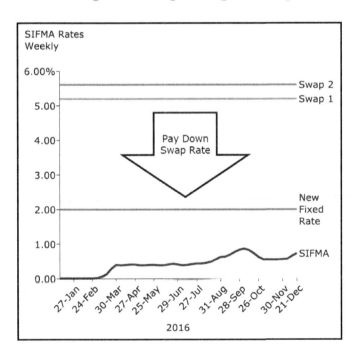

Note: The SIFMA rate is the weekly average of interest rates of high-grade, variable-rate, tax-exempt municipal bonds compiled and published by the Securities Industry and Financial Market Association.
Source: MBTA Interest Rate Swap Portfolios, Amendment Opportunities.
Retrieved from http://www.mbta.com/uploadedfiles/About_the_T/Board_Meetings/K.%20%20Interest%20Rate%20Swap%20Amendments.pdf.

The proposed modification was made in January 2017, but the swap contracts that were signed in early 2000 continue to haunt MBTA and, if not terminated, will continue to do so until 2030. Looking back at how MBTA became a counterparty for long-term swap contracts and joining the Swap Mania, the story is simple. MBTA had a short-term (five-year)

Massachusetts Bay Transportation Authority Exhibit 3
The Disclosure Ushering Joining the Swap Mania

Interest Rate Swap (for Massachusetts Bay Transportation Authority)

- In fiscal 2000, the Authority entered into an interest rate swap agreement for its General Transportation System Bonds, Variable Rate Demand Obligations, 2000 Series (the "2000 Bonds").
- The interest rate swap matures in fiscal 2006.
- Under this agreement, the Authority pays to the swap counterparty fixed interest rates of 4.9284% on a notional amount equal to the total outstanding principal of the 2000 Bonds.
- The swap counterparty (the bank) pays interest on the same notional amount based on the Municipal Bond Average Interest Rate [SIFMA].
- Only the net difference is exchanged with the counterparty.
- The Authority continues to pay interest to the holders of the 2000 Bonds at the variable rate provided by the bonds.
- However, during the term of the swap agreement, to the extent that the Municipal Swap Index is equivalent to the variable interest rate on the 2000 Bonds, the Authority effectively pays a fixed rate on the 2000 Bonds. (The synthetic fixed rate which was assumed to be 4.9284%.)

  ○ In fiscal 2002, the Authority entered into a five-year option for a swap agreement effective from September 1, 2005 up to September 1, 2010 to execute a new swap agreement in connection with the 2000 Bonds after the existing one expires.
  ○ If exercised, the Authority will enter into a swap with a counterparty under which the Authority will pay a fixed interest rate of 5% and
  ○ Receive a floating rate equal to 67% of LIBOR.
  ○ The swap agreement would terminate on March 1, 2030. From the sale of this option, the Authority will receive $5,663(000) in August 2002 and 2003.

Note: The reproduced statement refers to "fiscal 2002" although it appeared as part of the footnote disclosures in the Financial Statements of June 30, 2001.
Source: Massachusetts Bay Transportation Authority. Financial Statements June 30, 2001.
Retrieved from http://www.mbta.com/uploadedFiles/Documents/Financials/kpmg2001.pdf.

swap contract in 2001, and it did not lose money on the swap in the first year. This was a good cause for big banks to encourage MBTA to enter into other swap contracts for longer terms, and to sweeten the deal, they offered MBTA upfront money of $5,663,000. By accepting the money for a swaption contract, MBTA had effectively given away the right to decide.

The annual report of 2001 relates this story as if it were a simple fact of life like any other daily activity. "Massachusetts Bay Transportation Authority Exhibit 3" is an annotation of the relevant parts.[2]

Interpretation

MBTA sold bonds in 2000 at a variable rate. Simultaneously, MBTA entered into a swap contract having a notional amount equal to the face amount of the bond issue. The terms of the swap required MBTA to pay big banks 4.9384% and to receive the Municipal Bond Average Interest Rate (SIFMA). If SIFMA covers the interest rate on the bond issue, then the net cost of borrowing would be close to 4.9289%, which would be the synthetic rate (while excluding transaction cost). The swap would terminate in five years.

However, the related bonds have a term ending in 2030. In 2002, MBTA got into the game in a big way; it sold a swaption contract to big banks for an upfront payment of $5,663,000, giving big banks the right, but not the obligation, to have a swap contract with MBTA in 2005. If the banks decided to exercise this option, MBTA would be obligated to agree to it. When exercised, the swap contract calls for MBTA to pay a fixed rate of 5% and receive a variable rate equal to 67% of LIBOR. The contract has a 25-year term and terminates in 2030 just like the related bond issue. In September 2005, LIBOR averaged 3.85%, which meant that 0.67% of LIBOR was 2.58% at that time. At the same time, the forward rates were projected to go up to 4.6% at the end of 30 years, which was still much lower than the 5% fixed rate that MBTA was paying.

---

[2]Massachusetts Bay Transportation Authority. Notes to Financial Statements, June 30, 2001.

Retrieved from http://www.mbta.com/uploadedFiles/Documents/Financials/kpmg2001.pdf.

In other words, there was no time on the horizon when the forward rates would increase sufficiently to ensure that the fair value of the *fixed leg* of the swap would equal the fair value of *the floating leg* at the time of signing the contract. Clearly, such a swap contract would not be a fair exchange, as discussed later in this book in Chapter 34.

By 2015, MBTA had eight swap contracts on notional amounts of $632 million. Also in 2015, MBTA disclosed that total losses on these swaps amounted to $113 million. While that amount of loss was lower than the $120 million loss in 2010, it appears that officials at MBTA began to realize having made a mistake in getting into a speculative/gambling game about which they had little knowledge or competence. This led to two actions:

○ In 2016, MBTA terminated five swap contracts and paid a termination penalty of $73.3 million in termination fees.
○ The three remaining swap contracts had a total expected loss of $39.2 million, which MBTA would have had to pay if it had decided to terminate these contracts at the year's end.

Just like all others, the gambles failed and all the money paid to big banks was and is simply paid for nothing.

CHAPTER 31

A Couple of Other Port Authorities

(a) The Port Authority of New York and New Jersey Paid Big Banks $242 Million to Exit Swaps

The financial statements of the Port Authority of New York and New Jersey began to show items related to interest-rate swaps in 2003 when the authority joined the Swap Mania and entered into four swaps having notional amounts of $377 million. By the end of the year, the port Authority owed big banks a total of $59 million for losses on the swaps. By 2005, the notional amounts of the swaps increased to $794 million, and the related expected long-term loss increased to $162 million after the annual settlements were paid in cash. By 2008, the Port Authority had entered into more swap contracts and the total notional amounts of swaps increased to $805 million. These activities had also increased the Port Authority's swap loss-related obligations to $235 million or 29% of the notional amounts, once again after settling the recurring loss for that year. By 2012, the Authority realized it had been paying millions of dollars every year since 2003 to settle swaps' liabilities while continuing to be indebted to big banks for huge amounts of swap losses payable in the future. Because some of the swap contracts were scheduled to terminate in 2036, and 2038, the Authority decided to avoid the annual financial bleeding of cash for another quarter of a century and *terminated all outstanding swap contracts by making a one-time payment of $228 million.* This amount was, of course, in addition to the cash paid that year for the annual settlement (amounts were not disclosed) and the $14.1 million the Authority had paid to terminate one of the swaps in 2010.

This is truly a story of swift end of joining the Swap Mania: the Port Authority had entered into swaps to avoid paying higher interest rates but instead ended up paying hundreds of millions of dollars in additional costs. With the decision to terminate all swaps, the word *swap* did not appear in the 2013 annual report!

(b) Pennsylvania Turnpike Authority Confounds the Financing

On October 7, 2014, the Pennsylvania Turnpike Commission issued a preliminary documentation to raise over $210 million in subordinated bonds. In that document, the commission noted that toll revenues would go toward covering certain obligations, including obligations arising from interest-rate swaps on $1.5 billion notional amounts. This disclosure followed the findings and related recommendation of Auditor General Jack Wagner[1]:

> **Finding Six** — The Turnpike Commission's use of interest rate "swaps" has cost the taxpayers and its toll paying customers at least $108.9 million dollars *more than if the Turnpike had instead financed with conventional fixed rate bonds.* [Emphasis Added]
>
> To address Finding Six, we recommend that the Turnpike Commission should, (1) terminate all remaining swaps as soon as it is fiscally responsible to do so and refinance, if necessary, with conventional fixed-rate bonds; and (2) promptly adopt a resolution unequivocally and permanently prohibiting the use of swaps in the future.

---

[1] Jack Wagner, "Pennsylvania Turnpike Commission: A Performance Audit," January 2013.

Retrieved from https://www.paturnpike.com/pdfs/business/finance/PTC_Report_final_01082013.pdf#search=%22swaps%22.

Wagner's auditing report shows that the Turnpike Commission paid $59 million between 2001 and 2009 for terminating other swap contracts.

Although the Commission disagreed with Wagner's finding and recommendation, it continued to lose money and pay cash for settlements year after year. Auditor General Wagner also raised concern about the impact of interest-rate swaps on the operations of the Pennsylvania Turnpike Commission because the Commission had already paid $109 million in interest and swap settlements in relation to its swap portfolio.

In its Comprehensive Annual Financial Report dated May 2014, the commission reported having 19 interest-rate-swap contracts with maturity dates going from 2015 to 2039. The financial statements also revealed confusing information intended to understate the commission's obligations for swap losses; an arbitrary and meaningless distinction was made between (a) book-fair values and (b) full-fair values due to banks. The reported information reveals that total notional amounts of the pay-fixed, receive-variable swaps were $685 million, and the book-fair value of the swaps reflecting swap-related loss liabilities to big banks was $49 million, but curiously, the "full-fair value due to banks" was $196 million. The explanation provided for the difference makes little or no sense[2]:

> The full value (to) from Counterparty listed is the mid-market value at May 31, 2014. The difference between full value and book fair value is related to the value of the swaps at the time the related bonds were refunded and/or the swap was novated.

Adding this uniquely inventive explanation to the technical nature of the entire financial report and the various financial jargon guaranteed that no one in the public could have understood a thing about the obligations arising from interest rate swap contracts. For the same total of notional

---

[2] Comprehensive Annual Financial Report, Pennsylvania Turnpike Commission, A Component Unit of the Commonwealth of Pennsylvania Fiscal Years Ended May 31, 2014 and 2013., p. 92.

Retrieved from https://www.paturnpike.com/pdfs/business/PTC_CAFR_14_13_Final.pdf#search=%22swaps%22.

amounts, the book-fair value of the swaps amounted to $134 million in 2016, but no information was provided for the so-called full-fair value.

Just like many other nonprofit entities, the Pennsylvania Turnpike Commission was obsessed with interest rate swaps. In its 2016 Comprehensive Annual Financial Report, the word *swap* was repeated 89 times as compared to repeating the word *toll* only 38 times.

The LIBOR Scandal:

Big Banks' Colluded & Conspired to Siphon More Money from the Public Service Sector & Everyone Else

No, This Was Not a Lover's Plea

On September 7, 2006, a London desk head [of Deutsche Bank] attempted to obtain a low EURIBOR (interest rate benchmark) submission from an external banker at Barclays, "I'm begging u, don't forget me... pleasssssssssssssssseeeeeeeeee... I'm on my knees..." The external banker replied, "I told them 1 m [one month] up is that right?" The London desk head continued, "please pal, insist as much as you can... my treasury is taking it to the sky... we have to counter balance it... I'm beggin u... can u beg the [a panel bank] guy as well?" The external banker agreed, "ok, I'm telling him."

Source: *NYDFS Announces Deutsche Bank to pay $2.5 billion, terminate and ban individual employees, install independent monitor for interest rate manipulation.*

Retrieved from http://dfs.ny.gov/about/press/pr1504231.htm.

Why Manipulate the Benchmark "LIBOR"?

In long-term swap contracts having face amounts of hundreds of trillions of dollars for which big banks receive specified fixed interest rates and pay adjustable interest rates linked to the London Average Interest Rate (LIBOR). Deflating LIBOR reduces the amounts of money that big banks pay on interest-rate swaps and increases their profits. If deflating that rate could be achieved by colluding and conspiring among big banks, so be it. The US Department of Justice found the foreign domiciled big banks doing business in the United States criminally liable for sustaining conspiracies and collusion to manipulate LIBOR for many years. Many injured entities filed class-action suits against the involved banks, which continued running the normal course through the US court system.

CHAPTER 32

The London Connection: London Average Interest Rate (LIBOR)

With the assistance of the Bank of England and large international banks, the British Bankers Association (BBA) designed a process to calculate an interest rate that would be acceptable worldwide. The newly designed system began operation in 1986. In designing that process, BBA got almost all giant international banks involved. In principle, the envisioned system was simple and straightforward as summarized in the following five steps:

i. BBA designated ten major currencies — e.g., the US dollar, the euro, the Australian dollar, the Yen, and the British Pound.
ii. BBA negotiated with large international banks to be members of, what amounted to be like, "voting" panels, one panel for each currency. These are the *bank panels of submitters*. For the US dollar, for example, the panel of submitters in 2009 consisted of three US banks, nine European banks, two banks from Japan, a Canadian bank, and a bank from Hong Kong[1].

---

[1] These banks were

Bank of America (USA)   Bank of Tokyo-Mitsubishi UFJ Ltd (Japan)
Barclays Bank plc (UK)   Citibank NA (USA)

iii. By 11:10 a.m. London time every day, each bank submits interest rates in response to the following question:

   At what rate could you borrow funds, were you to do so by asking for and then accepting interbank offers in a reasonable market size just prior to 11:00 a.m.?

   Each bank submitted rates for each of 15 short-term loans varying from one day to one year.

iv. BBA retained an agency that was later sold to Thomson Reuters to calculate the average rate for each loan term using a specific procedure.

v. At 11:30 a.m. London time, BBA announces the obtained averages as the rates at which big banks could borrow short-term loans from one another.

The designation of the final averages of interest rates is the London Interbank Offered Rate (LIBOR). To avoid complication, the presentation in this book use the made-up simple name of "London Average Interest Rate." In order for the system of BBA to function as intended, two conditions must always be present:

(1) All banks on the submission panels must report honestly.
(2) Each bank must make its own submission totally independent of all other banks.

In the 30 years, that followed since the start of this system, LIBOR has become the most important global-interest-rate reference or benchmark for all types of contracts, especially as a benchmark (or index) for interest rates of mortgages, loans, and about $400 trillion

---

Credit Suisse (Switzerland)	Deutsche Bank AG, (Germany)
HSBC (UK and Hong Kong)	JPMorgan Chase (USA)
Lloyds TSB Bank plc (UK)	Rabobank (The Netherlands)
Royal Bank of Canada	Société Générale (France)
The Norinchukin Bank (Japan)	The Royal Bank of Scotland (UK)
UBS AG (Switzerland)	West LB AG (Germany)

[$400,000,000,000,000] of interest-rate-derivatives contracts worldwide.[2]

Later on, financial markets questioned the validity of a statement made by Martin Wheatley, the former chair of the United Kingdom regulator Financial Services Authority (FSA), in which he told the UK Parliament that LIBOR is "the most important figure in finance." The doubt was fueled by rumors that the panels of bank submitters were in violation of the appropriate rules of conduct — they colluded and conspired to orchestrate their submitted rates to benefit themselves and their traders.

On March 15, 2011, the evidence of collusion and conspiracy among members of the bank panels of submitters was revealed. On that day, the Swiss bank UBS AG, which is also cross-listed on the New York Stock Exchange, disclosed the following bombshell in its annual filing of the 10-K form with the US Securities and Exchange Commission (SEC):

> UBS has received subpoenas from the SEC, the US Commodity Futures Trading Commission and the US Department of Justice in connection with investigations regarding submissions to the British Bankers' Association, which sets LIBOR rates. UBS understands that the investigations focus on whether there were improper attempts by UBS, either

---

[2]Bank for International Settlements, Statistical release, "OTC derivatives statistics," Monetary and Economic Department. Notional amounts of interest rate contracts (and corresponding fair market values) were:

Notional (Market Value)

$ 76 trillion ($ 1.7 trillion) in 2001. Retrieved from https://www.bis.org/publ/otc_hy0112. pdf, p. 5.

$204 trillion ($ 6.0 trillion) in 2005. Retrieved from https://www.bis.org/publ/otc_hy0511. pdf, p. 7.

$479 trillion ($19.0 trillion) in 2010. Retrieved from https://www.bis.org/publ/otc_hy1011. pdf, p. 13.

$561 trillion ($15.0 trillion) in 2013. Retrieved from https://www.bis.org/publ/otc_hy1311. pdf, p. 19.

$438 trillion ($16.0 trillion) in 2016. Retrieved from https://www.bis.org/publ/otc_hy1611. pdf, p. 13.

acting on its own or together with others, to manipulate LIBOR rates at certain times. In addition, UBS has received an order to provide information to the Japan Financial Supervisory Agency concerning similar matters. UBS is conducting an internal review and is cooperating with the investigations.[3]

This note marked the first public acknowledgment of an undercover investigation of the LIBOR scandal by the Commodity Futures Trading Commission (CFTC), the Securities and Exchange Commission and the Department of Justice. The CFTC and the Department of Justice began their investigation in 2008 following the public circulation of a special report titled "Is LIBOR Broken?" The report authors, Scott Peng, Chintan (Monty) Gandhi, and Alexander Tyo, were analysts at Citigroup Global Markets, Inc.[4] The report noted that "LIBOR touches everyone from the largest international conglomerate to the smallest borrower in Peoria," but it may be understated by 20–30 basis points (0.2–0.3%; a basis point is 0.01%). In the week following the publication of Peng, Gandhi and Tyo report, the *Wall Street Journal* published two articles by Carrick Mollenkamp (April 16, 2008), and Carrick Mollenkamp and Mark Whitehouse (May 29, 2008).[5] In his April 16, 2008, article, Mollenkamp quoted a mortgage banker who said he depended on LIBOR to tell him how much he owed his bank, adding that concerns about LIBOR's reliability are "actually kind of frightening if you really sit and think about it."

---

[3] UBS AG. Annual Report 2010, p. 318.

Retrieved from https://www.google.com/#q=ubs+form+10-k+2010.

[4] Scott Peng, Chintan (Monty) Gandhi, and Alexander Tyo, "Special Topic: Is LIBOR Broken?" (Citigroup Global Markets, Inc., April 10, 2008).

Retrieved from http://www.moneyscience.com/mod/file/download.php?file_guid= 393006.

[5] Carrick Mollenkamp, "Bankers Cast Doubt On Key Rate Amid Crisis," *The Wall Street Journal*, April 16, 2008.

Retrieved from http://online.wsj.com/article/SB120831164167818299.html.

Carrick Mollenkamp and Mark Whitehouse, "Study Casts Doubt on Key Rate," *The Wall Street* Journal, May 29, 2008.

Retrieved from http://online.wsj.com/article/SB121200703762027135.html.

To highlight the significance of what might be mistakenly taken as a minor manipulation in the world of finance; UBS AG trading records confirmed that each 0.01% (one basis point) movement in LIBOR would generate profits of approximately $459,000 for the book of Thomas Hayes, one of the bank's most notorious derivatives traders. Additionally,[6]

> Citibank, N.A. reported it would make $936 million in net interest revenue if rates would fall by 25 basis points (0.25%) per quarter over the next year and $1.935 Billion if rates fell 1% instantaneously.
>
> JPMorgan Chase reported that if interest rates increased by 1%, the bank would lose over $500 million in interest revenue.
>
> HSBC and Lloyds also estimated that interest rate changes of less than 1% would affect their profits by hundreds of millions of dollars in 2008 and 2009.

Up to that point in time, many financial experts had missed the significance of a change in the benchmark rate of interest by one basis point. Even the former governor of the Bank of England could not mask his surprise upon reading a transcript provided by the UK Financial Services Authority[7]:

> In a telephone call on 12 September 2007, the Submitter [of the bank's interest rate] indicated that Barclays' Derivatives Traders had an interest in high three month LIBOR submissions "for about a couple of million dollars a basis point. Ah, but I don't know how much longer I'm gonna be able to keep it up at seventy seven."

---

[6] United States District Court. Northern District of California. The Regents of the University of California vs. Bank of America Corporation, etc. Case4:13-cv-02921-DMR Document1 Filed06/25/13, June, 2013, p. 30.

Retrieved from http://web.stanford.edu/group/lawlibrary/cgi-bin/liborlitigation/wp-content/uploads/2013/06/UCRegents-complaint-NDCalif-25Jun2013.pdf.

[7] House of Commons, United Kingdom. "Treasury Committee Fixing LIBOR: some preliminary findings," *Second Report of Session 2012–13 HC 481–I.*

Retrieved from https://publications.parliament.uk/pa/cm201213/cmselect/cmtreasy/481/481.pdf.

To this, the governor of the Bank of England noted:

I was very struck and surprised, when reading these three reports [from regulatory authorities], to discover that changing LIBOR by one basis point was the kind of rigging that people were interested in. You would never have noticed that from market activity. We were worried about tens of basis points.

CHAPTER 33

The Discovery of Cheating

(a) Litigating LIBOR Manipulation

Following the publicity about the conspiracy and collusion to manipulate LIBOR, many investors and counterparties to interest-rate swaps filed class-action suits. For example, on August 8, 2012, the investors Elizabeth Lieberman and Todd Augenbaum filed a class-action suit claiming that[1]

> "The banks communicated with each other and colluded to artificially depress Libor." As a result of such actions, Preferred Equity Securities purchased by the Plaintiffs, with dividends tied to the U.S. Dollar Libor rate, received a lower rate of return.

But none of the class-action suits got as much public attention as the one filed on October 14, 2012, by Annie Bell Adams — a citizen of Mobile, Alabama, who was 65 years old at the time and lost her house to foreclosure. The suit included a large number of homeowners who had adjustable-rate mortgages linked to London Average Interest Rate (LIBOR). In the suit, the homeowners allege that banks intentionally raised LIBOR

---

[1] SFC Associates, Court Cases Involving the Manipulation of London Interbank Offered Rate, March 3, 2013.

Retrieved from http://sfcassociates.com/wp-content/uploads/2013/03/LIBOR-Cases-As-of-3_13_13.pdf.

on the first day of each month, "resulting in Libor-based adjustable rate mortgages paying two basis points higher than average."[2] John Sharbrough, the Alabama-based attorney for the case, said the class might include as many as 10,000 plaintiffs. The plaintiffs alleged that banks conspired and colluded to manipulate LIBOR upward on the day their adjustable mortgage rates were scheduled for resetting. Adams' mortgage rate was set at LIBOR plus 6%, updated every six months on the first day of the month. The lawsuit claims that the "statistical analysis shows LIBOR rose consistently on the first day of each month between 2000 and 2009...Between 2007 and 2009 LIBOR moved by as much as 7.5 basis points on certain reset days."[3]

Financial Times

October 14, 2012 9:52 pm
US woman takes on banks over LIBOR
By Caroline Binham in London

A pensioner whose home was repossessed is taking on some of the world's leading banks in the first known class-action lawsuit claiming that alleged LIBOR manipulation made mortgage repayments for thousands of Americans more expensive than they should have been.

Retrieved from https://www.ft.com/content/6b912248-1496-11e2-8cf2-00144feabdc0.

---

[2] Caroline Binham, US Woman Takes on Banks over LIBOR. *Financial Times*, October 14, 2012.

Retrieved from https://www.ft.com/content/6b912248-1496-11e2-8cf2-00144feabdc0. *See also,* Halah Touryalai, Banks Rigged Libor To Inflate Adjustable-Rate Mortgages: Lawsuit, *Forbes,* October 15, 2012.

Retrieved from https://www.forbes.com/sites/halahtouryalai/2012/10/15/banks-rigged-libor-to-inflate-adjustable-rate-mortgages-lawsuit/#6d2b4c6ba85b.

[3] The originating bank of Adams's mortgage loan was Ameriquest, which sold the mortgages it had originated to Deutsche Bank. In turn, Deutsche Bank pooled the plaintiffs' mortgages with others and used them to back issuing special types of bonds known as residential mortgage-backed securities (RMBS) for sale to the public. *United States District Court for the Southern District of New York, Case 1:12-cv-07461-UA Document 1 Filed 10/04/12.*

The two claims noted above made contradictory allegations as to whether big banks colluded to inflate or deflate LIBOR away from its representative values. The alleged motivation for this manipulation consists of two arguments:

a. Deflating the submitted interest rates would make banks look less risky and more creditworthy such that the banks themselves could borrow at lower interest rates.
b. The manipulation up or down was motivated purely by profit making — reducing the adjustable interest payable on interest-rate swaps and similar instruments.

More class-action suits against the bank panel of submitters began to accumulate very quickly. The lead plaintiffs included the Federal Deposit Insurance Corporation; the National Association of Credit Unions; the

Regents of the University of California; the New York Metropolitan Transportation Authority; the Bay Area Toll Authority; and the cities of Baltimore, Philadelphia, Houston, Oakland, San Diego, and Sacramento among many others. On March 29, 2013, Judge Naomi Buchwald of the Southern District Court of New York, issued a ruling not granting the plaintiffs their wishful decision against big banks concerning antitrust violation.[4] The legal service site *LEAGLE* provides a detailed listing of these cases.[5]

In its class-action complaint, the City of Baltimore, a lead plaintiff, indicated that it had "purchased hundreds of millions of dollars in interest rate swaps directly from at least one Defendant in which the rate of return was tied to LIBOR and was injured as a result of Defendants' anticompetitive conduct"[6] In particular, the city followed the bankers' advice to issue bonds at adjustable (floating) rates and entered into a large number of interest-rate-exchange (swap) contracts that are linked to LIBOR. Under these agreements, the city and the class in the suit paid fixed rates and received adjustable rates linked to LIBOR. When banks colluded and conspired to deflate LIBOR, the city claimed to have lost millions of dollars on its interest-rate swaps.

To provide evidence that big banks had artificially depressed LIBOR, the plaintiffs used three measures for comparison with LIBOR:

i. The first measure is the correlation between the rates of interest submitted by the bank panel which was on average lower than their credit risk would indicate. This correlation was calculated by Kamakura Co, a leading establishment of credit analysis and scoring which was one

---

[4]United States District Court, Southern District of New York. In Re LIBOR-Based Financial Instruments Antitrust Litigation. Memorandum and Order relates to all cases. Case no. 1:11-md-02262-NRB, March 29, 2013.

Retrieved from http://www.nysd.uscourts.gov/cases/show.php?db=special&id=280.

[5]LEAGLE. In Re LIBOR-based Financial Instruments Antitrust Litigation, April 29, 2016.

Retrieved from https://www.leagle.com/decision/infdco20160502c87.

[6]United States District Court. The Southern District of New York. Mayor and City Council of Baltimore and City of New Britain Firefighters' and Police Benefit Fund. Plaintiffs on behalf of themselves and all others similarly situated. In Re: Libor-based Financial Instruments Antitrust Litigation. Master File No. 1:11 -md-2262-NRB. April 30, 2012, p. 5.

Retrieved from https://www.unitedstatescourts.org/federal/nysd/383368/130-0.html.

of the expert witnesses.[7] The consultant calculated the association (correlation) between the probabilities of default and the interest rates submitted by 26 banks. The normal expectation is to obtain a positive association, suggesting the rates at which banks can borrow would increase as their default risks increase, but the analysis showed negative correlations for 2007 and 2008. Negative correlations meant that the high probabilities of default — i.e., higher credit risk — were accompanied by low interest rates, which is impossible to obtain under normal market conditions free of manipulation.

ii. The second measure used for comparison was the relationship between London Average Interest Rate (LIBOR) and the interest rates the Federal Reserve Bank pays on Eurodollar deposits (the deposits of US dollars outside the United States).[8]

iii. The third measure used for comparison was the correlation between LIBOR and the rates at which these panel banks could borrow funds from the Federal Reserve. Normally these two rates should be positively correlated but that was not always true.

The expert witnesses assisting in the legal case of the City of Baltimore presented these correlations and other measures to support their claim that LIBOR was understated according to a pattern that could not have happened without an orchestrated effort to lower it artificially. According to the US Department of Justice, this artificial setting of the London Average Interest Rate (LIBOR) was the making of at least one of the bank's management:[9]

> Barclays often submitted inaccurate Dollar LIBORs that under-reported its perception of its borrowing costs and its assessment of where its

---

[7]One of the main specialties of Kamakura is estimating the probability of default of all publicly listed companies globally.

[8]In recent years, Eurodollar deposits consist of US-dollar deposits anywhere outside United States. Initially counting these deposits was limited to US-dollar deposits in Europe only, but the name did not change after expanding the scope to include all US-dollar deposits anywhere outside the US mainland or properties.

[9]US Department of Justice. Barclays Bank PLC Admits Misconduct Related to Submissions for the London Interbank Offered Rate and the Euro Interbank Offered Rate and Agrees to Pay $160 Million Penalty. June 27, 2012.

Retrieved from https://www.justice.gov/iso/opa/resources/9312012710173426365941.pdf.

Dollar LIBOR submission should have been. Certain members of management of Barclays, including senior managers in the treasury department and managers of the money markets desk, directed that the Barclays Dollar LIBOR submitters contribute rates that were nearer to the expected rates of other Contributor Panel.

While the alleged main goal of big banks in carrying on this manipulation was to avoid revealing their own true credit risk, the goal of derivatives traders and rate submitters was different. They wanted to earn more money for themselves by increasing the gains of the banks' portfolios of interest-rate swaps and other derivatives. In chasing the money, the credit ratings of the involved banks appeared to be far from the minds of derivatives traders: they were thinking of one trade at a time merely to make profits for their books and increase their own bonuses. This meant that at times derivatives' traders could have been working on increasing LIBOR while the bank management was working on lowering it. Derivatives traders and rate submitters cooperated with their competitors at other banks to achieve their own goals, as the excerpts of "cheating chats" in the following sections reveal.

(b) Cheating Chats and
Why Manipulating LIBOR Matters

A Given:

Depressing LIBOR will artificially lower the dollar amounts of interest that banks pay to counterparties in plain vanilla swap contracts for which banks pay variable and receive fixed.

In its capacity as the receiver of 38 banking institutions that failed between 2008 and 2011, the Federal Deposit Insurance Corporation (FDIC) filed, on March 14, 2014, a class action lawsuit before the US District Court, Southern District of New York. The complaint consists of

33 counts against the banks on the panel submitting input for US dollar LIBOR to the British Bankers Association. The filing documentation presented a number of mishaps, including the following:

(i) *Internal communication showing that executives were aware of and involved in the manipulation.* For example,[10]

> 53. On August 20, 2007, RBS's [Royal Bank of Scotland] London-based head of money markets trading and the person responsible for USD LIBOR submissions, Paul Walker, call his counterparty in Tokyo and stated "People are setting to where it suits their book...LIBOR is what you say it is."

> 54. Also in August 2007, senior managers at Barclays instructed their USD LIBOR submitters to lower their USD LIBOR submissions so that they would stay "within the pack" and be nearer to the suppressed rates of other Panel Bank Defendants rather than rates that were consistent with the BBA's definition of LIBOR.

(ii) *Informing the Federal Reserve Bank of New York of the manipulation as early as October 2008, but the Fed took no action.*[11]

> According to UBS's admissions, an internal discussion took place among UBS employees in September 2008 that confirmed that the Panel Bank Defendants were continuing to make artificially low LIBOR submissions. In a documented discussion, a UBS employee stated, "LIBORs currently are even more fictitious than usual." On October 10, 2008, a Barclays' employee privately reported to the New York Federal Reserve Bank ("NY Fed") that Barclays's USD LIBOR submissions were "unrealistic." An October 17, 2008 email from a Rabobank LIBOR submitter stated, "We are now setting all libors [sic] significantly under the market levels." On October 24, 2008, another Barclays employee privately reported to the NY Fed that USD LIBOR

---

[10] United States District Court, Southern District of New York, Federal Deposit Insurance Company, plaintiff, Case No. 1:14-cv-01757-GHW, March 14, 2014, pp. 28–29.

Retrieved from http://web.stanford.edu/group/lawlibrary/cgi-bin/liborlitigation/wp-content/uploads/2014/03/SDNY-14-1757-LIBOR-related-COMPLAINT-vs-16-banks.pdf.

[11] Federal Deposit Insurance, Plaintiff, pp. 37–38.

rates were "absolute rubbish," citing submissions by Portigon [formerly, WesLab] and Deutsche Bank as being too low. The employee told the NY Fed that he was aware of banks that were making LIBOR submissions that were below what they actually paid in comparable transactions.

However, the UK House of Commons report *"Fixing LIBOR"* reveals some preliminary findings. With the second report of Session 2012–2013 came the finding that

> [I]t stretches credibility to suggest that Barclays was trying to alert regulators to inconsistencies in the LIBOR submissions of other banks yet had no idea about the repeated "low-balling" of its own submissions during the financial crisis set out in the FSA Final Notice. We have found no evidence that the board of Barclays sought to conduct an investigation.[12]

(iii) *Responses to the US Commodity Futures Trading Commission and the Department of Justice probes.*

On March 15, 2011, UBS made an admission of being investigated in a note in its 10-K Annual Report for the year ended December 31, 2010 stating that

> UBS and others received subpoenas from the Antitrust Division of the US Department of Justice (DOJ) and the US Securities and Exchange Commission (SEC) seeking information relating to the investment of proceeds of municipal bond issuances and associated derivative transactions. In addition, various state Attorneys General have issued subpoenas seeking similar information. The investigations are ongoing, and UBS is cooperating. Several putative class actions also have been filed in Federal District Courts against UBS and numerous other firms. In the SEC investigation, on 4 February 2008, UBS received a "Wells notice" advising that the SEC staff is considering recommending that the SEC

---

[12]The Treasury Committee, House of Commons, United Kingdom, "Fixing LIBOR: some preliminary findings," Second Report of Session 2012–2013. HC 481–I, August 9, 2012.
  Retrieved from https://publications.parliament.uk/pa/cm201213/cmselect/cmtreasy/481/481.pdf.

bring a civil action against UBS in connection with the bidding of various financial instruments associated with municipal securities.[13]

This note marked the first public acknowledgment by any Defendant of the hitherto secret investigation by the Department of Justice and the Commodity Futures Trading Commission, which began in late 2008. The Annual Report stated that the investigations focused on whether there were improper attempts by UBS, either acting on its own behalf or together with others, to manipulate LIBOR rates.

One of the worst cases was related to IndyMac, a bank in California that thoughtlessly entered into 10 interest-rate-exchange contracts between 2000 and 2006:

> 146. The IndyMac Contracting Defendants [big banks on the LIBOR submitters panel] knowingly breached and defaulted on the IndyMac Master Agreements through their fraudulent and collusive conduct, their failure to disclose fraudulent and collusive conduct, their intentional misrepresentation and manipulation of USD LIBOR, and their underpayments [on swap contracts] to IndyMac tied to the artificially suppressed USD LIBOR.[14]

As we shall see, the conspiracy and collusion were widespread, as the recorded conversations in chat rooms have documented. In its preliminary report, the regulatory agency "Financial Services Authority" in the United Kingdom was among the first regulators that referred to a conversation between two employees in different banks conspiring to alter the rates to fit themselves (unedited):

> Trader C requested low one month and three month US dollar LIBOR submissions at 10:52 am on 7 April 2006 (shortly before the submissions were due to be made); "*If it's not too late low 1m* [one month LIBOR] *and 3m* [three months LIBOR] *would be nice, but please feel*

---

[13] UBS. Annual Report, 2010, p.315.

Retrieved from https://www.ubs.com/global/en/about_ubs/investor_relations/annualreporting/2010.html.

[14] The Federal Deposit Insurance Corporation, Plaintiff, p. 62.

free to say "no"...Coffees will be coming your way either way, just to say thank you for your help in the past few weeks". A Submitter responded *"Done...for you big boy."*[15]

The class action lawsuit filed by the Regents of the University of California against the LIBOR bank panels makes this point clear (unedited)[16]

> In the simplest terms, LIBOR is intended to represent the interest rate that a Defendant LIBOR member bank could borrow from other LIBOR member banks on any given date, depending on the currency and the duration of the loan. This rate is set by the LIBOR member banks each day and is intended to reflect the true cost of borrowing in any given economic environment, representing the amount of interest that one financial institution would charge for lending money to another financial institution in an arms-length transaction.

The case continued to provide evidence of violating the rules set for LIBOR[17]

> On November 29, 2007, Barclays learned the confidential USD LIBOR submissions of every defendant [other banks on the panel] before they were made public and adjusted its LIBOR submission downward by 20 basis points in order to stay within the pack of other banks' low LIBOR submissions. Barclays' managers issued standing instructions to stay within specific ranges of other panel banks' LIBOR submissions, indicating that Barclays believed that it would have continued access to every other panel bank's confidential LIBOR submissions before they were published. According to the CFTC's review of the evidence it collected,

---

[15] The Treasury Committee, House of Commons, p. 17.

[16] United States District Court, Northern District of California, The Regents of the University of California vs. Bank of America Corporation, etc. Case4:13-cv-02921-DMR Document1 Filed06/25/13. June 2013 pp. 1–2.

Retrieved from http://web.stanford.edu/group/lawlibrary/cgi-bin/LIBORlitigation/wp-content/uploads/2013/06/UCRegents-complaint-NDCalif-25Jun2013.pdf.

[17] United States District Court. The Regents of the University of California, June, 2013. p. 8.

Senior Barclays Treasury managers provided the [LIBOR] submitters with the general guidance that Barclays' submitted rates should be within 10 basis points of the submissions by the other U.S. Dollar panel banks…
That same day, on November 29, 2007, a Barclays manager explained that "other panel banks 'are reluctant to post higher and because no one will get out of the pack, the pack sort of stays low.'" Barclays and UBS admitted that they issued and obeyed instructions to stay within the pack of other banks' low LIBOR submissions during large portions of the Relevant Period.

When law-enforcement agencies finally obtained the recorded conversations documenting the collusion and conspiracy among derivatives traders and rate submitters within the bank and across other banks, the senior management of Barclays did not persist in denying knowledge of, and involvement in, the manipulation. The cat was let out of the bag at a Parliamentary inquiry in London on July 16, 2012, when "Barclays' chief operating officer Jerry del Missier told MPs he was instructed by [the CEO] Diamond to lower the bank's LIBOR submissions. He also told them that he believed the Bank of England alone instructed Barclays to lower them."[18]

Asked if a 2008 phone call from his former boss [Diamond, CEO of Barclays] was an instruction to cut the LIBOR rate submissions, Mr del Missier said "yes it was". Barclays has said Mr del Missier told his traders to lower LIBOR following a misunderstanding over an email sent from Mr Diamond. The email had summarised a call between Mr Diamond and Paul Tucker, deputy governor of the Bank of England. It appeared to suggest the Bank [of England] might turn a blind eye if Barclays reduced its high LIBOR submissions, to avoid appearing under financial stress at the height of the international banking crisis. However, Mr del Missier told MPs he acted on the basis of a phone call from Mr Diamond. "It was an instruction, yes," he told the MPs.[19]

---

[18]"Timeline LIBOR Fixing Scandal," *BBC News,* February 6, 2013.
  Retrieved from http://www.bbc.com/news/business-18671255.
[19]"Barclays: FSA regulator criticizes 'culture of gaming,'" *BBC News*, July 16, 2012.
  Retrieved from http://www.bbc.com/news/business-18854193?print=true.

But did the Bank of England actually suggest that Barclays Bank report false numbers? That remains ambiguous, although Jerry del Missier read out loud Diamond's internal memo as instruction to lower the rates. BBC News has reproduced this internal memo summarizing his conversation with Paul Tucker, the Governor of the Bank of England back then.[20]

Bob Diamond's notes of phone conversation with Paul Tucker Emailed to then chief executive John Varley on 30/10/2008. Copied to Jerry del Missier.

Date: 29th October 2008

Further to our last call, Mr Tucker reiterated that he had received calls from a number of senior figures within Whitehall to question why Barclays was always toward the top end of the *LIBOR* pricing. His response was "you have to pay what you have to pay." I asked if he could relay the reality, that not all banks were providing quotes at the levels that represented real transactions, his response "oh, that would be worse."

I explained again our market rate driven policy and that it had recently meant that we appeared in the top quartile and on occasion the top decile of the pricing. Equally I noted that we continued to see others in the market posting rates at levels that were not representative of where they would actually undertake business. This latter point has on occasion pushed us higher than would otherwise appear to be the case. In fact, we are not having to "pay up" for money at all.

Mr Tucker stated the levels of calls he was receiving from Whitehall were "senior" and that while he was certain we did not need advice that it did not always need to be the case that we appeared as high as we have recently.

---

[20] "Barclays reveals Bank of England LIBOR phone call details," *BBC News*, July 3, 2012. Retrieved from http://www.bbc.com/news/business-18695181.

However, the files of the FBI at the U. S. Department of Justice explain this issue more clearly[21]:

> On October 29, 2008, a senior Bank of England official contacted a senior Barclays manager. The Bank of England official discussed the external perceptions of Barclays's LIBOR submissions and questioned why Barclays's submissions were high compared to other Contributor Panel banks. As the substance of the conversation was passed to other Barclays employees, certain Barclays managers formed the understanding that they had been instructed by the Bank of England to lower Barclays' LIBOR submissions, and instructed the Barclays Dollar and Sterling LIBOR submitters to do so even though that was not the understanding of the senior Barclays individual who had the call with the Bank of England official.

By suppressing the submitted rates, the bank followed the guidance from the top.[22]

> According to internal Barclays communications, for certain time periods, Barclays management instructed the Barclays Dollar LIBOR submitters not to be an "outlier" compared to other Contributor Panel banks, even if Barclays contributed the highest rate; Barclays could be "at the top of the pack" but not too far above the next highest contributor. (FBI Files)

As the court cases evolved, the incentive for Barclays's actions to deflate LIBOR became clear. If Barclays submits to BBA rates of interest higher than the rates submitted by "the pack," other banks would perceive Barclays as having higher credit risk. This concern was based on the fact that the submitted rates were the interest rates at which Barclays could

---

[21] U. S. Department of Justice, "Barclays Bank PLC Admits Misconduct Related to Submissions for the London Interbank Offered Rate and the Euro Interbank Offered Rate and Agrees to Pay $160 Million Penalty," *Appendix A. Statement of Facts*, June 27, 2012. p. 21.

Retrieved from https://www.justice.gov/iso/opa/resources/9312012710173426365941.pdf.

[22] Barclays Bank PLC Admits, p. 16.

borrow money. By suppressing the submitted rates, Barclays had effectively achieved two goals:

(i)   giving credit markets signals that the credit risk of the bank was not too high, and
(ii) deflating the adjustable interest rates payable to counterparties for the trillions of dollars of swap contracts held by Barclays.

According to the US Department of Justice, this artificial setting of US dollar LIBOR was the making of the bank's management[23]:

> Barclays often submitted inaccurate Dollar LIBORs that under-reported its perception of its borrowing costs and its assessment of where its Dollar LIBOR submission should have been. Certain members of management of Barclays, including senior managers in the treasury department and managers of the money markets desk, directed that the Barclays Dollar LIBOR submitters contribute rates that were nearer to the expected rates of other Contributor Panel.

(c) Evidence from the Files of the Financial Services Authority (UK) and the FBI (USA)[24]

Regulatory authorities in the UK and the USA took more interest in looking at Barclays's books, emails, chat rooms, and any documentation that could help in their investigations. They wanted to use their knowledge of Barclays' activities as an anchor for their search into the manipulation by other banks. It was not long after the investigation began that Barclays's management admitted to the bank's participation in a wide-ranging conspiracy and collusion at all levels, conspiracy and collusion to massage and change London Interbank Interest Rate (LIBOR) in ways that

---

[23] Barclays Bank PLC Admits, p. 15.
[24] Financial Services Authority (UK). Report of Barclays Final Notice, June 17, 2012.
    Retrieved from http://www.fsa.gov.uk/static/pubs/final/barclays-jun12.pdf; http://www.fbi.gov/washingtondc/press-releases/2012/barclays-bank-plc-admits-misconduct-related-to-submissions-for-the-london-interbank-offered-rate-and-the-euro-interbank-offered-rate-and-agrees-to-pay-160-million-penalty; https://www.justice.gov/opa/pr/barclays-bank-plc-admits-misconduct-related-submissions-london-interbank-offered-rate-and.

benefitted the bank without regard to who else would be harmed. The management also revealed that derivatives' traders and rate submitters were rewarded for doing a good job in cheating and for coordinating the manipulation with other banks. The UK Financial Services Authority (FSA) issued a final report summarizing the investigations carried out by both itself and the UK's Serious Fraud Office (SFO). Parallel investigations were going on in the USA within the Department of Justice's Federal Bureau of Investigation (FBI), the Office of the Comptroller of the Currency (OCC), and the Commodity Futures Trading Commission (CFTC). Because of these investigations, all agencies have issued reports on the crimes committed by Barclays. The bank was convicted of both civil and criminal violations, but in the common tradition of dealing with the crimes of big banks, the bank was charged civil penalties after admitting to the manipulation, the conspiracy, and the collusion, but admitted no guilt! The no-guilty-plea agreement (NPA) is now the maxim of big banks as it had been for so many years, and there is nothing on the horizon to suggest any change in the regulators' modus operandi.

The investigation lasted close to three years, although some hidden ruts may resurface and require further investigation. At the end, Barclays paid fines for civil penalties and continued on its merry way of getting fatter and bigger with the use of derivatives and its interest-rate swaps. The degree and magnitude of working hard at Barclays to massage LIBOR by derivatives traders, rate submitters, managers, and senior managers are clearly laid out in the FSA's Final Notice and in the US Department of Justice's "Statement of Facts."

> 71. On the majority of occasions where Barclays's submitters were contacted by Barclays's derivatives traders with requests, Barclays's submissions (for US dollar LIBOR and EURIBOR) were consistent with those requests[25]:
>
> i. [T]he FSA analysed 111 requests made by Barclays' Derivatives Traders in the period from 3 January 2006 to 6 August 2007 relating to US dollar LIBOR submissions. On around 70% of those occasions the submissions were consistent with the requests. On 16%, of

---

[25] Financial Services Authority (UK), *Report of Barclays Final Notice*, June 27, 2012, p. 14. Retrieved from http://www.fsa.gov.uk/static/pubs/final/barclays-jun12.pdf.

occasions it was unclear if the submissions were consistent with the requests. On 14% of occasions the submissions were inconsistent with the requests; and

ii. [T]he FSA analysed 42 requests made by Barclays' Derivatives Traders in the period from 23 February 2006 to 3 June 2008 relating to EURIBOR submissions. On 86% of those occasions the submissions were consistent with the requests. On 2% of occasions it was unclear if the submissions were consistent with the requests. On 12% of occasions the submissions were inconsistent with the request.

Annotated Chatting Excerpts (as reported) from

The Criminal Division of the U. S. Department of Justice (DOJ) DOJ: *Appendix A: Statement of Facts.*
Retrieved from https://www.justice.gov/iso/opa/resources/9312012710173426365941.pdf.
&
Financial Services Authority (FSA in the UK) Report of Barclays *Final Notice*, June 27, 2012.
Retrieved from http://www.fsa.gov.uk/static/pubs/final/barclays-jun12.pdf.

Example 1 (Item 12 in the DOJ Statement of Facts, and Item 59 in the Final Report of the UK Financial Service Authority

On Friday, 10 March 2006, two US dollar Derivatives Traders made email requests for a low three month US dollar LIBOR submission for the coming Monday:

   i. Trader C stated *"We have an unbelievably large set on Monday (the IMM). We need a really low 3m fix, it could potentially cost a fortune. Would really appreciate any help"*;

   ii. Trader B explained *"I really need a very very low 3m fixing on Monday — preferably we get kicked out. We have about 80 yards* [billion] *fixing for the desk and each 0.1* [one basis point] *lower in the fix is a huge help for us. So 4.90 or lower would be fantastic."* Trader B also indicated his preference that Barclays would be kicked out of the average calculation; and

---

(Continued)

(Continued)

---

iii. On Monday, 13 March 2006, the following email exchange took place:

Trader C:	*"The big day* [has] *arrived... My NYK are screaming at me about an unchanged 3m libor. As always, any help wd be greatly appreciated. What do you think you'll go for 3m?"*
Submitter:	*"I am going 90 altho 91 is what I should be posting."*
Trader C:	*"[...] when I retire and write a book about this business your name will be written in golden letters [...]."*
Submitter:	*"I would prefer this* [to] *not be in any book!"*

The Result*: Barclays's 3-month Dollar LIBOR submission on March 13, 2006 was 4.90%, which was a rate unchanged from the previous trading day and was tied for the lowest rate submitted.*

Example 2: Item 14 (p. 6 in DOJ *Statement of Facts*)

On February 22, 2006,

- Swap trader I:
  "Hi (again) We're getting killed on our 3m resets, we need them to be up this week before we roll out of our positions. Consensus for 3m today is 4.78 - 4.7825, it would be amazing if we could go for 4.79...Really appreciate ur help mate." (ellipses in original).

- Submitter-2
  "Happy to help."

The Result*: Barclays's 3-month Dollar LIBOR submission on February 22, 2006 was 4.79%.*

(Continued)

(Continued)

Example 3: Item 67 (p. 13) in the *FSA Final Report*

On 6 August 2007, a Submitter even offered to submit a US dollar rate higher than that requested:

Trader F:	*"Pls set 3m libor as high as possible today"*
Submitter:	*"Sure 5.37 okay?"*
Trader F:	*"5.36 is fine"*

Example 4. (Item 83 (p. 19) in *FSA Final Report* and Item 26 (p. 11) in U. S. DOJ *Statement of Facts*

83. For example, on 26 October 2006, an external trader made a request for a lower three month US dollar LIBOR submission. The external trader stated in an email to Trader G at Barclays *"If it comes in unchanged I'm a dead man."* Trader G responded that he would *"have a chat."* Barclays' submission on that day for three month US dollar LIBOR was half a basis point lower than the day before, rather than being unchanged. The external trader thanked Trader G for Barclays' LIBOR submission later that day: *"Dude. I owe you big time! Come over one day after work and I'm opening a bottle of Bollinger."* Thanks for the libor." Trader-6 replied, "know [sic] worries!!!"

The Result: Barclays's 3-month Dollar LIBOR submission on October 26, 2006 was 5.375%, which was lower than Barclays's submission on the previous trading day.

Example 5. Item 22 (p. 9) in U. S. *DOJ Statement of Facts*

Because of the high value of the notional amounts underlying derivative transactions tied to LIBOR and EURIBOR, even very small movements in those rates could have a significant impact on the profitability of a trader's trading portfolio. As an example of the potential impact of this activity, on September 28, 2005, in a series of electronic messages, Trader-3 and Trader-I discussed the next day's 3-month LIBOR submission.

(Continued)

(Continued)

On September 28, 2005, in a series of electronic messages, Trader-3 and Trader-1 discussed the next day's 3-month LIBOR submission.

- Trader-3 stated, "WE WANT TOMORROW'S FIX TO BE 4.07 MINIMUM," repeating, "4.07....NOTHING LESS..." (Emphasis and ellipses in original).
- Trader-3 explained: "We have turn exposure of 837 futures contracts. [F]or every .25 bps tomorrows [sic] fix is below 4.0525 we lose 154,687.50 usd [United States Dollars]...if tomorrows [sic] fix comes in at 4.0325 we lose 618,750 usd." (Ellipses in original).
- Trader-1 replied in part, "I'll ask [Submitter-1] to go for 4.07."

The Result: Barclays's 3-month Dollar LIBOR submission on September 29, 2005 was 4.07%, which was the highest rate submitted by any Contributor Panel bank.

Example 6: Item 27 (p. 11) in the U. S. DOJ *Statement of Facts*

○ Former Trader-1:
"I know I 'm asking for much, but ONLY if u guys care, a low 3m libor would be great...anywhere below 5.35...thanks dude." (Ellipses in original).
○ Former Trader-1 (later):
"Dude, thanks a lot for the LIBOR, can you PLEASE thank [Submitter-I] as well."
○ Trader-6:
"anything for you!!!"
○ Trader-1:
"seriously, thanks a million dude."

The Result: *Barclays's 3-month Dollar LIBOR contribution on March 29, 2007 was 5.345*

(Continued)

(Continued)

Example 7: Item 71(pp. 35–36) in the in *FSA Final Report* and Item 45 (pp. 20–21) in U. S. DOJ *Statement of Facts*

On the bright side, however, the investigation reports show that Barclays has some bankers who found the conspiracy to manipulate LIBOR to be dreadful. In one of those cases, the submitter raised concern and expressed his worries in a chat on December 4, 2007 stating[26]

> that he was "*Feeling increasingly uncomfortable about the way in which USD libors are being set by the contributor banks, Barclays included.*" He went on to note that his one month submission was 5.30 but he was paying in the market at 5.40. "*Given a free hand I would have set at around 5.45% […] one contributor was paying [x%] in the market at 11 am* [and setting at y%]. *This is not an uncommon phenomenon. The same kind of thing is happening in all the periods although 1 month is the most distorted. My worry is that we (both Barclays and the contributor bank panel) are being seen to be contributing patently false rates. We are therefore being dishonest by definition and are at risk of damaging our reputation in the market and with the regulators.*"

More Chat-room reports are in Appendix 12.

(d) Collusion and Conspiracy at UBS AG: The Rain Man & Company

In its legal filings against UBS AG, the US Commodity Futures Trading Commission (CFTC) summarized the basis for imposing a $700 million fine on UBS[27]:

In summary, CFTC's Order finds:

- For at least six years UBS regularly tried to manipulate multiple benchmark interest rates for profit, and at times succeeded in manipulating the official fixing of Yen LIBOR;

---

[26] *Ibid.*, p. 20.

[27] CFTC Orders UBS to Pay $700 Million Penalty to Settle Charges of Manipulation, Attempted Manipulation and False Reporting of LIBOR and Other Benchmark Interest Rates. Retrieved from http://www.cftc.gov/PressRoom/PressReleases/pr6472-12.

- More than 2,000 instances of unlawful conduct involving dozens of UBS employees, colluding with other panel banks, and inducing interdealer brokers to spread false information and influence other banks; and
- UBS made false U.S. Dollar LIBOR and other submissions to protect its reputation during the global financial crisis.

In a dramatization of the collusion and conspiracy that took place at UBS regarding LIBOR manipulation, William D. Cohan wrote an article in *Bloomberg* titled "UBS LIBOR Manipulation Deserves the Death Penalty" (December 23, 2012). He was probably referring to specific traders such as Thomas Alexander Hayes, aka the Rain Man. Hayes was the derivatives trader at a UBS subsidiary in Japan after having worked for other large banks, and his collaborators inside and outside the bank orchestrated many nefarious activities. When he was arrested and charged with fraud in 2012, Hayes was only 33 year old, which is revealing another example of a rarely discussed crisis of the upper echelons and senior management at big banks: namely hiring youngsters to manage huge derivatives' portfolios in the billions of dollars then punishing them hard for misbehaving.[28] In July 2015, a jury in

---

[28]This is a repeat of the most egregious socio-economic syndrome. Big banks play with financial derivatives just as poker chips with which anyone could play and carry around. Simply stated, they hire young people in their twenties, give them financial derivatives' portfolios of billions of dollars and when they lose, they prosecute them and seek severe penalties of jail and money. No one has ever asked the question "why would smart executives in big banks trust people just out of college to deal with billions of dollars and succeed?" Where does the responsibility of failure lies? This was the case of Nick Leeson who destroyed Barings Bank (1995), Jerome Kerviel who caused *Société Générale* a loss of $7 billion (2007); John Rusnak who caused Allied Irish Bank (USA) a loss of $691 million; Kewke Adoboli who caused UBS — London to lose at least $2.0 billion (2012), Tom Hayes at UBS (Japan) whose illicit activities contributed much damage to many big banks, and Joseph Jett at Kidder Peabody (GE) who lost $350 million in early 1990s. The oldest one of that bunch was Jett who was 36 years old when his fraud was discovered.

Sylvia Nasar, "Behind the Kidder Scandal: The Overview; Kidder Scandal Tied to Failure Of Supervision," *The New York Times*, August 5, 1994.

Retrieved from http://www.nytimes.com/1994/08/05/us/behind-kidder-scandal-overview-kidder-scandal-tied-failure-supervision.html?pagewanted=all.

Southwark Crown Court in the United Kingdom convicted Thomas Alexander Hayes of eight counts of conspiracy to defraud and sentenced him to 14 years in prison, a very harsh sentence in the British system of jurisprudence. The sentence was later reduced later to 11 years. As of today, February 12, 2017, other trials of co-conspirators in the LIBOR scandal continue.

Hayes started his career at the Royal Bank of Scotland at the age of 27 after earning a degree in mathematics and computer science, then moved to RBC, to UBS, to Citibank, and back to UBS. Making all these moves in the span of six years gave him exposure to all styles of trading derivatives and taught him the tricks of the trade. His style of communication and interaction with other people was basic, idiosyncratic, not flashy, and to the point. These characteristics earned him the nickname the Rain Man, after the 1998 movie with Dustin Hoffman. The reports of investigators in the matter in the UK, USA, Japan, and Switzerland detail the actions of a young man who was more like the "mother of the bride" to all of his co-conspirators, seeking and paying for the cooperation and advice of everyone in his bank and in several other banks. The stakes were high and were evidently clear in Hayes' communication with other traders, as reported by the Financial Services Authority's *Final Notice* (December 19, 2012)[29]:

> For example, on 18 September 2008, a Trader explained to a Broker:
> *"if you keep 6s* [i.e., the six-month JPY LIBOR rate] *unchanged*

Mark Tran, "The AIB Scandal," *The Guardian*, February 20 2002.

Retrieved from https://www.theguardian.com/business/2002/feb/20/theissuesexplained.

Nicola Clark and David Jolly, "Société Générale loses $7 billion in trading fraud," *The New York Times*, January 24, 2008.

Retrieved from http://www.nytimes.com/2008/01/24/business/worldbusiness/24iht-soc-gen.5.9486501.html.

Jason Rodrigues, "Barings collapse at 20: How rogue trader Nick Leeson broke the bank," *The Guardian*, February 15, 2010.

Retrieved from https://www.theguardian.com/business/from-the-archive-blog/2015/feb/24/nick-leeson-barings-bank-1995-20-archive.

Lindsay Fortado, "Kweku Adoboli: a rogue trader's tale." *Financial Times*, October 12, 2015.

Retrieved from https://www.ft.com/content/0fa0b42a-783a-11e5-a95a-27d368e1ddf7.

[29] Financial Services Authority (UK). *Report of Barclays Final Notice*, June 17, 2012, p. 30.

Retrieved from http://www.fsa.gov.uk/static/pubs/final/barclays-jun12.pdf.

today...I will f—g do one humongous deal with you...Like a 50,000-buck deal, whatever...I need you to keep it as low as possible...if you do that...I'll pay you, you know, 50,000 dollars, 100,000 dollars...whatever you want...I'm a man of my word". UBS entered into at least nine such wash trades using this Broker Firm, generating illicit fees of more than £170,000 [more than $250,000] for the Brokers.

In its complaint against Thomas Hayes, the US Department of Justice noted the following[30]:

On at least approximately 335 of the 738 trading days from in or about November 2006 through or August 2009, HAYES or the UBS Junior Trader, at HAYES's direction, requested that Darin, UBS Junior Submitter 1, or UBS Junior Submitter 2, accommodate HAYES's requests when setting UBS's Yen LIBOR.

Availability of chat-room texts allowed the Serious Fraud Office and the Financial Services Authority in the UK and the Department of Justice (FBI) and CFTC in the USA to obtain information on the depth and breadth of the management's involvement in the conspiracy to manage LIBOR. Unlike the case at Barclays where the pressure aimed at lowering LIBOR, Tom Hayes at UBS directed his troops at different banks in different directions to increase, lower, or not change LIBOR in ways and at times that fit his large portfolio of trading derivatives.

(e) The Rain Man's Long Reach to RBS (from the FBI Files)

The Royal Bank of Scotland (RBS) was another bank on the submission panel of the London Average Interest Rate (LIBOR) for the US Dollar. RBS is also one of the very large banks that lacked effective coordination, control, and management. As a result, it was not a

---

[30] United States of America Complaint –V – Tom Alexander William Hayes and Roger Darin,

18 u.s.c. §§ 1349, 1343 & 2; 15 u.s.c. § 1.

Retrieved from https://www.justice.gov/sites/default/files/ag/legacy/2012/12/19/Hayes-Tom-and-Darin-Roger-Complaint.pdf.

difficult issue for its derivatives traders and LIBOR submitters to also engage in the collusion and conspiracy to manipulate LIBOR. Thomas Hayes at UBS knew that information and also knew some of the employees by virtue of having started his career at RBS, although that was not relevant to him because he was able to call anyone and chat about pushing LIBOR up or down whenever he wanted and by as much as he wanted. The FBI files include some of Hayes's chats with RBS employees, such as the following[31]:

> RBS employees also allegedly furthered their collusive scheme with Hayes to fix the price of derivative instruments tied to Yen LIBOR through electronic communications. For instance, in an electronic chat on April 20, 2007, Hayes requested that an RBS derivatives trader ("Trader-3") ask Submitter-1 for a low three-month Yen LIBOR submission: Hayes:…if you could ask your guys to keep 3m low wd be massive help as long as it doesn't interfere with your stuff…tx in advance.

Approximately 30 minutes later, Hayes and Trader-3 had the following exchange:

Hayes: mate did you manage to spk to your cash boys?
Trader-3: yes u owe me they are going 65 and 71
Hayes: thx mate yes i do…in fact i owe you big time

Approximately 45 minutes later, Hayes sent the following message to Trader-3:

Hayes: mater they set 64…thats beyond the call of duty!
Trader-3: no worries

---

[31] Federal Bureau of Investigation, Washington Field Office. "RBS Securities Japan Limited Agrees to Plead Guilty in Connection with Long-Running Manipulation of LIBOR Benchmark Interest Rates," February 6, 2013.

Retrieved from https://archives.fbi.gov/archives/washingtondc/press-releases/2013/rbs-securities-japan-limited-agrees-to-plead-guilty-in-connection-with-long-running-manipulation-of-libor-benchmark-interest-rates.

(f) Deutsche Bank's High Cost of Denial

In its report on what appeared to be a final settlement with Deutsche Bank, the U. S. Commodity Futures Trading Commission states the following[32]:

> [F]rom at least 2005 through early 2011 (the "relevant period"), by and through the acts of certain, Deutsche Bank's employees engaged in systemic and pervasive manipulation of the London Interbank Offered Rate ("LIBOR") and the Euro Interbank Offered Rate ("Euribor"), two critical international financial benchmark interest rates. Deutsche Bank's profit-driven misconduct undermined the integrity of LIBOR and Euribor and the integrity of the U.S. and global financial markets. (CFTC)

The amounts of cash and profitability of its trading in derivatives were the factors Deutsche Bank used to determine the interest rates submitted to Thomson Reuters on behalf of the British Bankers Association for both Euribor (European InterBank Offered Rate) and LIBOR for several currencies (US dollar, Yen, Sterling, and Swiss Franc). Deutsche Bank traders coordinated their LIBOR submissions with dealers at other banks, including Barclays (the United Kingdom), BNP Paribas SA (France), Citigroup Inc. (USA), Bank of America — Merrill Lynch (USA), Société Générale SA (France), and UBS (Switzerland). The uncovered evidence shows that the manipulation was carried out systematically by interest rate submitters and derivatives' traders and involved higher echelons of management. For example, the bank had rearranged the physical layout of its London office to have rate submitters, cash traders, and derivatives' traders located adjacent to one another, which allowed for easy flow of information and effortlessly coordinating actions across these functions. To

---

[32] United States of America before the Commodity Futures Trading Commission. Deutsche Bank AG, Respondent. (CFTC Docket No. 15-20). In the Matter of *Order Instituting Proceedings Pursuant to Sections 6(c) and 6(d) of the Commodity Exchange Act, Making Findings, and Imposing Remedial Sanctions*," April 23, 2015, P. 2

Retrieved from http://www.cftc.gov/idc/groups/public/@lrenforcementactions/documents/legalpleading/enfdeutscheorder042315.pdf.

facilitate that flow of information and coordination, traders shouted their requests or goals out loud across the aisles.[33]

> From London, the Global Senior Manager instructed all traders to have open communication across offices and instilled an expectation that the derivatives traders and submitters would communicate routinely about relevant market conditions and individual trading positions. (CFTC, p. 8)
>
> ....
>
> By failing to separate responsibilities for making LIBOR and Euribor submissions from its trading functions, Deutsche Bank allowed an environment to exist that yielded significant opportunities for traders and submitters to attempt to manipulate LIBOR and Euribor submissions to the benefit of the bank's trading positions, and the traders and submitters took full advantage of those opportunities. As a result, the submitters routinely skewed Deutsche Bank's LIBOR and Euribor submissions to benefit the bank's trading positions by attempting to manipulate the fixings of LIBOR and Euribor. At times, their attempts to manipulate U.S. Dollar, Yen, Sterling, and Swiss Franc LIB OR and Euribor were successful. (CFTC, 9)

Deutsche Bank permitted traders to have a culture of acting solely in their own self-interest and created an environment in which traders found mutual benefits by colluding and conspiring with rate submitters. Information sharing was encouraged, not discouraged. This encouragement went far beyond any acceptable protocols; the bank permitted derivatives traders to make rate submissions to British Bankers Association for the purpose of determining London Average Interest Rate (LIBOR) and Euribor, a task in which they should have never been involved. Derivatives' traders had no way of ascertaining the rates of interest at which Deutsche Bank could have borrowed funds from other banks on the panel in the preceding 24 hours. Instead, they submitted the rates they believed would help move LIBOR in directions profitable to their own portfolios of derivatives.

---

[33] Commodity Futures Trading Commission. Deutsche Bank AG, April 23, 2015, pp. 8–9.

This dysfunctional structure extended beyond the boundaries of Deutsche Bank itself. In one particular case, the derivative' trader who casually took over the role of rate submitter faked the submission and made up rates to help a derivatives trader at another bank — UBS AG. This episode gives a gaudy picture of loss of coordination and management control such that perpetrating fraud was not confined to the participating Deutsche Bank employees but had also been exported to other banks.

Unlike Barclays, the management of Deutsche Bank did not cooperate with investigators and persistently denied having any documentation of fraud. But regulatory agencies in the USA and the UK continued to pursue the truth, and when the bank finally came through with the recorded conversations among the conspirators, the regulators were outraged. Georgina Philippou, the acting director of enforcement and market oversight at the British Financial Conduct Authority, commented that "Deutsche Bank's failings were compounded by them repeatedly misleading us…The bank took far too long to produce vital documents and it moved far too slowly to fix relevant systems and controls."[34] It is possible that senior executives did not want to reveal their totally inept management style by disclosing the content of chat rooms.

Taking a look at their chat-room conversations is probably adequate for anyone to lose faith in anything these big banks say or do. Snippets of these chats are reproduced in Appendix 12 as "LIBOR Cheating Chats at Deutsche Bank and other banks."

---

[34] Strowmatt, Shane, Suzi Ring, and Greg Farrell. "Deutsche Bank to Pay $2.5 Billion to End LIBOR Probe." *Bloomberg.* April 23, 2015.

Retrieved from https://www.bloomberg.com/amp/news/articles/2015-04-23/deutsche-bank-to-pay-record-2-5-billion-to-resolve-libor-probes.

Unconscionability:

Dancing with the "Snakes" of Modern Times

CHAPTER 34

Are Interest Rate Swaps with Nonprofit Entities Unconscionable Contracts?

Dancing with snakes in their ceremonial rituals and related magic shows has been a long-held tradition of the Native American Hopi tribe in Arizona. Starting in 1990s, big banks began performing their own form of dance. They scattered their sales forces across the land to entice nonprofits to a perpetual grand dance with a special type of intangible snakes that were not defanged — snakes known otherwise as interest rate swaps or interest-rate-exchange contracts.

For swap contracts, we will consider "unconscionability" as replacing snake "poison" in the traditional ritual dancing. Unconscionability is a doctrine in law presented in Section 2-302 of the US Uniform Commercial Code.[1] The courts and the legal literature have partitioned unconscionability in contracting into procedural and substantive, although the subtle distinction between these two forms escapes many attorneys and many others outside the circle of legal scholars. A procedural

---

[1] Unconscionability is a doctrine in law presented in Section 2-302 of the US Uniform Commercial Code addressing the legal consequences of a contract that might be deemed unconscionable.

unconscionability is said to arise in cases of unequal bargaining power with the party drafting the contract using terms and technical jargon unfamiliar to the counterparty. Larry DiMatteo and Bruce Rich provide a comprehensive summary of the rather scant literature and cases on the subject.[2] Of relevance is their reference to the case of Williams v. Walker-Thomas Furniture.

> The seminal case in this regard was delivered in 1965 in Williams v. Walker-Thomas Furniture Co. 21 Its precedential power was restated in a 2002 case: For the most part, the unconscionability cases follow Williams v. Walker-Thomas and look for two factors: (1) unfairness in the formation of the contract, and (2) excessively disproportionate terms. ... Most courts have looked for a sufficient showing of both factors in finding a contract unconscionable.

Suppose, for example, the contract had "buried very complicated, technical language that most people wouldn't understand or recognize," then the two contracting parties do not have equal bargaining power, and

---

§ 2-302. Unconscionable Contract or Clause

(1) If the court as a matter of law finds the contract or any clause of the contract to have been unconscionable at the time it was made the court may refuse to enforce the contract, or it may enforce the remainder of the contract without the unconscionable clause, or it may so limit the application of any unconscionable clause as to avoid any unconscionable result.

(2) When it is claimed or appears to the court that the contractor any clause thereof may be unconscionable the parties shall be afforded a reasonable opportunity to present evidence as to its commercial setting, purpose and effect to aid the court in making the determination.

Source: Legal Information Institute. Cornell University. Retrieved from https://www.law.cornell.edu/ucc/2/2-302.

---

[2]Larry A. DiMatteo and Bruce Rich, A Consent Theory of Unconscionability: An Empirical Study of Law in Action. Florida State University Law Review, Vol. 33. Summer 2006.

Retrieved from http://scholarship.law.ufl.edu/facultypub/524.

the courts might deem the contract unconscionable and thus unenforceable.[3]

However, the legal community in the United States has not tackled this challenge with respect to financial derivatives and swap contracts although, other than the distances traveled in space, the magnitudes of OTC derivatives overtakes everything else known to humans. (Appendix 3 provides information about the size of global OTC derivatives as reported by the Bank for International Settlements.) This problem was highlighted in each case presented in this book. Simply put, all available evidence strongly suggests the existence of unequal bargaining power between swap dealers, the knowledgeable, and nonprofit officials who generally had no idea about the risks posed by the contracts they signed. Admitting ignorance was not easy and, in an attempt to reduce their culpability, they hired swap advisors who, in most cases, knew as much about swaps as the officials themselves. Negotiated contracts having expertise knowledge on one side and casual knowledge on the other side created fertile grounds for unconscionable contracting. Based only on the structures and forms of the contracts as reported in publicly available documentation, all available evidence strongly suggests the existence of unequal bargaining power between swap dealers, the knowledgeable, and the officials at nonprofit entities who generally had no idea about the risks posed by the contracts they signed. Admitting ignorance was not easy and, in an attempt to reduce their perceived culpability, they hired swap advisors who, in most cases, knew as much about swaps as the officials themselves. It does not take rocket science to conclude that negotiated agreements having expertise

---

[3] Akhbari, Kourosh. What is an Unconscionable Contract? LegalMatch, March 9, 2013.

Retrieved from http://www.legalmatch.com/law-library/article/what-is-an-unconsciona-ble-contract.html.

An unconscionable contract is one that is so one-sided that it is unfair to one party such that the courts might render it unenforceable under the law. Paul Marrow puts it differently; it is an agreement "as no man in his senses and not under delusion would make on the one hand and as no honest and fair man would accept on the other." Unconscionability could arise from major difference in bargaining power between the parties before signing the contract. "Unequal bargaining power" exists when one party is aware that the other party did not understand the contract terms.

knowledge on one side and casual knowledge on the other side create fertile grounds for unconscionable contracting. This problem is addressed in every case presented in this book. In addition, this chapter provides below five more indicators of the described problem.

The five indicators of unconscionability considered here are:

- COLLECTING MONEY FOR SERVICES THAT WILL NEVER BE PROVIDED
- UNBALANCED CONTRACTING
- BIG BANKS CONTROL BOTH SIDES OF INTEREST PAYMENTS OF SWAP CONTRACTS
- EXPROPRIATING FUTURE RESOURCES UPON TERMINATION. THIS IS A ROAD TO UNJUST ENRICHMENT
- PRETENDING TO OFFER SYNTHETIC FIXED RATE EVEN WHEN IT IS NOT REALLY FIXED

FIRST INDICATOR:
COLLECTING MONEY FOR SERVICES THAT WILL NEVER BE PROVIDED

It is fair to ask "what service do interest rate swaps really provide?" The economic motivation for nonprofit entities to enter into interest rate swap contracts might be viewed as limiting exposure to the risk of paying higher cost for their variable rate debt. In this sense, and putting the gambling aspects aside, it is possible to view interest rate swaps as quasi insurance policies. Also in this sense, the losses payable for a swap contract may be considered a quasi-insurance premium. Yet, over the past 25 years, as counterparties to swap contracts, nonprofits had been paying and continue to pay enormous amounts of money for a quasi "insurance" services not rendered and will never be rendered.

Take for example the case of the State of New Jersey and Bank of Montreal. In 2007, the State of New Jersey planned issuing bonds for a school construction. For reasons related to the State's own budget, the issuance of these bonds was deferred to 2009. That would not have been a problem if the officials in the state government did not assume the role of financial wizards and signed up with the Bank of Montreal (BOM) to buy a forward interest rate swap with the intent of hedging interest rates on the planned bond issue after it was sold. The details of the agreement remain private because the related debt was never issued. In 2008, the State of

New Jersey reversed course and decided to cancel the sale of the planned bond issue. Somehow, the penalty payments to BOM on the swaps worked out to $21,892.00 <u>a day</u> for three years. When the bond for which the swap contract was intended did not exist, the need to hedge interest rate risk or to reduce the cost of debt was no longer a relevant issue. However, under the conventions of swap markets, the State of New Jersey could not just terminate the swap contract and go home free. BOM worked out what would have been the expected loss of the State of New Jersey for the entire term of the swap contract if the bonds were sold. The estimate came to $21.3 million in present value dollars. BOM demanded the entire amount and the State of New Jersey obliged by paying $21.3 million over a period of three years.[4] The related bonds were not sold, the risk of exposure to changing interest rate was not relevant, and BOM did not offer any service whatsoever to deserve this or any other amount of money from the State of New Jersey. However, that was not money paid for nothing; it was money paid for compliance with a contract written according to the "Master Agreement," and for the lack of financial sophistication of financial offices at the state level. The essence of this deal was that the State of New Jersey had to "pay" if there was actually a risk to hedge and also had to "pay" if there was no risk to hedge. The existence of the "Pay & Pay" form of adhesion contract is uniquely attributable to financial derivatives.

However, it is important to ask "why should the State of New Jersey or any other counterparty pay for termination of interest rate swap contracts?" It is of import to know that terminating swap agreements has two unharmonious effects: (a) it results in termination of all hopes for using swaps to manage interest rate risk. (b) It does not alter the object of these contracts and would not preclude any bank from selling similar swap agreements to others. In particular, interest rate swap contracts are bets on the change in the term structure of interest rates in the marketplace.[5]

---

[4]Cited in Ryan Chittum, "Bloomberg Covers Yet Another Swap Flop," *Columbia Journalism Review*, December 4, 2009.

Retrieved from http://archives.cjr.org/the_audit/bloomberg_covers_yet_another_s.php. David Lazar, "New Jersey Losing $22,000-a-Day With Swap for Bonds Never Sold," *NJ Internet Marketing*, December 4, 2009.

Retrieved from http://njinternetmarketing.blogspot.com/2009/12/new-jersey-losing-22000-day-with-swap.html.

[5]Known in the finance literature as "The Term Structure of Interest Rate."

Macroeconomic forces such as inflation, international trade and the supply of, and demand for, money determine the term structure of interest rate and neither purchasing, nor terminating swap contracts by any organization would have any effect on it. Thus, terminating or canceling interest rate exchange (swap) contracts does not diminish or damage the ability of big banks to carry on the same business. More specifically, termination of interest rate swaps causes no harm to either the object of the gamble — the term structure of interest rate — or to big banks' ability and scale to sell other contracts. Furthermore, the termination penalties are calculated not based on free market conditions but on contrived clauses in the self-serving design of the ISDA template "Master Agreement."

In the same articles about the contract with BOM and the State of New Jersey, the reporters noted, "The state's transportation trust fund was giving almost $1 million a month to a Goldman Sachs Group for an agreement linked to bonds that were redeemed." This was another episode of the state's failure to manage interest rate risk. Because of the financial and legal problems with Auction Rate market in 2008, the Transportation Trust Fund Authority of New Jersey converted $341 million of Auction Rate bonds to fixed rate bonds. Once the conversion was complete, the Transportation Trust Fund Authority no longer faced the risk of interest rate movements adversely affecting its cash flow. Nonetheless, a serious problem remained and that stemmed from the related interest rate swap contracts. While the swaps lost their use for anything good, the contracts will not terminate until 2019. This simply means that between 2008 and 2019, the Transportation Trust Fund Authority would be paying and will continue to pay money to hedge a risk to which it is no longer exposed. Thus, for 11 years, the State of New Jersey's Trust Fund Authority will be paying Goldman Sachs about $12 million a year for nothing received in return — nothing whatsoever.

Incidentally, Goldman Sachs is also the same counterparty of swap contracts with the City of Oakland. As noted above in Chapter 7, the City of Oakland paid off the debt for which the city acquired interest rate exchange (swap) agreements to hedge interest rate. After paying off the related debt fully in 2008, the risk being hedged no longer existed but the City of Oakland must continue paying for the swaps until the end of its original maturity in 2021.

Let us also not forget the case of State College Area School District in Pennsylvania. As discussed in Chapter 13, the District had planned a $57 million dollar bond issue for floating (sale) in 2007. In the meantime, the District was eager to hedge interest rate risk and entered into a (forward) interest rate exchange (swap) contract with Royal Bank of Canada. Changes in plans led to canceling the sale of the planned bond issue. There were no bonds, no interest rate risk but the cost of terminating the interest rate exchange (swap) contract remained. In less than two years, the court ordered State College Area School District to pay $10 million in termination penalty, but settled with RBC for $9 million. That was, $9 million for hedging risk the District never had.

Generally speaking, counterparties use interest rate swap contracts for one or more of the following reasons:

- Hedging (offsetting or counteracting) interest rate risk. That is the risk of paying more interest on a variable rate bond.
- Managing exposure to interest rate risk by altering the patterns of receivable and payable cash flow with the goal of lowering the cost of borrowing.
- Betting or gambling on the movement of interest rates for profit making.

Purchasing interest rate exchange (swap) contracts has the potential of achieving any or all of the three objectives. However, when swap contracts are terminated, the results are not ambiguous:

(a) The hedge is no longer a possibility and the buyer of the swaps loses that benefit completely.
(h) Managing interest rate risk and lowering the cost of borrowing would be an impossibility since the swap contracts will not be active to modify the patterns of cash flow.
(c) Succeeding in gambling is also an impossibility because the instrument of gambling will no longer exist.

More specifically, upon terminating interest rate swap contracts, all of the desired services also terminate. Therefore, it is beyond reason and ethical boundaries for big banks to require the buying counterparties to pay termination penalties equal to what could have been the losses of the terminated services from the time of termination to maturity. While these specific cases are compelling, termination penalties of interest rate swaps anywhere have the same implications. Namely, termination of swap contracts does not change the market term structure of interest rates or diminish the ability of big banks to enter into other swap contracts. These assertions apply to all cases including the $1.25 billion penalties or fees paid by Harvard University; the $1.043 termination fees and penalties paid by the City of Detroit; the more than $500 million penalties and fees paid by the City of Chicago; the $921 million penalties paid and payable by the State of New Jersey; and many more.

SECOND INDICATOR
UNBALANCED CONTRACTING

i. *Excessive Time to Maturity*

There is at least one distinct difference between swap contracts written for the corporate sector and those written for nonprofits — a major difference in the contracts' tenor or time to maturity. According to OTC statistical analysis reported by the Bank for International Settlements, more than 75% of interest rate swaps have time to maturity of five years or less, and about 25% have time to maturity of one year or less.[6] These statistics are for all OTC interest rate swaps including both the corporate and nonprofit sectors. Similarly, according to reports released by the Office of the Comptroller of the Currency of the U. S. Treasury, more than 75% of interest rate contracts held by the largest 25 U. S. commercial banks have time to maturity shorter than five years.

Comparing these statistics with the information obtained for OTC interest rate swaps sold to nonprofits is nothing short of shocking; the vast majority have time to maturity longer than 20 years. For example, the time to maturity of the portfolio of swaps held by the city of Chicago in 2008 (Chapter 6, page 145) ranged between 20 and 35 years

---

[6]Torsten Ehlers and Egemen Eren. The changing shape of interest rate derivatives markets BIS Quarterly Review | December 2016
Retrieved from https://www.bis.org/publ/qtrpdf/r_qt1612f.htm

with an average of 29 years. Chicago Exhibit 1 in this chapter presents four swap contracts held by the city in 2016. The average time to maturity of these four contracts is 33.75 years. This pattern is typical for nonprofits. For example, the swap portfolio of The Johns Hopkins Health in 2016 had an average time to maturity of 33 years (Hopkins Exhibit 2, p 295).

These statistics suggest that swap contracts purchased by nonprofits represent outliers in the distribution of time to maturity of OTC interest rate swaps. These outliers were on the high side and have contributed to increasing the average time to maturity of interest rate swaps for the OTC market in the US economy to 7.8 years in 2014 and to 11.8 in 2016.[7]

This information brings us to the main point of this subsection. It is clear that big banks and nonprofits operate under different incentives and strategies. Banks aim at maximizing profits irrespective of the consequences to social cost and, thus, bankers and swap dealers have all incentives to aggressively sell interest rate swaps but have no incentive to correct bad decisions that others make if those decisions add to the banks profits. In contrast, the business model of nonprofits is very different. Nonprofits are in the business of using public money to provide essential services to the public and society — education, transportation, health care, etc. They have absolutely no comparative advantage in matters of money management and high finance. By the same token, hedge funds and financial institutions do not venture into the business of providing education, health care, building roads and bridges; they had no comparative advantage in doing so. It is not possible for nonprofits to enter into offsetting swaps as banks do. Furthermore, nonprofits have no mechanisms or flexibility to deal with interest rate fluctuations and market uncertainty both of which increase exponentially as time to maturity increases. It is therefore mind boggling to see nonprofits take actions to become heavily involved in financial management and compete head on against big banks and swap dealers. Ever since OTC market started in the mid-1980s, the evidence shows that many nonprofits have added hedge-funds-like functions to their activities and, almost without

---

[7]Barnes, Chris. The Average Maturity of Swaps is Increasing. *Clarus Financial Technology.* January 25, 2017.
Retrieved from https://www.clarusft.com/the-average-maturity-of-swaps-is-increasing/

exception, ended up holding the losing buckets. The behavior displayed by the sample of cases presented in this book reveals that nonprofits operate in environments characterized by loss of control and possibly not highly competent management that big banks were able to exploit to their benefit.

Operating in a setting of incomplete information, nonprofits suffered damage from ignorance of one critical feature of interest rate swaps and that is the low likelihood that they could end being the winners. It is not conceivable that swap dealers (big banks) were so magnanimous to the point of informing executives at nonprofits that an interest rate swap contract has only one winner and that winner may not be the nonprofits themselves. It is also highly unlikely that the swap advisors hired to assist the nonprofits in making decisions about committing to interest rate swaps had the fortitude to provide this specific disclosure to the executives at nonprofits. Neither group had any financial incentive in providing full disclosure to the buying nonprofits. Swap dealers wanted to sell swap contracts and swap advisors wanted to close the deals in order to get paid. Yet, the managements of nonprofits all over the country had the unwarranted overconfidence to commit their organizations to non-cancelable bets on interest rate movements for thirty years or longer.

These considerations lead to pondering several questions.

a. Who in the management ranks of nonprofits — hospitals, public school districts, universities, state and local governments, transit authorities, etc. — had the skill, knowledge or ability to manage interest risk for periods as long as 30 years, while being subject to a very high cost to exit?

b. Who gave executives at nonprofits the right to endanger public service money (whether funded by taxpayers or donors) by committing their organizations to bet on the movement of interest rate benchmarks for periods of 30 years or even longer?

c. Would these officials have taken that much risk if they were subject to unambiguous systems of accountability?

d. Would these officials have taken that much risk if they were dealing with their own funds?

Chicago Exhibit 1
Disclosure of a Partial List of the City of Chicago
Swap Contracts as of June 30, 2016

Bond Issue	National Amounts	Date	Pay	Receive	Fair Value	Maturity
GO VRDB (Series 2007EFG).	$ 200,000	11/08/2007	3.998%	SIFMA	$ (41,116)	01/01/2042
GO VRDB (Series 2005D).	222,790	08/17/2005	4.104	SIFMA	(50,034)	01/01/2040
Chicago Midway International Airport Revenue Bonds (Series 2004C&D)	152,150	12/14/2004	4.174	SIFMA Plus .05%	(25,216)	01/01/2035
Wastewater Transmission Variable Rate Revenue Bonds (Series 2004A).	332,230	07/29/2004	3.886	67% of 1 Mo. LIBOR	(81,112)	01/01/2039

Average Maturity = 33.75 Years   Pay   Receive

- SIFMA was 1.65% (2004), 2.55% (2005) and 3.41% (2007) & 0.67 of LIBOR was 1.2328% (2004).
- In 2016, SIFMA was 0.84% and LIBOR 0.5%

Questions:

1. Given the Forward Yield Curve at inception, in 2004 and 2007, how could anyone claim that the present values of the "pay" and "receive" sides of any of these contracts were equal at inception or at any time thereafter?
2. No rational decision maker would choose this combination of pay/receive for 33 years and remains sane.

ii. *Flawed Analysis and Valuation*

In principle, swapping interest rates is like "bartering" two different products having equal values at the time of initiating the barter. For example, in old cultures, especially in the countryside, it was not unusual to exchange essential products such as exchanging a measure of rice for another measure of wheat. In modern times, financial and abstract products replaced physical and tangible commodities. The two financial products exchanged (in the most common interest rate swap contract) are commitments to exchange fixed rates of interest for variable rates of interest for a period of time. These contracts are known as plain vanilla swaps in which one party pays variable and receives fixed rates of interest and the counterparty pays fixed and receives variable rates of interest. The structure of these plain vanilla swaps are subject to two critical criteria.

Criterion 1: Presumed Equality of Values

As in the traditional bartering of commodities, in an interest rate swap contract the present value of the over-time stream of fixed interest equals the present value of the over-time stream of variable interest. This equality meant that the two counterparties are engaged in an arms-length exchange or a fair transaction. The Theoretical [Fair] Swap Exhibit in this chapter, which is adapted from a publication by PIMCO,[8] provides a good description of the presumed theoretical structure of an interest rate swap contract at inception. This exhibit is for a plain vanilla swap contract having a tenor (time to maturity) of four years and is exchanging interest at a 2.5% fixed rate for a floating, variable rate based on an acceptable benchmark such as LIBOR. During the first one-half of time to maturity, the fixed rate is expected to be higher than the variable rate according to a certain pattern. During that period, the fixed-rate payer is expected to experience cash outflow (losses), which would be gains for the fixed rate receiver. Based on the behavior of the determinants of the variable rate,[9] it is expected that the variable rate will increase overtime until it exceeds the fixed rate during the second one-half of time to maturity of the contract. During the second half, the variable rate will be above the fixed rate generating gains for the fixed rate payer (loss for the fixed rate receiver). This structure resulting in a loss in the first one-half of the life of a swap contract and a gain in the second half describes the expectation of a nonprofit entity that

---

[8] PIMCO. Interest Rate Swaps. Understanding Investing. Undated.
  Retrieved from https://global.pimco.com/en-gbl/resources/education/understanding-interest-rate-swaps
[9] These include the Yield Curve, the Zero-Coupon Curve and the Forward Rate Curve

pays fixed and receives variable. When all gains and losses are brought to the present time and represented by current dollars (discounted to present values) the present value of the loss zone should be equal the present value of the gain zone. This expected equality of gains and losses over the life of the contract means that the value of the swap contract at inception is zero — i.e., the contract is a fair gamble.

Criterion 2: Ignoring Transaction Cost

In almost all of the writing about interest rate swaps that I had examined, the equality of the present values of the two sides of a plain vanilla swap contract at inception is touted as a virtue — i.e., a clear indication of a fair transaction (gamble). In making these calculations, none of the books, research reports

The Theoretical [Fair] Swap Exhibit
The Expected Cash Flow at the Time of Initiating an Interest Rate Swap

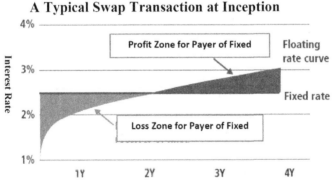

A Typical Swap Transaction at Inception

When an investor enters into a swap, the difference between the fixed rate payments and the expected future floating rate payments should be zero.

Adapted from PIMCO

Source: PIMCO. Interest Rate Swaps. Understanding Investing. Undated.

Retrieved from https://global.pimco.com/en-gbl/resources/education/understanding-interest-rate-swaps

or websites has ever discussed, or gave consolidation to the existence and magnitude of the transaction cost of entering into a swap contract. The only possible exception of which I am aware is a presentation by Andrew Kalotay, which noted the existence of cost other than interest rates.[10]

Big banks have encouraged and sometimes required, as in the case of the city of Atlanta, that the nonprofit entity refund fixed rate bonds and replace them with variable rate bonds in order to facilitate entering into interest rate swap agreements. In some cases, as in the case of the University of North Carolina, variable rate bonds were refunded by selling other variable rate bonds that are more favorable for exchanging interest rates. This behavior suggests that the transaction cost of interest rate swaps consists of two components:

a. The incremental transaction cost of issuing floating rate bonds above the transaction cost of maintaining fixed rate bonds.
b. The transaction cost of the interest rate swap contract itself.

These costs are contract specific (idiosyncratic) but include the following:

(a) The cost of underwriting the swap agreement and perhaps the incremental cost of underwriting the floating bond contract. The latter were in cases where the switch from fixed to floating rate bonds was undertaken to create a setting for entering into a swap agreement.
(b) The additional cost of insurance. This cost could be high and is, most likely recurring for the entire life of the swap.
(c) The cost of remarketing auction rate bonds consisting of a fee ranging from 0.3% to 0.7% payable to the marketing banks plus the cost of maintaining a staff and a marketing agent on the premises (all are recurring costs).
(d) Swap advisors fees.
(e) The fees of retaining legal counsel (which could be recurring).

---

[10] Andrew Kalotay. "Municipal Swaps: Realities and Misconceptions." Global Association of Risk Professionals. December 11, 2012. http://kalotay.com/sites/default/files/private/GARP_Muni_Swaps.pdf

(f) The cost of obtaining liquidity facility from other financial institutions. This also could be substantial. The state of Illinois, for example, acquired a liquidity facility from Depfa Bank at a cost of 0.32% of the principal amount of a specific variable-rate bond issue plus interest for thirty-five days. However, in 2013, Depfa Bank was replaced by a syndicate of five banks at an annual cost of 2.35% of the outstanding par amount of bonds. Thus, the fixed rate payable for the swaps would be higher than the rate specified in the contract by 2.35% a year.

(g) The administrative cost of maintaining a staff to remarket auction rate bonds, to process the documentation and keep up with the flow of funds

(h) The cost of putting up collateral for the swap debt. Funds restricted or used for collateral become essentially idle assets for the entity.

Most of these items are not covered by swap dealers and big banks. Instead, the burden of paying these cost items falls on the nonprofit counterparty. More specifically, when transaction cost is factored into the analysis, the actual and true cost payable by the nonprofit counterparty is the fixed rate of interest stated in the contract plus the nonprofit's burden of the swap transaction cost. In other words, from the vantage point of the nonprofit entity, the true structure of a plain vanilla swap contract is as shown in Exhibit of Swap's True Cost Structure.

The result of accounting for transaction cost is the divergence between the expected present value of gains and losses. As shown in "The True [Unfair] Swap Exhibit," the "loss zone" is much larger than the "gain

Exhibit of Swap's True Cost Structure
For the Nonprofit Counterparty

Receive	Variable Rate based on a known benchmark (LIBOR or SIFMA)
Pay	A predetermined Fixed Rate + Swap Contract Transaction Cost

zone." More specifically, from the vantage point of the nonprofit counterparty, the expected present value of the swap contract at inception is negative — the nonprofit is losing from the start.

The True [Unfair] Swap Exhibit
The Expected Cash Flow at the Time
of Initiating an Interest Rate Swap

> The true cost to the fixed rate payer is actually the fixed rate stated in the contract plus the embedded cost of several items: underwriting fees, insurance cost, legal consulting fees and swap advisors' fees among others. Adding these items to the contractual interest rate, the present value of the swap contract at inception would be negative, a loss to the fixed rate payer—usually the nonprofit entity.

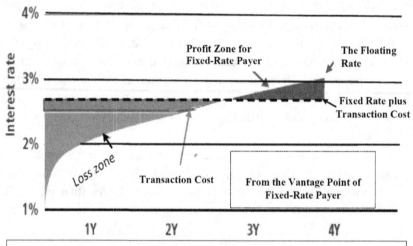

When an investor enters into an interest rate swap contract, the true cost structure should include the payable interest rate plus transaction cost. When the transaction cost is factored in, the loss zone becomes larger than the gain zone for the fixed-rate payer and the initial present value of the swap contract is negative.

Why Big Banks Do Not Lose on These Swap Deals

As private companies, swap dealers (big banks) have complete flexibility to enter into offsetting swap contracts at will. When a bank enters into a swap contract with a nonprofit entity to receive fixed and pay variable the bank would be exposed to interest rate risk in the sense that any increase in the benchmark rate would cost the bank more money. However, the bank has the opportunity and the ability to enter into an offsetting swap contract with a third party almost immediately requiring the bank to pay fixed and receive variable. Exposure to interest rate risk would thus be neutralized. Although this offset alleviates their economic obligations, it may or may not alleviate their legal obligations.

This possibility is not available to non-profits. As public organizations subject to budgetary and inflexible administrative constraints, nonprofits have neither the ability nor the funds that enable them to enter into offsetting swaps. Stated differently, once a nonprofit entity enters into a swap contract, it is stuck for the long haul.

THIRD INDICATOR:
BIG BANKS CONTROL BOTH SIDES OF THE INTEREST PAYMENTS ON SWAP CONTRACTS

Banks have developed a mastery of financial engineering for which the buyers do not have a comparable match because the officials at nonprofit institutions completed their formal education long before the appearance of interest-rate-swap contracts. They also came to know that such contracts are unlike any other finance contracts that have ever existed in the marketplace. For one thing, no investment of funds are involved, and unlike big banks, nonprofit entities do not have any influence over the movements of interest rates in the market. Big banks do. They vote to decide on the level of the benchmark interest rate LIBOR, and when movements in that rate did not go their way, they colluded and conspire to twist it to benefit themselves. The fact that one party of the contract has fixed the rate it receives and also has control over the interest rate it pays the counterparty is a connection most people would not expect.

Additionally, the contracts are often written in technical jargon bordering on being an exotic alien language, adding to the difficulty of deciphering their complex structures. The fact that officials at nonprofit entities were unaware of the complexities of the new financial instruments has created opportunities for many "old" finance specialists to learn the new jargon and pretend-to-be qualified swap advisors. The cases reported in this book reflect some of the most unintelligent advice provided by some of them, and these cases represent only a sample of a much larger population. The faults of these structures are clearly apparent in the cases of the City of Chicago and its public school district; Denver Public Schools; the University of California System; the City of Detroit; IU Health; the University of North Carolina; the states of New Jersey, New York, Illinois, and Texas; the City of Atlanta, and hundreds of other cases. In the land of the blind, nonprofit entities retained those pretend swap specialists, paid them lots of money, and went ahead to implement their lousy advice.[11]

---

[11] A notable exception known to me is Andrew Kalotay, the founder of Kalotay Analytics, who knows the stuff well and shares the view that all the pretend swap advisers cared about was getting paid.

The cases that shine with blatant unconscionability, including hiring the pretend swap advisers, are the cases of Jefferson County; the City of Detroit; and the public school systems of Denver, Chicago, and Pennsylvania, especially small school districts. All hired swap advisers who knew as little as anyone outside the new finance arena.[12] One cannot forget the case of the Erie City School District, which borrowed $780,000 from JPMorgan Chase that ended up costing the district $2.9 million. Also among the $17.4 billion swap contracts in the State of Pennsylvania were the cases of Bethlehem Area School District, the State College Area School District, and Philadelphia School District. Like many others, the financially naïve members of school boards of those districts appear to have feared the indignity and ramifications of saying "we do not understand these contracts."

However, it is not possible to find a case which is not tainted by unconscionability for several reasons.

(a) Unfair exchange,
(b) Making false promises while knowing that synthetic rate is not really fixed, especially when the related bonds have weekly adjustable rates,
(c) Embedding and concealing other costs to keep them out of view when comparing the cost of debt with and without coupling bonds with swap contracts.

The US Uniform Commercial Code did not limit the types of contracts to which Section 2-302 applies. In general, however, the unconscionability clause has been applied in cases of sales of goods, leasing agreements, and family law. Few cases in financial contracts went through the U.S. courts. Charles Knapp presented two of these

---

[12] Sharon Ward, *Too Big to Trust? Banks, Schools and the Ongoing Problem with Interest Rate Swaps.* Pennsylvania Budget and Policy Center, Harrisburg, PA 17101. January 17, 2012.

Retrieved from http://pennbpc.org/sites/pennbpc.org/files/TooBigSwaps.pdf.

cases: (a) The Massachusetts Supreme Court used unconscionability to rule against Citibank for continually raising the interest rate on the credit card of one customer until the rate came to more than 47% per annum. (b) A Florida court ruled against banks for overdraft charges, arguing that unconscionability existed because of unequal bargaining power.[13]

The Florida court noted that the plaintiffs had sufficiently pled *procedural* unconscionability, noting the "disparity in sophistication and bargaining power" between the parties, the "voluminous boilerplate language" in the banks' documentation, the lack of any "meaningful opportunity to negotiate on equal footing," and the lack of notice to customers that they could decline the overdraft-fee arrangement.[14]

Unequal bargaining power also arises in almost all other cases.[15] Even the most financially educated school superintendents and finance officers in municipalities, state agencies, universities, or hospitals could not claim to have too much knowledge of the terminology and modeling of swap contracts as far back as the 1990s or even 2000s when interest-rate Swap Mania began. By then, financial-engineering models and terminology had been developed far beyond the abilities of some of the most successful chief financial officers to detect the pitfalls in the specific terms in the contracts to which they had agreed.[16]

---

[13] Knapp, Charles L. Unconscionably in American Contract Law: A Twenty-First Century Survey. University of California Hastings Research Paper No. 71, 2013 pp. 25–27.

Retrieved from https://papers.ssrn.com/sol3/papers.cfm?abstract_id=2346498.

[14] Knapp, Ibid, p. 27.

[15] Except perhaps the case of Harvard Management Corporation, where two former secretaries of the Department of the Treasury (Robert Rubin and Larry Summers) discussed, approved, and signed the contracts with big banks.

[16] The contract between Procter & Gamble and Bankers Trust of New York in early 1993 is a case in point. To show the complexity and indecipherability of the contract, consider the following terms of one of the interest-rate-swap contracts written by Bankers Trust New York for Procter & Gamble as presented in the court report.

FOURTH INDICATOR:
EXPROPRIATING FUTURE RESOURCES UPON TERMINATION — UNJUST ENRICHMENT?

In the first chapter, I made a comparison between a long-term lease and interest-rate swap as a financial contract. Leasing a property, whether real estate or equipment, for a long term, say 30 years, and canceling the contract before maturity leads to the question of penalty. The party canceling the contract would be responsible for compensating the counterparty for damages. The lessee must leave the property in good condition and also pay for any economic loss the lessor would encounter because of the cancelation. In general, the terms of the contract explicitly specify the penalty conditions in these cases. Nevertheless, no one encountered a

---

During the fall of 1993, the parties began discussing the terms of an interest rate swap which was to be customized for P & G. After negotiations, the parties agreed to a swap transaction on November 2, 1993, which is referred to as the 5s/30s swap; the written Confirmation is dated November 4, 1993.

In the 5s/30s swap transaction, BT agreed to pay P & G a fixed rate of interest of 5.30% for five years on a notional amount of $200 million. P & G agreed to pay BT a floating interest rate. For the first six months, that floating rate was the prevailing commercial paper ("CP") interest rate minus 75 basis points (0.75%). For the remaining four-and-a-half years, P & G was to make floating interest rate payments of CP minus 75 basis points plus a spread. The spread was to be calculated at the end of the first six months (on May 4, 1994) using the following formula:

$$\text{Spread} = [(98.5 * [5 \text{ year CMT}] - 30 \text{ T Price}) 5.78\%] / 100$$

In this formula, the "5 year CMT" (Constant Maturity Treasury) represents the yield on the five-year Treasury Note, and the "30 T Price" represents the price of the 30-year Treasury Bond. The leverage factor in this formula meant that even a small movement up or down in prevailing interest rates results in an incrementally larger change in P & G's position in the swap.

United States District Court, S.D. Ohio, Western Division. **PROCTER & GAMBLE CO. v. BANKERS TRUST CO.** No. C-1-94-735. 925 F.Supp. 1270 (1996). *The PROCTER & GAMBLE COMPANY, Plaintiff, v. BANKERS TRUST COMPANY and BT Securities Corporation, Defendants.*

Retrieved from http://www.leagle.com/decision/19962195925FSupp1270_12043/PROCTER%20 &%20GAMBLE%20CO.%20v.%20BANKERS%20TRUST%20CO.

contract that says, "When you cancel, you must pay the full rent for the entire term of the lease."

Nonetheless, what is forbidden for lessors became acceptable for banks starting with the establishment of the International Swap and Derivatives Association (ISDA) in 1985. Through the design of the Master Agreement by the ISDA as the banks' true agent, big banks legitimized the forbidden fruit for interest-rate swaps. Canceling an interest-rate-swap agreement before maturity has a totally different penalty structure than canceling a long-term lease contract before maturity. If you cancel a 30-year-term interest rate swap contract before maturity, say in the third year, you would be required to pay the counterparty (the bank) the present value of the amount of money you could have lost for the entire 27 years remaining in the life of the contract. In this case, there is no property involved because interest-rate swap is simply a bet on future changes in the market term structure of interest rates. If you bet on the wrong side, it would not matter to the counterparty when you wanted to exit the contract because (i) exiting an interest rate swap contract will not change the term structure of interest rate, and (ii) there are other trusting gullible people out there whom the bank could convince to buy alternative bets. If you cancel in year three, for example, your penalty would be equal to the loss in year three multiplied 27 times adjusted for the behavior of the forward yield curve and the time value of money. You do not have many other choices and the bank does not have to show any damage. The only implicit claim the bank could offer is that you were not foolish enough to stay in the contract and lose so that the bank could gain every year till maturity. You made a bet for 30 years, and if you wish to leave early, the bank has the inalienable right to take from you the future resources that could have been the bank's profits. A simplified procedure of calculating the penalty of premature contract termination is in "Termination Penalty Exhibit 2."

(a) This calculation of penalty makes the absurd assumptions that the bad economic conditions that led you to lose this year will continue in the future, and we expect you to lose a similar amount every year upto the end of the contract's original maturity date.

(b) After termination, it is absolutely irrelevant if the market interest-rate benchmark changes to be in your favor and you could have had profits going forward. The calculation of loss made by the banks does not take these contingencies into account. The banks' assumption remains unchanged: you were destined to lose future resources, which would compensate the bank for your gambling loss, but you would not receive any service or benefits whatsoever. You gambled on interest rate, you lost currently, and the bank sentenced you to lose for the remaining life of the contract whether it does or does remain in force!

Termination Penalty Exhibit 2

The penalty of terminating an interest rate swap contract is the (present value) of the total amount of money that you could have lost if you stayed in the contract. That is also the amount of money of which the counterparty would be deprived due to your terminating the contract.

Penalty = The loss in the year of cancelation
@
The number of years remaining to maturity (assuming a flat yield curve).

In our example:
Loss in the third year = $10 million
Remaining life in the contract = 27 years
Equal penalty for termination = $270 million (discounted to present value)*

Thus, in this type of contract,

- The termination penalty is the amount of money that the losing (defaulting) party would have lost had he/she stayed with the contract to maturity.
- This amount of money is calculated on the basis of the current year's loss.* In many cases the bank and counterparty enter into negotiation to lower this huge amount of money, eve if so slightly.
- The assumption that the defaulting party will lose the same amount annually till maturity is not exactly the process that big banks apply because, in reality, the forward yield curve is not flat.
- Why should anyone pay for future losses after all services are terminated?
- Because so says the Master Agreement of the International Swap and Derivatives Association.
- Who formed the ISDA and made that policy?
- None other than big banks and other swap dealers?

* To be discounted to present value to report it in current dollars.

FIFTH INDICATOR:
PRETENDING TO OFFER SYNTHETIC FIXED RATE EVEN WHEN IT IS NOT REALLY FIXED

The obscure terms that complicate swap contracts make these contracts unlike any other in the business world. To entice nonprofits to enter into swap contracts, big banks offered to help them fix the interest rate on variable-rate bonds synthetically (artificially). "Synthetic Fixed Rate Exhibit 3" portrays the story that swap dealers sold to nonprofit entities throughout the country.

A Necessary Assumption:

The fixed rate achieved in this artificial fixing process is presumed to be lower than the fixed rate the entity would have paid on a traditional fixed rate municipal bond. While this might be the case at the start, nothing was guaranteed for any time or level during the long term (30 years or more) of the swap contract.

The bankers selling swaps found it convenient to highlight the point that the synthetic fixed rate was lower than the fixed rate at which plain-vanilla municipal bonds were sold. This result is true in theory, academic circles, and blue skies; the reality over the past 20 years has proved it to be false. See, for example, doubling the rates in some years for the Bay Area Toll Authority (Chapter 29), the City of Philadelphia (Chapter 5) and the City of Atlanta. That the two contracts — a variable-rate bond and a

Synthetic Fixed Rate Exhibit 3
The Theoretical Notion of Converting a
Variable-Rate Bond to a Fixed-Rate Bond

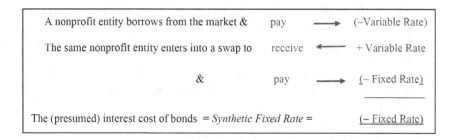

swap to pay fixed and receive variable — would lower the cost of borrowing is a story nonprofits seemed to believe and repeat ad nauseam in their annual reports since the year 2000, while showing exactly the opposite.

Because of bankers' persuasion, each of the nonprofit entities involved in swap transactions would have two types of contracts: (a) a variable (adjustable or floating) rate bond and (b) a swap contract. Each of the two contracts is a self-contained stand-alone agreement. However, the two contracts are related in terms of achieving certain goals, not in terms of structure because the benchmark rate used for interest rate swaps is typically different from the benchmark or auction rate used for the bond issue. Additionally, each of these two contracts entails obscure or hidden transaction cost that add materially and significantly to the cost of borrowing far more than the cost indicated by the synthetic fixed rate. Below is a partial list of some of these embedded, costly terms, which economists call "transaction cost" and which are conveniently ignored in making cost comparison.

Examples of "Synthetic" Fixed Rates

The variable rate on the bond was either indexed to a benchmark rate such as LIBOR or was left wide open as an Auction Rate, requiring the bond to be remarketed and repriced *every week, every two weeks, or every 35 days*. Every time a bond issue is remarketed, the bondholders change, and a new interest rate is set. Therefore, the issuer takes on market credit risk in addition to interest-rate risk. Examples from cases presented in this book are as follows:

a. *From Jefferson County (Chapter 3)*

This county in Alabama was driven into bankruptcy by issuing bonds beyond its needs or ability to pay back and coupling them with swap contracts promoted to them by JPMorgan Chase, the same underwriter of the bonds. Two executives, LeCroy and MacFaddin, from JPMorgan Chase conspired with the president of the county council, Larry Langford, to have the council take action on whatever the bank wanted the county to do. For the purpose of this section, the following quote suggests the depth of the damage to the county:

Based on this recommendation, the [County] Commission voted to issue $3.0 billion of adjustable and *auction rate* (all floating rate) bonds and authorized Langford to sign for the Commission.[17]...The County's risk increased further when one of its *auction rate bonds failed* and there was no taker even at the highest auction interest rate.[18]

b. *From the Report of the Massachusetts Bay Transportation Authority (Chapter 30)*

The 2003 Series Bonds are Auction Rate bonds. The Auction Rate is reset every 28 days. The Authority has a SWAP arrangement on these bonds to enable the authority to pay a fixed rate of 5.2% over the life of

---

[17] An auction-rate bond means that interest rates are set for a very short period at a time. A remarketing agent places the bond issue back in the marketplace seeking bids on interest rates. The remarketing could be set for periods from one week to 35 days. A weekly auction-rate bond requires remarketing and resetting interest rates on the bond weekly. The use of auction-rate bonds began in the mid-1980s with the dawn of the Swap Mania but collapsed in 2008. See the Securities and Exchange Commission, Auction Rate Securities, at

https://www.investor.gov/introduction-investing/basics/investment-products/auction-rate-securities.

[18] In his ruling of January 6, 2012, Judge Bennett noted the following:

A fundamental, yet terrible error made by the county's experts in municipal finance is not paying attention to the fact that markets fail. This is the process that commenced in what is called the auction rate securities market in late 2007: purchasers of auction rate securities stopped purchasing them. There was no market for these and other types of securities. Once this occurred, the county's sewer system debt's fate was sealed and default was likely to follow with respect to the warrants. Despite being a simplistic explanation, the county's use of auction rate warrants was essentially taking advantage of short term interest rates to finance long term debt. To do this requires the existence of a market for short term debt refinancing, and when it became nonexistent, a critical part of the scheme collapsed (footnote 1, page 7).

Source: United States Bankruptcy Court, Northern District of Alabama, Southern Division. In Re: Jefferson County, Alabama, Alabama, a political subdivision of the State of Alabama. Case No.: 11-05736-TBB.

Retrieved from http://www.gpo.gov/fdsys/pkg/USCOURTS-alnb-2_11-bk-05736/pdf/USCOURTS-alnb-2_11-bk-05736-0.pdf.

the bonds while the third party pays the Authority BMA (Bond Municipal Association) Index (a variable rate).[19]

c. *From Denver Public Schools (Chapter 15)*

In 2008, Denver Public Schools (DPS) sold $750 million of bonds to JPMorgan Chase, Bank of America, and Royal Bank of Canada at the weekly auction rate. DPS coupled all these bonds with interest-rate swaps to pay fixed at 4.859% and receive variable at London Average Interest Rate (LIBOR). The relationships between the two financial instruments as shown in "Denver Schools Exhibit 1" led to having a highly undetermined synthetic "fixed" rate equal to 2.074% plus the unknown weekly auction rate of the related bonds. Thus, there was no reason whatsoever to claim either one of the two highly hyped benefits: (a) attaining a fixed rate of interest on variable-rate bonds or (b) reducing the cost of borrowing.

d. *From the School District of Philadelphia* (SDP, Chapter 12)

The School District of Philadelphia Interest-Rate Swaps: SDP entered into ten (10) floating-to-fixed swaps effective June 29, 2004 with a total initial notional amount of $691.1 million, to synthetically advance refund certain outstanding bonds. *Each swap is associated with either 7-day reset auction-rate securities or 35-day reset auction-rate securities.* The combination of auction-rate securities and a floating-to-fixed swap creates synthetic fixed-rate debt at a rate lower than was available in the cash bond market. 58.5% of LIBOR + 27 basis points swaps were used to hedge the 7-day auction-rate securities and 60.4% of LIBOR + 32 basis points swaps were used to hedge the 35-day securities.[20]

---

[19]MASSACHUSETTS BAY TRANSPORTATION AUTHORITY Financial Statements and Required Supplementary Information June 30, 2004 and 2003, p. 20. Note that the BMA index has changed to become SIFMA, as noted earlier in the book.

Retrieved from http://www.mbta.com/uploadedFiles/Documents/Financials/642MBTA-FS-2004-FINAL.pdf.

[20]City of Philadelphia, Pennsylvania. Comprehensive Annual Financial Report Fiscal Year Ended June 30, 2006, p. 79.

Retrieved from http://www.phila.gov/investor/pdfs/Financial%20Statements/FY%20 2006%20Financial%20Statements/FY%202006%20Phila%20CAFR.pdf.

[Emphasis added; with 35-day Auction Rate, the fixity of the synthetic rate could last for 35 days only]

e. *From the City of Chicago — Midway Airport Bonds (Chapter 6)*
    Bond Series 2004C-D, which has notional amounts of $152 million.

The Series 2004C-D bonds were sold in December with an initial *auction rate* of 1.55 percent and 1.45 percent and maturity dates ranging from January 1, 2012 to January 1, 2035. [Emphasis added]
...
At the discretion of the City, the Series 2004C-D bonds may bear interest at a weekly, flexible, adjustable long, auction rate or fixed rate. *The City issued the bonds in the auction rate mode for a seven-day auction period.*

Concurrently with the sale of these bond series, the city entered into swap contracts having notional amounts and terms to maturity set to match the bond series. These swap contracts required the city to pay a fixed interest rate at 4.14% and receive a variable rate at Municipal Bond Average Interest Rate (SIFMA). The city's 2004 Comprehensive Annual Financial Report displays the city council's apparent disbelief — and confusion — that entering into a swap contract would convert an auction-rate bond into a synthetic-fixed-rate bond.

At the discretion of the City, the Series 2004C-D bonds may bear interest at a weekly, flexible, adjustable long, auction rate or fixed rate. The City issued the bonds in the auction rate mode for a seven-day auction period. Accrued and unpaid interest on the bonds shall be due in a daily Auction Period on the first business day of the month immediately succeeding the Auction Period, if the Auction period is more than seven days but less than 92 days the unpaid interest is payable immediately following such Auction Period and if the Auction Period is longer than 92 days interest is payable on the thirteenth Thursday after the first day of the Auction Period.

Synthetic Fixed Rate Exhibit 4
The City of Chicago's So-Called Synthetic Fixed
Rate That Is Not Fixed

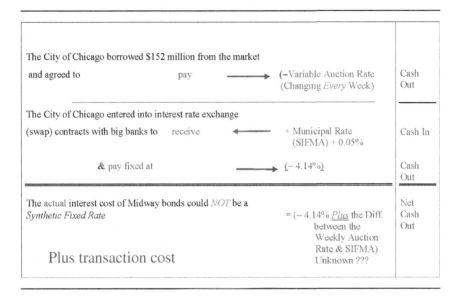

The City of Chicago borrowed $152 million from the market and agreed to	pay →	(−Variable Auction Rate (Changing *Every* Week)	Cash Out
The City of Chicago entered into interest rate exchange (swap) contracts with big banks to receive ←		+ Municipal Rate (SIFMA) + 0.05%	Cash In
& pay fixed at →		(− 4.14%)	Cash Out
The actual interest cost of Midway bonds could *NOT* be a *Synthetic Fixed Rate*		= (− 4.14% *Plus* the Diff. between the Weekly Auction Rate & SIFMA)	Net Cash Out
Plus transaction cost		Unknown ???	

In connection with the issuance of the Series 2004C-D bonds, the City entered into three interest rate swap agreements to obtain a [synthetic] fixed interest rate.[21]

Because of signing to a bond contract at <u>auction rates</u>, what big banks had promised and the City of Chicago cited in its official documents as a synthetic fixed interest rate is false and misleading; with these terms "fixity" may exist only in a hypothetical world. "Synthetic Fixed Rate Exhibit 4" presents the interest-rate cost of the Chicago Midway Airport bond issues and the related swaps. As this exhibit shows, the so-called synthetic fixed rate consisted of 4.14% *plus* the difference between the weekly

---

[21] City of Chicago. Comprehensive Annual Financial Report for the year ended December 31, 2004.

Retrieved from https://www.cityofchicago.org/content/dam/city/depts/fin/supp_info/CAFR/2004/CAFR_2004.pdf.

auction rate and Municipal Bond Average Interest Rate (SIFMA). That difference does not remain stationary. Yet bankers sold it to Chicago City Hall as an instrument of fixing interest rate artificially, or "synthetically."

The more surprising is the double-talk one encounters in some annual reports assuming that the readers are simply idiots. For example, in the 2006 Comprehensive Annual Financial Report of the State of New York (Chapter 10), we have a statement sounding like "We have a synthetic fixed rate, but not really." The quotation from page 67 of the report is broken down into two components to highlight the problem[22]:

- The bonds and the related *synthetic fixed rate swap agreements* have final maturities occurring through March 17, 2033 and the swaps' total notional amount of $5 billion matches the $5 billion variable-rate bonds. Under the swap agreements, the State pays the counterparties a fixed payment at rates ranging from 2.86 percent to 3.66 percent and receives a variable payment computed as 65 percent of the one-month LIBOR rate.
- The bonds' variable rate coupons are based upon rates determined *by remarketing agents for bonds in the weekly interest rate mode and by auction rate agents for bonds in the auction rate mode.* (p. 67, emphasis added)

This obfuscated logic needs deciphering: if the interest rate on the bonds changes weekly but the variable rate on the swap is tied to LIBOR, these two rates could not be equal at any time, except by a random chance. When the difference between these two variable rates is added to the fixed rate payable on the swap, it is impossible to call the total product anything other than "floating" rate.

---

[22] State of New York, Comprehensive Annual Financial Report for Fiscal Year Ended March 31, 2006.

Retrieved from https://www.osc.state.ny.us/finance/finreports/cafr/cafr06.pdf.

CHAPTER 35

Epilogue

In 1982, the Student Loan Marketing Association (Sallie Mae) entered into an innocuous transaction with another financial institution to exchange interest dollars on a fixed-rate bond for interest dollars on a variable-rate instrument. Only one year earlier, the first known currency swap took place between IBM and the World Bank. Given the novelty and recency of these types of exchanges, officials at Sallie Mae did not expect this one-time transaction to be planting the seed that would grow at a rate faster than the growth rate of bamboo or mahi-mahi in the Pacific Ocean. It gave big banks and Wall Street merchants the idea of institutionalizing this form of contracting in a big way and kept on building it up until it grew to be several times the size of the U.S. Gross Domestic Product. It is overwhelming to think of the largest 25 U. S. Bank Holding Companies having derivatives contracts having face (reference or notional) amounts of over $250 trillion [$250,000,000,000,000] held by the largest 25 banks in the United States. This much level of OTC derivatives is neither needed nor intended to hedge the risks of an economy having Gross Domestic Product of $18 trillion [$18,000,000,000,000]! In fact, the statistics reported by the U.S. Office of the Comptroller of the Currency show that more than 98% of the financial derivatives, consisting mostly of interest rate contracts, held by the largest 25 U.S. banks are for "trading" purposes — i.e., profit making. Moreover, just like all betting instruments, interest-rate swaps are instruments for wealth transfer, *not* wealth creation.[1]

The basic and most common form of a swap contract is to exchange (swap) a fixed rate of interest for a variable rate of interest on some pre-specified face (reference, notional) amount. Typically, the variable rate is linked to a benchmark rate such as the London Average Interest Rate (which is London Interbank Offered Rate or LIBOR), the Average Municipal Bond Rate (which is the swap index of the Securities Industry and Financial Market Association or SIFMA), the Prime Rate of interest, Consumer Price Index (CPI) or other commonly known and acceptable benchmarks. In other cases the rate was determined by means of auctions held periodically for periods varying between one week and thirty five days.

The generic name of this contract is plain-vanilla swap. The two counterparties do not exchange the reference (face) amount, and neither party to the contract makes an initial investment (other than processing cost including hefty underwriting fees). In addition, typically the risk-and-reward relationships for the seller (the bank) and the buyer (the counterparty, such as a nonprofit organization) of the contract are very different. Interest rate swap contracts are not standardized and not permitted for sale to the public. Rather they are self-tailored to fit the two counterparties own specifications. The terms of these contracts include

* Paying the bank underwriter's fees;
* Conforming to the bank's demand of insuring the exchange (swap) through highly rated insurers;
* Agreeing to the conditions the seller (the bank) will use to determine the counterparty's credit events that would propel the banks to take action;
* Reserving the right to terminate the contract under some conditions at any time;
* Reserving the right to determine the terms of the variable-rate bonds to which the interest-rate swap contracts may be related. This condition includes asking the counterparty to issue the related bonds at any

---

[1] As the Bank for International Settlements report, this problem is huge in North America and Western Europe more than other places in the world.

of the auction rates that would change daily, weekly, or monthly.[2] For that facility, the counterparty must pay an annual fee for remarketing the bonds; and

✳ Setting up the terms for collateral to secure the debt of the counterparty in the case of accumulating losses.

In short, the risk of loss, or the downside risk, for the seller of a swap contract (the bank) is relatively low. However, the risk of loss for the counterparty is relatively high; especially when the counterparty is a nonprofit organization whose officials had foolishly agreed to maturity terms as long as 30 or 40 years, have little or no possibility of entering into costless offsetting contracts and in addition facing costly exit.

Shortly after the Sallie Mae transaction in 1982 and before the birth of the Swap Mania, big banks being the majority of swap dealers, wanted to write more of these contracts, but they faced two obstacles:

i. The first obstacle was the local and state prohibition on betting on prices of securities and commodities. It all goes back to the stock-market crash and Bank Panic of 1907 that raised concerns about investors leaving the stock market to gamble on stock and grain prices. Up until that time, the New York Stock Exchange required 10% margin and did not permit odd lot trading. These requirements made trading on the floor of the exchange accessible only to the wealthy.

The aspiring investors from the poor and middle class found a different way to bet on securities and commodity prices. Starting around 1867, entrepreneurs had found a way to draw in the customers who could not participate in either the New York Stock Exchange or the Chicago Board of Trade. They established shops that appeared as if they were legitimate stock brokerage houses and allowed customers to place

---

[2]While the Auction Rate market collapsed in 2008 as noted in this book, this change affected the new contracts for which the market developed other forms of floating rates that mimics the Auction Rate.

bets on future changes in the prices of securities and commodities, especially grain. These alternative establishments, which are known as Bucket Shops, required margins of less than 1%. At the end of the day, the shop owners and customers settled by exchanging the difference between the bet price and the actual price posted by organized exchanges. The name given to these establishments was "bucket shops" which drew many customers away from the legitimate stock and grain exchanges. Following the Bank Panic and stock-market crash of October 1907, the State of New York took action to eradicate these gambling shops that formed illegal competition to the stock market.

In May 1908, the State of New York enacted a legislation prohibiting the operation of bucket shops. Other states followed suit and enacted similar laws.[3] Largely, these laws *remained in effect until December 20, 2000* when this state of affairs changed with the assistance of extensive lobbying by Senator Phil Gramm of Texas.[4] The bankers back then charted a path to build up the gaming segment of their business. All worked hard to repeal and preempt state and local laws and regulations against bucket shops and gambling on prices of securities and commodities. This achievement came in the form of nothing less than a section inserted into a major federal law. Section 117 of the Commodity Futures Modernization Act (CFMA), signed by President Clinton on December 20, 2000, states[5]:

---

[3] David Hochfelder, September 2006. "Where the Common People Could Speculate": The Ticker, Bucket Shops, and the Origins of Popular Participation in Financial Markets, 1880–1920. *The Journal of American History,* pp. 335–358.

Retrieved from https://academic.oup.com/jah/article/93/2/335/830224.
Brendan Sapien. 2010. Financial Weapons of Mass Destruction: From Bucket Shops to Credit Default Swaps. *Southern California Interdisciplinary Law Journal.*

Retrieved from http://clhc.usc.edu/why/students/orgs/ilj/assets/docs/19-2%20Sapien.pdf.
[4] Eric Lipton and Stephen Labaton. November 16, 2008. Deregulator Looks Back, Unswayed. *The New York Times.*

Retrieved from http://www.nytimes.com/2008/11/17/business/economy/17gramm.html.
[5] Commodity Futures and Modernization Act. December 14, 2000. The 106 Congress.

Retrieved from http://www.cftc.gov/files/ogc/ogchr5660.pdf.

This Act shall supersede and preempt the application of any State or local law that prohibits or regulates gaming or the operation of bucket shops (other than antifraud provisions of general applicability. (105).

The impact of this section in CFMA was significant and lasting. For example, Resolution no. 120147 of the Council of the City of Philadelphia in 2012 used CFMA in justifying the city's use of interest rate swaps[6]:

WHEREAS, Qualified interest rate management agreements, also known as interest rate "swaps," belong to the class of financial instruments known as derivatives. The use of swap agreements in public financial management was encouraged by the federal Commodity Futures Modernization Act of 2000, and authorized by the Pennsylvania Legislature in Act 23 for use by local government units in 2003.

ii. The second obstacle resulted from state laws prohibiting any government agency from transacting in interest-rate swaps or any other financial derivative. State and local laws and regulations enforced the prohibitions. To overcome this obstacle, big banks dispatched emissaries to lobby state legislatures to undo the prohibitions against contracting in interest-rate swaps or other financial derivatives by state or local government agencies. In 2002 and 2003, legislatures in the states of Illinois and Pennsylvania, for example, adopted laws to permit public and government agencies to enter into interest-rate swaps and other contracts of financial derivatives. In the State of New York, approval of transacting in financial derivatives started in 1988 and came in piecemeal authorization in response to requests from different banks.[7]

---

[6]Council of the City of Philadelphia. Office of the Chief Clerk. Resolution No. 120147. March 1, 2012.
Retrieved from http://legislation.phila.gov/attachments/12751.pdf.
[7]Banking Interpretations. April 25, 2003. Department of Financial Services. State of New York.
Retrieved from http://www.dfs.ny.gov/legal/interpret/lo030425.htm.

In the meantime, a herd of swap sellers targeted nonprofit organizations and roamed the country from north to south and from east to west seeking customers. They worked hard and used all means of persuasion to convince officials at nonprofit organizations that entering into interest-rate-swap contracts, under specific structures, could help lower the costs of their borrowing. However, other than the initial relationships, the bankers selling these contracts did not provide any evidence to substantiate their claims. Nor did they offer guarantees of any kind. In addition, it appears that bankers selling these swap contracts did not inform the officials of counterparties that, in any one bilateral contract, there can be only one winner! That was easy to skip since they did not think much of the financial abilities and skills of the nonprofit officials with whom they were dealing. Greg Smith, a former vice president of Goldman Sachs, noted this phenomenon clearly. When he left the bank in 2012, he wrote an article in *The New York Times* noting that bankers at Goldman Sachs referred to their clients in these types of contracts as the "muppets."[8] Sure enough, the "muppets" have been falling into the traps of interest-rate-swap contracts that increased their costs of borrowing and slowly drained their cash reserves beyond any wild expectation. When bankers made the promises to nonprofits to lower the cost of debt by coupling variable rate bonds with plain vanilla (pay fixed, receive variable) swaps, those promises as stipulated in circuitous contracts were like fishhooks dangled from the jaws of sharks. Once on the hook — non-profits paid dearly, painfully, for many years, without any benefits purportedly represented by the executed documents.

The evidence suggests that swap dealers from big banks practiced skillful sales tactics that notoriously avoided full disclosure and, at times, included deception and occasional bribing of officials to incentivize them to buy losing swap contracts. Collectively, participating nonprofit entities lost billions of dollars in wealth transfers to big banks while receiving nothing in return. More blatantly, these contracts have undermined the social fabric of this society and added nothing to national wealth. The

---

[8]Greg Smith, March 14, 2012. Why I am leaving Goldman Sachs. *The New York Times*. Retrieved from http://www.nytimes.com/2012/03/14/opinion/why-i-am-leaving-goldman-sachs.html?_r=0.

damage spread throughout the country, spanning the range of agencies having different financial strength from the most financially disadvantaged such as the City of Detroit and Jefferson County, Alabama, to the richest and most sophisticated institutions, such as Harvard University, the University of Texas, and the University of California among others. Hospitals and medical centers did not escape the serious damage incurred from being parties to interest-rate-swap contracts either. Even charity hospitals like the Sisters of Charity of Leavenworth Health System and Dignity Health, Inc. did not fare any better in dealing with swap contracts than the Johns Hopkins Health System Corporation, the health centers at Indiana University and the University of Florida among others.

Big banks used all means of persuasion to convince officials of all the involved nonprofit organizations to write swap contracts for terms as lengthy as the maturities of related bonds — up to 30 or 40 years. Swap contracts are typically noncancelable and enforceable under the law. Interestingly, swap dealers did not discriminate among their customers in that they used interest-rate-swap contracts to draw money from every type and size of nonprofit organization in all parts of the USA. Some of the injured parties had to file for bankruptcy. Jefferson County and the City of Harrisburg, the capital city of Pennsylvania, are prominent cases. Other injured parties took different actions when swap contracts turned sour; they cut services and dismissed employees — schoolteachers, nurses, municipal employees and others — to release funds to pay big banks for the swaps. A third group is holding steady; the organizations in this group kept on paying the annual losses and pleading with the archangels for eventual turnaround. Examples from our sample include the Bay Area Toll Authority (BATA), the Johns Hopkins Health System and the University of Texas System. A fourth group could not justify the large payments for the recurring annual losses on interest-rate swaps and decided (or forced) instead to terminate their contracts and pay the high termination fees and penalties. From our sample, the latter group includes the NY/NJ Port Authority, the State of New Jersey, Harvard University, and the City of Detroit (though this action was not by choice). The saga of Detroit is particularly painful; it cost the city more than one billion dollars to terminate disastrous interest rate swap contracts while struggling to manage its way out of bankruptcy.

The contrast between the incentives of the sellers (bankers) and buyers (nonprofit organizations) of interest-rate swaps could not be more striking. While bankers were looking after their own personal self-interests as well as the interests of their banks, it is perplexing to think of any reasonable incentives or positive scenarios for the buyers. This would be true especially when they bind their organizations to 30- or 40-year commitments and deprive them from the flexibility of responding to changes in the market. Clearly, the longer maturity periods entailed bearing higher degrees of uncertainty, exposing these counterparties to high risk, and incurring huge termination penalties.

Without taking a complete survey of the hundreds of nonprofit entities that fell into the swap trap, it is not possible to estimate the total amount of funds transferred to big banks via the cash sinkholes created for and by interest-rate swaps. However, others have estimated the transferred funds from 1999 to this day to be in the hundreds of billions of dollars. It is not difficult to imagine the enormity of the amounts lost if we know, for example, that the State of New Jersey paid nearly $800 million to terminate its swap contracts *after* having paid many millions of dollars more in annual recurring losses for periods of 10–15 years while receiving nothing. In another case, Harvard University paid $1.25 billion to terminate swap contracts on notional (reference) amounts of $4.8 billion after having paid $217 million for annual recurring losses before termination. The public schools district of the City of Denver paid at least $216 million in 2012 alone to terminate its interest-rate-swap contracts. For Denver, this amount of penalty was more than 66% of the total instruction budget in 2012. In addition, the City of Detroit paid $900 billion in cancelation penalties and termination fees. In 2015, the City of Chicago (excluding Chicago public schools) paid over $408 million in penalties for terminating one half of its swap portfolio and, additionally, paid close to $300 million in recurring annual losses including the high interest rates the City paid to borrow money to manage its swap portfolio.

This book concludes by reasoned economic arguments that these swap agreements have the elements of "unconscionable contracts" under Section 2-302 of the US Uniform Commercial Code and, as such, they would be unenforceable. Furthermore, all nonprofit organizations that paid high termination fees and penalties seem to have the basis for recapturing these penalties. According to this presentation, it is the "unconscionability" of contracting, not "the antitrust violation" that is the essence of big banks culpability. It is true that case law on unconscionable contracts in the USA is very sparse as compared to the situations in the United Kingdom, Australia, or Malaysia, for example. Nevertheless, no contracts have ever come close to the multi-billion dollars magnitudes and penetration of all public service segments as the spread of interest rate swaps reveals. The most salient of these reasons is that the counterparties in nonprofit entities signed onto contracts they were not able to fully understand or comprehend. It is true that the agreed upon contracts had adopted the "Master Agreement" of the International Swap and Derivatives Association (ISDA), but that model contract has two serious failings:

(a) Ten large banks established ISDA in 1985. Currently, a board of 26 member, 19 of whom are large banks, manage ISDA. It is thus unrealistic to claim that anyone other than these banks made the rules that govern the swap contracts they write and the payments they receive as swap dealers as well as estimating fair values. The recurring annual losses and the long-term expected losses are what big banks claim as if it is their legacy and gave them the name of "fair" market values. When either side terminates the contract, all expected services also terminate and the officials at these banks know they would not be providing any service to allow them to claim having earned the so-called "fair" market termination values.

(b) I gave the 40-page, single-spaced and small font "Master Agreement" to two contract law attorneys, one has practiced writing and litigating contracts for more than 20 years and the other practices and teaches contract law. Weeks later, both of them wrote and independently expressed their dismay that they found the Master Agreement incomprehensible. These responses create a predicament. Specifically, if contract attorneys could not decipher the ISDA "Master Agreement," how could anyone claim that city mayors and financial officers in municipalities, hospitals, universities or transit authorities do? In fact, it would be a worthwhile challenge for big banks to set up a contest to see if any one of their swap counterparties in any nonprofit entity had really understood the contracts to which they had agreed. Furthermore, it was not possible to rectify this deficiency by retaining the so-called "swap advisors." Many of these advisors have displayed lack of sufficient knowledge of the burdensome technicalities of interest rate swap contracts to allow them to match the tactics of swap dealers.

The cases presented in this book constitute only a small fraction of the cases for which the negative social, human, and economic effects of entering into long-term swap contracts have been shockingly pernicious to the public service institutions of our nation. An outline of a sample of other cases is in Appendix 7. All are selected without any sampling plan. Writing special types of noncancelable interest rate exchange (swap) contracts with expiry dates lasting many decades ahead was uniquely tailored means of transferring large amounts of funds to big banks while causing waste and damage to public interest. Moreover, when nonprofit organizations did not have the resources to pay for these swaps, they took two dysfunctional actions: (a) they borrowed the needed funds at high cost, and (b) they cut down the provision of basic services for education, health care, transportation, and local and state governance. Nonprofit organizations at all levels have diverted enormous resources from providing basic services that fuel the engines of stability and growth to paying big banks for these swap contracts while receiving nothing tangible in return. Because many of these contracts with nonprofits mature in 30–40 years, it is not likely that big banks will take any action to right the wrong without facing public outrage and intervention of regulators and perhaps Congress. In addition, nonprofits must change their incentive and accountability system. For example, resigning or changing jobs should not absolve nonprofit officials of accountability for their use of public service money. They cannot simply march to the drum beat of big banks offering exotic contracts without serious concern for public interest.

A Final Word:
Creative Destruction

The opening up of new markets, foreign or domestic, and the organizational develop-ment from the craft shop to such concerns as U.S. Steel illustrate the same process of indus-trial mutation — if I may use that biological term — that incessantly revolutionizes the economic structure from within, incessantly destroying the old one, incessantly creating a new one. This process of Creative Destruction is the essential fact about capitalism.

Source: Schumpeter, Joseph A., Capitalism, Socialism and Democracy (London, Routledge, 1942, 3rd ed.), p. 83.

APPENDIX 1

Basic Concepts of Dancing with the Swaps

**An Appendix On Swap Contracts
to Support the Introduction**

Assume that a hospital and a public school were seeking to borrow funds from the municipal bond market. The hospital administration had the view that market interest rates will decline in the near future. In contrast, the public school board had the opposite view and believed that the direction of interest rate is on the rise. This difference in expectations led them to issue bonds with different features:

- The hospital issued bonds at an adjustable, variable rate of interest.
- The public school issued bonds at a fixed rate of interest.

After one year, the hospital administration came in possession of information to suggest that market interest may actually increase. The

(*Continued*)

(Continued)

administration had two choices: (a) to sell a fixed interest rate bond and use the proceeds to refund the variable rate bond it had already issued, or (b) to use the new finance tools and enter into a contract to exchange (swap) interest rates. The first choice is essentially a refinance of an existing bond, which has a high transaction cost. The management opted for the second approach. The flow of cash for the different types of interest would then look like the following pattern:

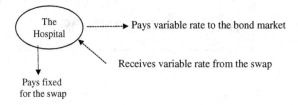

If the cash receivable from the swap covers the cash payable to bondholders, the hospital will end up paying only the fixed rate on the swap as the cost of debt. This fixed rate is not contractually fixed by arrangements with bondholders, it is artificially (synthetically) obtained. The cost of debt will differ from the presumed synthetic fixed rate by the extent to which cash receivable from the swap and the cash payable for the bond have different amounts.

Each one of these contracts entails transaction cost for underwriting, insuring, legal counseling, swap and financial advisors among others. However, the typical discussion and analysis of swaps ignores the role of the relatively high transaction cost.

Let us now turn to the school transaction. Assume that the public school board also has a change of expectations and believed that interest rate is on the decline and the school could save money by switching from fixed rate to a variable rate. In the new finance, the school also enters into an interest rate swap contract to receive fixed rate and pay variable rate. The flow of cash for the school transactions would be as shown below.

(Continued)

(Continued)

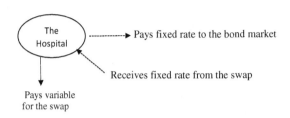

Pays fixed rate to the bond market

Receives fixed rate from the swap

Pays variable
for the swap

What Is a Notional Amount?

Understanding the differences between bonds and swaps and the meaning of *notional amounts* is necessary in order to appreciate the disastrous consequences of marketing and using swap contracts. To do so, let us first think of two contracts between a B (a bank) and an H (a hospital, for example).

Contract 1: B agrees to loan $1 million to H at a fixed rate.

Contract 2: H agrees to loan B $1 million at an adjustable rate.

For these two contracts, the $1 million is a wash, does not exist, and thus remains hypothetical or simply "notional". Taking this illustration a step further, the parties B and H could achieve the same goal by entering into one bilateral agreement that says the following: on $1 million, H pays a fixed rate of interest, and B pays an adjustable rate. This single bilateral agreement is a swap accomplishing the same goals as the two bond contracts noted earlier. In both cases, the notional amount is $1 million.

A simple form of an adjustable rate is typically written as follows:

A designated benchmark interest rate + a specified percentage

The adjustable rate changes if the designated benchmark changes. If, for example, the designated benchmark is the Federal Reserve Funds Rate, an adjustable rate might be written as follows:

(Continued)

(Continued)

The Federal Reserve Funds Rate + 2%, for example.

The fixed interest payment stream is referred to as the *fixed leg*, and the adjustable-rate payments are referred to as *the floating or variable leg*. At inception, the fixed leg has the same present value as the variable leg, and therefore, the value of the swap contract itself is zero.

- Afterward, the value of the swap contract changes if the Federal Reserve Funds Rate changes:
  - If the Federal Reserve Funds Rate increases, the bank would owe the buyer (the public school, in this case) money.
  - If the Federal Reserve Funds Rate decreases, the buyer (the hospital) would owe the bank money.

The losses of the buyer are the gains of the bank and vice versa. Nothing else happens — no change in production or wealth.

APPENDIX 2

Relative Magnitude of Over-the-Counter Financial Derivatives

Total Notional (Face) Amounts of Over-the-Counter

Financial Derivatives Outstanding as of the End of 2016

(≥ $552 Trillion)

[$552,000,000,000,000]

Worldwide GDP
In 2016
(≈ $78 Trillion)
[$78,000,000,000,0000]

USA GDP
($18 Trillion)
[$18,000,000,000,000]

APPENDIX 3

The 2017 Report of the Bank for International Settlements on Global OTC Derivatives

Global OTC derivatives market

In billions of US dollars

	Notional amounts				Gross market Value			
	H1 2016	H2 2016	H1 2017	H2 2017	H1 2016	H2 2016	H1 2017	H2 2017
All Contracts	**552,925**	**482,422**	**542,439**	**531,912**	**21,119**	**14948**	**12,683**	**10,956**
Foreign Exchange Contracts	85,567	78,781	88,429	87,117	3,578	3,324	2,626	2,293
Interest Rate Contracts	446,462	385,514	435,206	426,649	16,417	10,636	2,626	2,293
Equity-Linked Contracts	6,761	6,253	6,964	6,570	523	447	524	575

Notes: H1 = first one half of the year.

      H2 = second one half of the year

Source: Bank for International Settlements

https://www.bis.org/statistics/d5_1.pdf

APPENDIX 4

OTC Financial Derivatives in the Top Four US Banks

Over-the-Counter Face (Notional) Amounts on December 31
(In Trillion [\$1,000,000,000,000] US Dollars)

	2000	2006	2012	2016
JPMorgan Chase	\$25	\$66	\$69	\$53
Citibank	\$8	\$29	\$55	\$52
Bank of America	\$8	\$32	\$42	\$26
Goldman Sachs	NA	NA	\$41	\$44

Source: US Office of Comptroller of the Currency.
Retrieved from https://www.occ.gov/topics/capital-markets/financial-arkets/derivatives/derivatives-quarterly-report.html.

Notes:
- Interest-rate contracts are about 80% of total over-the-counter derivatives.
- The statistics in this table do *not* include the exchange-traded derivatives.
- According to the global statistics provided by the Bank for International Settlements, the fair-market value, which is also the termination fee, is estimated to be between 3% and 3.5% of total notional amounts. For example, the fair-market values for JPMorgan Chase and Citibank in 2016 would be close to \$1.6 trillion [\$1,600,000,000,000] each.

Source: Retrieved from http://www.bis.org/statistics/d5_1.pdf.

APPENDIX 5

Three Reasons to
Use Financial Derivatives

Hedging
- → Managing risk to which buyers of the derivatives are currently exposed.

Speculation
- → Managing risk to which buyers of the derivatives expect to be exposed.

Gambling
- → Taking on more risk for the sole expectation of making profit.

APPENDIX 6

An Example of a Swap Sales Presentation Having an Odd Ending

DAUPHIN COUNTY BOARD OF COMMISSIONERS

COMMISSIONERS WORKSHOP MEETING

WEDNESDAY, April 13, 2005

10:00 A.M.

Retrieved from http://www.dauphincounty.org/government/About-the-County/Meetings/Minutes/WS041305.pdf

Lou Verdelli and Scott Shearer of Public Financial Management (pp. 2–5)

Proposal for SWAP transaction.

Mr. Verdelli: What we wanted to talk to you about this morning is an opportunity to potentially lower the cost of the taxable debt that the County has outstanding right now.

On page 2 of the handout that I just passed out, the first bullet point, you will see that the County currently has about $19 million of taxable bonds outstanding. The rest of your bonds that are outstanding are tax exempt. From the restructuring last year, you may recall that tax exempt bonds have a lower interest rate, taxable bonds have a rate that is usually about a point and a half higher than tax exempt bonds. Of that $19 million, there was $14.8 million that was part of last year's restructuring that was done on a taxable basis. So we were looking at ways to potentially lower the cost of the taxable bonds, get it a little bit closer to tax exempt, even though we can't get the whole way there. There is an opportunity out there to use an instrument called a Basis Swap that allows us to try and take advantage of variable rate indexes and lower the cost of the taxable debt to kind of understand what the risk of a transaction like this is, it is important to understand the benefit of issuing tax exempt debt. When we issue tax exempt debt the investors that buy those bonds, the interest you pay them, they can deduct that from their federal income taxes. Therefore, when we look at the ratio of where do tax exempt bonds trade versus taxable bonds, it is really a factor of where are the tax brackets in the income levels that we all pay on a personal basis. If those were to be changed, if tax rates were to be either increased or decreased, the value in the interest rates that you borrow tax exempt money would change if tax rates were eliminated. You would be borrowing at pretty much corporate tax rates, if that were ever to happen because there would be no value to an investor that buys your bonds to be able to deduct any interest costs. That is really the important thing to think about with this proposal.

On your taxable bonds right now, you had not assumed any tax risk. On the tax exempt bonds you have outstanding, and when we think about any financing that the County may have to do over the next fifteen years, you are assuming tax risks because if tax rates change between now and then, when you go out to borrow that money, it is going to be either at a higher rate or a lower rate. So, we have no tax risk on this $19 million of taxable bonds. To potentially lower the cost of it, we're proposing that we introduce some tax risk on those taxable bonds. We've specifically focused on the $14 million Series D of 2004. That is the one piece of last year's restructuring. It goes out to the year 2019. So it is about fifteen years of risk we would be looking at. The potential to lower the cost on that is by entering into this instrument called a Basis Swap.

How that actually works, is described on page 3. The mechanics of it, you are agreeing to exchange variable rate payment streams. There are indexes out there that represent variable rate bonds. One index that we talked about last year on one of the swaps is the LIBOR Index (London Inter Bank Offering Rate). It is a big internationally used index for quoting variable rate bonds. You would agree to receive a percent of that index and you would agree to pay the bond market association index. That is a basket of tax exempt bonds by issuers just like you all across the country where their variable rates are trading. It is indicative of the value of tax exempt securities. You are agreeing to basically exchange those payments. If those payment streams match up over time like they have done over the last fifteen or twenty years, we'll show you that illustration, basically the benefit that you would either take up front in the form of a cash payment or over time in terms of an annual credit, would be all preserved as long as those two indexes match up.

On page 4, really just graphically illustrates that on the left, the County would pay the top line going across to a potential swap counterparty. The counterparty, again on the right side is a large bank, like we did the interest rate swap last year a very, very large highly rated entity is who you would enter into this agreement with. You would agree to pay them the BMA index. They would pay you 67% of whatever the LIBOR Index is. The benefit of doing that can either be received in terms of an upfront cash payment or a payment over time.

On page 5, really what this all comes down to, is what are the chances that if we agree to exchange these payments, that they perfectly match up? Page 5 shows you these two indexes since 1984. You will see that the lines of course don't perfectly match up if you are looking on each week to week basis which is when these rates would be changing. Certainly, they don't match up perfectly but when you look in the box, when we average that period of time over the last twenty years, you can see the average works out to 3.643% for the BMA Index versus 67% of LIBOR at 3.649. So very, very close but certainly there will be months where one index is higher and the other is lower. In those situations your payment may be higher than what you are receiving. There would be months potentially the payment you are making is less than what you are receiving. It would basically equally even out. This 67% of LIBOR is an important point that basically you are looking at twenty years of historical data. There are entities that if you were entering into one of these transactions they would be more aggressive and pick a percent of LIBOR of about 65%. There is a better chance there that they may not perfectly match up. If you wanted to be more conservative with this proposal, you could pick 70% of the LIBOR Index. There should be some additional benefit if you were to do that. Again 67% is what is used nationally in the swap market to be indicative of where this relationship has been over the last twenty years.

In terms of the potential benefit for the County, why would you do this? On page 6, how does it potentially lower the cost on the taxable financing? On the left side of the page, it is labeled option I, there we have assumed there would be no upfront payment to the County and over time, column 3, if you don't take a payment upfront, one of the swap providers would say is, we'll pay you the index plus and extra 31 basis points each year. If they were to do that, column 2 shows what the principal amount is in your Series D of 2004. You can see right now, it would be $14.8 million. Obviously, you pay principal down each year and through the year 2019 which is your final payment. If you were to agree to take payments over time, column 3 approximately 31 basis points is what you would receive. What does that mean in dollars saving for the debt service on those bonds? Column 4, you can see you would save on average, over the next ten years, a number like $40,000 per year on the debt service payment on that $14 million bond issue. You can see that it gets smaller obviously because you are getting the 31 basis points paid on a declining amount of debt that is outstanding. While your benefit goes away, so does your risk in those later years because if those indexes were not matching up, it is still calculated on however much principal is outstanding. If you got to 2019 and the index was off by 10 basis points, that 10 basis points that you would be paying is just calculated on $2.3 million as opposed to if it happened right away on the $14.8 million that you have now.

At the bottom of column 4, you can see that the benefit over time would be $451,000 of savings on that issue. On the right side of the page, we've illustrated, if you say you would like 100% of that benefit paid at closing, in the upper right, you can see the $350,000 number. Column 7 then, you would not be getting any payment over time. You would just be exchanging those two indexes. The only way there would be additional savings, in column 8, would be if the one index was trading in your favor. What would allow that to happen? Potentially if income tax rates were increased and were higher, those indexes would change. If you took the upfront payment and said, okay, what happens if tax rates are decreased we could end up with column 8, where you would actually have a payment to make over and above what the current debt service is right now.

Basically, this transaction really does not have interest rate risk. It doesn't depend upon the level of interest rates. If interest rates are 10% five years from now, there really should be no differential in this index. If in fact if you look, on page 5, we obviously have twenty years of history where interest rates have been all over the place at very high levels in the 1980's that the index still matches up. So it is not really interest rate sensitive. Not really interest rate risk The real sole tax risk here, is that if the tax code undergoes a significant change potentially the two indexes in the value of tax exempt bonds goes away if there was a dramatic reduction in income tax rates. [Emphasis Added]

APPENDIX 7

More Fell for Dancing
with the Swaps: Another Sample

An Incomplete Sample of Universities

University	Long-term Swap Obligations in millions 2015/2016
Arizona State University	$ 8
Boston University	$297
Carnegie Mellon	$ 34
Columbia University	$ 68
Cornell University	$207
Dartmouth College	$250
Duke University	$117
Northwestern University	$ 33
Stanford University	$215
University of Chicago	$ 67
University of Illinois	$ 19
University of Mass	$ 90
University of Michigan	$ 28
University of Virginia	$ 39
University of South Carolina	$ 34
Virginia Commonwealth University	$ 11
Yale University	$358

Hospitals

An Incomplete Sample of Other Hospitals

Other Community Hospitals	Additional Information	Swap Debt in Million Dollars	
Stanford Health Care		$331 (in 2016)	$215 (in 2015)
Baylor Scott & White Health		$203 M (in 2014)	$258 M (in 2015)
The University of Chicago Medical Center		$110 M (in 2015)	$165 M (in 2016)
Mercy Hospital (CA)		$40.6 M (in 2014)	$39.6 M (in 2015)
St. Anthony's Medical Center (Saint Louis, MO)		$21 M (in 2011) 9% of all debt	$40 M (in 2012) 17% of all debt
Community Health Systems, Inc. (Indiana)		$68 M (in 2014)	$76 M (in 2015)
El Camino (CA)	Paid $ for terminating interest-rate-exchange contracts in	$7.0 M (in 2014)	$6.8 M (in 2015)
United Health Services (multiple states)	From the 2015 annual report: "However, at December 31, 2014, each swap agreement entered into by us was in a net liability position that would require us to make the net settlement payments to the counterparties. We do not anticipate nonperformance by our counterparties. We do not hold or issue derivative financial instruments for trading purposes (but no disclosure of numbers)."		

(Continued)

(*Continued*)

Other Community Hospitals	Additional Information	Swap Debt in Million Dollars	
Palomar Health	Swap Liability	$26 M	$28 M
Rady Children's Hospital and Health Center (CA)	Money put for collateral	$49 M	$50 M
		$40 M	$40 M
Scripps Health		$20 M (2014)	$25 M (2015)
Sharp HealthCare		$2.0 M	$2.3 M
St. Joseph Health System		$37 M (2013)	$86 M (2014)
St. Mary's College of California		$14 M	$13 M
Trinity Health (CA)	Liability for the interest-rate-exchange contracts	$117 M (net of assets)	$111 M (net of assets)
Anne Arundel Health System (Maryland)	Collateral posted for the interest-rate-exchange contracts	$68 M	$58 M
		$62 M	$51 M
Ascension Health Alliance		$142 M (2015) net	$120 M (2014) net
Franciscan Alliance and Associates	Paid $26.7 million in 2013 to terminate two swap contracts. Has a mix of pay fixed for variable that has negative termination values (fair-value liability) and pay variable for variable that has positive termination values (fair-value assets)	$83 M (in 2015)	$84 M (in 2014)

(*Continued*)

(*Continued*)

Other Community Hospitals	Additional Information	Swap Debt in Million Dollars	
Seattle Children's Hospital	Eleven swap contracts, $2.3 billion notional	$20 M (in 2014)	$24 M (in 2015)
Community Health System Inc., headquartered in Tennessee (203 affiliated hospitals in 29 states, 31,000 licensed beds)	Six swap contracts, notional amounts of $1.027 billion (net of collateral)	FV debt was $88 M (in 2013)	$68 M FV loss (in 2014)

APPENDIX 8

The Formula for the Swap Contract between Procter & Gamble and Bankers Trust of New York

The contract between Procter & Gamble and Bankers Trust of New York in early 1993 is a case in point. To show the complexity and indecipherability of the contract, consider the following terms of one of the interest-rate-swap contracts written by Bankers Trust New York for Procter & Gamble as presented in the court report.

During the fall of 1993, the parties began discussing the terms of an interest rate swap which was to be customized for P & G. After negotiations, the parties agreed to a swap transaction on November 2, 1993, which is referred to as the 5s/30s swap; the written Confirmation is dated November 4, 1993.

In the 5s/30s swap transaction, BT agreed to pay P & G a fixed rate of interest of 5.30% for five years on a notional amount of

(Continued)

(Continued)

$200 million. P & G agreed to pay BT a floating interest rate. For the first six months, that floating rate was the prevailing commercial paper ("CP") interest rate minus 75 basis points (0.75%). For the remaining four-and-a-half years, P & G was to make floating interest rate payments of CP minus 75 basis points plus a spread. The spread was to be calculated at the end of the first six months (on May 4, 1994) using the following formula:

$$\text{Spread} = [(98.5 * [5 \text{ year CMT}] - 30 \text{ T Price}) \, 5.78\% \,] / 100$$

In this formula, the "5 year CMT" (Constant Maturity Treasury) represents the yield on the five-year Treasury Note, and the "30 T Price" represents the price of the 30-year Treasury Bond. The leverage factor in this formula meant that even a small movement up or down in prevailing interest rates results in an incrementally larger change in P & G's position in the swap.

United States District Court, S.D. Ohio, Western Division. **PROCTER & GAMBLE CO. v. BANKERS TRUST CO.** No. C-1-94-735. 925 F.Supp. 1270 (1996). *The PROCTER & GAMBLE COMPANY, Plaintiff, v. BANKERS TRUST COMPANY and BT Securities Corporation, Defendants.*

Retrieved from http://www.leagle.com/decision/19962195925FS upp1270_12043/PROCTER%20&%20GAMBLE%20CO.%20 v.%20BANKERS%20TRUST%20CO.

APPENDIX 9

The State of Illinois Hedge-Fund-Like Portfolio of Financial Derivatives in the *Illinois Teachers Retirement System*

Table 14-4   (amounts expressed in thousands)

Investment Derivatives	Fair Value at June 30, 2016	Change in Fair Value	Notional*
Rights	$ 393	$ (548)	$ 6,272
Warrants	20,512	(540)	3,735
Currency Forwards			
Purchases	3,746,468		
Sales	(3,781,675)		
	(35,207)	(50,806)	-
Futures**			
Equity Futures Long	-	(28,532)	99,039
Equity Futures Short	-	3,354	(46,828)
Fixed Income Futures Long	-	28,393	414,353

(*Continued*)

(Continued)

Fixed Income Futures Short	-	(32,165)	(1,302,219)
Commodity Futures Long	-	(11,401)	18,662
Commodity Futures Short	-	12,17	(29,438)
		(28,194)	(846,431)
Options**			
Equity Options Purchased	-	(808)	-
Equity Options Written	-	57	-
Currency Forward Options Purchased	3,339	123	72,839
Currency Forward Options Written	(497)	2,948	20,657
Inflation Options Written	(116)	704	3,498
Options on Futures Purchased	-	(379)	23,080
Options on Futures Written	-	1,070	8,580
	2,726	3,715	128,654
Swaptions			
Swaptions Purchased	4,527	(6,319)	25,714
Swaptions Written	(4,474)	5,269	44,166
	53	(1,050)	69,880
Credit Default Swaps			
Credit Default Swaps Buying Protection	(401)	(176)	12,921
Credit Default Swaps Selling Protection	(1,920)	1,395	232,284
	(2,321)	1,219	245,205
Index Swaps	1,488	(4,028)	22,756
Interest Rate Swaps			
Pay Fixed Interest Rate Swaps	(67,564)	(108,317)	1,258,000
Received Fixed Interest Rate Swaps	3,915	2,174	143,226
	(63,649)	(106,143)	1,401,226
Inflation-linked Swaps			
Pay Fixed Inflation Swaps	(5,797)	(3,017)	213,238
Received Fixed Inflation Swaps	4,784	6,347	82,726
	(1,013)	3,330	295,964
Grand Totals	$ (77,018)	$ (183,045)	$ 1,327,261

*Notional amounts represent financial exposure to these instruments in U.S. dollars.
**Notional values do not represent actual values in the Statement of Fiduciary Net Position.
Source: Comprehensive Annual Financial Report, 2016, p. 125. file:///G:/ILLINOIS/*CAFR*_2016.pdf.

APPENDIX 10

The State of Texas Exhibit: Partial Listing of the Hedge-Fund-Like Portfolio of Swaps

Summary of Derivative Activity

(Amounts in Thousands)

	Change in Fair Value	Fair Value	Notional Amount
GOVERNMENTAL ACTIVITIES			
Investment Derivatives			
Basis Swaps	$ (1,131)	$ 25,121	$ 400,000
Futures	7,352		34,872
BUSINESS-TYPE ACTIVITIES		23%	
Cash Flow Hedges			
Pay-Fixed Receive-Variable Interest Rate Swaps	$(202,010)	$(770,766)	$3,345,785
Commodity Forwards	(2,244)	(2,244)	960 *
Investment Derivatives			
Pay-Fixed Receive-Variable Interest Rate Swaps	$ 539	$ 996	$ 135,040
Pay-Variable Receive-Fixed Interest Rate Swaps	32	32	28,225
Basis Swaps	374	7,729	954,975
Credit Default Swaps	(681)	152	137,273
Equity Swaps	1,554	1,554	596,856
Currency Swaps	(50)	(50)	5,054
Commodity Swaps	(214)	(214)	12,161
Forwards	(12,710)	(12,710)	2,451,993
Futures	(2,543)		1,336,261
Options	(89,216)	42,476	24,390,722
FIDUCIARY ACTIVITIES			
Investment Derivatives			
Pay-Fixed Receive-Variable Interest Rate Swaps	$ (3,415)	$ (699)	$ 60,532
Pay-Variable Receive-Fixed Interest Rate Swaps	2,561	777	41,192
Total Return Swaps	(197,909)	21,316	1,131,863
Credit Default Swaps	247		
Forwards	(42,750)	23,326	6,124,786
Futures	(635,424)		9,038,282
Warrants	6,427	32,821	10,445
Options	4,910	4,830	38,134

*The unit of measurement for the notional amount of the commodity forwards is expressed in million British thermal units (MMBTU). The notional amount of the commodity forwards is 960 thousand MMBTUs.

Source: 2102 Comprehensive Annual Financial Report. The State of Texas, p. 100.

Retrieved from https://comptroller.texas.gov/transparency/reports/comprehensive-annual-financial/2012/.

APPENDIX 11

The Commonwealth of Massachusetts Partial Listing of Swap Portfolio

Terms Fair value at June 30

Associated Bond Issue	Notional Amounts Outstanding	Effective Date	Replacement Agreement Effective Date	Fixed Rate Paid (Range)	Variable Rate Received	2016	2015	Change in Fair Value	Final Termination Date	Counterparty	Counterparty CreditRating Moody's/S&P/ Fitch
General Obligation Bonds:											
Series 1998A (refund) [1] Consolidated Loan of 2006, Series A Central Artery Loan of 2000,	$ 24,105	11/17/2008	11/17/2008	4.174%	60% 1-Month LIBOR + 25 basis points	$ (219)	$ (1,637)	$ 1,418	9/1/2016	Wells Fargo Bank	Aa2/AA-/AA
Series 1998A (refunding)	10,185	9/17/1998	9/1/2016	4.174%	Cost of Funds	(95)	(751)	656	9/1/2016	Wells Fargo Bank	Aa2/AA-/AA
Series 2000A	97,092	8/16/2007	8/16/2007	3.942%	SIFMA - 3 basis points	(1,866)	(5,430)	3,564	8/1/2018	Merrill Lynch Cap Svcs	Baa1/NR/A
Series 2000A	49,308	8/16/2007	8/16/2007	3.942%	SIFMA - 3 basis points	(920)	(2,735)	1,815	8/1/2018	JP Morgan formerly Bear Stearns	Aa3/A+/AA-
Series 2001B & C	421,000	2/20/2001	2/20/2001	4.15%	Cost of Funds	(40,717)	(51,165)	10,448	1/1/2021	Morgan Stanley Capital	A1/A+/t/N/A
Series 2006B, Series 2000D	294,000	4/2/2009	4/2/2009	4.515%	67% 3-Month LIBOR	(100,369)	(81,690)	(18,679)	6/15/2033	Barclays Bank PLC	A2/A-/A

(Continued)

(Continued)

Series 2006C	100,000	1/1/2007	1/1/2007	3.73% - 3.85%	CPI-based formula	(4,939)	(5,795)	856	11/1/2020	Wells Fargo Bank	Aa2/AA-/AA
Series 2007A	400,000	10/8/2008	10/8/2008	4.42%	67% 3-Month LIBOR + 0.57%	(13,588)	(25,376)	11,788	5/1/2037	Barclays Bank PLC	A2/A-/A
Series 2007A (refunding)[1]	31,665	10/8/2008	10/8/2008	3.936%	67% 3-Month LIBOR + 0.46%	(3,900)	(3,786)	(114)	11/1/2020	Wells Fargo Bank	Aa2/AA-/AA
Series 2007A (refunding)	414,130	10/8/2008	10/8/2008	4.083%	67% 3-Month LIBOR + 0.55%	(75,327)	(62,871)	(12,456)	11/1/2025	Bank of NY Mellon	Aa2/AA-/AA
Series 2013A, 2014E, 2015C	475,000	3/15/2005	3/15/2005	3.672% - 4.004%	SIFMA	(93,099)	(79,637)	(13,462)	2/1/2028	Wells Fargo Bank	Aa2/AA-/AA
Subtotal	2,316,485					(335,039)	(320,873)	(14,166)			

> Same question as all others:
>
> Why would any rational person sign onto contracts with these featuresand commit the state for decades to come?

Source: Comprehensive Annual Financial Report, Commonwealth of Massachusetts, 2016, p. 99.

http://www.macomptroller.info/comptroller/docs/reports-audits/cafr/2016-cafr.pdf.

APPENDIX 12

LIBOR Cheating Chats: Deutsche Bank and Other Banks (as Reported)

Source: Commodity Futures Modernization Committee. In the Matter of Deutsch Bank, Respondent. ORDER INSTITUTING PROCEEDINGS PURSUANT TO SECTIONS 6(c) AND 6(d) OF THE COMMODITY EXCHANGE ACT, MAKING FINDINGS, AND IMPOSING REMEDIAL SANCTIONS. April 23, 2015. https://www.cftc.gov/sites/default/files/idc/groups/public/@lrenforcementactions/documents/legalpleading/enfdeutscheorder042315.pdf

(Continued)

From the Files of the Commodity Futures Trading Commission

[Various boxes include plain English explanations for the conversation right above each.]

March 22, 2005: (emphasis added)

U.S. Dollar LIBOR Submitter:	if you need something in particular in the LIBORs i.e., you have an interest in a high or a low fix let me know and there's a high change I'll be able to in a different level just give me a shout the before or send an email from your Blackberry first thing
New York U.S. Dollar Trader 1:	Thanks — our CP guys have been looking for it a bit higher — not a big deal
U.S. Dollar LIBOR Submitter:	if anything the cash has actually cheapened up since yesterday too albeit by 1/2 tick — true could get some sub 75 days thru the next week

April 1, 2005: (emphasis added)

London U.S. Dollar Trader 1: Could you pls have a low 6 MTH fix today old bean?

> **Could you please have a low six-month fix (rate) today?**

September 21, 2005: (emphasis added)

London MMD Manager: Subject: "$ LIBORS: 83, 89, 96 and 11 lower mate lower!!

> Subject: US Dollar LIBOR rates: 83. 89. 96 and 11. Please set it lower mate...lower

U.S. Dollar LIBOR Submitter: will see what i can do but it'll be tough as the cash is pretty well bid

> I will see what I can do, but it will be tough as the cash is pretty well bid (out)

(Continued)

(*Continued*)

	[Another U.S. Dollar Panel Bank] Is doing it on purpose because they have exact opposite position-on which they los 25 MIO so far — let us take them on!!
	Subject: US Dollar LIBOR bank panel member is doing it on purpose because they have exact opposite position on which they have lost 25 million so far — let us take them on.
U.S. Dollar LIBOR Submitter:	ok, let's see if we can hurt them a little bit more then

February 28, 2007: (emphasis added)

New York U.S. Dollar Trader 2:	LIBOR HIGHER TOMORROW?
U.S. Dollar LIBOR Submitter:	shouldn't be
New York U.S. Dollar Trader 2:	COME ON. WE ALWAYS NEED HIGHER LIBORS !!! HAHA
U.S. Dollar LIBOR Submitter:	haha, i'll do my best fkcer
New York U.S. Dollar Trader 2:	NO WORRIES. JUST CURIOUS, U SURVE THE DEBACLE OF TH PAST 24 HRS>

August 13, 2008: (response to U.S. Dollar LIBOR Submitter's email) (emphasis added)

New York U.S. Dollar Senior Trader:	**Subject: $ lsbors unch** oh bullshit....strap on a pair and jack up the 3m. hahahaha
	Subject: US Dollar LIBOR unchanged. Oh, bullshit,,, strap on a pair and jack up the three month LIBOR. hahahaha

November 28, 2006: (email to London Pool Trading Manager) (emphasis added)

New York U.S. Dollar Senior Trader:	Altho I don't have a huge 1 mL fix tomw, I am paying 1 mL on about 40 BN throughout December so I was hoping for a low 1m fix to MW to set the tone

(*Continued*)

(Continued)

	Although I do not have a huge one month LIBOR fix (rate) for tomorrow, I am paying one month LIBOR on about 40 Billion throughout December. So, I was hoping for a low one month fix to Monday-Wednesday to set the tone

August 12, 2007: (emphasis added)

New York Regional Manager:	If possible, we need in NY 1 mo LIBOR as low as possible next few days....tons of pays coming up overall....thanks!
	If possible, we need one month LIBOR as allow as possible in New York in the next few days…tons (huge amounts) of pays coming up overall….thanks!
U.S. Dollar LIBOR Submitter:	**Will do our best** [New York Regional Manager]. **I'll coordinate the overnight in the same way as we did last week with (New York U. S. Dollar trader 1) tomorrow**

December 13, 2007: (emphasis added)

Frankfurt Non-Euro Desk Manager:	
[London Pool Trading Manager],	**I NEED YOUR HELP…IF IT SUITS YOU CAN PUT IN A HIGH LIBOR TILL NEXT TUESDAY IN THE 3MTS?**
POLO	
London Pool Trading Manager:	ok
Bank A Euro Swaps Trader:	Amigo checked with my FFT their 3m euribor Contribution which seems v low at 2.11 like ur FFT have u checked with your guys???

(Continued)

(Continued)

	My friend, I checked with my rate submitters. Their three month Euribor contribution which seems low at 2.11 like your submitters. Have you checked with your guys?
London MMD Manager:	**will tell them from tomorrow to put a higher fix..its way too low**
	I will tell them tomorrow to put a higher fix (rate). It is way too low

EXAMPLES OF COORDINATION WITH DERIVATIVES DEALERS AT OTHER BANKS TO MANIPULATE **LIBOR**

August 28, 2008: (emphasis added)

UBS Senior Yen Trader:	look i appreciate the business and the calls **we should try to share info where possible also let me know if you need fixes one way or the other**
Senior Yen Trader-Submitter:	sure sorry mate have to go too busy on many things
UBS Senior Yen Trader:	**and i'll do the same if you have any joy with your setters**
Senior Yen Trader-Submitter:	**no prob**
	No problem

September 1, 2008:

Senior Yen Trader-Submitter:	[. . .] but going to put high LIBORs today
UBS Senior Yen Trader:	sure i think you guys are top in 1m anyways
Senior Yen Trader-Submitter:	i am mate need it high!
	Sure. I think you guys are high in one month LIBOR anyway. My mate, I need it high!

(Continued)

(Continued)

September 18, 2008: (emphasis added)

UBS Senior Yen Trader:	**you got any ax on 6m fix tonight?**
	Do you have any axe (to cut) the six month rate tonight?
Senior Yen Trader-Submitter:	**absolutely none but i can help**
UBS Senior Yen Trader:	**can you set low as a favour for me?**
Senior Yen Trader-Submitter:	**done**
UBS Senior Yen Trader:	i'll return favour when i can just ask have 75 mm jpy a bp tonight
	I will return the favor when I can. Jussk. I have 75 million Japanese Yen a basis point tonight
Senior Yen Trader-Submitter:	np (no)
UBS Senior Yen Trader:	thanks so much
Senior Yen Trader-Submitter:	[. . .] 73/90/99 am putting LIBORs
	I am submitting LIBOR rates at 73, 90, 99 basis points (for different loan durations)
UBS Senior Yen Trader:	great thanks mate

IN A FOLLOW-UP MESSAGE THE NEXT DAY, THE UBS SENIOR YEN TRADER OFFERED THE SENIOR YEN TRADER-SUBMITTER A DEAL, STATING, "**IN FACT CAUSE YOU HELPED ME ON 6M YDAY.**"

May 21, 2009: (emphasis added)

UBS Senior Yen Trader:	**cld you do me a favour would you mind moving you 6m LIBOR up a bit today, i have a gigantic fix i am limit short can't sell anymore just watch**
	Could you do me a favor? Would you mind moving your (submission for) six month LIBOR up a bit today? I have a gigantic fix (rate) and I am limited because of shorting so I cannot sell anymore today
Senior Yen Trader-Submitter:	**i can do that**
UBS Senior Yen Trader:	thx

(Continued)

(Continued)

Follow-up message the next day:	
Senior Yen Trader-Submitter:	**u happy with me yesterday?**
	Were you happy with me yesterday?
UBS Senior Yen Trader:	**thx** i don't see it going up again today Senior Yen
Trader-Submitter:	me too
UBS Senior Yen Trader:	only you and [Yen Panel Bank A] moved
JUNE 15, 2009:	
UBS Senior Yen Trader:	is there any chance you cld set a high 6m tonight, just tonight, i have 1..5m usd bp fix no worries if you can't god knows where that all came from
	Is there any chance you could set a high six month rate tonight? Just tonight? I have (a large US Dollar) basis points fix. No worries if you cannot. God knows where all of that came from
Senior Yen Trader-Submitter:	hum i think my LIBORs will be unch for a while now….my led is quite high and i do not want 3m LIBOR up
	Well. I think my LIBOR rates will be unchanged for a while now. My yield is quite high and I do not want three month LIBOR to increase
UBS Senior Yen Trader:	me neither i need low 3m no prob ustnd you will help me out when 6m goes over the turn tho? i have 1m usd a bp that day too
	Me too. I need low three month LIBOR. No problem, I understand. You will help me out when the six month LIBOR goes over the turn though. I have 1 month USD a basis point that day too

(Continued)

(Continued)

Senior Yen Trader-Submitter:	Hello big boy
UBS Senior Yen Trader:	hi
Senior Yen Trader-Submitter:	is there a date u see we could have 6m LIBOR ot is no point being stubborn in that direction an i do sthing else sorry 6m lower hopeviuosly no for teh next 3 weeks

[. . .]

> Is there a date you see in which we could have six month LIBOR? Or is there no point being stubborn in that direction? And, I will do something else [for you]. Sorry,. The six month LIBOR lower but hopefully not for the next three weeks.

UBS Senior Yen Trader:	basically i will help you in 2 weeks time i am the saem way
Senior Yen Trader-Submitter:	perfect

> Basically I will help you in two weeks' time. I am the same way…the Senior Yen trader-submitter. Perfect.

UBS Senior Yen Trader:	but **for the next two weeks i really really need you to put 6m HIGFHER**

> But I really, really need you to put the six month LIBOR higher for the next two weeks

[. . .]

UBS Senior Yen Trader:	**after that i need 6m to crash off like you**
Senior Yen Trader-Submitter:	**that is no problem for me, i do nothing with the cash guys UNTIL THEN**
UBS Senior Yen Trader:	i need you to move 6m up for two weeks mate

[. . .]

(Continued)

(*Continued*)

<u>UBS Senior Yen Trader:</u>	but please move 6m up on Monday
	But please move the six-month LIBOR up on Monday
<u>Senior Yen Trader-Submitter:</u>	understood
<u>UBS Senior Yen Trader:</u>	thx i need you in the panel on Monday
<u>Senior Yen Trader-Submitter:</u>	ok enough cheers
<u>UBS Senior Yen Trader:</u>	i will then get our 6m way down after July 18th it is . . . and will try to get everyone else down too
[. . .]	
<u>UBS Senior Yen Trader:</u>	only reason i on bid is i have huge huge position that way so am happy for to come lower after the 17th
	The only reason I was to bid is that I have a huge, huge position that way. So I am happy to see it come lower after the 17th.
<u>Senior Yen Trader-Submitter:</u>	ok enough enough **on my fra switch it is your best?**
	Ok. Enough, enough on my forward rate arrangement, it is your best?
<u>UBS Senior Yen Trader:</u>	tell me what you need to see i have a vested interest in making sure our fixings match just don't rip me off too much i had those round mid i got to go soon
<u>Senior Yen Trader-Submitter:</u>	**ok -1.5 and -1 am i asking too much?**
<u>UBS Senior Yen Trader:</u>	**thats fine**
[. . .]	

APPENDIX 13

A Sample of Regulatory Penalties
(In Connection with Manipulating LIBOR)

	In Million	Country	Agency
Deutsche Bank	$800	USA	Commodity Futures Trading Commission
	$600	USA	NY Department of Financial Services
	$775	USA	US DOJ Criminal Penalties
	$344	UK	United Kingdom Financial Conduct Authority
Royal Bank of Scotland	$612	USA	Securities and Exchange Commission
	$395	UK	Financial Services Authority
		USA	Department of Justice
	€260	EU	European Union
Barclays	$710	USA	Department of Justice
	$485	USA	NY Dept. of Financial Service
	$400	USA	CFTCs
	$443	UK	Financial Services Authority
JPMorgan Chase	$550	USA	Department of Justice
	€80	EU	European Union
Citibank	$925	USA	Department of Justice
	€80	EU	European Union

References and Sources

Clusters

City of Chicago

City of Chicago Comprehensive Annual Financial Reports for the period 2003–2016.

Retrieved from https://www.cityofchicago.org/city/en/depts/fin/supp_info/comprehensive_annualfinancialstatements.html.

Chicago Public Schools

Chicago Public Schools. Comprehensive Annual Financial Reports for the period 2003–2016.

Retrieved from http://cps.edu/About_CPS/Financial_Information/Pages/Annualreport.aspx.

City of Detroit

The City of Detroit Comprehensive Annual Financial Reports for the period 2002–2016.

Retrieved from http://www.detroitmi.gov/How-Do-I/City-of-Detroit-CAFR-Find-How-Do-I-City-of-Detroit-MI; http://citymobiletest.detroitmi.gov/How-Do-I/City-of-Detroit-CAFR-Find-How-Do-I-City-of-Detroit-MI.

City of Gainesville, Florida

Comprehensive Annual Financial Reports for the period 1996–2016.

Retrieved from http://www.cityofgainesville.org/GOVERNMENT/City
DepartmentsAM/BudgetFinance/CAFR/tabid/189/Default.aspx.

City of Philadelphia
Comprehensive Annual Financial Reports for the period 2006–2016.
Retrieved from http://www.phila.gov/investor/cafr.html.

Harvard University
Annual Financial Report for the period 2004–2016.
Retrieved from https://finance.harvard.edu/annual-report.

Metropolitan Transportation Commission, California, Bay Area Toll Authority
Comprehensive Annual Financial Reports for the period 2002–2017.
Retrieved from https://mtc.ca.gov/digital-library/search/%22
comprehensive%20annual%20financial%20report%22?solrsort=ds_
created%20asc.

The City of New York
Comprehensive Annual Financial Reports for the period 2001–2017.
Retrieved from https://comptroller.nyc.gov/reports/comprehensive-
annual-financial-reports/.

State of Illinois
The State of Illinois. Comprehensive Annual Financial Reports for the period
1981–2016.
Retrieved from https://illinoiscomptroller.gov/financial-data/find-a-report/
comprehensive-reporting/comprehensive-annual-financial-report-cafr/

State of New Jersey
Comprehensive Annual Financial Report for the period 1987–2016.
Retrieved from http://www.nj.gov/treasury/omb/publications/archives.shtml.

University of Chicago Health Center
Audited Financial Statements for the Period 1999–2016.
Retrieved from http://finserv.uchicago.edu/reporting/statements.shtml.

University of California
Annual Financial Report for the period 2007–2017.
Retrieved from http://www.ucop.edu/financial-accounting/financial-
reports/annual-financial-reports.html.

University of North Carolina
The University of North Carolina at Chapel Hill. Comprehensive Annual Financial Report. Digital Collections for the period 1994–2016. Retrieved from http://digital.ncdcr.gov/cdm/ref/collection/p249901coll22/id/418915; http://finance.unc.edu/about/reports-data/.

Individual References

ABC News, Clinton: I Was Wrong to Listen to Wrong Advice Against Regulating Derivatives. April 18, 2010. Retrieved from http://blogs.abcnews.com/politicalpunch/2010/04/clinton-rubin-and-summers-gave-me-wrong-advice-on-derivatives-and-i-was-wrong-to-take-it.html.

ABC Action News. 3,783 Being Laid off from Philadelphia School District. June 7, 2013. Retrieved from http://6abc.com/archive/9130566/.

Admati, Anat and Martin Helwig, *The Bankers' New Clothes: What's Wrong with Banking and What to Do About It.* Princeton University Press. Princeton. 2013.

Akhbari, Kourosh. "What is an Unconscionable Contract?" *Legal Match,* March 9, 2013. Retrieved from http://www.legalmatch.com/law-library/article/what-is-an-unconscionable-contract.html.

Alameda County, CA. The Civil Grand Jury of Alameda County CA. Final Report 2010–2011. June 27, 2011. Retrieved from https://www.acgov.org/grandjury/final2010-2011.pdf.

American Enterprise Institute, AEI Newsletter. The Largest Municipal Bankruptcy Ever? October 1, 2008. Retrieved from http://www.aei.org/publication/the-largest-municipal-bankruptcy-ever/.

Arizona State University. Comprehensive Annual Financial Report. Year ended June 30, 2016. Retrieved from http://www.asu.edu/fs/documents/annual_reports/ASU-2016-CAFR.pdf.

"Auditor General Jack Wagner Calls on General Assembly to Ban Risky 'Swap' Contracts by Schools, Local Governments," *Cision, PR Newswire,* November 18, 2009.

Retrieved from http://www.prnewswire.com/news-releases/auditor-general-jack-wagner-calls-on-general-assembly-to-ban-risky-swap-contracts-by-schools-local-governments-70388252.html.

Arvedlund, Erin, "Kenney bill seeks to ban city deposits with Citigroup, Bank of America," *The Inquirer,* January 22, 2015.
Retrieved from http://www.philly.com/philly/news/breaking/20150123_Kenney_bill_seeks_to_ban_city_deposits_with_Citigroup__Bank_of_America.html.

Badger, Emily, "The U.N. says water is a fundamental human right in Detroit," *The Washington Post,* October 23, 2014.
Retrieved from https://www.washingtonpost.com/news/wonk/wp/2014/10/23/the-u-n-says-water-is-a-fundamental-human-right-in-detroit/?utm_term=.4a10302d2db6.

Baker, Marcia Merry, "Swaps'/Gambling Slams School Districts," *EIR*, September 6, 2013.
Retrieved from http://larouchepub.com/eiw/public/2013/eirv40n35-20130906/44-47_4035.pdfB.

Bank for International Settlements, Statistical release, "OTC derivatives statistics," Monetary and Economic Department.
For 2001 Retrieved from https://www.bis.org/publ/otc_hy0112.pdf.

For 2005 Retrieved from https://www.bis.org/publ/otc_hy0511.pdf.

For 2010 Retrieved from https://www.bis.org/publ/otc_hy1011.pdf.

For 2013 Retrieved from https://www.bis.org/publ/otc_hy1311.pdf.

For 2016 Retrieved from https://www.bis.org/publ/otc_hy1611.pdf.

Retrieved from https://www.bis.org/publ/otc_hy0112.pdf, p. 5.

$204 trillion ($ 6.0 trillion) in 2005

Retrieved from https://www.bis.org/publ/otc_hy0511.pdf, p. 7.

$479 trillion ($19.0 trillion) in 2010

Retrieved from https://www.bis.org/publ/otc_hy1011.pdf, p. 13.

$561 trillion ($15.0 trillion) in 2013

Retrieved from https://www.bis.org/publ/otc_hy1311.pdf, p. 19.

$438 trillion ($16.0 trillion) in 2016

Retrieved from https://www.bis.org/publ/otc_hy1611.pdf, p. 13.

"Barclays reveals Bank of England LIBOR phone call details," *BBC News*, July 3, 2012.
Retrieved from http://www.bbc.com/news/business-18695181.

"Barclays: FSA regulator criticizes 'culture of gaming," *BBC News*, July 16, 2012.
Retrieved from http://www.bbc.com/news/business-18854193?print=true.

Bhatti, Saqib and Carrie Sloan, *"Turned Around: How the Swaps that were Supposed to Save Illinois Millions Became Toxic,"* The Roosevelt Institute Refund America Project, January 2016.
Retrieved from http://rooseveltinstitute.org/wp-content/uploads/2016/01/Turned-Around-Jan-2016.pdf.

Binham, Caroline, "US Woman Takes on Banks over LIBOR." *Financial Times*. October 14, 2012.
Retrieved from https://www.ft.com/content/6b912248-1496-11e2-8cf2-00144feabdc0.

Black, Fisher, Emanuel Derman, and William Toy, "A one-factor model of interest rates and its application to Treasury bond options." *Financial Analysts Journal*, January–February 1990. pp. 33–39.
Retrieved from http://www.emanuelderman.com/media/faj-one_factor_model.pdf.

Blodget, Henry, "Bill Clinton: Larry Summers and Bob Rubin Gave Me Lousy Advice About Derivatives." *Business Insider*. Apr. 19, 2010.
Retrieved from http://www.businessinsider.com/henry-blodget-bill-clinton-larry-summers-and-bob-rubin-gave-me-lousy-advice-about-derivatives-2010-4.

BondGraham, Darwin, "Oakland Toxic Deal with Wall Street," *East Bay Express*, February 15, 2012.
Retrieved from http://www.eastbayexpress.com/oakland/oaklands-toxic-deal-with-wall-street/Content?oid=3125660.

Broadwater, Luke, "City shuts off water to delinquent residents; hits Baltimore Co. homes hardest." *The Baltimore Sun*. May 15, 2015.
Retrieved from http://www.baltimoresun.com/news/maryland/baltimore-city/bs-md-ci-water-shutoffs-20150515-story.html.

Braun, Martin Z., Darrell Preston and Liz Willen. "The Banks that Fleeced Alabama." *Bloomberg Markets*. September 2005.
Retrieved from http://www.mobilebaytimes.com/alabama.pdf.

Braun, Martin Z. and William Selway, "Hidden Swap Fees by JPMorgan, Morgan Stanley Hit School Boards," *Bazaarmodel Posts*. February 1, 2008.
Retrieved from http://bazaarmodel.net/phorum/read.php?1,5487.

Braun, Martin Z. and William Selway, "Schools Flunk Finance," *Bloomberg Markets*, March 2008.
Retrieved from http://www.bloomberg.com/apps/news?pid=nw&pname=mm_0308_story2.html.

Caplan, Andrew, "City Sets Budget, Bumps Up GRU Rates," *The Gainesville Sun*, July 18, 2017.
Retrieved from http://www.gainesville.com/news/20170718/city-sets-budgets-bumps-up-gru-rates.

Chicago Tribune "Watch Dog, Various dates." Borrowing Troubles. *Chicago Tribune*.
Retrieved from http://www.chicagotribune.com/news/watchdog/cpsbonds/.

Chicago Public School. Comprehensive Annual Financial Report for the year ended June 30, 2007.
Retrieved from http://cps.edu/About_CPS/Financial_information/Documents/FY07_CAFR.pdf.

For the year ended June 30, 2015.

Retrieved from http://www.cps.edu/About_CPS/Financial_information/Documents/FY15_CAFR.pdf.

Chittum, Ryan, "Bloomberg Covers Yet Another Swap Flop," *Columbia Journalism Review*, December 4, 2009.
Retrieved from http://archives.cjr.org/the_audit/bloomberg_covers_yet_another_s.php.

City of Atlanta. Comprehensive Annual Financial Report. December 31, 2004.
Retrieved from https://www.atlantaga.gov/home/showdocument?id=729; https://www.atlantaga.gov/government/departments/finance/controller.

City of Atlanta. Comprehensive Annual Financial Report. December 31, 2006.
Retrieved from https://www.atlantaga.gov/home/showdocument?id=731.

City of Atlanta. Comprehensive Annual Financial Report. December 31, 2009.
Retrieved from https://www.atlantaga.gov/home/showdocument?id=734.

City of Philadelphia, Pennsylvania. Comprehensive Annual Financial Report, Fiscal Year Ended June 30, 2006.
Retrieved from http://www.phila.gov/investor/pdfs/Financial%20Statements/FY%202006%20Financial%20Statements/FY%202006%20Phila%20CAFR.pdf.

City of Philadelphia Comprehensive Annual Financial Report, Fiscal Year Ended June 30, 2009,
Retrieved from http://www.phila.gov/investor/pdfs/Financial%20Statements/FY%202009%20Financial%20Statements/FY%202009%20Phila%20CAFR.pdf.

City of Philadelphia Comprehensive Annual Financial Report, Fiscal Year Ended June 30, 2016.
Retrieved from http://finreports.universityofcalifornia.edu/index.php?file=13-14/pdf/fullreport-1314.pdf.

Clark, Nicola and David Jolly, "Société Générale loses $7 billion in trading fraud," *The New York Times*, January 24, 2008.
Retrieved from http://www.nytimes.com/2008/01/24/business/worldbusiness/24iht-socgen.5.9486501.html.

"New York Department of Financial Services (NYDFS) Announces Deutsche Bank to pay $2.5 billion, terminate and ban individual employees, install independent monitor for interest rate manipulation." April 23, 2015.
Retrieved from http://dfs.ny.gov/about/press/pr1504231.htm.

Commodity Futures and Modernization Act, The 106 U. S. Congress. December 14, 2000.
Retrieved from http://www.cftc.gov/files/ogc/ogchr5660.pdf.

Commodity Futures Modernization Committee. In the Matter of Deutsch Bank, Respondent.ORDER INSTITUTING PROCEEDINGS PURSUANT TO SECTIONS 6(c) AND 6(d) OF THE COMMODITY EXCHANGE ACT, MAKING FINDINGS, AND IMPOSING REMEDIAL SANCTIONS. April 23, 2015.https://www.cftc.gov/sites/default/files/idc/groups/public/@lrenforcementactions/documents/legalpleading/enfdeutscheorder042315.pdf

Consolidated Financial Statements Indiana University Health Inc. and subsidiaries Years Ended December 31, 2011 and 2010. With Report of Independent Auditors.
Retrieved from https://www.in.gov/isdh/files/2011_Indiana_University_Health_AFS.pdf.

Consolidated Financial Statements Indiana University Health, Inc. and subsidiaries Years Ended December 31, 2013 and 2012. With Report of Independent Auditors.
Retrieved from https://www.in.gov/isdh/files/2013_Indiana_University_Health_AFS.pdf.

Consolidated Financial Statements Indiana University Health, Inc. and subsidiaries Years Ended December 31, 2015 and 2014. With Report of Independent Auditors.
Retrieved from https://www.in.gov/isdh/files/2015_Indiana_University_Health_AFS.pdf.

Corfman, Thomas A. "Despite Vitale's business experience, CPS flunks Finance 101. Scool Chief's Strong Financial Background hasn's cured CPS' ills." Crain's Chicago Business. May 02, 2015.
Retrieved from http://www.chicagobusiness.com/article/20150502/ISSUE01/305029991/despite-vitales-business-experience-cps-flunks-finance-101.

Cornyn, John. Office of the Attorney General of the State of Texas. "Opinion No. JC-0068. Re: Whether a hospital district is authorized to execute a contract to hedge against interest rate fluctuations." June 15, 1999.
Retrieved from https://texasattorneygeneral.gov/opinions/opinions/49cornyn/op/1999/pdf/jc0068.pdf.

Council of the City of Philadelphia, Office of the Chief Clerk. Resolution No. 120147. March 1, 2012.
Retrieved from http://legislation.phila.gov/attachments/12751.pdf.

Dale, Daniel, "Baltimore, Detroit threaten thousands with water shut-off." The Star. April 22, 2015.
Retrieved from https://www.thestar.com/news/world/2015/04/22/baltimore-detroit-threaten-thousands-with-water-shut-off.html.

Daniels, Melissa, "In Pennsylvania, swaps are a $17.2 Billion problem," *Pennsylvania Watchdog,* May 29, 2013.
Retrieved from http://watchdog.org/217204/paindy-in-pennsylvania-swaps-are-a-17-2-billion-problem/.

Darragh, Tim and Steve Esack, "Firms Reap Millions from Interest Rate Swap Deals," *The Morning Call*, June 7, 2009.
Retrieved from http://www.mcall.com/news/local/swaps/all-news-swaps-060709-pt2-story.html.

Davis, Owen, "In Financially Distressed Chicago, Public and Private Lines are Blurred," *International Business Times*, March 15, 2016.
Retrieved from http://www.ibtimes.com/financially-distressed-chicago-public-private-lines-are-blurred-2336392.

Dawson, Mike, "State College Area school board agrees to pay $9 million in swap settlement with Royal Bank of Canada," *Central Daily Times*. January 14, 2013. Retrieved from http://www.centredaily.com/2013/01/14/3465128_state-college-area-school-board.html?rh=1.

City and County of Denver, Colorado. Comprehensive Annual Financial Report for the Year Ended December 31, 2016. Retrieved from https://www.denvergov.org/content/dam/denvergov/Portals/344/documents/CAFR/2016_CAFR.pdf.

Denvir, Daniel, "Who's killing Philly public schools?" *My City Paper,* February 5, 2012. Retrieved from https://mycitypaper.com/cover/whos-killing-philly-public-schools/.

DeVito, Lee, "All charges dismissed against the 'Homrich 9' Detroit water shutoff protestors," *Detroit Metro Times,* June 20, 2017. Retrieved from https://www.metrotimes.com/news-hits/archives/2017/06/20/all-charges-dismissed-against-the-homrich-9-detroit-water-shutoff-protestors.

Dignity Health and Subordinate Corporations, Consolidated Financial Statements as of the Years Ended June 30 2015 and June 30, 2014 and Independent Auditors' Report. September 22, 2015. Retrieved from https://emma.msrb.org/ES730463-ES572510-.pdf.

Dignity Health and Subordinate Corporations, Consolidated Financial Statements as of the Years Ended June 30 2016 and June 30, 2015 and Independent Auditors' Report. September 21, 2016. Retrieved from https://emma.msrb.org/ES823341-ES646022-ES1041174.pdf.

Dignity Health Religious Sponsors. Retrieved from https://www.supportdhfglobalmissionprogram.org/about-us/religious-sponsors

DiMatteo, Larry A. and Bruce Rich, "A Consent Theory of Unconscionability: An Empirical Study of Law in Action." Florida State University Law Review, Vol. 33. Summer 2006. Retrieved from http://scholarship.law.ufl.edu/facultypub/524.

DiStefano, Joseph N., "Philly Deals: Interest-rate swap strategy backfires, costs city $186M," *The Philadelphia Inquirer,* October 24, 2012.

Retrieved from http://www.philly.com/philly/columnists/joseph-diste-fano/20121024_PhillyDeals__Interest-rate_swap_strategy_backfires__costs_city__186M.html.

Eaton, Charley, Jacob Habinek, Mukul Kumar, Tamera Lee Stover, Alex Roehrkasse and Jeremy Thompson, *"Swapping Our Future: How Students and Taxpayers are Funding Risky UC Borrowing and Wall Street Profits,"* Department of Sociology at the University of California at Berkeley, 2012. Retrieved from https://publicsociology.berkeley.edu/publications/swapping/swapping.pdf.

Eisenbrey, Ross, "Detroit's Deals with Financial Institutions Led to Disaster," *Economic Policy Institute*. December 24, 2013. Retrieved from http://www.epi.org/blog/detroits-deals-financial-institutions-led/.

Federal Bureau of Investigation, Washington Field Office. "RBS Securities Japan Limited Agrees to Plead Guilty in Connection with Long-Running Manipulation of LIBOR Benchmark Interest Rates," February 6, 2013. Retrieved from https://archives.fbi.gov/archives/washingtondc/press-releases/2013/rbs-securities-japan-limited-agrees-to-plead-guilty-in-connection-with-long-running-manipulation-of-libor-benchmark-interest-rates.

Fettig David, David S. Dahl, and Kathy Cobb, "Interstate branch banking: Opt in or opt out?" *Fedgazette*. The Federal Reserve Bank of Minneapolis. January 1, 1995. Retrieved from https://www.minneapolisfed.org/publications/fedgazette/interstate-branch-banking-opt-in-or-opt-out.

Fichera, Joseph S, "Were Detroit's Interest-Rate Swaps Not Fair," *Bloomberg*. January 27, 2014. Retrieved from https://saberpartners.com/press/bloomberg-view/.

Financial Services Authority (UK). *Report of Barclays Final Notice*, June 17, 2012. Retrieved from http://www.fsa.gov.uk/static/pubs/final/barclays-jun12.pdf.

Financial statement Audit Report of the University of North Carolina at Chapel Hill for the year ended June 30, 2003. Retrieved from http://www.ncauditor.net/EPSWeb/Reports/Financial/FIN-2003-6020.pdf. Retrieved from http://www.unc.edu/finance/fd/c/docs/2009_cafr.pdf.

"Finding Cure for Financial Derivatives: The Market Cancer," *The American Almanac*. 1993.
Retrieved from http://american_almanac.tripod.com/derivs.htm.

FINRA, *Auction Rate Securities — What Happens When Auctions Fail.* November 18, 2008.
Retrieved from https://www.investor.gov/introduction-investing/basics/ investment-products/auction-rate-securities; https://www.sec.gov/investor/ ars.htm.

Fortino, Ellyn. "CTU Closes Bank of America Account Over 'Toxic' Interest Rate Swaps," *Progress Illinois*, February 3, 2016.
Retrieved from http://www.progressillinois.com/quick-hits/content/2016/ 02/03/ctu-closes-its-account-bank-america-over-toxic-interest-rate-swaps.

Fortino, Ellyn, "Chicago Activists, Lawmakers Deliver Petitions To SEC For Action On 'Toxic' Interest-rate swaps," *Illinois Progress*, July 7th, 2016.
Retrieved from http://progressillinois.com/quick-hits/content/2016/07/07/ chicago-activists-lawmakers-deliver-petitions-sec-action-toxic-swaps.

Fortado, Lindsay, "Kweku Adoboli: A Rogue Trader's Tale," *Financial Times*, October 12, 2015.
Retrieved from https://www.ft.com/content/0fa0b42a-783a-11e5-a95a- 27d368e1ddf7.

Fusco, Chris, "The Watchdogs: CPS' pain is these firms' gain." *Sun Times.* July 4, 2015.
Retrieved from http://chicago.suntimes.com/the-watchdogs/7/71/740413/ watchdogs-cps-bond-fee.

Grotto, Jason & Heather Gillers, "Risky Bonds Prove Costly for Chicago Public Schools," *Chicago Tribune,* November 7, 2014.
Retrieved from http://www.chicagotribune.com/news/watchdog/cpsbonds/ ct-chicago-public-schools-bond-deals-met-20141107-story.html.

Gillers, Heather & Jason Grotto, "Banks Kept CPS in Shaky Bond Market," *Chicago* Tribune, November 10, 2014.
Retrieved from http://www.chicagotribune.com/news/watchdog/cpsbonds/ ct-chicago-public-schools-bonds-banks-met-20141107-story.html.

Guyette, Curt. "Bad interest rate swaps contribute to Detroit water crisis and financial crisis." *Detroit MetroTimes,* August 6, 2014.
Retrieved from https://www.metrotimes.com/detroit/water%C2%ADwoes% C2%ADand%C2%ADthe%C2%ADswaps%C2%ADswamp/Content? oid=2214702.

Hansen, Jeff, "Timeline: How Jefferson County, Alabama's financial crisis unfolded" — The Birmingham News. August 5, 2011.
Retrieved from http://blog.al.com/birmingham-news-stories/2011/08/timeline_how_jefferson_countys.html.

Hansell, Saul, "P. & G. Sues Bankers Trust Over Swap Deal." *The New York Times.* October 28, 1994.
Retrieved from http://www.nytimes.com/1994/10/28/business/p-g-sues-bankers-trust-over-swap-deal.html.

Hansell, Saul, "Bankers Trust Settles Suit with P. & G." *The New York Times.* May 10, 1996.
Retrieved from http://www.nytimes.com/1996/05/10/business/bankers-trust-settles-suit-with-p-g.html.

Harvard University Financial Report, Fiscal Year 2009.
Retrieved from http://finance.harvard.edu/files/fad/files/2009fullreport.pdf?m=1389978230.

Hazlett, Chelsea, "The Scandalous Baseline of Your Utility Bill," *Gainesville Scene,.* July 6, 2015.
Retrieved from http://gainesvillescene.com/2015/07/06/the-scandalous-baseline-of-your-utility-bill/.

Hochfelder, David, "Where the Common People Could Speculate": The Ticker, Bucket Shops, and the Origins of Popular Participation in Financial Markets, 1880–1920. *The Journal of American History,* September 2006, pp. 335–358.
Retrieved from https://academic.oup.com/jah/article/93/2/335/830224.

Hochfelder, David, "How Bucket Shops Lured the Masses Into the Market," *Bloomberg.* January 10, 2013.
Retrieved from https://www.bloomberg.com/view/articles/2013-01-10/how-bucket-shops-lured-the-masses-into-the-market.

Holland, Kelley, Linda Himelstein, and Zachary Schiller, "The Bankers Trust Tape," *BusinessWeek*, October 16, 1995.
Retrieved from https://www.bloomberg.com/news/articles/1995-10-15/the-bankers-trust-tapes.

House of Commons, United Kingdom, "Treasury Committee Fixing LIBOR: Some Preliminary Findings," *Second Report of Session 2012–13 HC 481–I.*
Retrieved from https://publications.parliament.uk/pa/cm201213/cmselect/cmtreasy/481/481.pdf.

Hutchinson, Bill, "New $1.5 Billion Goethals Bridge Will Provide Pedestrian, Bike Paths to N.J." *New York Daily News*. April 25, 2013.
Retrieved from http://www.nydailynews.com/new-york/1-5b-goethals-bridge-provide-bike-route-n-article-1.1326769.

Infographics, "A Philadelphia Political Hall of Shame," *The Inquirer,* (undated).
Retrieved from http://www.philly.com/philly/infographics/383865751.html.

Interest-rate swaps in India, "Derivatiff: A Retiring Official Raises the Alarm About Derivatives in India," *The Economist*, February 16, 2013.
Retrieved from https://www.economist.com/news/finance-and-economics/21571901-retiring-official-raises-alarm-about-derivatives-india-derivatiff.

Ivry, Bob, *The Seven Sins of Wall Street: Their Washington Lackeys and the Next Financial Crisis*. Public Affairs Publisher. New York. March 11, 2014.

Johnson, Simon and James Kwak, *13 Bankers: The Wall Street Take Over and the Next Meltdown*, (New York, Vintage, 2010).

Kaske, Michelle, "Keystone State Talks Swaps," *The Bond Buyer*. May 5, 2010.
Retrieved from http://www.bondbuyer.com/issues/119_335/pennsylvania_prohibit_local_governments_derivatives-1011756-1.html.

Kalotay, Andrew, "*SEC Hearing on The State of Municipal Securities Market Birmingham, AL*," Securities and Exchange Commission, July 29, 2011.
Retrieved from https://www.sec.gov/spotlight/municipalsecurities/statements072911/kalotay.pdf.

Kalotay, Andrew. "Municipal Swaps: Realities and Misconceptions." Global Association of Risk Professionals. December 11, 2012. http://kalotay.com/sites/default/files/private/ GARP_Muni_Swaps.pdf.

King, Sharon, "Market Place; Municipal Bond Investors Could Wind Up in an I.R.S. Crackdown," *The New York Times*, July 25, 1996.
Retrieved from http://www.nytimes.com/1996/07/25/business/market-place-municipal-bond-investors-could-wind-up-in-an-irs-crackdown.html.

Kirby, Fiona, "UC CFO Refutes Accusation of Interest Rate Swap Losses," *Daily Bruin*, February 28, 2014.
Retrieved from http://dailybruin.com/2014/02/28/uc-cfo-refutes-accusation-of-interest-rate-swap-losses/.

Knapp, Charles L., "Unconscionably in American Contract Law: A Twenty-First Century Survey." University of California Hastings Research Paper No. 71. 2013. pp. 25–27.
Retrieved from https://papers.ssrn.com/sol3/papers.cfm?abstract_id=2346498.

Kwak, James, "Clinton Confesses: Rubin and Summers Gave Bad (strike that) Excellent Advice on Derivatives," *The Baseline Scenario: What happened to the global economy and what we can do about it*, April 20, 2010.
Retrieved from https://baselinescenario.com/2010/04/20/clinton-rubin-summers-derivatives/.

Kwesell, Allison, "In Detroit, City-Backed Water Shut-offs 'Contrary to Human Rights,' say UN experts," *UN News Center*, October 20, 2014.
Retrieved from http://www.un.org/apps/news/story.asp?NewsID=49127#. WdjTx2hSyUk.

Lamont Investment Advisory Corporation, "State of New Jersey Interest Rate Swap Valuation-Portfolio Summary," November 30, 2010.
Retrieved from http://www.nj.gov/transparency/bond/pdf/20100531_swap_portfolio.pdf.

Lapavitsas, Costas and Alexis Stenfors, "A Fine for Royal Bank of Scotland will not Fix LIBOR," *Financial Times*, February 7, 2012.
Retrieved from https://www.ft.com/content/1054054a-7052-11e2-85d 0-00144feab49a?mhq5j=e1.

Lazar, David, "New Jersey Losing $22,000-a-Day With Swap for Bonds Never Sold," *NJ Internet Marketing*, December 4, 2009.
Retrieved from http://njinternetmarketing.blogspot.com/2009/12/new-jersey-losing-22000-day-with-swap.html.

Reproduced by *Derivatives Investing Net*.
Retrieved from http://www.derivativesinvesting.net/article/743273432/new-jersey-losing-22-000-a-day-with-swap-for-bonds-never-sold/.

LEAGLE, *In Re LIBOR-Based Financial Instruments Antitrust Litigation*, April 29, 2016.
Retrieved from https://www.leagle.com/decision/infdco20160502c87.

Lipton, Eric and Stephen Labaton, "Deregulator Looks Back," Unswayed, *The New York Times*, November 16, 2008.
Retrieved from http://www.nytimes.com/2008/11/17/business/economy/17gramm.html.

Long, Cate, "Pennsylvania's Worthy Debate Over Swaps, *Reuters*," September 10, 2013.
Retrieved from http://blogs.reuters.com/muniland/2013/09/10/pennsylvanias-worthy-debate-over-swaps/.

Loomis, Carol, "Untangling the Derivatives Mess," *Fortune*. March 20, 1995.
Retrieved from http://archive.fortune.com/magazines/fortune/fortune_archive/1995/03/20/201945/index.htm.

Mahon, Ed., "The Swap. State Swap College goes National," *Ed Mahon Sample of Journalism.* May 21, 2011.
Retrieved from https://edmahon.wordpress.com/clips/enterpriseinvestigative/the-money-swap/.

Massachusetts Bay Transportation Authority. Financial Statements and Required Supplementary Information June 30, 2004 and 2003.
Retrieved from http://www.mbta.com/uploadedFiles/Documents/Financials/642MBTA-FS-2004-FINAL.pdf.

Massachusetts Transportation Authority. Interest Rate Swap Portfolio: Amendment Opportunity. January 2017.
Retrieved from https://www.mbta.com/uploadedfiles/About_the_T/Board_Meetings/K. Interest Rate Swap Amendments.pdf.

Masterson, Matt, "CPS to Cut More Than 1,000 Teaching, Support Staff Positions," WTTW. August 5, 2016.
Retrieved from http://chicagotonight.wttw.com/stories-by-author/matt%20masterson.

Massachusetts Bay Transportation Authority, Notes to Financial Statements, June 30, 2001.
Retrieved from http://www.mbta.com/uploadedFiles/Documents/Financials/kpmg2001.pdf.

Massachusetts Bay Transportation Authority, "Interest Rate Swap Portfolios, Amendment Opportunities," January 2017.
Retrieved from http://www.mbta.com/uploadedfiles/About_the_T/Board_Meetings/K.%20%20Interest%20Rate%20Swap%20Amendments.pdf.

McDonald, Michael and David Scheer . "SEC 'Missed Opportunity' to Save Auction-Rate Market Investors. Bloomberg. September 07, 2008
Retrieved from http://www.pluris.com/printer/sec-missed-opportunity-to-save-auction-ratemarket-investors

Methodist Health System, Financial Assistance Policy, September 28, 2016.
Retrieved from http://www.methodisthealthsystem.org/workfiles/financial/Financial-Assistance.pdf.

Methodist Health System, Media Center, Methodist Health System Uses Progressive Financing to Save Millions of Dollars. January 1, 2008.
Retrieved from https://www.methodisthealthsystem.org/body.cfm?id=93&action=detail&ref=59.

Metropolitan Transportation Commission, Financial Statements for the year ended June 30, 2002.
Retrieved from https://mtc.ca.gov/sites/default/files/MTC2002AR_Financials.pdf.

Metropolitan Transportation Commission, Financial Statements for the years ended June 30, 2003 and 2002.
Retrieved from http://mtc.ca.gov/sites/default/files/Financial_Report_03.pdf.

Metropolitan Transportation Commission, Comprehensive Annual Financial Report for Fiscal Year Ended June 30, 2008.
Retrieved from http://mtc.ca.gov/sites/default/files/CAFR-financials_07-08.pdf.

Metropolitan Transportation Commission, Financial Statements for years ended June 30, 2009 and 2008, p. 65.
Retrieved from https://mtc.ca.gov/sites/default/files/CAFR_June30-2009.pdf.

Metropolitan Transportation Commission, Financial Statements for years ended June 30, 2013 and 2012.
Retrieved from https://mtc.ca.gov/sites/default/files/CAFR_2013.pdf.

Metropolitan Transportation Commission, Financial Statements for the years ended June 30, 2016 and 2015.
Retrieved from https://mtc.ca.gov/sites/default/files/FY_16_MTC_CAFR.pdf.

"Minutes. Dauphin County Board of Commissioners Workshop," April 13, 2005.
Retrieved from http://www.dauphincounty.org/government/About-the-County/Meetings/Minutes/WS041305.pdf.

"Minutes. Dauphin County Board of Commissioners' Workshop Meeting," July 26, 2006.
Retrieved from http://www.dauphincounty.org/government/About-the-County/Meetings/Minutes/WS072606.pdf.

"Minutes Dauphin County Board of Commissioners Workshop," July 9, 2014.
Retrieved from http://www.dauphincounty.org/government/About-the-County/Meetings/Minutes/WS%2007%2009%202014.pdf.

Mollenkamp, Carrick, "Bankers Cast Doubt On Key Rate Amid Crisis," *The Wall Street Journal*, April 16, 2008,
Retrieved from http://online.wsj.com/article/SB120831164167818299.html.

Mollenkamp, Carrick and Mark Whitehouse, "Study Casts Doubt on Key Rate," *The Wall Street Journal*. May 29, 2008.
Retrieved from http://online.wsj.com/article/SB121200703762027135.html.

Morgenstern, Gretchen, "Exotic Deals Put Denver Schools Deeper in Debt," *The New York Times*. August. 5, 2010.
Retrieved from http://www.nytimes.com/2010/08/06/business/06denver.html.

"Muni Swap Index Data. SIFMA 1989–2014 Swaps Historical Data" (Ending August 13, 2014) (xls).
Retrieved from http://www.sifma.org/swapdata/index.html.

Municipal Securities Rules Board, "Synthetic Refunding," *MSRB Glossary of Municipal Securities Terms*.
Retrieved from https://www.definedterm.com/a/definition/97780.

Nasar, Sylvia, "Behind the Kidder Scandal: The Overview; Kidder Scandal Tied to Failure Of Supervision," *The New York Times*, August 5, 1994.
Retrieved from http://www.nytimes.com/1994/08/05/us/behind-kidder-scandal-overview-kidder-scandal-tied-failure-supervision.html?pagewanted=all.

"New York Department of Financial Services (NYDFS) Announces Deutsche Bank to pay $2.5 billion, terminate and ban individual employees, install independent monitor for interest rate manipulation." April 23, 2015.
Retrieved from http://dfs.ny.gov/about/press/pr1504231.htm.

Office of High Commissioner, "Detroit: Disconnecting water from people who cannot pay — an affront to human rights, say UN experts," United Nations Human Rights, June 24, 2014.
Retrieved from http://www.ohchr.org/EN/NewsEvents/Pages/DisplayNews.aspx?NewsID=14777.

North Penn Water Annual Report 2015.
Retrieved from http://northpennwater.org/uploads/Annual%20Financial%20Report.pdf.

"Orange County Case." *Finance Train,* (Undated).
Retrieved from http://financetrain.com/orange-county-case/.

Otis, Ginger Adams, "MTA is Losing Money and Headed to Financial Disaster, Despite Attempts to Find Revenue," *Daily News New York*. April 28, 2015.
Retrieved from http://www.nydailynews.com/new-york/mta-losing-money-headed-financial-ruin-article-1.2202720.

Palmer, Maija, "You Get a Thick Skin and You Learn When not to be at the Bar," *Financial Times.* September 27, 2017, p. 5.
Retrieved from https://www.ft.com/content/743cfdc2-715c-11e7-93ff-99f383b09ff9.

Partnoy, Frank. *F.I.A.S.C.O.: Blood in the Wall Street*, (New York, W.W. Norton. 1997).

Partnoy, Frank. *Infectious Greed: How Deceit and Risk Corrupted the Financial Markets.* (London, Profile Books, 2003).

Peng, Scott, Chintan (Monty) Gandhi, & Alexander Tyo, *"Special Topic: Is LIBOR Broken?"* Citigroup Global Markets, Inc. April 10, 2008.
Retrieved from http://www.moneyscience.com/mod/file/download.php?file_guid=393006.

Pennsylvania Turnpike Commission, A Component Unit of the Commonwealth of Pennsylvania Comprehensive Annual Financial Report, Fiscal Years Ended May 31, 2014 and 2013.
Retrieved from https://www.paturnpike.com/pdfs/business/PTC_CAFR_14_13_Final.pdf#search=%22swaps%22.

Peralta Community College District "Final Report, Other Post-Employment Benefits Program." KNN Public Finance. June 28, 2011.
Retrieved from http://web.peralta.edu/accreditation/files/2012/01/3.-OPEB-Final-Report-June-28-2011-KNN.pdf.

Perez Jr., Juan, "CPS lays off more than 500 teachers, another 500 school-based workers." *Chicago Tribune.* August 5, 2016.
Retrieved from http://www.chicagotribune.com/news/local/breaking/ct-chicago-schools-teacher-layoffs-0806-20160805-story.html.

Petersen, Melody, "UC Lost Millions on Interest-rate Bets," *The Orange County Register.* December 17, 2014.
Retrieved from http://www.afscme3299.org/2014/02/21/uc-lost-millions-on-interest-rate-bets/.

Retrieved from http://www.ocregister.com/articles/university-602769-interest-rate.html?page=1.

PIMCO. "Understanding Interest Rate Swaps." (Undated).
Retrieved from https://global.pimco.com/en-gbl/resources/education/understanding-interest-rate-swaps.

PR Newswire. "Auditor General Jack Wagner Calls on General Assembly to Ban Risky "Swap" Contracts by Schools, Local Governments." November 18, 2009.

Retrieved from http://www.prnewswire.com/news-releases/auditor-general-jack-wagner-calls-on-general-assembly-to-ban-risky-swap-contracts-by-schools-local-governments-70388252.html.

Pollack, Andrew and Leslie Wayne, "Ending Suit, Merrill Lynch to Pay California County $400 Million," *The New York Times,* June 3, 1998.
Retrieved from http://www.nytimes.com/1998/07/22/business/the-master-of-orange-county-a-merrill-lynch-broker-survives-municipal-bankruptcy.html.

Preston, Darrell, "Denver Pays Wall Street $216 Million as Swaps Fail: Muni Credit" *Bloomberg.* May 10, 2013.
Retrieved from http://saberpartners.com/press/articlepages/bloomberg_05_10_13.html.

Preston, Darrell and Steven Church, "Detroit Swap Banks Go First as Bankruptcy Looms: Muni Credit," *Bloomberg.* June 20, 2013.
Retrieved from https://www.bloomberg.com/news/articles/2013-06-21/detroit-swap-banks-go-first-as-bankruptcy-looms-muni-credit.

Prupis, Nadia, "Detroit Teachers Hold Sick-Out to Demand Fixes to School's 'Abominable' Problems," *Common Dreams,* January 15, 2015.
Retrieved from http://www.commondreams.org/news/2016/01/11/detroit-teachers-hold-sick-out-demand-fixes-schools-abominable-problems.

Reed, Robert, "Mayor, Treasurer Summers at Odds Over Antitrust Lawsuit Against Big Banks," *Chicago Tribune*, November 3, 2016.
Retrieved from http://www.chicagotribune.com/business/columnists/ct-kurt-summers-versus-banks-robert-reed-1103-biz-20161102-column.html.

Refund Transit Coalition, "Riding the Gravy Train: How Wall Street Is Bankrupting Our Public Transit Agencies by Profiteering off of Toxic Swap Deals," June 2012.
Retrieved from http://www.nowandfutures.com/large/GravyTrainWallStBanksRipOffTransitAuthoritiesVariousCities-Strat-Transitswaps.pdf.

"Regents of the University of California Meeting as a Committee of the Whole." November 15, 2012.
Retrieved from http://regents.universityofcalifornia.edu/minutes/2012/cw15.pdf.

Rodrigues, Jason, "Barings Collapse at 20: How Rogue Trader Nick Leeson Broke the Bank," *The Guardian*, February 15, 2010.
Retrieved from https://www.theguardian.com/business/from-the-archive-blog/2015/feb/24/nick-leeson-barings-bank-1995-20-archive.

Russ, Hillary, "Exclusive: New Jersey paid $720 million to exit all swaps under Christie" *Reuters*. August 20, 2015.
Retrieved from http://www.reuters.com/article/us-usa-new-jersey-swaps-idUSKCN0QP29520150820.

Russel, Dominic, Carrie Sloan, Aman Banerji, and Alan Smith, "It's Time for Universities to Pick Students over Swaps," *Roosevelt Forward: Rewrite the Rules*, September 20. 2016.
Retrieved from http://rooseveltforward.org/its-time-our-universities-pick-students-over-swaps/.

Sapien, Brendan, "Financial Weapons of Mass Destruction: From Bucket Shops to Credit Default Swaps," *Southern California Interdisciplinary Law Journal*. Vol. 19. 2010, pp. 411–442.
Retrieved from http://clhc.usc.edu/why/students/orgs/ilj/assets/docs/19-2%20Sapien.pdf.

Schoen, John W., "Damage to City Budgets: Self-inflicted with Help from Wall Street," *NBC News*, November 18, 2013.
Retrieved from http://www.nbcnews.com/business/damage-city-budgets-self-inflicted-help-wall-street-2D11603593.

School District No. 1 in the City and County of Denver and State of Colorado Comprehensive Annual Financial Report for the Year Ended June 30, 2012.
Retrieved from http://static.dpsk12.org/gems/generalaccounting/CAFR2012.pdf.

Schumpeter, Joseph A., *Capitalism, Socialism and Democracy*, (London, Routledge, 1942, 3rd ed.).

"Securities Industry Financial Markets Association, SEC No-Action Letter." March 14, 2008.
Retrieved from http://www.sifma.org/capital_markets/docs/SEC—ARSLetter.pdf.

"Securities Industry and Financial Markets Association. *Wikipedia*." October 26, 2017.
Retrieved from https://en.wikipedia.org/wiki/Securities_Industry_and_Financial_Markets_Association.

SEIU Local 1021 Members Visit Goldman Sachs to Demand a Fair Deal for Oakland. August 6, 2012.
Retrieved from http://www.seiu1021.org/tag/city-of-oakland/page/2/.

Selway, William and Martin Z. Braun, "JPMorgan Swap Deals Spur Probe as Default Stalks Alabama County," *Bloomberg.* May 22, 2008.
Retrieved from http://www.bloomberg.com/apps/news?pid=newsarchive& sid=aF_f8gLLNvn0.

Selway, William, "Jefferson County, Alabama's Path from Scandal to Settlement: Timeline," *Bloomberg Busin*ess. September 16, 2011.
Retrieved from http://www.bloomberg.com/news/articles/2011-09-16/ jefferson-county-alabama-s-path-from-scandal-to-debt-settlement-timeline.

Sexton, Elisabeth, "Unconscionable Conduct Still a Grey Area. Laws to Protect Investors are Constantly Changing, but the Ideal Test Case is Yet to Come Along," *The Sydney Morning Herald.* July 15, 2011.
Retrieved from http://www.smh.com.au/business/unconscionable-conduct-still-a-grey-area-20110714-1hgdq.html.

SFC Associates. March 3, 2013. Court Cases Involving the Manipulation of London Interbank Offered Rate.
Retrieved from http://sfcassociates.com/wp-content/uploads/2013/03/ LIBOR-Cases-As-of-3_13_13.pdf.

Shah, Prateek and Michael Sadler, "Watch Your Swaps and Derivatives Termination Payments," *Law 360.* June 10, 2013.
Retrieved from https://www.law360.com/articles/448512/watch-your-swaps-and-derivatives-termination-payments.

Sisters of Charity of Leavenworth Health System, Inc. Annual Financial Reporting Information for the Year Ended December 31, 2016. May 25, 2017.
Retrieved from https://www.sclhealth.org/-/media/files/shared/about/financials/sclhealthannualdisclosure2016final.pdf?la=en.

Shands Teaching Hospital and Clinics, Inc. and Subsidiaries. Consolidated Basic Financial Statements. June 30, 2016 and 2015.
Retrieved from https://ufhealth.org/sites/default/files/media/PDF/2016-shands-financial-statement.pdf.

Skarr, Douglas, "The Fundamentals of Interest Rate Swaps," *Issue Brief*, California Debt and Investment Advisory Commission, October 2004.
Retrieved from http://www.treasurer.ca.gov/cdiac/reports/rateswap04-12.pdf.

Sloan, Carrie, "The Unexpected Cause of Water Crises in American Cities," *Talk Poverty.* March 9, 2016.
Retrieved from https://talkpoverty.org/2016/03/09/unexpected-cause-water-crises-american-cities/.

Sloan, Carrie, "How Wall Street Caused a Water Crisis in America's Cities: Vulnerable Residents are Paying the Price for Dangerous Financial Deals," *The Nation.* March 11, 2016.
Retrieved from https://www.thenation.com/article/how-wall-street-caused-a-water-crisis-in-americas-cities/.

Smith, Robin, "Southern Discomfort: An Examination of the Financial Crisis in Jefferson County, Alabama." Houston Business and Tax Law Journal. 2010. pp. 376.
Retrieved from http://www-lexisnexis-com.proxy2.library.illinois.edu/hot-topics/lnacademic/?verb=sr&csi=250859.

Smith, Greg, "Why I am leaving Goldman Sachs," *The New York Times*, March 14, 2012.
Retrieved from http://www.nytimes.com/2012/03/14/opinion/why-i-am-leaving-goldman-sachs.html?_r=0.

Stannard, Matt, "What Wall Street Cost Denver's Schools," Public Banking Institute. March 28, 2016.
Retrieved from http://www.publicbankinginstitute.org/what_wall_street_cost_denver_s_schools.

"State College Area School District Agrees to $9 Million Payment in Interest Rate Swap Agreement with Royal Bank of Canada." *StateCollege.com.*
Retrieved from http://www.statecollege.com/news/local-news/state-college-area-school-district-agrees-to-9-million-payment-in-interest-rate-swap-agreement-with-royal-bank-of-canada,1222044/.

State of Illinois Comptroller. Comprehensive Annual Financial Report for the Year Ended June 30, 2016, February 28, 2017.
Retrieved from http://illinoiscomptroller.gov/ioc-pdf/CAFR_2016.pdf.

State of New Jersey. Comprehensive Annual Financial Report 2016.
http://www.state.nj.us/treasury/omb/publications/16cafr/pdf/fullcafr.pdf.
- Basic Financial Statements, 2011.
http://www.state.nj.us/treasury/omb/publications/11cafr/pdf/finstats.pdf.
- Basic Financial Statements, 2013.
http://www.state.nj.us/treasury/omb/publications/13cafr/pdf/finstats.pdf.
- Notes to Basic Financial Statements, State of New Jersey, 2015.
http://www.state.nj.us/treasury/omb/publications/15cafr/pdf/finstats.pdf.

State of New York. *Annual Performance Report — Interest Rate Exchange and Similar Agreements Fiscal Year 2016. New York State of Opportunity*, October 2016.

Retrieved from https://www.budget.ny.gov/investor/bond/Swaps PerformanceReport.pdf.

State of New York, Comprehensive Annual Financial Report, for Fiscal Year Ended March 31, 2006.
Retrieved from https://www.osc.state.ny.us/finance/finreports/cafr/cafr06. pdf.

Stech, Katy, "Judge Approves Jefferson County, Ala., Bankruptcy-Restructuring Plan. Residents to Shoulder Repayment Burden for Decades," *The Wall Street Journal.* November 21, 2013.
Retrieved from http://www.wsj.com/articles/SB10001424052702304337404 579212553163071992.

Stewart, Michael, *"Money for Nothing: How Interest Rate Swaps Have Become Golden Handcuffs for New Yorkers,"* SEIU December 14, 2011.
Retrieved from http://unitedny.org/files/2012/07/Money-For-Nothing-New-York-Interest-Rate-Swaps.pdf.

This site is currently inactive but the report may be retrieved from https:// www.coursehero.com/file/11150128/Report-on-New-York-Swaps1/.

Strauss, Valerie, "Philadelphia School District Laying off 3,783 Employees," *The Washington Post.* June 8, 2013.
Retrieved from https://www.washingtonpost.com/news/answer-sheet/ wp/2013/06/08/philadelphia-school-district-laying-off-3783-employees/ ?utm_term=.80c30f57bdb8.

Strowmatt, Shane, Suzi Ring, and Greg Farrell, "Deutsche Bank to Pay $2.5 Billion to End LIBOR Probe," *Bloomberg.* April 23, 2015.
Retrieved from https://www.bloomberg.com/amp/news/articles/2015-04-23/ deutsche-bank-to-pay-record-2-5-billion-to-resolve-libor-probes.

Stout, Lynn, "Testimony of Lynn A. Stout, Paul Hastings Professor of Corporate and Securities Law UCLA School of Law before the United States Senate Committee on Agriculture, Forestry and Nutrition," June 4, 2009.
Retrieved from https://corpgov.law.harvard.edu/wp-content/uploads/2009/06/ testimony3.pdf.

"Synthetic Refunding." MSRB Glossary of Municipal Securities Terms (Undated).
Retrieved from https://www.definedterm.com/a/definition/97780.

Taleb, N. N. "Skin in the Game," February 12, 2016.
Retrieved from http://www.fooledbyrandomness.com/rationality.pdf.

Tett, Gillian. *Fool's Gold.* The Free Press. New York, NY, 2009.

The Economist. "Derivatiff: A retiring official raises the alarm about derivatives in India," February 16, 2013.
Retrieved from https://www.economist.com/news/finance-and-economics/21571901-retiring-official-raises-alarm-about-derivatives-india-derivatiff.

The Johns Hopkins Health System Corporation and Affiliates Combined Financial Statements and Supplementary Combining Information June 30, 2013 and 2012.
Retrieved from https://emma.msrb.org/EA567941-ER545677-ER946910.pdf.

The Johns Hopkins Health System Corporation and Affiliates Combined Financial Statements and Supplementary Information June 30, 2016 and 2015.
Retrieved from http://hscrc.maryland.gov/Documents/Hospitals/Reports Financial/Audited/FY-2016/JHHS_AFS_FY16.pdf.

The Treasury Committee, House of Commons, United Kingdom, "Fixing LIBOR: some preliminary findings," Second Report of Session 2012–13. HC 481–I, August 9, 2012.
Retrieved from https://publications.parliament.uk/pa/cm201213/cmselect/cmtreasy/481/481.pdf.

The University of Texas System Annual Financial Report — Primary Financial Statements Fiscal Year 2015.
Retrieved from https://www.utsystem.edu/sites/default/files/documents/Consolidated%20Annual%20Financial%20Report%3A%20FY%202015/consolidatedafr15.pdf.

The University of Texas System. December 18, 2015. Consolidated Financial Statements for the Years Ended August 31, 2015 and 2014, p. 40.
Retrieved from https://www.utsystem.edu/sites/default/files/documents/Consolidated%20Annual%20Financial%20Report%3A%20FY%202015/auditedafr15.pdf.

The University of Texas System Consolidated Financial Statements for the Years Ended August 31, 2016 and 2015.
https://www.utsystem.edu/sites/default/files/documents/Consolidated%20Annual%20Financial%20Report%3A%20FY%202016/consolidated-audit-afr-2016.pdf.

"Timeline LIBOR Fixing Scandal," *BBC News,* February 6, 2013.
Retrieved from http://www.bbc.com/news/business-18671255.

Thomsen, Linda Chatman. "Testimony Concerning the SEC's Recent Actions with Respect to Auction Rate Securities." September 8, 2008.
Retrieved from https://www.sec.gov/news/testimony/2008/ts091808lct.htm.

Touryalai, Halah, "Banks Rigged Libor To Inflate Adjustable-Rate Mortgages: Lawsuit," *Forbes*, October 15, 2012.
Retrieved from https://www.forbes.com/sites/halahtouryalai/2012/10/15/banks-rigged-libor-to-inflate-adjustable-rate-mortgages-lawsuit/#6d2b4c6ba85b.

Townsend, Marty, "Detroit Cuts off Water to Poor People BUT not Delinquent Businesses!" *Liberal America.* June 1, 2014.
http://www.liberalamerica.org/wp-content/uploads/2014/06/detroit-water-shut-off.gif.

Tran, Mark, "The AIB Scandal," *The Guardian*, February 20, 2002.
Retrieved from https://www.theguardian.com/business/2002/feb/20/theissuesexplained.

UBS, Annual Report, 2010, p.315.
Retrieved from https://www.ubs.com/global/en/about_ubs/investor_relations/annualreporting/2010.html.

"Unconscionable Contract or Clause," Section § 2-302 in the U. S. Uniform Commercial Code. Legal Information Institute, Cornell University.
Retrieved from https://www.law.cornell.edu/ucc/2/2-30.

United Nations. Office of High Commissioner. "Detroit: Disconnecting water from people who cannot pay — an affront to human rights, say UN experts, United Nations Human Rights," June 24, 2014.
Retrieved from http://www.ohchr.org/EN/NewsEvents/Pages/DisplayNews.aspx?NewsID=14777.

United States Department of Justice, "Barclays Bank PLC Admits Misconduct Related to Submissions for the London Interbank Offered Rate and the Euro Interbank Offered Rate and Agrees to Pay $160 Million Penalty," *Appendix A, Statement of Facts*, June 27, 2012.
Retrieved from https://www.justice.gov/iso/opa/resources/9312012710173426365941.pdf.

United States Department of Justice. Federal Bureau of Investigation Washington Field Office, "RBS Securities Japan Limited Agrees to Plead Guilty in Connection with Long-Running Manipulation of LIBOR Benchmark Interest Rates," February 06, 2013.

Retrieved from http://www.fbi.gov/washingtondc/press-releases/2013/rbs-securities-japan-limited-agrees-to-plead-guilty-in-connection-with-long-running-manipulation-of-LIBOR-benchmark-interest-rates.

United States Department of Justice, "Two Former Deutsche Bank Employees Indicted on Fraud Charges in Connection with Long-Running Manipulation of Libor," June 2, 2016.
Retrieved from https://www.justice.gov/opa/pr/two-former-deutsche-bank-employees-indicted-fraud-charges-connection-long-running.

U. S. Department of the Treasury, "Treasury Deputy Secretary Lawrence H. Summers Testimony before the Senate Committee on Agriculture, Nutrition, and Forestry on the CFTC Concept Release," Press Center, the July 30, 1998.
Retrieved from https://www.treasury.gov/press-center/press-releases/Pages/rr2616.aspx.

United States District Court, S. D. Ohio, Western Division. Procter & Gamble Co. v. Bankers Trust Co. No. C-1-94-735. 925 F. Supp. 1270 (1996). The Proctor & Gamble Company, Plaintiff, v. Bankers Trust Company and BT Securities Corporation, Defendants. *Leagle*. May 9, 1996.
Retrieved from http://www.leagle.com/decision/19962195925FSupp1270_12043/PROCTER%20&%20GAMBLE%20CO.%20v.%20BANKERS%20TRUST%20CO.

United States Court of Appeals, Sixth Circuit. "The Procter & Gamble Company, Plaintiff-Appellee, v. Bankers Trust Company, BT Securities Corporation, Defendants-Appellees, The McGraw-Hill Companies, Inc., Appellant. No. 95-4078." FindLaw, March 5, 1996.
Retrieved from http://caselaw.findlaw.com/us-6th-circuit/1139948.html.

United States District Court, Northern District of California, "The Regents of the University of California vs. Bank of America Corporation, etc." Case4:13-cv-02921-DMR Document1 Filed06/25/13. June 2013 pp. 1–2.
Retrieved from http://web.stanford.edu/group/lawlibrary/cgi-bin/LIBORlitigation/wp-content/uploads/2013/06/UCRegents-complaint-NDCalif-25Jun2013.pdf.

United States Bankruptcy Court, Northern District of Alabama, Southern Division. "In Re: Jefferson County, Alabama, a political subdivision of the State of Alabama. Case No.: 11-05736-TBB." November 4, 2009.
Retrieved from https://www.sec.gov/litigation/complaints/2009/comp21280.pdf.

United States of America before the Commodity Futures Trading Commission. Deutsche Bank AG, Respondent. (CFTC Docket No. 15- 20). "In the Matter of Order Instituting Proceedings Pursuant to Sections 5(c) and 6(d) of the Commodity Exchange Ace, Making Findings, and Imposing Remedial Actions." April 23, 2015.
Retrieved from http://www.cftc.gov/idc/groups/public/@lrenforcementactions/documents/legalpleading/enfdeutscheorder042315.pdf.

United States Commodity Futures Trading Commission. Office of Public Affairs. *Examples of Misconduct from Written Communications.* (Undated).
Retrieved from http://www.cftc.gov/idc/groups/public/@newsroom/documents/file/writtencommunication_deutsche.pdf.

United States Department of the Treasury, "Daily Treasury Yield Curve Rate," Resource Center.
Retrieved from https://www.treasury.gov/resource-center/data-chart-center/interest-rates/Pages/TextView.aspx?data=yieldYear&year=2011.

United States District Court for the Northern District of Alabama, Southern Division. "Securities and Exchange Commission v. Larry P. Langford, William B. Blount, Blount Parrish & Co., Inc. and Albert W. LaPiere." Case CV-08-B-0761-S, filed on April 30, 2008.
Retrieved from https://www.sec.gov/litigation/complaints/2008/comp20545.pdf.

United States Securities and Exchange Commission. Northern District of Alabama, Southern Division. Case No. CV-09-~-2238-S. "Securities and Exchange Commission (Plaintiff) v. Charles E. LeCroy and Douglass McFaddin, (Defendants)." November 4, 2009.
Retrieved from https://www.sec.gov/litigation/complaints/2009/comp21280.pdf.

United States Securities and Exchange Commission. "*United States of America v. Larry P. Langford, William B. Blount, and Albert W. LaPiere,*" (United States District Court for the Northern District of Alabama, Case No. 2:08-CR-00245-LSC-PWG). December 5, 2008.
Retrieved from http://www.Securities and Exchange Commission.gov/litigation/litreleases/2008/lr20821.htm.

United States Department of Justice. "United States of America before the Securities and Exchange Commission. In the Matter of Michael Lissack. Order Making Findings and Imposing Sanctions and a Cease-and-Desist

Order. Securities Exchange Act of 1934. Release No. 39687 Administrative Proceeding File No. 3–9427, February 20," 1998.
Retrieved from https://www.sec.gov/litigation/admin/34-39687.htm.

United States of America Complaint –v– Tom Alexander William Hayes and Roger Darin, 18 u.s.c. §§ 1349, 1343 & 2; 15 u.s.c. § 1.
Retrieved from https://www.justice.gov/sites/default/files/ag/legacy/2012/12/19/Hayes-Tom-and-Darin-Roger-Complaint.pdf.

United States Bankruptcy Court, Northern District of Alabama, Southern Division." In Re: Jefferson County, Alabama, Alabama, a political subdivision of the State of Alabama. Case No.: 11-05736-TBB. January 6, 2012.
Retrieved from http://www.gpo.gov/fdsys/pkg/USCOURTS-alnb-2_11-bk-05736/pdf/USCOURTS-alnb-2_11-bk-05736-0.pdf.

United States District Court, Southern District of New York, Federal Deposit Insurance Company, Plaintiff, Case No. 1:14-cv-01757-GHW, March 14, 2014, pp. 28–29.
Retrieved from http://web.stanford.edu/group/lawlibrary/cgi-bin/liborlitigation/wp-content/uploads/2014/03/SDNY-14-1757-LIBOR-related-COMPLAINT-vs-16-banks.pdf.

United States District Court Southern District of New York. Case No. No. 15 Civ. 9319 (SAS) Amended Class Action Complaint. Jury Demanded. Public Schools Teachers' Pension and Retirement Fund of Chicago and Mayor and City Council of Baltimore on behalf of themselves and all others similarly situated, Plaintiffs, - against - BANK OF AMERICA CORPORATION; etc. February 25, 2016.
Retrieved from https://www.cohenmilstein.com/sites/default/files/IRS%20Amended%20Complaint.pdf.

United States District Court. The Southern District of New York. Mayor and City Council of Baltimore and City of New Britain Firefighters' and Police Benefit Fund. Plaintiffs on behalf of themselves and all others similarly situated. In Re: Libor-based Financial Instruments Antitrust Litigation. Master File No. 1:I 1 -md-2262-NRB. April 30, 2012.
Retrieved from https://www.unitedstatescourts.org/federal/nysd/383368/130-0.html.

United States District Court, Southern District of New York, In Re LIBOR-Based Financial Instruments Antitrust Litigation, Memorandum and Order relates to all cases, Case no. 1:11-md-02262-NRB, March 29, 2013.
Retrieved from http://www.nysd.uscourts.gov/cases/show.php?db=special&id=280.

United States District Court, Southern District of New York, In Re: Interest Rate Swaps Antitrust Litigation. This Document Relates to All Actions, Case 1:16-md-02704-PAE. July 28, 2017.
Retrieved from http://www.nysd.uscourts.gov/cases/show.php?db=special& id=562.

United States District Court Southern District of New York. In RE: Interest Rate Swaps Antitrust Litigation. 16-MD-2704 (PAE) & 16-MC-2704 (PAE). OPINION & ORDER. PAUL A. ENGELMAYER, District Judge. July 28, 2017.
Retrieved from http://www.nysd.uscourts.gov/cases/show.php?db=special& id=562.

United States Securities and Exchange Commission. Securities Act of 1933 Release No. 9078and Securities Exchange Act of 1934 Release No., 60928/ November 4, 2009 Administrative Proceeding file No. 3-13673 in the Matter of J. P. Morgan Securities Inc. Respondent. Order Instituting Administrative and Cease-and-Desist Proceedings. November 4, 2009.
Retrieved from https://www.sec.gov/litigation/admin/2009/33-9078.pdf.

United States Office of Comptroller of the Currency, "Quarterly Report on Bank Derivatives Activities," 1996–2017.
Retrieved from https://www.occ.gov/topics/capital-markets/financial-markets/derivatives/derivatives-quarterly-report.html.

United States Supreme Court, "The Bucket-Shop Decision," Cornell University Library, May 8, 1905.
An adequate summary is at http://caselaw.findlaw.com/us-supreme-court/198/236.html.

United States Supreme Court. November 16, 1906. ERNEST GATEWOOD, Plff. in Err., v. STATE OF NORTH CAROLINA. 203 U.S. 531 (27 S.Ct. 167, 51 L.Ed. 305). Legal Information Institute, Cornell University. December 24, 1906.
Retrieved from https://www.law.cornell.edu/supremecourt/text/203/531.

Varghese, Romy, "Pennsylvania Localities Tap Swaps for Upfront Cash: Muni Credit," *Bloomberg*, August 28, 2014.
Retrieved from http://www.bloomberg.com/news/articles/2014-08-28/pennsylvania-localities-tap-swaps-for-upfront-cash-muni-credit.

Watch Dog, Borrowing Troubles, *Chicago Tribune*, Multiple reports.
Retrieved from http://www.chicagotribune.com/news/watchdog/cpsbonds/.

Wagner, Jack, "A Special Investigation of the Bethlehem School District Leigh/ North Hampton Counties," Pennsylvania Department of the Auditor General, November 2009.

Retrieved from http://www.cftc.gov/idc/groups/public/@swaps/documents/dfsubmission/dfsubmission3_080910-afl-cio.pdf.

Wagner, Jack, "Pennsylvania Turnpike Commission: A Performance Audit," January 2013.
Retrieved from https://www.paturnpike.com/pdfs/business/finance/PTC_Report_final_01082013.pdf#search=%22swaps%22.

Ward, Sharon, *Too Big to Trust? Banks, Schools and the Ongoing Problem with Interest Rate Swaps.* Pennsylvania Budget and Policy Center, January 17, 2012.
Retrieved from http://pennbpc.org/sites/pennbpc.org/files/TooBigSwaps.pdf.

Wheeler, Brian, "The Scandal of the Alabama Poor Cut off from Water," *BBC News, Alabama.* December 14, 2011.
Retrieved from http://www.bbc.co.uk/news/magazine-16037798.

Whitmore, Kyle, "SEC settlement with JPMorgan bankers' just one more rotten deal for Jefferson County," December 2, 2016.
Retrieved from http://www.al.com/opinion/index.ssf/2015/12/sec_settlement_with_jpmorgan_b.html.

Zweig, Jason. 2015, *The Museum of Art and Finance, Gallery 1: Tulipmania.* September 3, 2015.
Retrieved from http://jasonzweig.com/the-museum-of-art-and-finance-gallery-1-tulipmania/?utm_content=buffer83e4a&utm_medium=social&utm_source=twitter.com&utm_campaign=buffer.

Zhu, Peter, "HMC Analyst Questions Dismissal: Analyst Says She was Fired for Criticizing Controversial Investment Practices," *The Harvard* Crimson, March 30, 2009.
Retrieved from http://www.thecrimson.com/article/2009/3/31/hmc-analyst-questions-dismissal-after-a/.

Index